This powerful collection of essays is part of a cresce... ...es emerging from the struggles of decolonization, the misunderstandings of postcolonialism, and the search for indigenization. It beautifully exemplifies two important aspects of this emergence and assertion of indigenous voices for the future: the presence of a uniquely Indigenous voice of inquiry, a voice beyond the confines of established academic discourses, and the importance of this voice for Philippine cultures and humanity beyond.

—*Jurgen W. Kremer, PhD. in Clinical Psychology and co-author of* Ethnoautobiography: Stories and Practices of Unlearning Whiteness, Decolonization, Uncovering Ethnicities

Back from the Crocodile's Belly is a book of power – a record of severe struggle to hang on to our soul and its unbroken link to the womb of our ancestral world wherever the Filipino may be. Dedicated to the babaylanes—our shamanic ancestors, many fed to crocodiles by the Spanish conquistador in the attempt to wipe out their world—this book offers a harvest of homecoming. Here the lived experiences of our *kababayan* carving expatriate lives in "the belly of the beast" links arms with the continuing struggle in the motherland to keep alive what it still remembers of that ancestral world. With passion, wit and grace, racial memory propels us to evolve as we meet ourselves and link hands in that blessed moment "before the invention of violent hierarchies and the beauty-killing empires, machines, markets, standing armies, corporations, and governments that now threaten life on the planet."

—*Sylvia Mayuga, thrice winner, Philippine National Book Award, journalist, essayist, poet, and documentary filmmaker*

Cover image: by Perla Daly
Ang Bai, Buaya, kag ang Kahoy sg Kaluluwa
(The Woman, Crocodile, and Tree of the Soul)

BACK FROM THE CROCODILE'S BELLY

PHILIPPINE BABAYLAN STUDIES AND THE STRUGGLE FOR INDIGENOUS MEMORY

EDITED BY S. LILY MENDOZA AND LENY MENDOZA STROBEL

PUBLISHED BY

CENTER FOR
BABAYLAN STUDIES

Back from the Crocodile's Belly:
Philippine Babaylan Studies and the Struggle for Indigenous Memory

Copyright © 2013 by the Center for Babaylan Studies

ISBN 978-1492775317

Published by
Center for Babaylan Studies
Santa Rosa, California

Copyright by
S. Lily Mendoza and
Leny Mendoza Strobel

Designer
Perla Paredes Daly

Library of Congress Cataloguing-in-Publication Data
Back from the crocodile's belly: Philippine babaylan studies and the struggle
for indigenous memory/edited by S. Lily Mendoza and Leny Mendoza Strobel
306 pages 30 cm
Includes bibliographical references
ISBN 978-1492775317
1. Indigenous Studies. 2. Postcolonial Studies.
3. Filipino American Studies – United States. 4. Intercultural Studies.

In memory of the Babaylan

women and men

who were fed to crocodiles

during the Spanish colonial times

Acknowledgments

This anthology owes its life to communities both in the Philippine homeland and in the diaspora that are linked together by a shared inspiration and vision of remembering the old magnificent ways of being human—before the invention of violent hierarchies and the beauty-killing empires, machines, markets, standing armies, corporations, and governments that now threaten life on the planet.

We walk this road because our academic ancestors upon whose work we are building and adding to the scaffold of learning have paved it for us: Virgilio Enriquez, N.V.M. Gonzalez, Reynaldo Ileto, Felipe de Leon, Jr., Albert P. Alejo, Zeus Salazar, and Prospero Covar and those who came after them.

For over a decade, we have been nurtured and enriched by conversations about decolonization and indigenization via listserves and online discussion groups. Special thanks to Perla Daly, Letecia Layson, Venus Herbito, Lane Wilcken, Virgil Apostol, Katrin de Guia, Jean Vengua, Eileen Tabios, Grace Nono, Beth de Castro, Mila Anguluan-Coger, Lizae Reyes, and Agnes Miclat Cacayan. Thank you to the tireless volunteers who have supported the Center for Babaylan Studies since 2009: Titania Buchholdt, Baylan Megino, Frances Santiago, Will Gutierrez, Jen Navarro, Marissa Barreras, Leng Cahambing, Holly Calica, Noemi Issel, Karen Pennrich, Flori Cabergas, Kriya Velasco, Geej Langlois, Rebecca Mabanglo Mayor, Vedel Herbito, Roque Bucton, Marybelle Bustos, Grace Duenas, Olivia Sawi, Jay Malvar, Carol Gamiao, Carol Kimbrough and the countless folks who have participated in CfBS events and continue to motivate us to serve our Kapwa.

Special thank you:

To Tera Maxwell for editorial assistance in the early phase of this book project.

To Leah Barker for her formatting and proofreading support.

To Perla Daly for book design and book production assistance.

To the undergrads and graduate students whose responses to our work continue to challenge and inspire us.

To Martin Prechtel, Linda Hogan, Vine DeLoria, Leslie Marmon Silko, Greg Sarris, David Abram, Ivan Illich, Paul Shepard, James C. Scott, Jurgen Kremer, Gerald Vizenor, Derrick Jensen, James W. Perkinson and other thinkers who not only ask difficult questions about modern civilization but ask them beautifully.

To Leny's spouse, Cal Strobel, who shares our passion for this work and supports us wholeheartedly because he believes "this work is bigger than our marriage."

To Jim Perkinson, Lily's spouse, who patiently pored over portions of the book and unselfishly lent his wordsmithing ability in reining in Lily's penchant for kilometric sentences and OCD for endless nuance.

To our siblings Ernie, Melinda, Millie, and Rox who keep us in check and remind us that "all your theorizing doesn't matter if you don't know how to cook."

To our parents and ancestors who watch over us and whose invisible hands have guided us in this path so that we may learn to weave words of beauty and fragrance that feed the Holy and that coaxes the Indigenous Soul out of its cave of hiding.

To Noah and his cousins – because the future belongs to them.

Ode to the Other World

S. Lily Mendoza

You call
Ever so gently
Like a sweet siren song
Wooing my heart
With courtship deliciousness
Steady
Like a samba note
Beating constant
Soothing
Rhythms of love
Breathing life
Weaving dreams
Reassuring me
That I'm still
Alive

You call
Amidst the dark
Of soul's night
The grating sound
Of dead machine
Plying its wares
Peddling its lies
Of overwrought
Fantasies and
Entombed desires
Instruments of torture

Like Potchikoo's hell[1]
Leaving in their wake
Dried up, wrinkled
Souls, walking zombies
Consuming flesh
Turning all living
Into dead

You call
And I, far gone
Hear you
And beg
To be ravished
Take me, I cry
But know I will
Fight you
Tooth and nail
Like a demoniac
Possessed
Or an addict
In withdrawal

---

[1] From the questing journey of Native American trickster Potchikoo, whose life after death found him wandering aimlessly, until he comes upon a giant warehouse with the metal door marked "ENTRANCE HELL." The story goes:

Potchikoo got a thrill of terror in his stomach. He carefully laid his ear against the door, expecting his blood to curdle. But all he heard was the sound of rustling pages. And so, gathering his courage, he bent to the keyhole and looked to see what it was the white race suffered.

He started back, shook his head, then bent to the keyhole again.

It was worse than flames.

They were all chained, hand and foot and even by the neck, to years and years of mail order catalogues. From the old Sears Roebuck to the Sharper Image, they were bound. Around and around the huge warehouse they dragged the heavy paper books, mumbling, collapsing from time to time to flip through the pages. Each person bent low beneath the weight. Potchikoo had always wondered where the millions of old catalogues went, and now he knew the devil gathered them, that they were instruments of torment.

The words of the damned, thin and drained, rang in his ears all the way home.

Look at that wall unit. What about this here recliner? We could put up that home gym in the basement....

(Louise Erdrich, *Original fire: Selected and new poems*, 2003, pp. 44-45)

But fight for me
I beg you
Fight for the seed
Of Aeta life
Of clanging gongs
And dancing feet
Fight for the life
That stirs
If ever so faintly
In my starving
Machine-fed belly

You—you've killed me
Once, but now
I sense
Another death is due
Only this time
Why does dying
Feel so much
Like love?
Quivering
Anticipating
Like seed-releasing
Nurturance
From the one
Earth Mother

Table of Contents

ACKNOWLEDGMENTS ii

FOREWORD 1

INTRODUCTION 5

PART I – ANCIENT SEEDS OF KNOWING

1. Audible Travels: Oral/Aural Traditional Performances and
   the Spread of Philippine Indigenous Religion 29
   Grace Nono

2. *Anting-anting* or Why *Bathala* Hides Inside the Stone: Colonialism,
   Myth, and Indigenous Potency 47
   Nenita Pambid

3. In the Mountain's Womb: Rizalista Practices as Cultural Memory 69
   Michael Gonzalez

4. Filipino Tattoos: Pigment as Spirit 85
   Lane Wilcken

5. As Healers Dance: A Processual View of Panay
   Bukidnons' *Babaylan*-in-Motion 107
   Christine Muyco

PART II – INDIGENOUS SOUNDINGS
IN CONTEMPORARY PRACTICES

6. The Death of Maria Clara and the Resurrection
   of *Babaylan*: Reclaiming the Filipina American Body 127
   Jane Alfonso

7. Glimpses into the Indigenous: Cultural Portals and Ethnic Identity
    Development among Second Generation Filipino Americans 159
    Maria Ferrera

8. Towards a *Kapwa* Theory of Art: Working towards Wholeness
    in Contemporary Practice 185
    Margarita Garcia

9. DJ Qbert as Cyber-Maniac Shaman: What Does Hip-Hop
    Tricksterism Have To Do With *Babaylan* Practice? 207
    James W. Perkinson

PART III – BABAYLAN RESURRECTIONS
OUT OF THE CROCODILE'S BELLY

10. Imperial Remains: Footnotes on an Energy Healer 225
    Tera Maxwell

11. B(e)aring the *Babaylan*: Body Memory,
    Colonial Wounding, and Return to Indigenous Wildness 243
    S. Lily Mendoza

12. The East-West Quest:
    Intergenerational Mythweaving and Cultural Identity 257
    Ethelyn Anguluan-Coger

13. *Pagbabalikloob,* Cyberactivism, and Art:
    Babaylan Provocations and Creative Responses 271
    Perla Daly

NOTES ON THE CONTRIBUTORS 298
ABOUT THE EDITORS 302

Foreword

Ver Enriquez, the guru of *Sikolohiyang Pilipino,* would be very happy to see that the indigenization of Filipino intellectual discourse is flourishing not only in the Philippines but also in diasporic communities. Ver, I am sure, would also congratulate, as I do now, the **Center for Babaylan Studies** for starting and sustaining this new tradition of re-enchanting both our secularized world and our institutionalized religions with the indigenous energies of babaylan spirituality. Their earlier work, the ***Babaylan: The Call of the Indigenous*** was audaciously published in Mindanao, Philippines. That book really touched me to the core. I knew then that Leny Mendoza Strobel, who compiled and edited that precious collection of babaylan essays, was giving birth to a different kind of movement.

Now, in ***Back from the Crocodile's Belly: Philippine Babaylan Studies and the Struggle for Indigenous Memory,*** Leny has done it again, this time with her sister and collaborator Lily, in gathering kindred spirits, as in an ancient bonfire. Around this bonfire, all faces are now aglow, each one taking turns in stoking the flame with chants and cheers, some swaying their painted bodies in rituals of healing, some others singing silenced stories to rebuff colonial noise, still others enkindling virtual identities with the warmth of cyber sisterhood, always touching ground while releasing sparks of new languages. Again, I can sense, I can feel, and I know that the spirit of Ver Enriquez, our shared ancestor-guide, is very much around in soulful solidarity.

In writing this Foreword, I feel the temptation—borne perhaps out of an assumed expectation—that I should highlight my being an anthropologist, or my dabbling as a poet, or do just anything to diplomatically hide my being a priest, a Jesuit priest, because babaylan spirituality has often been positioned as a critique of institutional religion, which I somehow represent.

Like most of the writers in this book, however, I must face my own struggle for decolonization and re-indigenization. Fortunately, many things have happened during my two decades of working with indigenous peoples, making this period a propitious moment for the work of liberation.

First is the emergence of *social movements* of the indigenous peoples themselves. Despite ethnocide and development aggression, the recent decades have witnessed not the predicted demise of indigenous peoples but the resurgence of self-determination. These movements have found an ally in international bodies that promote the collective rights of indigenous peoples.

Second are the stirrings that come from more global concerns, such as climate change. Indigenous peoples live in lands with extremely delicate environments, made many times more risk-prone because of the intrusion of huge extractive industries in their territories. The indigenous values, however, are probably what we need to survive in this planet. Don't we all campaign now for a renewal of the spiritual harmony with the earth, for going beyond the narrow-mindedness of individualism and consumerism into the inner joy of working for intergenerational common good, for reducing waste and recycling used resources? Aren't these virtues that can save our planet also the message of many indigenous sages?

And more touchingly, a powerful stirring comes from the widespread *dialogue and reconciliation* movements. The growth in interfaith dialogue among world religions serves as a challenge to its application in the intrafaith processes concerning our relationship with indigenous peoples. The realization of some Christians' own participation in discrimination against indigenous peoples and all kinds of marginalized peoples and cultures, is leading now to a series of collective asking for forgiveness by Christian missionaries from indigenous communities for the crimes and historical injustices committed against them.

Thirteen years ago, Pope John Paul II, on bended knees, prayed for forgiveness for all the sins of the Church against indigenous peoples: *"Lord of the world, Father of all, through your Son you asked us to love our enemies, to do good to those who hate us and to pray for those who persecute us. Yet Christians have often denied the Gospel; yielding to a mentality of power, they have violated the rights of ethnic groups and peoples, and shown contempt for their cultures and religious traditions: be patient and merciful towards us, and grant us your forgiveness!"*

The Franciscan missionaries echoed this papal apology, with a more ardent contrition: *"We ask forgiveness of the Mayan people for not having understood your world view and your religion and for having denied your deities; for not having respected your culture and for having imposed upon you for many centuries a religion that you did not understand"* (Mani, Yucatan 2009).

My brother Jesuits also admitted our inconsistency in missionary theory and practice: *"Our intuition is that the Gospel resonates with what is good in each culture. At the same time, we acknowledge that we have not always followed this intuition. We have not always recognized that aggression and coercion have no place in the preaching of the Gospel of freedom, especially in cultures which are vulnerable to manipulation by more powerful forces. We have often contributed to the alienation of the very people we wanted to serve"* (General Congregation 34).

I devote space to these apologies because to me they signal the existence of a clearing on the ground where a new bonfire could be lit and stoked by the new ways of reclaiming identities and celebrating indigenous energies such as those that are collected in this book.

I sincerely hope that cultural activists and contextual theologians, and all those interested in being human on this sacred planet, will pay attention to this book and all the future work of the Center for Babaylan Studies.

Albert E. Alejo, SJ

PhD in Anthropology (School of Oriental and African Studies, University of London) and author, *Ehemplo: Spirituality of Shared Integrity in Philippine Church and Society*

Pasakalye / Introduction

S. Lily Mendoza and Leny Mendoza Strobel

One of the legacies of the late Virgilio "Ver" Enriquez, father of *Sikolohiyang Pilipino* (also known as *Liberation Psychology*), is the founding of *Akademya ng Sikolohiyang Pilipino* (Academy of Filipino Psychology, formerly, the Philippine Psychology Research and Training House or PPRTH) in Quezon City, Philippines just a stone's throw away from the University of the Philippines main campus. The *Akademya* had one over-arching purpose: to nurture home-grown scholars and build their confidence and capacity in producing new knowledge and in theorizing the world as they see it, with integrity. In the classroom and in the various *kapihans* (coffee hours) and *balitaktakans* (informal exchanges) that the *Akademya* organized, Ver "sought to undermine the students' excessive awe and unquestioning acceptance of Western norms of scholarship by critiquing the whole citational tradition in Western social science where a self-perpetuating logical system tended to be built around the practice of name-dropping of published authorities as sole warrant for knowledge claims" (Mendoza, 2002/2006, p. 65). Instead, he motivated them to use their own creativity and trust their own instincts even as they looked to each other, as well as to other authors and scholars (whether local or foreign) for intellectual challenge and inspiration. In addition, a practice he instituted was that of placing students' term papers, theses, and other unpublished research reports at the *Akademya*'s library, thus, creating a body of work (on the study of psychology from indigenous perspectives, then a very marginal area of study in the Philippine academy still dominated by Western psychology) which he made publicly accessible, along with his own voluminous book collection.

Both editors of this book, Lily and Leny, have been privileged to have been mentored by Ver Enriquez (Lily having been a student in the very last graduate seminar that Ver taught at the University of the Philippines before his untimely demise, and Leny, having encountered Ver during his Visiting Professor stint in the United States in the first half of the 1990s, in addition to hosting him at her home at various points of his stay in the country). We realize that it is but fitting to continue that beautiful legacy of mentorship right here where we are—in the United States diaspora away from the homeland. For despite the now ubiquitous talk of "decolonization," "postcoloniality," and even the new buzz word, "indigenization," imperial perspectives remain ascendant and seductive, if not at times intimidating, to those of us, people of color, coming from the margins.

In this book offering, we not only seek to create space for new/old/forgotten knowledges pertaining to ancestry and indigenous practices, but also to honor a diversity of ways of speaking: from the typical voice of normative academic writing to the more personal and embodied language of ethnoautobiography (Kremer & Jackson-Paton, 2013) and creative artistic expression as represented in this collection of essays. Interestingly, we've noticed ourselves that the deeper we go in our own tutelage to older ways of being and knowing, the more our language begins to shift register: from the objective, bloodless, cerebral tone of expository discourse to that of passionate, florid, and exquisite *story*. For we are learning that the native gods are fed by, and delight in, a good story (as do we—once we're no longer afraid to reclaim our own native subjectivity). Thus, we open this Introductory Chapter with our respective stories as a way of marking this transformation and sharing the impetus behind the birthing of this volume.

TWO SISTERS, ONE PATH
FROM ROMANCE WITH MODERNITY TO ANCESTRAL AWAKENINGS

LILY'S STORY

During a trip to Lake Mullet two summers ago in the city of Cheboygan up north of the Michigan Peninsula, my sister's and niece's family, along with my husband and I, were treated to a rare event: the emergence of hundreds of bright blue green dragonflies from their nymph larva stage—first, the head, then slowly a bulge as the main body squeezes out of its brown nymph shell, its gossamer wings still tucked close. Then finally the worm-like tail follows as new life frees itself completely from its water-bound abode, leaving behind its old life forever. For a moment the newly-minted creature walks gingerly on its spindly legs, perhaps dazed by this expansive other world never before experienced in its previous mode of existence. Then slowly, out pops a set of wings, first one side and then the other, and before you know it, up and away the winged creature flies, alighting on a leaf only to take off again as if instinctively knowing there's a whole world out there to explore. It is said that it takes about four years to complete the process of gestation before this moment of metamorphosis. In that long period of seemingly nothing happening, I wondered whether the nymph thought of its water borne existence as the only world there was, or whether it actually spent its time dreaming of this one, with a deep knowing that this is what it was meant to be—a bright beautiful creature of the air, meant to fly free to kiss the sun and bathe in the warm generosity of its embrace.

I, too, have known the seeming nothingness of a long gestation period. It has been close to five years when I felt my life dry up and lose its nurturing sap. Used to the seasons of abundance and fallow that always accompanied rhythms of creativity and gestation in my experience of things, at first, I did not panic. I've just been through two major upheavals involving career and personal life, exacerbated by a radical shake up in my existential worldview with my encounter with deep ecology, critique of civilizational logic, and talk of planetary collapse propelled by predatory capitalism, and so I thought, this is hibernation time. Go into your cave and be content. Sit in the hard discipline of darkness and unknowing for a while; this is your needed pedagogy. Soon, your moment of *kairos* will come, and, desire, like unbidden longing, will once again find its flow. For now, sit and wait.

A few years earlier, I was scheduled to co-edit the volume *Babaylan: Filipinos and the Call of the Indigenous* (2010) with sister and collaborator Leny Strobel and have in fact begun work reviewing the essay contributions, but entombment in my cocoon of emptiness and hollow continued unabated, uninterrupted by anything auguring new life or any intimation of spring anytime soon. I have done what I thought was proper mourning: both for the loss of innocence brought on by the precipitating crises of the previous years and by the ending of the old without a clear sense of what comes next. Yet the dull trod of days, weeks, months, yes, even years, of uninspiration and hollow marched on for what seemed like eternity. To do the faithful work of simply putting one foot in front of the other when all motivation is lost required every ounce of will one could muster. Thankfully, the one place that still hosted, if ever so slightly, a sign that all isn't lost (yet) was the continuing appeal to me of anything indigenous, i.e., those ways and manners of human *being* as yet uncoerced or coopted into domestication and civilization—primitive cultures, languages, social organizations, fabrics, art, dances, practices of spirit, initiations, ceremonies and ritual. These signs of an-other way of human *being* now exist only in the remotest of areas as yet unreached—but I'm afraid not for long—by the long arm of the earth-devouring, earth-poisoning, and beauty-killing machine called the global economy. As well, they exist in hybrid forms among scattered indigenous communities around the world struggling to keep alive ancient memory, or in fragments of archive and re-invention among those who, once touched by their power and beauty, could not but be compelled to struggle alongside to recover what remains of such communities' witness.

That—the compelling vision of an other world steeped not only in meaning, beauty, and boundless generosity but also in the ungrudging acceptance of grief, pain, death, and loss as part of its cosmos—became my only tether to the world of the living in those days of fallow. Completely isolated from that (indigenous) world and enveloped instead in the ghost of a machine of a lost industrial city (Detroit)[1] on the one hand, and that other mega-machine of the corporate academy, on the other, what served as a lifeline were my books and conversations with others of like mind across geographic, cultural, and cyber, space, among them: my life partner, Jim Perkinson and his writings on the world of rhythm and indigenous spirituality in *Shamanism, Racism and Hip-hop Culture* (2005), Sheila Coronel and her beautiful book, *Memory of Dances* (2002), Stuart Schlegel's *Wisdom from*

---

[1] Albeit sprouting life of another kind through its urban gardens and soulful grassroots community life.

It is said that to awaken to critical consciousness, it is not enough to see and grieve what is wrong in the world; one needs also to fall in love.

a *Rainforest* (1998), Rane Willerslev's *Soul Hunters*, Paul Shepard's *Nature and Madness* (1982/1998), *The Tender Carnivore* (1973/1998) and other writings, Ivan Illich's *De-Schooling Society* (1971), *Tools for Conviviality* (1973), *Towards a History of Needs* (1978) and his other works, John Zerzan's *Against Civilization* (2005), Derrick Jensen's *Endgame* volumes (2006a, 2006b) and other works, and most especially Martin Prechtel's *Secrets of the Talking Jaguar* (1998), *The Toe Bone and the Tooth* (2002), *Long Life Honey in the Heart* (1999/2004), and his other writings. In particular, Prechtel's baroque descriptions of what used to be still an intact Mayan village life among the Tzutujil Indians in Guatemala before its utter decimation by U.S.-sponsored death squads helped joggle memory and lift the inertia of ennui and despair beginning to creep into my dark cocoon. Between laughter and tears at the exuberant joy, wild craziness, dangerous adventure, beautiful grieving, and fierce loving and commitment that knitted life together in that little village, I found myself slowly falling in love again. It is said that to awaken to critical consciousness, it is not enough to see and grieve what is wrong in the world; one needs also to fall in love. (That is how the tree-sitter Julia Butterfly Hill describes her reason for sitting for 738 days on a roughly 1500-year old, 180-foot tall California redwood tree named Luna in order to save it from being clearcut.)

How do these indigenous soundings affect how I now do my work in the world as a scholar and an academic? For the most part, it has meant schooling myself in an other world—a world that, in the discourse of the modern academy, signifies little more than abjected forms of human *being*—an unthinkable world of savages, jungles, and beast-like existence that no one in their right mind could ever imagine or remotely long for or desire. The relentless disinformation campaign is deliberate and systematic; as part of the colonizing project of modernity, its singular aim is to legitimize the system of plunder and takeover that now spans the globe and that involves the take over and decimation of indigenous lands, the enslavement of bodies, and the taming of all things wild and anarchic for the sake of control, profit, and domination. As I wrote elsewhere:

> The logic [of our modern culture] goes: "The peoples under whose feet are found the last remaining resources needed for industrial production don't look like us, don't live like us, don't value and think like us; are lazy and unmotivated or are otherwise incapable of developing such resources

for themselves; and are therefore undeserving of them. We[2] can negotiate and offer provisions for their relocation elsewhere, but if they refuse, we have no other choice but to do what we have to do; too bad if they don't know what's good for them." Whether we are speaking of the clear-cutting of tropical rainforests in the Amazon region to make way for biodiesel production, the disastrous Athabasca Tar Sands mining in Alberta, Canada, the devastating diamond mining by Gem and De Beers Corporations in the Central Kalahari Game Reserve or a host of other corporate incursions in the regions of hitherto unassimilated or previously uncontacted Indigenous peoples around the globe, the consequences for the regions' inhabitants— in the form of enslavement as cheap laborers for the corporations, cultural genocide, or their outright extinction—rarely inspires a serious cry of protest from the rest of us modern humans who, in the end, are the *de facto* beneficiaries of the projects of such extractive industries.[3] It is as though despite whatever protestations we make after the fact, underneath, we are all just social Darwinists by subconscious persuasion, believing that "whatever [is] happening to 'uncivilized' peoples around the world [is] not just natural and inevitable, but also an aspect of humanity's 'progress' upwards from the apes" (Brantlinger, 1995, p.54). (Mendoza, 2013, p. 4)

It is time that those of us who have begun to have the scales fall off our eyes, and seen the beauty, complexity, and differing rationality of indigenous life, push back and reclaim space in the public discourse for some serious truth-telling. At a time when we have now come to the endgame of a bankrupt civilizational system whose genocidal record, particularly in the last 500 years, is unmatched in all of human history, we need to learn one more time how to live beautifully on our shared planet. We do this by witnessing and listening deeply to the many and diverse ways of being that once constituted life on the planet before the invention of markets, empires, governments, and mega-corporations. In offering the stories, formal studies, and performances in this volume, our hope is to create alternative readings honoring of the rich tapestry of cultures and subjectivities that makes up the heritage and ancestry of our particular part of the world: the more than a hundred tribal and indigenous communities of the sun-kissed islands of the Philippine archipelago that now, in hindsight, emerge as haunting testament to another way of being human.

---

[2] The use of the collective personal pronoun here is deliberate and is meant to designate all modern subjects, this author included. To the extent that the majority of us now no longer live indigenously but by the industrial machine, *we* share complicity (albeit to varying degrees) with the decimation going on among the globe's last remaining indigenous peoples.

[3] See for example the film documentary by Christopher Walker, *Trinkets and Beads*, chronicling the cultural and environmental havoc wrought by oil drilling in the Huaorani and other neighboring tribes' territories in the Amazon heartland –all for the sake of a volume of oil extracted from the region sufficient to power cars in the U.S. for 13 days of driving.

LENY'S STORY

There are those of us who are drawn to the beauty of a theory or a concept, especially the one that ushers in an epiphany—that sudden surprise that comes from having received an unexpected gift or insight responding to a deep need or an ineffable longing. You trust your gut, your intuition, and you feel that if you only had the words and the courage, you could step outside into the wild and …dance.

The *Babaylan* is one such word. An encounter with the work of scholars and culture bearers[4] who have studied the precolonial history of the *babaylan* indigenous healer—was such a gift.

As I write this, a young Filipino American scholar has just finished interviewing me for her research on "how the lived experience of Pinay (colloquial for Filipina) scholars informs their work." Having to answer her questions gave me the chance to reflect on the last twenty years of my work. I mentioned that I am called many names: an organic intellectual, scholar/activist, leader; but the one I like most: the one who makes people cry (or angry) when she asks tough questions about Filipino identity, decolonization, and colonial mentality.

In the interview, I told her many stories about the mentors who opened doors for me and helped me get published; the Jungian therapists who helped me learn how to interpret my dreams; the authors whose books were lampposts along the path; the land that I am learning to dwell on; the role of family and friends who, together, create a beloved community where dreams are shared and the beauty of being from a people rooted in a land is sung and celebrated together.

The young scholar remarked that compared with the younger Pinay scholars she is interviewing, I, as an older scholar, provides a reflection that is contextualized within a frame that is larger than the academy. This seemed to reassure her of the rightness of her choice to become an academic, not in the narrow definition of discipline, but in the potential of an academic to offer gifts to the bigger world beyond the ivory tower. I told her that it takes more than intellectual passion for theorizing and knowledge building to move the work beyond the ivory tower. If she considers my work as trailblazing or groundbreaking, it is because there is a community that makes that possible. Ultimately it is the love that has been kindled in us that gives form to the work that we do. I recall a Martin Prechtel story about falling in love with the one sure small thing:

> To really make beauty, art, or to live artfully one must do it from a particular place, something focused that we get good at no matter how small…One flower is chosen, fertilized and hopefully goes to fruit, dries

---

[4] Like Carolyn Brewer, Fe Mangahas, Mila Guerrero, Zeus Salazar, Grace Nono, Sister Mary John Mananzan, Katrin de Guia, Ver Enriquez, Albert Alejo, among others.

and its seeds go to grow a new flowering beyond the individual. We no longer chase what we desire, we marry what we follow, and cultivate, hatch, raise up what we love. (Prechtel, *Disobedience of the Daughter of the Sun,* 2005, p.79*)*.

It is in hindsight that I now see more clearly what I have fallen in love with—the beauty of being an indigenizing and decolonizing Filipina. After all the circumnavigating around theories of identity and culture, postcoloniality, postmodernism, cosmopolitanism, nationalism, hybridity, etc., none has convinced me otherwise than that, surface evidence notwithstanding, to be a decolonized Filipina is a beautiful thing. None of the clichés about how we are all human beings, or are just one human race, or are all God's children, has made me sidestep the necessary work of convincing my *Kapwa-tao* (fellow human beings) that Filipina identity is more than being an unfortunate and hapless victim of history. Sure, history has been overdetermined and

> *It is in hindsight that I now see more clearly what I have fallen in love with— the beauty of being an indigenizing and decolonizing Filipina.*

it has wrought its consequences on our amnesiac psyches. I still hear N.V. M. Gonzalez's voice in my head when he said that we have inherited a cultural version of Alzheimer's disease. We, Filipinos, are cultural amnesiacs.

That, too, is a theoretical statement or a literary metaphor. But cultural amnesia is curable and it need not be a curse.

Part of the work that I do as a scholar of decolonization and indigenization is to articulate a criticism of empire and modern civilization. Many Filipino and Filipino American scholars are doing a good job of this as well.

Lately, however, I've noticed that I have come to yet another threshold. My growing dissatisfaction with the narrowness of the discourse on modernity made me want to seek alternative stories. The narrowness refers to the reduction of human history to only the last 500 years of modern civilization and its self-definition as a progressive evolutionary process. In this linear progression, human beings are assumed to be incessantly improving— from being pre-rational, mythic thinking beings to rational beings with highly evolved consciousness. This was unsettling to me because in order to subscribe to this story, I had to deny other stories that I felt in my body and in my soul.

In my younger days I remember reading Francis Schaeffer, a Christian evangelical writer popular in the 70s, and trying to grapple with "the God who is there" as he tried to convince the reader that he could prove the existence of God by way of reason alone.

Later, I wrestled in my mind with another author, Ken Wilber, a philosopher and Zen practitioner, who wrote about the linear evolutionary process of consciousness. Something in me just didn't quite agree with his position that indigenous/primitive peoples are archaic, mythic, and irrational and that humankind has been in the process of transforming itself into higher states of consciousness since. These are only two of the many authors that I read as I made my way out of the womb of my homeland into the big world outside.

Along the way, I made my bare bones acquaintance with many theories – postcolonial, postmodern, literary theory, cultural studies, multicultural studies, transformative learning and pedagogy, and feminist and womanist studies. Outside of the academic texts, I was drawn to poetry, short stories, novels, and creative non-fiction. But secretly, I was drawn to movement, sound, and rhythm. I didn't consciously acknowledge this until much later… until I succumbed to the gongs of the Cordillera at the 2008 *Kapwa* conference at the University of the Philippines in Iloilo and danced with the participants from indigenous communities. Here is a community that I felt already understood the wisdom of the body and that gave the body freedom to be creative, imaginative, visionary.

In a prior year, I listened to Agnes Miclat Cacayan's keynote talk at the *Babaylan* Conference at St. Scholastica College entitled "She Dances in Wholeness" where she talked about her research with primary *babaylans* in Mindanao. This and other encounters with modern *babaylans* in Mindanao drew me closer and closer. This tug wasn't coming from my intellect; it was coming from my body. For the first time in my life, I gave my body permission to lead and guide. I didn't know why. I only knew that it felt good and it made me feel at home.

In small steps, I gave this new body-wisdom more and more space. I read more books about shamanistic practices, the shamanic body, indigenous practices of survivance,[5] and, with these texts, I felt a sense of belonging to an intellectual community that was coming to its senses about the need to fully embody what we know in our heads. David Abrams, in *The Spell of Sensuous* (1996) and in *Becoming Animal* 2011) writes about the need to recover our oral consciousness through the written word. I learned that it is possible to develop synesthesia – the fusion of the senses.

However, at some level the textual community wasn't satisfactory enough. There was also a cyber community among Filipina Americans that emerged and flourished as we shared these awakenings, all of which led to the creation—in real time and space—of the *Center for Babaylan Studies*. And it is here that this present volume first found its fruitful gestation.

---

[5] Survivance is a word coined from "survival" and "resistance" by Anishinabe scholar and Professor of American Studies at University of New Mexico, Gerald Vizenor.

QUESTING FOR THE BABAYLAN
OUT OF THE CROCODILE'S BELLY

The story of the historical *Babaylan* resonates with both of us as diasporic Filipinas. The term "*babaylan*" refers to the indigenous shaman/priestess in Philippine indigenous cultures. *Babaylan* is a Visayan term. In other Philippine indigenous communities, s/he is the *mumbaki, dawac, balyan, katalonan, ma-aram, mangngallag, manbunong, beliyan.*

Babaylan is more than a term or a concept; it points to real persons bearing names that ring down the corridor of history like a distant gong: Cariapa, Bolandungan, Cabacungan, Estela BangotBanwa, Mendung Sabal. These bearers of the people's memory were (and are) healers, priestesses, ritualists, herbalists, and mediators between realms. They were also warriors who led resistance movements against colonial imposition.

A story is told that when the Spaniards (who colonized the Philippine islands beginning in the 16th century) began to understand the power and potency of the *babaylan*, they so feared the latter's spiritual prowess that they not only killed many of them but in some instances, fed them to crocodiles to ensure their total annihilation. While appearing in the archive primarily in connection with the 1663 *babaylan* uprising in Tapar, Iloilo,[6] the story captures a broad truth: colonial violence *did* consume indigenous culture (the 2001 account of religious historian Carolyn Brewer details the systematic demonization of *babaylans* and their ostracism and social "dismemberment" as *brujas* or witches).

The colonial enterprise was indeed a ravenous maw. Yet, the *babaylan* tradition never really died; it remained alive inside the colonial religious infrastructure. Across the centuries, its whispers and

> *The colonial enterprise was indeed a ravenous maw. Yet, the babaylan tradition never really died; it remained alive inside the colonial religious infrastructure. Across the centuries, its whispers and ache, its raw force and quiet upwellings, continue to speak.*

---

[6] Where the corpses of *babaylan* charismatic rebel leader Tapar and his followers, along with the group's blessed holy mother, Maria Santisima, were impaled on bamboo stakes and deliberately placed on the mouth of river Laglag to be eaten by crocodiles (cf. Diaz, C. [1890] Conquistas de las Islas Filipinas, covering 1616-1694 as cited in Blair & Robertson, 1998))

ache, its raw force and quiet upwellings, continue to speak. We two sisters are only slowly learning to open to the deep motions of our own interior continuity with the tradition from whence we have come. An inchoate *babaylan* energy has never ceased to course its way forward like some transgender Jonah awaiting a beach. It speaks of an "other" world, of possibilities for being, not imagined by colonial masters. That other Way is the matter of our amnesia, the tool and truth we seek to lend a voice and organize into a movement in our current hour of crises writ large.

For the past decade, a community of decolonizing Filipino Americans who were engaged in two online listserves—*Pagbabalikloob* (returning to indigenous self) and *Babaylan*—decided it was time to organize more formally and create a vehicle for disseminating the invaluable information that was being shared in these online spaces. Thus was formed the *Center for Babaylan Studies* (CfBS) in 2009. The Center was organized as an incubator and launching pad for scholarly research, culture-bearing creative expression, and political advocacy for indigenous peoples' rights. The various events (workshops, retreats, healing concerts, festivals) that CfBS organizes or participates in represent the integration of the body-mind-spirit approach that is simultaneously intellectually rigorous, physically nourishing, and spiritually grounding. It affirms the intersubjective orientation of Filipinos, which we call *kapwa* (shared being), an indigenous core value in Filipino Indigenous Psychology. In several brief videos[7] created by the Center for Babaylan Studies, we have tried to articulate how the indigenous *Babaylan* tradition speaks to us today. The work is introductory, a preliminary attempt to reach Filipinos in the diaspora who resonate with the feelings of alienation, homesickness, confusion, non-belonging, and overall disempowerment in the places where they find themselves, and to tell them that there are stories that we can gather and tell ourselves to make ourselves whole again.

Since its founding in 2009, the Center has organized an International *Babaylan* Conference in 2010, a symposium on decolonization and indigenization in 2011, a trek across the Pacific to participate in the International *Kapwa 3* Conference in Baguio in 2012, and a second CfBS-hosted International *Babaylan* Conference in 2013. The unanticipated success of the first conference signaled to us that the time is ripe to affirm this indigenous turn. A similar turn is also happening in some academic disciplines (e.g., American Studies, Ethnic Studies, Postcolonial Studies, and most especially, in the emergent field of Indigenous Studies) as well as in local sites in Filipino communities in the diaspora.

In the Philippines, we acknowledge the work of the National Commission on Culture and the Arts (NCCA) and the Heritage and Arts Academies of the Philippines (HAPI) in supporting the *Schools of Living Tradition* (NCCA-funded structures tasked with ensuring that indigenous knowledge and skills continue to be passed down to the next generations) all

---

[7] Cf. "Honoring our Babaylan Ancestors." (https://www.youtube.com/watch?v=JjygYiCsUwA); (https://www.youtube.com/user/Center4Babaylan/videos), among others.

over the country. Through the *Kapwa* conferences in the Philippines organized by HAPI and the conference organizers' openness to the participation of Filipino Americans at these events, we have been forging connections and collaboration on how to articulate the importance of indigenous perspectives in an age of globalization and increasing environmental catastrophe. Shared concerns over the many-faceted crisis of the global capitalist system—e.g., climate change, resource depletion, theft of ancestral domains, marginalization of Indigenous Peoples, increasing violence and militarization—call on us to work towards a more sustainable, humane, earth-friendly, and earth-honoring path as we work our way out of the conundrum and despair that our current way of life invariably fosters.

In the global South, we are already witnessing the effects of rising ocean levels and changing weather patterns that impact the growing of food, the health of the forests and rivers, the flow of water from the headwaters. In the affluent global North, we are also seeing the devastating consequences of typhoons, tornadoes, and fires. Furthermore, we have now come to the manic phase of resource extraction (fracking, oil extraction from the tar sands, dangerous deep sea drilling) in order to continue fueling the consuming habits of the "First World." We are also witnessing the social consequences of such changes as they disparately impact people of color, poor communities, and other disenfranchised groups.

The movement of refugees and workers across the globe, including Filipinos, as people from the South are displaced and uprooted by global treaties such as the North Atlantic Free Trade Agreement (NAFTA) and, even more devastatingly, the Trans-Pacific Partnership Agreement (TPP), also calls for a different lens of analysis capable of mounting, not just piecemeal critique, but a civilizational one—one that is able to get at the deep-rooted logic of domination and expansion that now threatens life on the planet as we know it.

At the 2013 International Indigenous Studies Conference organized by the University of the Philippines in Baguio, Cordillera Studies Center, and the Tebtebba organization, Cordillera scholars and other Filipino academics doing research on indigenous communities found themselves on a platform with internationally recognized indigenous scholars from Peru, Nicaragua, Nigeria, Tanzania, China, Nepal, Canada, and the U.S.—lending encouragement to the young researchers about the need for formalizing Indigenous Studies in Philippine university settings.

Within the Filipino American community (centered in California), there is also a growing decolonization and indigenization movement that has been influenced by a body of scholarly work including Enriquez' many texts on *Sikolohiyang Pilipino* (1990a; 1990b; 1992), Strobel's work on decolonization (2001, 2005, 2010), Mendoza's theorizing of Filipino and Filipino American cultural politics (2002/2006, 2006a, 2006b, 2006c, 2005/2006, 2001), De Guia's book entitled *Kapwa: The Self in the Other* (2005), Grace Nono's *The Shared Voice* (2008) and *Song of the Babaylan* (2013), Apostol's *Ancient Ways of Healing* (2010), and Wilcken's investigation of Filipino tattoo traditions in *Filipino Tattoos Ancient to Modern* (2010).

Indeed, indigenous worldviews are affirming of the fact that there are remarkably diverse ways of being human on the planet...and it is this diversity that needs to be recuperated as an antidote to the homogenizing logic of modernity.

In this volume, we present works by authors who are striving to construct more indigenously-grounded analyses in their attempt to understand contemporary history and to push back on the presumptions of modernity to define exclusively what it means to be human. Indeed, indigenous worldviews are affirming of the fact that there are remarkably diverse ways of being human on the planet—besides that of modern industrial culture—and it is this diversity that needs to be recuperated as an antidote to the homogenizing logic of modernity.

Today, we see a growing hunger for alternative visions of how to live within our Filipino American communities. We are becoming aware of the limits of regimes of accumulation and capitalist-sponsored development. Within the circles of the CfBS especially, we are also beginning to see a values re-orientation that reflects an emphasis on *Kapwa* in relational practices that seeks to create more intersubjective, interdependent, and reciprocal ways of relating to one another. We are seeing young people question their educational motivations and career choices. We are seeing elders take their mentoring potential more seriously. We are seeing people who hunger for sensuous connection to their own bodily wisdom, their own soul-life, and their own manner of embodying personhood and identity. We are seeing signs of the return of the mythic imagination that grounds us in a vision that is larger than the typical cosmologies of established religions and political ideologies. We hear the song of the *Babaylan*. We listen to her stories and she leads us into a wider scope of inquiry into our own ancestral moorings and, as the renowned Philippine independent filmmaker Kidlat Tahimik would say, our own *indio-genius*.

The book is also an offering to a wider audience that is not always able to attend CfBS events. We want to inspire and encourage, to make visible our deepest longings to go back to the Source, the ground of our being – our Indigenous Soul.

ATANG
OFFERINGS TO THE ANCESTORS

Various aspects of Philippine Indigenous Knowledge Systems and Practices (IKSP) both in the homeland and in the diaspora are represented in the narrative and discursive essays in this volume. By including authors coming from a diversity of locations and positions—from scholars and academics (in the homeland and in the U.S.), to artist-activists and body practitioners—we have sought to widen the book's scope of representation and inclusiveness, and, as well, the range of styles of writing. An ethic undergirding the book's conception is the commitment to creating a venue for hybrid practices that nonetheless reflect respect for primary *babaylan* practice and critical thinking about acts of appropriation and engagement with primary sources (e.g., indigenous peoples' crafts, chants, songs, rituals, and other practices).

The first section of the book, "Ancient Seeds of Knowing," presents a wealth of primary research about living indigenous traditions that continue to be kept alive among ethnic communities in the Philippines and, interestingly, in certain parts of the United States. Grace Nono's chapter on oral/aural traditions and the diasporic spread of indigenous religions as an unintended consequence of the Western and Christian missionary impulse points us to the shift of religious influence "from the margins to the metropole." In this piece, Nono's study of this curious phenomenon is done primarily through the story of the Ifugao *babaylan/mumbaki* Mamerto Tindongan who currently resides in Ohio. Nono documents how Mamerto was led to receive belatedly a transmission of a healing gift from his Ifugao *mumbaki*-father as a *balikbayan* (returning Filipino) after falling ill with a debilitating disease (and how his new-found openness had been enabled through the ministrations of a half Native American shaman and through apprenticing to other shamanic healing modalities from other diasporic cultures in the United States before he was able to go home). Returning to Ohio after his *mumbaki* initiation from his father, he became a healing practitioner and today carries on the tradition away from the homeland. What this diasporic trend in the spread of Philippine indigenous religions portends is a question that Nono asks and invites us to engage.

The second chapter in this section is a fascinating study by Nenita Pambid Domingo on *anting-anting* (or amulets) that explores what "really" happened when the Spanish Catholic God purportedly "vanguished" the "heathens" and their god(s) after the 16th century invasion and colonization of the islands. Most Filipinos are aware of the popularity and ubiquity of the *anting-anting* as artifacts but have never had access to the history recounting how "God" or the *Nuno* (Ancestor) came to reside in the stone in the first place. In this chapter, Pambid tells the story of *Infinito Dios* or *Nuno* or *Bathala* as the god who refused to be baptized by the Christian Three Persons except on his own terms—in effect, performing judo on the Christian God and remaining alive underneath the conquering religion. The native humor that permeates the duel between the pagan *Nuno* and the Christian Jesus serves up rib-cracking "trickster delight" and begs the question, "Who's really zooming whom?" as the two deities matched wits and powers using *oracion* (power words) as weapons. Far from capitulating to the dismissal of the belief in *anting-anting* as nothing more than superstition, this piece restores the living story to the orphaned modern practice, revealing native genius and adeptness in keeping indigenous belief alive under the surveilling radar of colonial religion.

Closely related to the foregoing piece is Michael Gonzalez' recuperation of another living indigenous religion by a Philippine peasant movement known as the *Rizalistas,* built around the person of the Philippine national hero, Dr. Jose Rizal. In the piece, Gonzalez tracks the beliefs and practices, prominently encoded in song and shared across numerous Rizalista healing communities around the country, that effectively transmutes the official Rizal into a Christ-like figure—one that continues to walk among them as healer, wise elder, friend, and defender of the poor and oppressed (a belief likewise noted by other scholars like the renowned Philippine historian, Reynaldo Ileto in *Pasyon and Revolution* (1979). This Rizal is a virtual *babaylan.* Interesting in the piece is the seamless embrace and navigation of the official story (in community events and celebrations) right alongside the sustaining narrative of the "other Rizal" that is maintained without any experience of contradiction. (Was he killed by the Spaniards in Bagumbayan on December 30, 1896? Yes. Is he alive and moving among us today, healing, guiding, bestowing spirit and energy? Also yes.). In inviting us to explore the larger *babaylan* semantic field as performed by the Rizalista indigenous communities, Gonzalez challenges our severely impoverished Western rationalistic worldviews and underscores the need to be tutored in another way of seeing that is far more expansive, richly creative, and deeply appreciative of indigenous popular imagination.

Lane Wilcken's chapter on the spiritual and cultural meanings of Filipino traditions of tattooing offers a much-needed context for understanding the difference between modern and indigenous tattooing practices. In this study, Wilcken tells of the metaphors and symbolism in creation stories of Filipino indigenous communities that often serve as sources of sacred designs and motifs and their link to the same among Pacific Islanders; but mostly, he focuses on the tattooing tradition as found among the various Philippine indigenous communities. A practicing tattoo artist and wearer of traditional tattoos himself, in addition to having published scholarly studies on the subject, his piece in this volume pulls together his extensive knowledge of the beliefs and spiritual meanings that anchor tattooing as an indigenous practice—from the belief in deified ancestral spirits or *anitos* that animate much of the healing/shamanic practices (including that of his own *mangngilut* grandmother), through the communal marking or conferment of particular tattoo motifs upon individuals as a symbol of the person "having earned the inscribed trait" and/or as a sign of "commitment to uphold community responsibilities," to the thorny issue of being marked after successfully performing headhunting as part of an initiatory rite of passage into manhood. (In acknowledging the complexities of this latter tradition which historically is not only found in the Philippines, but, as well, in other parts of the world including South Asia, West and Central Africa, Oceania, Mesoamerica, and among certain Celtic and West Germanic peoples, among others—we have appended a brief response by scholar and fellow contributor, James W. Perkinson contextualizing the practice in relationship to our own complicity with a kind of globalized "headhunting" today.) Overall, Wilcken's essay calls on those of us inclined to appropriate indigenous practices such as tattooing, to do so with circumspection, mindful of their meanings and context as well the responsibility they demand for those who would dare adopt them.

This book section ends with Christine Muyco's essay on the dance tradition of *binanog* among the healers of Panay Bukidnon, an indigenous tribe in the Philippine Visayan Islands. Using the frame of the body-in-motion "as a communicative body," Muyco unpacks the significance of the structure and performance of the healing dance—in ritual, chant, and voice—and its achievement of a transcendent "flow" called *tayuyon* that signals that the healer has connected with the spirits in an altered state of consciousness. A trained ethnomusicologist, Muyco does not end merely with a scholarly exploration of the tradition. Fascinating as the study is in and of itself, she shares as well (in characteristic modesty), the personal impact that her encounter with the indigenous healing dance tradition of this highland people has had on her own life and cultural practice as founder of a non-governmental organization called *Balay Patawili, Inc.* established to support projects of the Schools of Living Tradition in the highland Visayas. In keeping with her opening premise that *binanog* dancers heal both the sick and themselves, she tracks some of her own experience of such when her ethnographic study finally pushes her into becoming a dancer herself.

These scholarly research studies into *babaylan* practices gives us a glimpse into the richness and continuing vibrancy of these indigenous traditions despite the steamrolling efficiency of global monoculture (and governments) at tribal incorporation. But the "glimpse" can only be turned into an edifying *ouvre* through patient tutelage into the grief of not seeing and comprehending as quickly and as easily as one might want.

In the next section, the set of essays brings indigenous perspectives into conversation with contemporary practices across a range of topics, including somatic embodiment of Filipino womanhood, decolonization struggles among second generation Filipino Americans, art theory and cultural practice, and, last but not the least, Filipino American hip hop virtuosity.

Starting with Jane Alfonso's "Death of Maria Clara and the Resurrection of the Babaylan" the question is posed: "What does it mean to have a Filipina American body?" As a practitioner of somatic therapy (or body-oriented psychotherapy), Alfonso queries the social functioning of (Philippine hero and novelist) Jose Rizal's character, Maria Clara, whose profile as a "devoted, suffering, self-sacrificial, and self-denying mother" is circulated as the archetypal embodiment of what it means to be a Filipina. Citing that Maria Clara's only choice under colonial rule was either "death or the nunnery" (and the latter as itself a place of death!), Alfonso tracks in detail the ways in which the Filipina body under colonial rule was forcibly socialized into this Maria Clara mold. In a powerfully written autobiographical narrative, she traces the intergenerational trauma of such construction in her own experience. Ironically, the saga of her bodily search for home finds a path not outside, but through, her process of interpellation as "other." Like the archaeological task of recuperating the abjected *babaylan* turned *bruja* (witch) within the discourse of the Spanish church, she tells of her long process of self-reclamation/resurrection through her encounter with indigenous ancestry, finding a home in the strong healing arms of "the *Babaylan*" as both identity and community.

Continuing the focus on intergenerational trauma, Maria Ferrera's chapter examines the effects of colonial mentality on second generation Filipino Americans (SGFA). Coming from the discipline of psychology, Ferrera grounds her study in a vast review of the literature on minority identity development (as informed by the growing field of postcolonial psychology) as it relates to the struggles and experiences of SGFAs dealing with marginalizaton, depression, and, in a number of cases, even suicide. Central to her study is her notion of "cultural portals" designating "points of access that provide exposure to, and an understanding of, Filipino history and culture" as catalysts in SGFA's decolonization process. While noting the widespread phenomenon of cultural alienation among many SGFA youth, her research nonetheless offers an encouraging and inspiring look at the struggles of a generation twice or thrice removed from the homeland whose search for ethnic connection yet remains profound and deep. Just here, the gift of indigenously-informed cultural portals augur deep into underground currents connecting such youth with their Filipino heritage, thereby opening a way toward a more affirming and creative elaboration of their ethnic identity development issues.

"Towards a *Kapwa* Theory of Art" is Margarita Garcia's contribution on how a Filipino American contemporary artist struggles to deal with the issue of being "Other" in the mainstream contemporary art world. Could *Kapwa* help create a coherent practice out of an agonizing dialectic whose possibilities reproduced stereotypes whichever way she chose to represent herself (either as "just an artist" or as specifically a "Filipina artist")? Garcia's positioning as "hybrid" offered no "out"—"a 'good' immigrants' daughter [who simultaneously functioned as] a highly paid executive and card carrying member of the digerati launching dot.coms in Times Square, with an Ivy League degree on the wall that didn't stop [her] colleagues from occasionally asking [her] for their take-out food deliveries." Her unplanned extended stay in the Philippines—specifically in the province of Batanes in the northernmost part of Luzon—and her eventful stint as Director of the Pacita Abad Center for the Arts, along with her encounters with the various indigenous communities and artists in the area, introduced her to the salience of *Kapwa*. Here was a complex of relations, a fluidity of being, and a subtlety of communication protocols that, in hindsight, would enable her to ground her aesthetic in a different sense of doing art as a diasporic Filipina.

Her narrative is rich, replete with stories of serendipitous enactments and revelations of the indigenous logic of *kapwa*, auspiciously matched in the essay by a smorgasbord of deliciously striking, creative innovations that such an indigenous practice inspired in her art.

From high art we move to the street. James Perkinson's essay explores the ways Filipino American hip hop icon of the 1990s, DJ Qbert, and his posse, Invisible Skatch Piklz, blazed a "sonic trail into the inner ether by melding human hand and vinyl disc into a mestizo mix of tricks, doing judo on the diasporic clash of cultures defining California's coast at the millennial crossover." Spitting words like a scratched record, Perkinson juxtaposes diasporic DeeJaying and *babaylan* healing in an unlikely conjunction. To what degree might these "wobble-fingered" young masters of today's "wheels of steel" (turntables) be grasped as channeling a much older sensibility and energy? The essay argues that despite wildly different modalities and geographies, Filipino American turntablists and *babaylan* travelers to the spirit-world of ancestors and healing are both alike auguring an indigenous current. Detouring through Amazonian shamanic practices orchestrating vision and sound in a synesthesia of "healing attunement," the argument provokes by opening up strange possibilities. Breakdown of patterns of energy and their re-assembly under a different structure and rhythm is common to both scratch-mixing and shamanic spirit-wrestling. Perhaps DJ Qbert and the Filipina *babaylan* matriarch indeed sip at the same well of ancestry.

Finally, the third and final section of the book presents what we call ethnoautobigraphical narrations (Kremer & Jackson-Paton, 2013), focusing on the deep affective processes of ancestral storytelling whose cathartic effects issue into various personal and psychic transformations.

Tera Maxwell's poignant essay, "Imperial Remains: Footnotes on an Energy Healer" grapples with the unnamed trauma and grief that has inexplicably haunted her family across generations, including her own. She discovers that it is only through sifting through what she calls the "official and unofficial archives" of history ("memories, oral histories, art, literature, films, websites, and museums") that she finds the connection between the haunting of her family and the unrecorded grief and trauma of Empire. In her essay, Maxwell traces the enmeshment of individual, familial, and political histories to reveal what she calls "imperial remains:" that which lie hidden, un-storied, and untold in the official version of the archive of Empire. She refers to her approach to storytelling as "shamanic," as having the effect of creating a different archive "that serves the discerning of the present" and the "moving of energy" in ways that heal individuals and community. Yet, the work itself is fraught. As she forewarns, "But although I excavate traditional archival remains… these are simply touchstones for the more elusive, intangible remains that make up my archive: affective remains that span generations and continue to define the present." The challenge of working with the dynamic of those affective "ghosts," or what she calls "energetic imprints" that often span generations, takes her to what she calls a *"babaylan* journey," and, ultimately, to her current vocation as an energy practitioner.

Continuing on the theme of body memory and colonial wounding, S. Lily Mendoza's narration takes us through her journey of transformations from constraining religious asceticism, the sacred wounding of intimate betrayal, and the painful decay of a dying (industrial) city to the freeing embrace of embodied indigenous wildness, the hallowing of intimate wounding, and the struggle to rebuild sustainable forms of community. Through her story, we catch glimpses of what could be called shades of the *babaylan* path—seen in the beginning articulation of her own personal story (a story of personal wounding and overcoming) to the Larger Story that is longing to be told (the wounding of Earth Mother and the need for her children to recover the original instructions given to the ancestors on how to live). Her story is an invitation for us, "inheritors of ancient Filipino memory and history," to struggle to weave this Larger Story together.

Mila Anguluan-Coger's essay on "mythweaving" reintroduces us to the myth of Bernardo Carpio, the legendary Filipino hero "with superhuman strength, and the journey that led him to seek clarity and fulfillment by confronting the mythical mountain with two clashing rocks within its bowels." Taking the story of Bernardo Carpio as a trope of the story of immigrants in a hostile country, she develops a process of mythweaving that moves back and forth between the timeless strands of ancestral myth and those of the present, "regarding the past not as a fading relic of a bygone era, but a dynamic continuum of timeless strands being woven purposively to unfold the meaning of our lives." In this chapter, Anguluan-Coger shows the transformative impact of this process in the way she manages to "interweave" the Carpio story with the story of her own struggles as a single mother in the Philippines, and then as an immigrant in the U.S. in a mixed race marriage, with those of other elders in Los Angeles with whom she explored the uses of expressive arts therapies in discovering the strength of their indigenous stories. In particular, Mila shows how the collective exploration of the myth of Bernardo Carpio with these elders eventually evolved into intergenerational exchanges with university students where young and old alike found a "healing sanctuary" in the very act and performance of mythtelling—one we may call a beautiful way of composting grief into life-giving artistic expression.

Finally, Perla Daly's "*Pagbabalikloob*, Cyberactivism, and Art" narrates the author's cultural and political awakening in the homeland, beginning in her college days, that led her to search for ways to address more broadly the problem of colonial mentality among Filipinos. As part of her own process of decolonization, she tells of how she was drawn to the history and stories of the *Babaylan* through the pain of encountering the negative stereotyping of Filipinas online when she first attempted to find sources on the internet that could help her discover her ancestral roots. In this essay, she tells of her remarkable journey in creating the website, *Bagong Pinay* at newfilipina.com, her serendipitous meeting with various Filipino women that would inspire her in her search for ancestry (and that would in turn be inspired by her courage and passion), her establishing of two online listserve communities, *Pagbabalikloob* and *Babaylan*, and her work of organizing a nationwide conference for Filipino American Women's Network (FAWN) in 2005. In many ways, these amazing accomplishments are what helped seed the founding of what is now the *Center for Babaylan Studies.* How the *Babaylan* spirit figured in all of Daly's endeavors permeates her narration and her *babaylan*-inspired work—a glowing testament to the ingenuity of creative imagination in reclaiming indigenous consciousness.

> *But the truth is that all of us (Filipinos or otherwise), at one time in our ancestry... knew how to live on the land.... That is to say, we were indigenous and can learn to be so again.*

This collection of works is our beginning response to the need for alternate discourses and representations (whether in the high places of the academy or in the streets) that can mirror back to us images of native subjectivity that are not always already warped, primitivized, or cast as nothing more than "romanticized nativism." Rather the need is for discourses that truly make possible at last what Mendoza calls in her 2013 essay, "nativist longing." Typically this latter has been cast as a desire for a way of being that colonialist logic tells us we should abhor and fear becoming: the way of being of the abjected indigene—"uncivilized," loathingly uncouth, dirty, superstitious, "primitive"—one whose greatest sin today is that of being a non-consumer, of daring to live outside the industrial machine, or, most serious of all, of sitting on top of the last remaining precious raw materials needed to keep our cherished industrial civilization going without any interest or desire to exploit or develop them (or let others exploit or develop them). In a way, this Primitive Subject now stands as Modernity's only true (unconquered) "Other," whose very capacity to survive and thrive outside its trappings stands as the lone silent testament to the fact that civilization is neither inevitable nor destined, and that without mandatory assimilation into its civilizing project, another way of life, another world is truly possible. To do this kind of work is to engage in a symbolic struggle, in the words of Ann Stoler (2006), "to extend our historical imaginations in often unrehearsed and awkward [and, we would add, groping] ways" (p. 5), for none of our formal degrees or training, or socialization, have trained us to think outside of the default logic of the imperial mind that sees only good in accumulation and "progress," and bad in anything else. But the truth is that all of us (Filipinos or otherwise), at one time in our ancestry, before our conscription into civilization, knew how to live on the land, did things for ourselves without the mediation of corporations, had access to unlimited means for meeting limited wants, understood the ethic of reciprocity with living Earth and other living beings, and did not view comfort, convenience, and ease to be our highest purpose but embraced death, grief, and struggle as all part of being human. That is to say, we were *indigenous* and can learn to be so again. To that end—to ancestral remembrance—we dedicate this book.

Siya Nawa. May it be.

References

Abram, D. (1996). *The spell of the sensuous: Perception and language in a more-than-human world*. New York: Vintage Books.

Abram, D. (2011). *Becoming animal: An Earthly cosmology*. New York: Vintage Books.

Alejo, A. (1990). *Tao Po! Tuloy! Isang Landas ng Pag-unawa ng Loob ng Tao*. Quezon City, Philippines: Office of Research and Publications, Ateneo de Manila University.

Apostol, V. (2010). *Way of the ancient healer: Sacred teachings from the Philippine ancestral traditions*. North Atlantic Books.

Blair, E. H., & Robertson, J. A. (1998). *The Philippine Islands, 1493-1898*. Bank of the Philippine Islands [commemorative CD re-issue]. Retrieved from http://www.elaput.org/chrmtpar.htm

Brewer, C. (2001). *Holy confrontations: Religion, gender, and sexuality in the Philippines, 1521-1685*. Manila, Philippines: Institute of Women's Studies.

Coronel, S. (2002). *Memory of Dances*. Quezon City, Philippines: Philippine Center for Investigative Journalism.

DeGuia, K. (2005). *Kapwa: The Self in the Other: Worldviews and lifestyles of Filipino culture-bearers*. Manila, Philippines: Anvil Publishing, Inc.

Enriquez, V. (Ed.). (1990a). Indigenous Personality Theory. In *Indigenous Psychology: A Book of Readings* (pp.185-208). Quezon City, Philippines: Philippine Psychology Research and Training House.

Enriquez, V. (Ed.). (1990b). Towards a Liberation Psychology. In *Indigenous Psychology: A Book of Readings* (pp.123-136). Quezon City, Philippines: Philippine Psychology Research and Training House.

Enriquez, V. (Ed.). (1992). *From colonial to liberation psychology*. Quezon City, Philippines: University of the Philippines Press.

Gonzalez, N. V. M. (1983). Whistling up the Wind: Myth and Creativity. In *Philippine Studies*. Quezon City, Philippines: Ateneo de Manila University Press.

Ileto, R. (1979). *Pasyon and revolution: Popular movements in the Philippines, 1840-1910*. Quezon City, Philippines: Ateneo University Press.

Illich, I. (1971). *Deschooling society*. NY: Harper & Row.

Illich, I. (1973). *Tools for conviviality.* NY: Harper & Row.

Illich, I. (1978). *Towards a history of needs.* NY: Pantheon Books.

Jensen, D. (2006a). *Endgame, Volume I: The problem of civilization.* NY: Seven Stories Press.

Jensen, D. (2006b). *Endgame, Volume II: Resistance.* NY: Seven Stories Press.

Jürgen W. K., & Jackson-Paton, R. (2013). *Ethnoautobiography – Stories and practices for unlearning whiteness, decolonization, uncovering ethnicities.* ReVision Publishing.

Mendoza, S. L. (2002/2006). *Between the homeland and the diaspora: The politics of theorizing Filipino and Filipino American identities.* (Routledge Series on Asian Americans: Reconceptualizing Culture, History and Politics). NY & London: Routledge. Revised Philippine edition, University of Santo Tomas Publishing House.

Mendoza, S. L. (2001). Nuancing anti-essentialism: A critical genealogy of Philippine experiments in national identity formation. In D. T. Goldberg, M. Musheno, & L. C. Bower (Eds.). *Between law and culture: Relocating legal studies* (pp. 224-245). Minneapolis, MN: University of Minnesota Press.

Mendoza, S. L. (2005/2006). Tears in the archive: Creating memory to survive and contest empire. In R. Lustig & J. Koester (Eds.*). Among US: Essays on identity, belonging, and intercultural competence* (Rev. ed., pp. 233-245). Boston: Pearson.

Mendoza, S. L. (2006a). New frameworks in Philippine postcolonial historiography: Decolonizing a discipline. In J. E. Braziel & J. Young (Eds.). *Race and the foundations of knowledge* (pp. 155-173). Urbana and Chicago: University of Illinois Press.

Mendoza, S. L. (2006b). 'Strategic parochialism:' Philippine insurgent nationalism and the search for a constituent public. In A. Dirlik (Ed.). *Pedagogies of the global: Knowledge in the human interest* (pp. 187-216). Boulder & London: Paradigm Press.

Mendoza, S. L. (2006c). A different breed of Filipino balikbayan: The ambiguities of (re-)turning. In T. Tiongson, E. Gutierrez, & R. Gutierrez (Eds.). *'Positively no Filipinos allowed:' Situating Filipino American formations in U.S. racial politics* (pp. 199-214). Philadelphia: Temple University Press.

Mendoza, S. L. (2013). Savage representations in the discourse of modernity: Liberal ideology and the impossibility of nativist longing. *Decolonization, Indigeneity, Education & Society, 2*(1), 1-19.

Nono, G. (2008). *The shared voice: Chanted and spoken narratives from the Philippines.* Anvil Publishing and Fundacion Santiago.

Nono, G. (2013). *Song of the Babaylan: Living voices, medicines, spiritualities of Philippine ritualist-oralist-healers.* Quezon City, Philippines: Institute of Spirituality in Asia.

Prechtel, M. (1998). *Secrets of the talking jaguar.* New York, NY: Penguin Putnam.

Prechtel, M. (1999/2004). *Long life, honey in the heart.* Berkeley, CA. North Atlantic Books.

Prechtel, M. (2002). *The toe bone and the tooth.* Hammersmith, London: Thorsons.

Prechtel, M. (2005). *The disobedience of the daughter of the sun.* Berkeley, CA: North Atlantic Books.

Schlegel. S. (1998). *Wisdom from a rainforest.* Athens, GA: University of Georgia Press.

Shepard, P. (1973/1998). *The tender carnivore and the sacred game.* Athens, GA: The University of Georgia Press.

Shepard, P. (1982/1998). *Nature and madness.* Athens, GA: The University of Georgia Press.

Stoler, A. L. (2006). (Ed.). *Haunted by empire: Geographies of intimacy in North American history.* Durham and London: Duke University Press.

Strobel, L. M. (2001). *Coming full circl: The process of decolonization among post-1965 Filipino Americans.* Quezon City, Philippines: Giraffe Books.

Strobel, L. M. (2005). *A book of her own: Words and images to honor the Babaylan.* San Francisco, CA: Tiboli Press.

Strobel, L. M. (2010). *Babaylan: Filipinos and the call of the indigenous.* Davao City, Philippines: Ateneo de Davao University Research and Publications Office.

Wilcken, L. (2010). *Filipino tattoos ancient to modern.* Schiffer Publishing.

Willerslev, R. (2007). *Soul hunters: Hunting, animism, and personhood among the Siberian Yukaghirs.* Berkeley & Los Angeles, CA: University of California Press.

Zerzan, J. (Ed.). (2005). *Against civilization.* Los Angeles: Feral House.

PART I

ANCIENT SEEDS
OF KNOWING

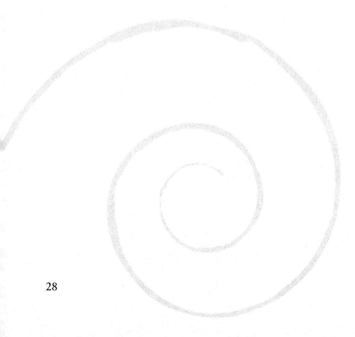

Audible Travels
Oral/Aural Traditional Performances and the Global Dispersal of a Philippine Indigenous Religion[1]

Grace Nono

Below are the first stirrings of an exploration I have been undertaking on what may fall under the purview of religion and globalization. The vast literature on how the so-called world religions that trace back to the Middle East, Rome, England, and North America, have been spreading out to the far reaches of the globe is increasingly complemented by a literature on how the religions of Asia, Africa, and other so-called margins, have, themselves, been penetrating the seats of world power (Csordas, 2007, p. 260). My own

[1] An earlier version of this paper was presented at the 2013 Buhay Babaylan Lecture-Ritual Series at the University of the Philippines-Diliman, Quezon City, Philippines on January 18, 2013. The author thanks her research hosts and collaborators led by Mamerto Tindongan in Ifugao, Philippines, and in Ohio, U.S.A., and Hospicio Dulnuan in New York, U.S.A. The author further thanks New York University's Global Research Institute in Florence, Italy, for hosting the paper's further development, Dr. Suzanne Cusick, her academic adviser at New York University, New York, U.S.A., and Dr. Martin Cohen of Boston College, Massachusetts, U.S.A. for his editorial inputs and valuable contributions.

interest is on how the indigenous religions of the Philippines are traveling out of their places of origin and thriving in foreign lands like North America, the Middle East, Europe, and other parts of the world. Sometimes the Philippine religions that win attention in new lands have already themselves absorbed and appropriated currents from world religions such as Christianity or Islam (Joson, 2007; Reed, 2001). At other times it is indigenous Philippine shamanisms that exert religious influence in a reverse direction, "from the margins to the metropole" (Csordas, 2007, p. 264).

With admiration, I have been scanning the growing literature on indigenous religions' current dispersal around the world, a development leading observers to refer to some of them as the new global religions. Examples include the religions of the *orisha* (deities) of West Africa (Nigeria and Benin), and of the *mansin* (shaman) of Korea. Regular pilgrimages are held in the African temples and festivals of the *orisha* attended by devotees from different continents. Conferences, books, recordings, films are being organized, published, and released about this fast globalizing religion. *Orisha* priests and priestesses who are based in continents other than Africa also travel regularly to their religious homeland, paving the way for the ongoing traffic of ritual knowledge and paraphernalia, among other manifestations of this increasingly globalized religion (Cohen, 2009, pp. 205, 214-216).

As for the Korean *mansin*, who for centuries were labeled as purveyors of superstition, persecuted by Christian missionaries and proponents of Western-style modernity alike, their fortunes have likewise shifted since the 1970s. The Republic of Korea instituted the Cultural Properties Protection Program, and, since then, has valorized the *mansin* as bearers of Korean cultural heritage. The *mansin*'s ritual, *kut*, has also taken on the valence of a national treasure. In the 1980s, some *mansin* were invited to perform their ritual activities at the Smithsonian Folklife Festival in Washington D.C. In 1990, a conference on *mansin*-related topics was organized by the International Society for Shamanistic Research in Seoul, Korea (Kendall, 2009). When a Korean *mansin* was invited to New York City in 2003 to help commemorate 9/11, she staged a *kut* (shamanic ritual) and called on the souls of the terror attack's victims (Kendall, 2009, pp. 11-31).

Besides their reconstitution as national heritage, *mansin* practices have also become viewed as religion by the Korean associations that promote them, even if the term does not quite capture *mansin* life given the absence of either a unified church or doctrine in its actual practice (Kendall, 2009, p. 30). Scholars like Talal Asad (1993, p. 29), Richard King (1999), and Tisa Wenger (2009), among others, have tackled the inappropriateness of the term "religion" in describing non-European and non-Western experiences. But because the term has already become part of many non-European populations' present-day vocabularies, its usage has continued, contributing to its ongoing process of redefinition (Marcos, 2010; Wenger, 2009).

When I read these studies, I asked myself, what of the Philippine indigenous religions like that of the *babaylan*, or the *mumbaki*, among others? What is happening to them in this day and age of global dispersal of Filipino bodies around the world? Considering that almost ten million Filipinos, constituting about ten percent of the Philippines' overall population, work and live outside of the homeland, what are the implications of this in the distribution of Philippine indigenous religions?

In his study on religion and globalization, Thomas Csordas (2007) raised the question: "What portable practices allow religious traditions to traverse geographical and cultural boundaries?" (p. 261). What I would like to explore in this study are the ways in which the performance of oral/aural traditions by functionaries and practitioners of Philippine indigenous religions constitute some of the portable practices that are responsible for the growing spread of Philippine indigenous religions around the world. The role of individuals as carriers and performers of these oral/aural traditions cannot be overstated, particularly in the face of accusations of globalization studies as "faceless" (Robbins, 2009, p. 218).

What of the Philippine indigenous religions like that of the babaylan, *or the* mumbaki…? *What is happening to them in this day and age of global dispersal of Filipino bodies around the world?*

THE BAKI OF MAMERTO TINDONGAN

After years of searching for a *babaylan* in the United States, I was introduced in December 2012 to an Ohio-based initiated Ifugao *mumbaki*. The *mumbaki* is the *babaylan* (indigenous priest, healer, oralist/auralist) among the people of the Ifugao province in the Cordillera Administrative Region of Northern Luzon, Northern Philippines. While the *babaylan* in the Philippines are predominantly women (Brewer, 2004; Mamanzan, 1999; Mangahas, 2006), the Ifugao mumbaki have been mostly men, though there have been women mumbaki in history (Huwan Candelario, personal communication, February 5, 2013).

Mamerto "Lagitan" Tindongan is a fifty-five year old *mumbaki*, wood sculptor, champion atlatlist (spear thrower), and healer. He is also an initiated *paqo* and *laika*, a 4th level priest and earth keeper, respectively, in the *Quero* (Native South American) tradition.

Born and raised in barangay Kinakin, municipality of Banaue, province of Ifugao, Mamerto had been living in Albany, Ohio, over the last twenty years. He first moved to the US in 1991 to join his wife, Cynthia White, who once served as a Peace Corps Volunteer in an Ifugao village. Mamerto finished two masters degrees at Ohio University, in Geography and in International Relations. After a year of living in the U.S., Mamerto was struck with

Menier's disease, a malady that ails the inner ear, causing exhaustion, loss of balance, and vomiting whenever the pupils of the eyes are moved. Mamerto consulted two American specialists who told him that Menier's disease had no known cure. Even if he underwent surgery, there was a forty percent chance that the procedure would fail. Mamerto suffered for many years. Then in 2005, he met a shaman of half Native-American descent in an International Health Exposition. This shaman performed soul retrieval ceremonies that interested Mamerto because this was something the *mumbakis* of Banaue also did. While Mamerto wanted to go home to Banaue then, he could not do so because of the lack of funds. So he decided to undergo soul retrieval with this half Native American shaman, a process that he believes, put him on the road to recovery. Mamerto's growing engagement with Native American ways, which, in his estimation, resembled those of the Ifugao—at the very least, the non-volunteering of spiritual knowledge, and the non-charging of fees for healing services—led him to undergo nine *munay ki* initiation rites that that gave him the title of *laika* or earth keeper in the *Quero* tradition. He also underwent the *hatun karpay* rite to become a fourth level priest (the *Quero* are the descendants of the Incas in the Andes mountains of Peru). When, finally, he was able to go home to Banaue—"My illness brought me back to the baki," he said—he voluntarily asked to be initiated by his father, Bruno "Buwaya" Tindongan, who was their family's seventh generation *mumbaki*.

Mamerto's initiation was a highly auspicious event because for a long time, his father had been looking for someone to inherit his *baki*. The first thing that Mamerto learned was to connect with his clan's *mumbaki* ancestors who had passed on. His next task was to memorize some of the *baki* of the Ifugao priesthood. The baki performances, he explained, were taught to the Ifugao by their higher *maknongan* (Ifugao deities), like Lidchum, the head of the *Kabunian* or skyworld. For millennia, the *baki* had been the oral/aural means through which Ifugao priests summoned their spirits. "The *maknongan* know the *baki's* sound. When they hear it they know that they are being called, so they come immediately, he said." To aid his learning, Mamerto has been using a digital audiotape to record the first three of his father's twelve *baki*. To obtain a complete record of his father's knowledge, he also plans to visit anthropologist Harold Conklin whose *baki* research was mostly informed, transcribed, and interpreted by Buwaya Tindongan, Mamerto's father. These technological and literate methods depart from traditional pedagogy that consists of sitting with, listening to, and participating in the rituals of the older *mumbakis* over a long period of time. "It's not that I'm in a hurry," Mamerto said. "But the digital recorder and my father's transcriptions are helpful too." This innovation is particularly relevant to Mamerto who is not always in Banaue. The one thing that Mamerto observed with the baki chants and recitations is that they are both effective in eliciting the *maknongan's* response. And because chanting is so much more difficult than reciting, not to mention, highly time consuming, a luxury not readily available in the much faster pace of life in America, Mamerto had only been reciting his baki. But while reciting is so much easier and takes much less time than chanting, Mamerto still wishes to master his father's chants someday.

When Mamerto first returned to Banaue, he saw that his father was sick. He offered him healing, using methods that he learned from his Native American teachers. Conversely, when he came back to Ohio, he carried with him his father's knowledge of the Ifugao *maknongan* whose names he had since been committing to memory so that he can invoke these anytime, anywhere he is in need. In other words, there transpired between Mamerto and his father an exchange of healing and spiritual knowledge. After Mamerto's initiation, his father, himself, felt encouraged to continue his own *baki*, after years of being forced by Mamerto's younger siblings to stop the practice due to fundamentalist Christian pressures. His father regained his energy after realizing that the *baki* will live on through Mamerto who became initiated as their family's 8th-generation *mumbaki*. Here, we note the impetus for the dispersal of indigenous religion as not only moving outward from the homeland, but also inward, back to the homeland.

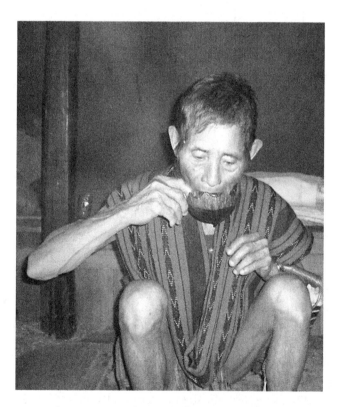

Figure 1. Senior Ifugao mumbaki Bruno "Buwaya"
Tindongan, Kinakin, Banaue, Ifugao, Philippines, 2011
(*Photo by Pedro "Abluyon" Tindongan*)

Figure 2. Ifugao mumbaki initiate Mamerto "Lagitan"
Tindongan, Kinakin, Banaue, Ifugao, Philippines, 2011
(*Photo by Pedro "Abluyon" Tindongan*)

In Mamerto's story we find the overriding importance in becoming a *mumbak*i of learning to connect with one's spirit sources through time-honored means. To the Ifugao, this is done through the performance of the *baki* that are oral/aural traditions introduced by and known to the *maknongan*. Because these voice performances that hold the endless potential for the confluence of sound and spirit have little material weight, and are portable and easy to travel with, they have served as some of the ways for Philippine indigenous religions to traverse geographical and cultural boundaries. Although Mamerto learned to practice many other spiritual paths and healing systems from his engagements with the Natives of his adoptive land, he still needed to return to his homeland to relate these with the practices he grew up with. By embracing his *baki* inheritance, by re-rooting himself in his ancestral traditions, by introducing innovations based on the demands of his own lived context in the diaspora, Mamerto is championing the history of *mumbaki.* He is, for example, following the prompting of his heart and conviction about the baki's original intention to promote only good in the world when he insists on doing away with the practice of cursing that is widespread in many religious traditions. He does the same when he promotes bypassing spirit intermediaries to go straight to the highest deities, as well as when he conducts rituals without the customary animal sacrifices whenever these are not available.

On January 23, 2013, Mamerto sent me a facebook message to inform me that he was coming home to Banaue because his father, Buwaya Tindongan had died from cardiac arrest. Since I was in Manila then, I decided to catch the final days of the wake. On February 1st, I took an overnight trip to Banaue.

It was drizzling when the bus pulled up at the Banaue terminal where Mamerto was waiting. "We had a compromise," Mamerto told me upon our arrival. After our introductions, we proceeded to his sister Estela's house, then drove to his old

In Mamerto's story we find the overriding importance [of]… learning to connect with one's spirit sources through time-honored means…

home in barangay Kinakin where the second and final part of the vigil took place. From the road, we descended on slippery stone steps to about a hundred meters below, into a sound world of human mourning, the slaughter of sacrificial animals, endless cooking, serving, and convivial chatter in Ifugao, Ilocano and English amongst the vigilers and hosts. There were between fifty to several hundred elders, middle-aged community members and children present at each time during the wake. The center of all the activity was the wooden Ifugao house on stilts with galvanized iron roofing, under which lay Buwaya Tindongan's body, dressed in a *barong* Tagalog, inside a beautiful wooden coffin adorned with Ifugao woven fabrics.[2] "We did a compromise here," Mamerto told me upon our arrival. With that he meant that some of the manner in which the vigil was conducted subscribed to the preferences of Christianized and modernized family members, while others were more in accordance with those who, like him, were just as modernized, but equally upheld their father's *baki* tradition. This compromise also meant that being at the place of vigil, one heard gong beaters take turns at playing and dancing to simulate eagles that once inhabited Banaue, but also the sounds of phonograph music playing American country western songs with Christian lyrics like "Standing on the Promise of God" and "How Great Thou Art." In one of the evening vigils, Mamerto organized a *liwliwa* chanting session so that the elders could sing and listen about Buwaya's life and deeds. While this transpired, the *liwliwa* singers' voices were drowned out by a Hollywood movie that featured Mel Gibson, and by evangelist fire and brimstone speeches by "Christ is the Answer" members who

---

[2] This was a departure from the older way (up to the 1990s) of having the body of the dead, donning native Ifugao attire, sit, tied to a chair made from the betel nut trunk, under the Ifugao house, while continuously being smoked to delay the process of decomposition. One reason put forward for the change was sanitation (personal communication, Ambrocio Dulnuan, February, 2013).

had the benefit of a loudspeaker. "The *liwliwa*," these evangelized Ifugaos, claim, "are nonsense. They have no Biblical basis, and constitute the devil's work." Thus, Ambrosio Dulnuan, Mamerto's brother in-law, noted, "The family and community are divided. Some are against the *baki*, while others uphold it. We were told," he added, "that there would have been more vigilers had the family not invited *mumbakis* to perform rituals. But we, Ifugao Catholics, continue to perform the *baki* because inculturation allows us to do so."[3] Mamerto added that just like disenfranchised Native Americans, many Ifugaos are confused, having been told that their ancestors were demons. He believes, however, that the Ifugaos continue to have strong ancestral connections with their ancestors.

Of the eight night and day vigil (three days in Estela's house where their father died, and five days in Mamerto's where their father lived), *baki* were performed on the first and sixth days. The rest were devoted to Christian services and Bible sharing. Mamerto told me that in one of the *baki*, Buwaya's soul was asked for the spiritual reason of his death. Through a mourner/medium, Buwaya replied, "It was the god of pahang that took me because I never performed the pahang (one form of baki). Even when I was sick, it was still not celebrated. I would have lived longer had the pahang been performed." Mamerto's youngest sisters, who, out of their great concern for their father's health, sent him to doctors of western medicine in their conviction that these, alone, not baki, could cure him, cried upon hearing this. Ambrosio explained, "There are illnesses that could not be cured by doctors and hospitals. This is especially the case if these are caused by the souls of ancestors who are asking for rituals." It is for this reason that many younger generation Ifugaos, however modernized, still choose to become initiated in the *baki* tradition. There is a sixteen year-old high school student who now practices *baki*. There is also one who has a Ph.D. and who serves as a school district supervisor," he said.

On the day of Buwaya's burial, a medium chanted over his coffin. Through this medium Buwaya spoke to express his gratitude and satisfaction over how the whole wake was conducted.

Very early the following morning, Estela came up to me to ask if I was interested in videotaping the *baki* that was about to commence. Called *lawet*, the purpose of this *baki* was to summon to Kinakin the deity responsible for ushering Buwaya's soul to Lagud (downstream in the spirit world), where all the dead go. It was additionally performed to cleanse the surviving kin of impurities. The reason why *lawet* is performed early in the morning is because the stream is still clear then, and the water trail not yet muddied by farmers. That morning's *lawet* was to be officiated by Huwan Candelario who was Buwaya's mentor, with the assistance of Jose "Nabbud" Pagaddut, Buwaya's nephew, a

---

[3] "Inculturation is the term that Catholic leaders and theologians have used in recent decades to denote a process of engagement between the Christian Gospel and a particular culture. The term is intended conceptually both to safeguard the integrity of the Gospel and to encourage sensitivity to various cultural contexts" (Doyle, 2012).

younger *mumbaki*. The reason for having many mumbakis in attendance, Ambrosio told me, is that if the one who does the calling gets possessed by the spirit, losing his will in the process, it becomes the responsibility of the other *mumbakis* present to converse with the spirit who has arrived, or to do its bidding.

I climbed the bamboo ladder to the interior of the Ifugao house where the *mumbakis*, together with Mamerto's eldest brother, Pedro, had gathered. I set up my computer while Mamerto readied his iPhone to record the proceedings. The fire on the hearth was burning, casting a soft glow on Huwan's silhouette draped with a red Ifugao blanket. Huwan faced the ritual paraphernalia that consisted of the *punamhan*, a wooden box that contained betel nut and leaves, ashes, and the blood of sacrificial chickens, among other items. The *punamhan*, Mamerto explained to me, was where the power of the *maknongan* was stored. There was also the *chuyu* or *pamanhan*, a wooden container for the *bayah* or rice wine, or in its absence gin, rum, or coke; coconut shell cups called *ongot*; and Huwan's sugarcane shoot. Sitting on a wooden bench, Huwan covered his right ear with his right palm and began to chant the *baki* in a soft drone for the next almost four hours. He paused along the way, to drink coke (Mamerto's family was not able to ferment rice wine, and even if they did, Huwan's doctor prohibited him from dinking any kind of liquor), to let Mamerto slaughter the sacrificial duck, to tell stories while the cooking took place, to call the spirits again, then to partake of the ritual food. Mamerto explained to me that in the baki, Huwan called on all the Lagud deities who conferred amongst themselves, then decided it was *maknongan* Hinogwakan who was to travel to Kinakin to fetch Buwaya's soul. Through the *baki*, Huwan guided Hinogwakan from Bagabag, outside of Ifugao, where the maknongan started his journey, through the Ifugao towns of Lamut, Lagawe, Hingyon, then Banaue. Hinogwakan did not, however, go through the towns proper but through the known old settlements. When he came close to Kinakin, for example, he went through the old settlement Guilot. Then he examined the river tributaries to determine which one to follow. Eventually, he came to another old settlement, within Kinakin, called Gohang, where he asked the descendants of an old settler there where the people who were calling him were located (referring to Huwan, Mamerto, and Mamerto's eldest brother, Pedro). Then he passed through Ellong, where he again inquired. Eventually, he arrived in Punlutaan, where Mamerto's house stood. After Hinogwakan was offered wine, Huwan, Pedro and Mamerto presented him with their animal offering. He then cleansed and blessed them, afterwards giving his assurance that he would take care of their father's soul. Taking Buwaya soul with him, he journeyed back to Lagud, following the river. Huwan no longer needed to guide Hinogwakan upon his return (Mamerto Tindongan, personal communication, July 26, 2013).

Figure 3. Three Ifugao mumbakis. From left: Jose "Nabbud" Pagaddut, Huwan Candelario
(senior mumbaki), Mamerto "Lagitan" Tindongan, Kinakin, Banaue, Ifugao, Philippines, 2013.
(*Photo by Myra-Ann Tindongan Dulnuan*)

In the foregoing description we glimpse the *baki's* crucial role in the ongoing
performance of human-spirit relations, as mediated by the *mumbaki*. The *baki's* sonic and
linguistic aspects are heard simultaneously in both the Ifugao human and spirit worlds that
may be seen as constituting one community of listeners. A community of listeners, Judith
Becker wrote, may not necessarily hear uniformly but there are overlaps in their audition's
salient features. They approach sound with a "pregiven set of expectations, a 'forestructure'
of understandings' (Becker, 2004, p. 69).

Besides providing a sonic point of convergence between Ifugao spirits and humans,
the *baki's* words are not mere statements or descriptions but constitute "performative
utterances" (Austin, 1962, 1975, pp. 5-7) that provoke spirit beings to cross the dimensional
divide to the site of encounter in ritual.

Hinogwakan's journey from the spirit world of Lagud to the human world of Kinakin
and back, and Buwaya's journey from Kinakin to Lagud, assume what J. Lorand Matory
refers to as a particular "logic of personhood, geography, and history" that determine
how translocal flows are conducted by particular groups . This is of particular importance
to discussions of globalization that confine the globe to its material manifestations, like
capitalism, and do not/ could not account for such interdimensional, translocal exchanges
(Matory, 2009, pp. 231- 233). Matory wrote:

> The ontology of any given religion is closely connected to an implicit
> geography and to its real-world geopolitics. [T]ransactions with the

divine [are described] in terms of the "paths," "roads," "journeys," and other trans-territorial conduits that connect us, collectively or individually, to the divine Other Place [spirit world]. In many religions, those paths are literally trans-territorial pilgrimage routes that cross-cut numerous political boundaries. [W]orshipers focus far less on the literal or metaphorical journey *to* the Other Place and far more on the continual movement of beings *between* Places. (Matory, 2009, pp. 239-240)

Matory's emphasis on interdimensional movement and spiritually-charged mobility is not necessarily incompatible with the critique advanced by certain Native groups against the notion of a global religion or spirituality that is not linked to any specific place. The critique states that "When non-Native people use the idea of spirituality to refer to a 'religion' that transcends time and space,

What remains to be seen, however, is if a community of mumbakis, *clients, entourage, and supporters can be forged in the U.S. to support the* baki's *transplantation into the foreign land.*

(atemporal and acultural) it continues the legacy of Christianity, which, by considering itself a religion of no particular time and place, became, in its own eyes, the religion of all times and places" (Grimes, 2001, pp. 18-19; Swanson, 1994, pp. 241-263). Matory clarifies that locality in global religious practice does not necessarily lose its relevance. Rather, "[t]he religious transaction between the Other Place and the Present Place cannot do without the reality of the Present Place," he wrote (2009, p. 240).

I asked mumbaki Nabbud and others if they thought summoning the *maknongan*, not from Banaue, Philippines, but from Ohio, USA, will provoke such deities to come to such unfamiliar grounds. The answer I received was a yes. The *baki*, the customary offerings, and the ordained *mumbaki*, himself, will make the unfamiliar grounds familiar. Hence, if a *mumbaki* in Ohio is able to successfully summon his spirits to his ritual site in the diaspora, these spirits' attendance is expected to contribute much to the efficacy of his ritual actions. What remains to be seen, however, is if a community of *mumbakis*, clients, entourage, and supporters can be forged in the U.S. to support the *baki's* transplantation into the foreign land. Without clients to request the *baki* regularly, for example, the *mumbaki* will have no opportunities to apply and master his knowledge. According to Hospicio Dulnuan, a respected Ifugao cultural leader who was responsible for introducing me to Mamerto, the Ifugaos in America are not only dispersed across vast distances, they are also too busy with their work to converge on a regular basis. And when these bear children from mixed marriages, language becomes a problem because the children end up learning English in school, thereby impeding the transmission of oral/aural traditional knowledge. There is also no other *mumbaki* who can officiate in rituals besides Mamerto who happens to live very far from Long Island, New York, where Hospicio has been residing.

Figure 4. Hospicio Dulnuan,
US-based Ifugao cultural leader, Ronkonkoma,
Long Island, New York, USA, 2012.
(*Photo by Grace Nono*)

For Hospicio's *baki* needs, he has, all this time, been calling upon *mumbakis* in Ifugao to perform rituals for him, long distance. He recounted that in 2011, he requested *mumbaki* Kindipan and another one to conduct a *baki*, the *pahang*, specifically, for his healing and good health. This was after Hospicio underwent surgery in the groin due to clogged veins, causing him extreme difficulty in walking. While the ritual took place in Banaue, he said, "my nephew here in Ronkonkoma, Jun, set-up skype on his large TV screen to connect with my family in Ifugao who were directly overseeing the ritual proceedings. Skype allowed *mumbaki* Kindipan to ask me questions and to give me instructions in real time, while the ritual was going on. Kindipan sacrificed seven native hens and showed me the chicken biles– their sizes, positions, and colors—all of which indicated an auspicious outcome."

Just like Mamerto's utilization of the iPhone as an aid to mastering his father's *baki*, here is another instantiation of how modern technology is utilized towards the dispersal of a Philippine indigenous religion outside of its land of origin. This technological form of mediation relies on oral/aural forms of engagement, and generates further oral/aural forms of engagement. .All this is reminiscent of Walter Ong's notion of secondary orality that is "technologically powered, demanding the use of writing and other technologies in designing and manufacturing the machines which reproduce voice" (Klein & Gale, 1996, pp. 65-86).

Figure 5. Iphone technology in the service of baki transmission.
Senior Ifugao mumbaki Huwan Candelaria (left) and
Mamerto "Lagitan" Tindongan (right), Kinakin, Banaue, Ifugao,
Philippines, 2013. (*Photo by Grace Nono*)

Despite the challenges that face the *baki* in Mamerto's adoptive land, Mamerto feels a measure of optimism. He has been invited by several US-based Philippine groups to bless their events and to speak about his *baki* practice. He dreams one day of inviting Huwan to America, and of performing the *baki* for Hospicio, and for Harold Conklin, among others. There will be other matters to consider if one extends the *baki* to non-Ifugaos, to non-Filipinos, and to the younger generations. One is language. How can those who do not speak Ifugao learn to perform the *baki*? Another is the US government's strict laws concerning the licensing of health practitioners. If *baki* practitioners submit to the certification process, thereby justifying the commercial exploitation of their practice, this will go against the time-honored practice by Philippine healers of desisting from charging payment for their services. A third challenge that faces the baki is the patriarchy that characterizes the current *mumbaki* ranks that may not sit well with the younger and more educated populations committed to overthrowing practices that marginalize women.

For now I will rest in the observation that oral/aural traditional performances like the *baki* provide a measure of portability and transposability that allow Filipinos, wherever

The global dispersal of Philippine indigenous religions may not be a very visible phenomenon. Yet it is audible to those who listen.

they are in the world, to access ancestral connections and knowledge. Csordas (2007) conceives of transposability as connoting susceptibility to "being transformed or reordered without being denatured, and the valuable musical metaphor of being performable in a different key" (p. 265). On this basis, Csordas alludes to a different understanding of universality, that is, not "the sense of being dominated by a single master narrative," but universality in the sense that "any element can be transposed onto or transported into any other cultural setting" (p. 265).

Just like the African *orisha* priest and the Korean *mansin*, Ifugao *mumbaki* Mamerto "Lagitan" Tindongan and his ancestral spirits are well poised to carry on with their ongoing movement across continents and dimensions, while keeping rooted in their spiritual and geographical homelands. Mamerto is joined by thousands of Filipinos—some of them indigenous priestesses and priests—in North America, in Europe, in the Middle East, among other places. They carry in their bodies, oral/aural traditions in the form of prayers, songs, and stories, whose performances are intended to activate ancestral spirit connections, anytime, anywhere, to heal the sick, to provide protection, guidance, and blessing. The global dispersal of Philippine indigenous religions may not be a very visible phenomenon. Yet it is audible to those who listen.

Figure 6. Ohio-based Ifugao mumbaki Mamerto "Lagitan" Tindongan (right) orally/aurally transmitting aspects of baki knowledge to his Filipino-American daughter, Amihan "Pinapin" Tindongan (left), Albany, Ohio, USA, 2013. *(Photo by Virgil Apostol)*

References

Asad, T. (1993). *Genealogies of religion: Discipline and reasons of power in Christianity and Islam.* Maryland: The John Hopkins Press.

Austin, J. L. (1962, 1975). *How to do things with words.* J. O. Urmson & M. Sbisa (Eds.). Massachusetts: Harvard University Press.

Becker, J. (2004). *Deep listeners: Music, emotion, and trancing.* Bloomington and Indianapolis: Indiana University Press.

Brewer, C. (2004). *Shamanism, Catholicism and gender relations in Colonial Philippines, 1521–1685.* Hampshire: Ashgate Publishing.

Cohen, P. (2009). The Orisha Atlantic: Historicizing the roots of a global religion. In T. J. Csordas (Ed.), *Modalities of transnational transcendence: Essays on religion and globalization* (pp. 205-229). Berkeley: University of California Press.

Csordas, T. (2007). Modalities of transnational transcendence. *Anthropological Theory, 7,* 259-272.

Doyle, D. M. (2012). The concept of inculturation in Roman Catholicism: A theological consideration. *U.S. Catholic Historian, 30*(1), 1-13.

Grimes, R. L. (2001). Global spirituality and ritual. In H. Phelan (Ed.), *Anail De: The Breath of God: Music Ritual and Spirituality.* Dublin: Veritas Publications.

Joson, V. (2007). Filipino missionaries in Europe: Witnesses for re-evangelization. In F. M. Hogsholm (Ed.), *In De Olde Worlde: Views of Filipino migrants in Europe* (pp. 364-375). Manila: Philippine Migration Research Network and Philippine Social Science Council.

Kendall, L. (2009). *Shamans, nostalgias, and the IMF: South Korean popular religion in motion.* Honolulu: University of Hawaii Press.

King, R. (1999). *Orientalism and religion: Postcolonial theory, India and 'the Mystic East'.* New York: Routledge.

Kleine, M., & Gale, F. G. (1996). The elusive presence of the word: An interview with Walter Ong. *Composition FORUM, 7.2,* 65-86.

Mananzan, M. J. (1999). Religion as a socializing force in the 'Women Question.' *Gender Construction: Review of Women's Studies, 9*(1 & 2), 1-15.

Mangahas, F. (2006). The babaylan: Historico-cultural context. In F. Mangahas & J. Llaguno (Eds.), *Centennial crossings: Readings on babaylan feminism in the Philippines.* Manila: C & E Publishing, Inc.

Marcos, S. (2010). Introduction: Perspectives of indigenous religious traditions from the Americas, Asia, and Australia. In S. Marcos (Ed.), *Women and Indigenous Religions*, vii-x. California, Colorado, Oxford: Praeger.

Matory, J. L. (2009). The many who dance in me: Afro-Atlantic ontology and the problem with 'transnationalism.' In T. J. Csordas (Ed.), *Modalities of transnational transcendence: Essays on religion and globalization.* Berkeley: University of California Press.

Reed, R. R. (2001). The Iglesia ni Cristo: From obscure Philippine faith to global belief system. *Bijdragen tot de Taal-, Land- en Volkenkunde, 157*(3), 561-608.

Robbins, J. (2009). The trans- in transnational. In T. J. Csordas (Ed.), *Modalities of transnational transcendence: Essays on religion and globalization.* Berkeley: University of California Press.

Swanson, T. (1994). To prepare a place: Johannine Christianity and the collapse of ethnic territory. *Journal of the American Academy of Religion, 62*(2), 241-263.

Wenger, T. (2009). *We have a religion: The 1920s Pueblo Indian dance controversy and American religious freedom.* Chapel Hill: University of North Carolina Press.

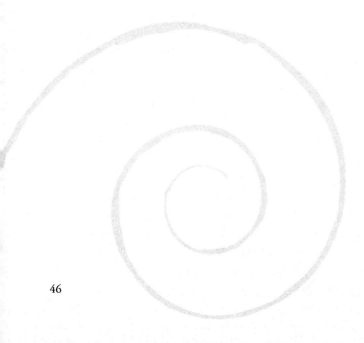

Anting-anting
Why Bathala Hides
Inside the Stone

Nenita Pambid Domingo

Figure 1. Anting-anting: Bronze amulets sold outside of Catholic Church in Quiapo, Manila (Photo by Tita Pambid)

"Our first task in approaching another people, another culture, or another religion is to take off our shoes, for the place we are approaching is holy, else we may find ourselves treading on man's [sic] dream; more seriously still, we may forget that God was there before our arrival."

—Cultural workers from Mindanao (in Crass & De Mesa, 1987, p. 26)

Before March 16, 1521 when Ferdinand Magellan claimed the archipelago presently known as the Republic of the Philippines and subsequently named in honor of King Philip the Second of Spain, the people of the islands believed in *anitu*, the spirit of the ancestor or of nature. According to western categories, this kind of belief is a form of animism. Animism is "the doctrine that all life is produced by a spiritual force separate from matter; that all natural phenomena have souls independent of their physical being; a belief in the existence of spirits, demons, etc." (Neufeldt, 1988, p. 55) To Filipinos, human beings have a spiritual component, a spirit or soul called *kaluluwa*.

The belief in the *kaluluwa* or spirit existed long before the coming of the Spaniards. The concept of the *kaluluwa* is widespread in different ethno-linguistic groups in the Philippines, and linguistic evidence supports this. In Tagalog, the term for the non-physical aspect of a human is *kaluluwa, carurua* in Ilocano (Carro, 1888, p. 82), *kaladuwa* in Kapampangan (Forman as cited in Lorenzo-Abrera, 1992, p. 135), *calag* in Bikol and Bisaya (De La Encarnacion, n.d., p. 6). The belief in the soul/spirit can be linked to the Southeast Asian belief in spirit possession and shamanism. In the Philippines, there is a belief that the physical body can be possessed or "occupied" by a good spirit such as one's ancestors or loved ones who have moved on to the "other life," or God the Father, God the Mother, or God the Son in the form of the Santo Niño. The Santo Niño or child Jesus is believed to have been brought over by Magellan in 1521, and was given as a gift to the wife of the chieftain of Cebu after undergoing baptismal rites in the Catholic faith.

The physical body can also be possessed by malevolent spirits or elementals such as the *tiyanak* or dwarfs, supernatural creatures native to the Philippines, and "naturalized" Hispanic ones such as the *cafre* (Patianak, 2013; Kapre, 2013). These supernatural creatures can cause harm or sickness to a person whose body was possessed. When a person's *kaluluwa* is out of its physical body and consciousness is absent, other spirits can occupy that physical body.

Spanish friars adapted the Tagalog word *kaluluwa*, something that detaches from the physical body, to signify the concept of soul. The Ilocano, Pangasinan, Kapampangan, Tagalog, Bikolano, and Bisaya who were at the epicenter of Spanish colonial rule, believed in one soul akin to Christian belief. The Ilocanos believe that everyone has a *cararua na bantay* (soul guard), the Tagalogs also equate the soul to *lagyo*[1] (having the same name with), *diwa*[2] (consciousness, the thing that animates), *buhay* (life), and the Spanish loan word *espiritu* (spirit) (Pambid, 1989). It can be conjectured that the Spanish friars tried to explain the concept of the soul to the natives by identifying a similar domain in the local culture and using vernacular terms that resonated with the indigenous concept of the soul for easy acceptance by the inhabitants of the islands.

Other ethnic groups like the Bagobo believe in two *kaluluwa*, the Negritos from two to three; the Tagbanuwa of Palawan believe in six, seven for the natives of Bukidnon, and eight for another group of Bagobo in Cibolan, Davao. Some groups share a belief in good and bad *kaluluwa* co-existing in the individual (Lorenzo-Abrera, 1992, p. 136).

---

[1] Lagyô. Alma. f.. Sinon. de hilagyo; kalulowa; sangay. Author found this in Pedro Serrano Laktaw's *Diccionario Tagalog-Hispano* Segunda Parte (Manila, Islas Filipinas: Imp. y Lit. de Santos y Bernal, 1914) p. 531. Kalulowa. See p. 438.

[2] Diwa. Def. 1. Espiritu; animo. Author's source: Serrano Laktaw, p. 225.

All the indigenous words mentioned above, except for *buhay, diwa,* and *espiritu,* denote "two" and something that detaches and departs from the earthen vessel that is the human body when breath expires. *Buhay* (life), *diwa* (consciousness), and *espiritu* (spirit) on the other hand refer to the function of the *kaluluwa, i.e.* it animates and gives life, movement, feeling, consciousness, and volition to the individual. According to Filipino belief, when the soul leaves, it signals the physical death of the person and all its attributes of feeling, willing, and thinking. The soul/spirit or *kaluluwa,* on the other hand, is deathless, i.e. continues to live without a "container."

In one of the myths of pre-Hispanic Filipinos, the first people of the islands were construed as the first people of the world borne of supernatural powers emanating from nature. The most popular creation myth is called *"calaque,"* the man and the woman *"cabaye"* who came out of the nodes of a bamboo (Quirino, 1958, pp. 389-396). The people, being a part and extension of the power in nature, hold feasts and rituals, and render offerings to the spirits called *anitu.* The creation myth was popularized during the Marcos dictatorial regime as "Si Malakas at si Maganda" (He, the Strong and She, the Beautiful), imparting a subliminal message that strengthened the power of the Marcoses.

. . . [W]hatever happened to the native God of the Filipinos when the Spanish Catholic God, Three Persons in One God or Holy Trinity and its host of angels vanquished the "heathens" and their gods?

When the Spaniards imposed their belief system, the concept of the Christian soul syncretically blended with the local belief in the *kaluluwa.* Christianity appropriated the native concept of the *kaluluwa* to contain the new Catholic theological concept of the soul. To the Filipinos, if a person's soul or spirit leaves its physical body, other spirits can possess the physical body. The possessing spirit can either be a good or a malevolent one.

Filipino indigenous worldview reflects a belief in numerous deities. The Igorots have numerous gods but believed in a supreme being called *Kabunian* (Kabunian, 2013). The Tagalogs on the other hand believed in a supreme being called *Bathala.* Any one of these spirits can possess a person's physical body. During the Spanish era, the Spanish friars labeled these spirits as demons or demonic.

One may ask, whatever happened to the native God of the Filipinos when the Spanish Catholic God, Three Persons in One God or Holy Trinity and its host of angels vanquished the "heathens" and their gods? After more than two years of library work and becoming a participant observer-researcher and an apprentice to a shaman/healer at Pateros, Rizal, Philippines, my research brought me to the gates of Quiapo Catholic Church at the heart of Manila, the capital city of the Philippines. In the days of pre-contact, these healers were called *babaylan,* or *catalonan.* At present, they are simply called *manggagamot* from the prefix *mang-* meaning office or profession/occupation, and *gamot,* meaning medicine. It was Ka[3] Ambo of the *Samahang Santisima Trinidad Samahang Santo Niño* (Association of the Holy Trinity Association of the Holy Child/Boy) who initiated me into indigenous healing and ushered me into the complex world of the Filipino psyche and view of the cosmos. He brought me into contact with the *Infinito Dios* (Infinite God) (See Figure 2) or *Nuno* (the Tagalog word for "ancestor" as well as grandchild), the God who refused to be baptized as engraved in the medallion/amulet or *anting-anting.* Over several years of contact with Ka Ambo and observing his healing practices and interaction with patients, he taught me many stories about Infinito Dios which were esoteric teachings that had direct application in healing. There are healers in my own family and this is the primary driving force behind my research on the healers and their use of amulets or anting-anting. Having been trained in western paradigms of knowledge, I had endeavored to find a theoretical framework for studying indigenous practices to make the topic on amulets acceptable as an academic field of study at the University of the Philippines in 1989 (cf. Pambid, 1989).

Figure 2. Infinito Dios
Bronze Amulet (Photo by Reuben T. Domingo)

---

[3] *Ka* is a social term for a male or a female to indicate respect. It is placed before the names of elders with whom one is acquainted with. Hence, *Ambo* is the name of the person. It is also used for distant uncles and aunts. *Ka* can also mean *kasama* which means companion or included. It is also a prefix which means co-, fellow, or mate as in ka*babayan*- fellow countryman.

According to a myth prevalent among the millenarians[4] in Mount Banahaw, Quezon Province, and other religious movements in the city, the belief in the Infinite God, *Nuno* (ancestor) or *Bathalismo* (from the name of the Tagalog God Bathala) was the indigenous belief of the Filipinos long before the coming of the Spaniards. In the course of time, either the Spanish Trinitarian God (Three Persons in One God) must have been indigenized, or Bathala, Hispanized.

In the myth of the Infinite God, the story avers that *Infinito Dios* was the first and the most powerful (Sabino, 1955, pp. 38-44). He created sixteen spirits, three of which were to play the role of Three Persons in One God. They are also known by other names: *Tatlong Persona sa Iisang Dios* (Three Persons in One God), *Sagrada Familya* (Holy Family[5]), and *Santisima Trinidad* (Holy Trinity). These three spirits were tasked to execute his plans of creation that the *Infinito Dios* and Maria or Gumamela Celis conceived. Maria in this myth is not the same persona as the Blessed Virgin Mary of the Catholic faith. Gumamela Celis is *Dios Ina* or God the Mother. According to the myth as told by Sabino (1955), the meaning of Gumamela Celis is *Bulaklak ng Langit* (Flower of Heaven) or *Rosa Mundi* (flower of the world). The name Maria, which, according to the myth means *Kataastaasan* (the highest or supreme) was *Infinito Dios*'s first thought. The *Infinito Dios* went down to the undermost part to prepare the *impierno* or *averni* (hell) and tasked Maria to guard his *Kaban ng Tipan* (Chest of Covenant).[6] The *Infinito Dios* strictly forbade Maria from opening the chest and if she does, she would have to go down to earth that would be created to take back the *virtud* (force or power; virtue) that were scattered and lost. Maria, however, did open the chest and three *virtud* flew away. (This part of the myth is similar to the story of Pandora's box and Eve's temptation in Genesis of the Bible; however, the tone is not punitive nor is the chest full of evil and disease.) When the *Infinito Dios* returned, he told Maria that now, Maria would have to go down to earth. Thereupon, the *Infinito Dios* created his plan and showed it to Maria.

When the Three Persons, God the Father (*Dios Ama*), God the Son (*Dios Anak*), and God the Holy Spirit (*Dios Espiritu Santo*) conferred and talked about the things that they would create, the *Nuno* or *Infinito Dios* would make his presence felt by interjecting his own thought on the matter, and played 'hide-and-seek' with them. The Three Persons thought they had the prerogative to plan and to create, and did not know that everything

---

[4] According to Reynaldo Ileto (1993), the millenarian movement rebellions were the bedrock of resistance during the colonial period. Millenarians believe in the transformation of society inspired by faith or in this case, by the magic of the anting-anting. Millenarian groups on Mt. Banahaw believe the world would come to an end in the millennium (year 2000 at the time of this study). Since the world didn't end in 2000, a new story has surfaced as to why the world did not end.

[5] In the Christian tradition, the Holy Family refers to the human parents Mary and Joseph and their divine child Jesus Christ.

[6] The other translation *of Kaban ng Tipan* is "Ark of the Covenant" (English, 2000, p. 1429).

In reality, according to the myth, it was God the Father—as he gave the order to God the Son to baptize the Nuno—who was baptized.

had already been planned before they had even envisaged the world and that they themselves were a product of the thought of that supreme being. The Three were greatly perplexed by this mysterious presence who would appear to them in the form of an eye with wings, a bright light, and an old man.

As the Three Persons pursued the enigmatic voice, they exchanged magic or power words called *oracion*[7] with the *Infinito Dios* or *Nuno* (a term used for both the ancestor and the descendant or grandchild) until they reached the gates of heaven. Here, the narration changes to the term *Sagrada Familya* to mean the Three Persons. The Three Persons did not know that they came from that One God- *Nuno,* that God the Father is the son of the *Nuno,* and God the Son, Jesus, is his grandson. God the Son and the two other Persons being oblivious of their provenance, tried to conquer and baptize the misconstrued God of the Savages or *erejes* (heretic) to save him. The chase ended when the *Nuno* hid inside a stone in Mt. Board.[8] After much struggle and persuasion, the *Nuno* acceded to the wish of his grandson to baptize him, but on condition that he would be baptized only through his own power, just like the elder in Philippine culture who gives way to the whims and caprice of the young but actually remains in control. The *Nuno* put out his finger through the stone to be baptized as shown in the *anting-anting*. In reality, according to the myth, it was God the Father—as he gave the order to God the Son to baptize the *Nuno*—who was baptized.

This very same myth handed down to me by Ka Ambo appeared in three different underground publications which can be bought from the manufacturers and dealers of *anting-anting*. All three texts were authored by Melencio T. Sabino: *Karunungan ng Diyos* (*The Wisdom of God,* 1955); *Kasaysayan ng Langit Kapangyarihan Laban sa Kasamaan* (*The History of Heaven Power over Evil,* n.d.), and *Secreto: Mga Lihim na Pangalan at Lihim na Karunungan* (*Secret Names and Occult Wisdom,* 1950). The texts from the three sources were identical except for the last one, which was in Spanish.

The following is an excerpt from the myth or Doctrine of *Infinito Dios,* translated from the Tagalog text, narrating how the Three Persons in One God struggled against

---

[7] From the Spanish *oracion* meaning "oration, speech, orison, prayer; dusk, beginning of the evening; (gram.) sentence. – the first part of catechism; the angelus." *Nuevo Diccionario Cuyas de Appleton Español-Ingles Ingles-Español por Arturo Cuyas* (Englewood Cliffs, New Jersey: Prentice-Hall, Inc., 1972) 395.

[8] Board is an ancient Anglo-Saxon family name. How it ended up in this myth is unknown. 12 July 2013 <http://www.houseofnames.com/xq/asp.fc/qx/boord-family-crest.htm>; 12 July 2013 <http://en.wikipedia.org/wiki/Wilpena_Pound?oldid=0>

the *Nuno* and how the myth and the *oraciones* or power words were put into symbols in the extant *Infinito Dios* amulet (Sabino, 1955, pp. 34+). From the *combate* (or fight using power words), one can glean from the myth, which is also the text of the *anting-anting*, a harbinger of the different powers attributed to the *Infinito Dios* amulet (See Figure 3).

Figure 3. Infinito Dios Hindi Binyagan (Pagan Infinite God). Artwork by Tita Pambid.

The Three Persons pursued the *Nuno* to Mt. Boord. Upon seeing the *Infinito Dios* (Infinito Dios), Jesus made known his intention of baptizing the Mighty M….. The Infinito Dios answered: "M…… E…..." which rendered him invisible to Jesus, though he was just beside him (Sabino, 1957, pp. 61-77).

Figure 4. "M...... E....."

Figure 5. "H..... N....."

Jesus countered: "H..... N....." With these power words, the *Infinito Dios* felt as though he was hit on the head, and thus did not know where to go. Incessantly, Jesus kept trailing him and enjoining him to acquiesce, pledging heaven and earth if he surrenders.

Figure 6. "C……….. V….. B….."

When the *Infinito Dios* became cognizant of what was happening, he sought to protect himself by uttering: "C……….. V….. B……"

With these power words, Jesus was dumbfounded.

Figure 7. "P…….. B…."

Upon seeing what had happened, God the Father who gave Jesus the order to baptize the *Nuno* said, "P…….. B….."

These power words paralyzed the *Infinito Dios*

Figure 8. "S……. H….. M…….. M…."

The *Infinito Dios* on the other hand retorted: "S……. H….. M…….. M….." These power words enabled him to move and he seized upon an ashlar stone which weighed 150 *arrobas* or 1,725 kilograms with the intent of hitting Jesus on the head.

Jesus retaliated by saying "I….," which froze the hands of the *Infinito Dios* in action and followed by "I…." which made the stone fall from the hands of the *Infinito Dios*. Finally, Jesus said, "I… H.. (E⁹H). This *oracion* knocked out the *Infinito Dios* unconscious. When Jesus saw what had happened, he reversed the *oracion* to revive the *Infinito Dios*

---

⁹ The letters "e" and "i" alternate in Filipino/Tagalog.

Figure 9. "I... H.. " (EH)

Figure 10. "L...... M...."

When the *Infinito Dios* regained consciousness, he uttered his most sacred name "L...... M....."

He uttered this with all his might, in a thunderous voice that shook the earth and shrouded the earth in darkness.

When the Virgin Mary saw what was happening, she said "M...... B......" Suddenly, the earthquake ceased and there was light.

Figure 11. "M…… B….."

Jesus rejoined by saying: "P……. E…..." The *Infinito Dios* sank into the stone and was enchanted.

Figure 12. "P……. E……"

Jesus thought of suspending Mt. Boord in the middle of the ocean but the Virgin Mary interfered by saying: "E…. G….. D….. DEUS DEUS DEUS E….. G…… D…"

Figure 13. "E…. …" (Unknown Photographer. Courtesy of Prof. Isagani Medina, University of the Philippines, Department of History, Diliman, Quezon City)

Whereupon Jesus pleaded with the *Nuno*. The *Nuno* said he could not by any means be baptized by Jesus since he is his forefather, the First and the only God who holds all the power and the well-spring of all the forces in the universe. Then God the Son replied:

"E…. M….." "Thou shalt be given that name, and anybody who calls on Thee would not undergo any suffering in the next life.

The Infinito Dios retorted: "Thou shalt be called the second person of my body."

In the end, the Infinito Dios finally succumbed to the wishes of his grandson Jesus, but only through his own power. Thus, he uttered the very words with which God the Son baptized him. And that was how *Nuno,* the ancestor, the ancient Tagalog God *Bathala,* had supposedly come to be baptized but actually not.

Infinito Dios: I am the Holy Trinity, incarnated and incarnates, that gives power. Enigmatic God. A true God, and you are Wisdom, Volition, and Remembrance… I

The Nuno *said he could not by any means be baptized by Jesus since he is his forefather, the First and the only God who holds all the power and the well-spring of all the forces in the universe.*

shall be baptized through my own power and my own strength, now baptize me, follow my dictates: "Nothing shall fall, no suffering, even darkness shall not pass, sunder hell and limbo dashed, heavens open I shall pass. I shall put out my finger, baptize me in my own name, from my own name emanate. I am a God the Father, the Son, wisdom, power and force, I shall be called God with Three Persons.

Figure 14. *Infinito Dios* Pagan (Di-Binyagan)　　　Figure 15. *Infinito Dios* Baptized (Binyagan)

It must have been difficult for recent converts to apprehend a God having three persons, and, at the same time, having Jesus, the second person of the trinity, not having human parents. To make matters comprehensible, the Three Persons (Holy Trinity, *Santisima Trinidad*) and the Holy Family (*Sagrada Familya*) were merged into that One God, who was actually *Bathala* or *Nuno,* but was given a Spanish name: *Infinito Dios* or Infinite God. The myth avers that the *Infinito Dios* or *Nuno* came first and in fact was the primordial origin of all the power in the universe, thereby eliminating the perplexity created by the mystery of the Holy Trinity in One God and the separate existence of the Holy Family— Jesus, Mary, and Joseph—with Jesus as the Second Person and, at the same time, the son of Mary and Joseph. The myth harmonized the indigenous ancestor worship and the Catholic faith imposed by the Spanish colonizers but in effect making the native God, *Bathala/ Infinito Dios*, the supreme forefather of the Spanish God; hence, the most powerful of all the other gods.

Before the Three Persons in One God went up to heaven, they left twenty-four names of the twenty-four elders surrounding God the Father or *Infinito Dios* in heaven.

Figure 16. 24 spirits

To my mind, *Infinito Dios* or *Nuno*, the ancient Tagalog God is the Filipino genius lodged in the stone or *anting-anting*. This indio-genius (to use a term coined by independent filmmaker Kidlat Tahimik) was repressed or submerged and was hidden during Spanish, American, or even in the present, administration. Under colonial rule, this indigenous belief came to be demeaned as demonic in an effort to eradicate indigenous belief.

One cannot fully understand the meaning of the continuing existence of the *anting-anting* and its significance without considering the various millenary[10] groups—the different cults and groups who believe in the second coming of Christ and who also believe in the *Infinito Dios*. History points to these marginalized groups as the users of the *anting-anting* in their noble fight against the invading colonizers.

During the 1896 Revolution against Spain, the Santisima Trinidad, which is also the *Infinito Dios*, was used by Emilio Aguinaldo, the first President of the Republic of the Philippines (1898). Other revolutionaries such as Andres Bonifacio, the founder of the revolutionary association called KKK or *Kataastaasang Kagalang-galangang Katipunan ng mga Anak ng Bayan* (The Supreme, Most Honorable Association of the Sons of the People), and General Antonio Luna—were also documented as possessing an anting-anting as a form of protection (Joven, 1929, p. 54). On the other hand, *Harper's History of War in the Philippines* published a photograph of the *Infinito Dios* drawn on a vest (as it is pictured

---

[10] Examples of millenary groups in the Philippines are: *Iglesia Sagrada ng Lahi* (Sacred Church of the Race), *Tatlong Persona Solo Dios* (Three Persons in One One God), *Ciudad Mistica de Dios* (The Mystic City of God), *Watawat ng Lahi* (Flag of the Nation), Bathalismo, Inc. *Cinco Vocales* (The Five Vowels). Most of these groups or associations have temples or headquarters at Mount Banahaw,which they believe is the Holy Land or *Santong Lugar*. See http://millenarianism. askdefine.com/ 2013, July 12 for other examples of social or political groups who believe that the corrupt and evil world would come to an end at the end of the millennium and only the devout and pure would survive and reign the world.

The anting-anting *is just one element of our indigenous mythology—richly textured, inverting worlds like a trickster, refusing capitulation to a monocultural rendering of reality and the world…*

now) worn by an *insurrecto* (rebel) who succumbed to the superior might of the American forces in 1900 (Wilcox, 1900, p. 69). From these examples, it can be gleaned that the *anting-anting*, specifically the *Infinito Dios* amulet played a significant role in the Filipino people's motivation and ideation in fighting for freedom and in defending the motherland. Ileto's work on the resistance movements during the revolutionary period reveals that the people's use of the *anting-anting* speaks of the richness, power, and resilience of indigenous culture in the face of overwhelming (physical and psychological) assault by colonial powers. Their employment of these amulets bespeaks of their agency. Because true freedom and equality were not obtained, the struggle of the masses was shifted to the spiritual plane to empower the poor and the oppressed (Marasigan, 1985). Stripped of power under consecutive oppressive regimes, it is in the spiritual realm that the poor and marginalized kept alive the indigenous soul so much so that until today, members of the various *samahan* (associations) collectively known as millenarians, as well as ordinary people, continue to believe in the spiritual potency of the *anting-anting*. In 1967, for example, Tatang Valentin de los Santos and his *Lapiang Malaya* (Freedom Party), carrying bolos and *anting-antings*, seeking reforms from the Marcos government, were massacred by the government forces (Ileto, 1989). Some would say that the stance of the poor has been noble, but that history is replete with not a few *anting-anting* fiascos. But perhaps it could be said that, at another level, the devotees' belief in the *anting-anting* did protect their integrity to the degree it enabled them to resist power with wholeheartedness, rather than merely capitulating to fear and being conformed to resigned silence. Instead of simply casting such belief as nothing more than naivete, we need to ask what the deepest values are. Perhaps the real naivete is believing that equipping ourselves with state of the art weaponry is going to protect us if we are to judge by the rates of PTSD (Post-Traumatic Stress Syndrome), suicide, and rape, and the group think devastation of human agency that is part and parcel of the life in the army in the conduct of modern warfare.

Eventually in the years to follow, the *anting-anting* would be mass-produced and used for various purposes—from the sacred to the profane as can be seen from the *anting-anting* catalogues given for free but the *anting-anting* themselves are sold by a few enterprising vendors at Quiapo, Manila. The most common uses of *anting-antings* are the following: for the exorcism of the *nakulam* or *naengkanto* (bewitched or hexed); for healing; for protection from physical danger such as snakes, storms, earthquakes, fire, accidents, ambushes, knives and bullets. These medals are also supposed to protect one from evil creatures such as *nuno sa punso*, (old spirit on the mound), *tikbalang* (half-horse, half-man creature) that makes one lose her way in the forest, *duwende* (earth spirit), and other *lamanlupa* (elemental spirit). Other *anting-antings* are used for good luck such as the wish for a successful business, a happy family, an easy delivery, or for safe travel by land, air, and sea. These are but a few of the magical powers the users of *anting-antings* hope to manifest in their lives.

In the present dispensation, when there is no longer an overt threat of invasion and danger from an invading force, the use of the *anting-anting* has shifted to serving the immediate needs of the people, e.g., protection from evil and physical harm, healing and good health, good livelihood, and economic sufficiency. Still and all, the *anting-anting* of today remains a symbol of the Filipinos' deeply rooted connection to the Filipino genius and the indigenous soul. Although on the surface, mainstream Filipinos may have been Christianized and westernized/modernized, these *anting-antings* continue to serve as holders of ancient memory commemorating stubborn resistance to colonial domination, encoding resilience and creativity in the face of impossible odds and overwhelming assault on indigenous cultural integrity. There is a saying that "in order to understand a people, [one has to] know their myth." The *anting-anting* is just one element of our indigenous mythology—richly textured, inverting worlds like a trickster, refusing capitulation to a monocultural rendering of reality and the world, i.e., for those who have the eyes to see and the ears to hear and listen.

Figure 17. Tatang Valentin de los Santos of "Lapiang Malaya" (Freedom Party). Photo by Romeo Vitug, published in the book, *Pasyon and Revolution, Popular Movements in the Philippines, 1840-1910,* Reynaldo Clemeña Ileto (Quezon City, Philippines: Ateneo de Manila University Press, 1989) xiv.

Figure 18. Cover of *Anting-anting* catalog.
Xerox copy from the original.

Figure 19. God the Mother amulets for
a successful business. (Photo by Rico Obusan)

References

"Aklat ng Dalit." (n.d.) Suprema dela Iglesia dela Ciudad Mistica de Dios, Kapulungan ng Malayang Pilipinas, Santa Lucia, Dolores, Quezon.

Alaras, C. R. (1988). *Pamathalaan: Ang pagbubukas sa tipan ng mahal na Ina.* Kolonya, Alemanya at UP Diliman: Zeus Salazar at Agnes R. Mendoza-Urban at Bahay Saliksikan ng Kasaysayan.

Almario, V. S. (1993). *Panitikan ng rebolusyon(g) 1896.* Quezon City, Philippines: University of the Philippines Press.

Azurin, A. M. (1995). *Reinventing the Filipino sense of being and becoming.* Quezon City, Philippines: University of the Philippines Press.

"Boord family crest and name history." (2013, July 12). Retrieved from http://www.houseofnames. com/xq/asp.fc/qx/boord-family-crest.htm

Carro, A. O.S.A., (1888). *Vocabulario Iloco-Español.* Manila: Establecimiento Tipo-Litografico de M. Perez, Hijo,.

Constantino, R. (1975). *The Philippines: A past revisited.* Quezon City, Philippines: Tala Publishing Services.

Crass , K., & De Mesa, J. M. (1987). With a Listening Heart. *In solidarity with the culture* (p. 26). Quezon City, Philippines: Maryhill School of Theology.

Cuyas, A. (1972). *Nuevo Diccionario Cuyas de Appleton Espanol-Ingles y Ingles-Espanol.* Englewood Cliffs, NJ: Prentice Hall, Inc.

De La Encarnacion, F. (1885). *Diccionario Bisaya-Español* (Tercera Edicion). Manila: Tipografia de "Amigos del Pais."

English, L. J. (1990). *Tagalog-English Dictionary.* Manila, Philippines: National Book Store. (Original work published 1986).

Eugenio, D. L. (Ed.). (1982). *Philippine folk literature, an anthology* (p. 462). Quezon City, Philippines: Folklore Studies Program, College of Arts & Sciences, University of the Philippines, Diliman and The U.P. Folklorists, Inc.

Ileto, R. C. (1989). *Pasyon and revolution: Popular movements in the Philippines, 1840-1910.* Quezon City, Philippines: Ateneo de Manila University Press. (Original work published 1979).

Ileto R. (1993). Religion and Anti-Colonial Movements. *Cambridge History of Southeast Asia, 2,* 197-248, http://dx.doi.org/10.1017/CHOL9780521355063

Joven, R. (1929). Anting-Antings, Las Armas mas Poderosas de la Revolucion. *Philippines Free Press, 54.*

Kabunian (Lumawig). (2013, July 12) Retrieved from http://en.wikipilipinas.org/index.php?search=K abunian+(Lumawig)&fulltext=Search)

Kapre. (2013, July 12) Retrieved from http://en.wikipedia.org/wiki/Kapre

Lorenzo-Abrera, M. B. G. (1992). *Ang Numismatika ng Anting-anting [Numismatics of Amulet].* Diliman, Lunsod Quezon: Programang Kaalamang Bayan, Tanggapan ng Dekano, Dalubhasaan ng Agham Panlipunan at Pilosopiya, Unibersidad ng Pilipinas.

Marasigan, S. J., V. (1985). *A Banahaw Guru.* Quezon City, Philippines: Ateneo De Manila University Press.

Meñez, H. (1996). *Explorations in Philippine folklore.* Quezon City, Philippines: Ateneo de Manila University Press.

Neufeldt, V. (Ed.). (1988). *Webster's New World Dictionary of American English, Third College Edition.* New York: Simon & Schuster, Inc.

Pambid, N. D. (2000). *Anting-anting o kung bakit nagtatago sa loob ng bato si Bathala.* Quezon City, Philippines: University of the Philippines Press.

Pambid, N. D. (1989, October). Ang Semiotika ng Anting-Anting. M.A. Thesis. Quezon City: College of Social Sciences and Philosophy, University of the Philippines, Diliman.

Patianak, (2013, July 12) Retrieved from http://www.enctype.de/Daemonen/1inhalpat.htm

Perez, Rev. C. R. (2001). "Sancta Animasola, Infinite God the Mother Supreme Omnipotente Universal Divine Creator," *Diaryo Pilipino.* Alhambra, California.

Pesigan, G. M. (1987). "Religion in society: Mythic qualities and social change: A study of charisma of religious leaders and social change in Ciudad Mistica." A typescript.

Pesigan, G. M. (1992). *Dulang-huhay ng Bundok Banahaw aranasan ng Ciudad Mistica.* Mandaluyong, Metro Manila: Bahay Saliksikan ng Pilipinolohiyang Simulain sa tulong ng Toyota Foundation, Inc.

Patianak. (2013, July 12) Retrieved from http://www.enctype.de/Daemonen/1inhalpat.htm

Quirino, C. (Ed.). (1958, December 4). The Manners, Customs, and Beliefs of the Philippine Inhabitants of Long Ago, being Chapters of "A Late 16th Century Manila Manuscript." (Transcribed, translated and annotated by C. Quirino & M. Garcia) *The Philippine Journal of Science, 87,* 389-396. Retrieved from http://en.wikipedia.org/wiki/Boxer_Codex

Rodriguez, M. J. B. (1999). *AngkKababaihan sa himagsikang Pilipino. Lathalain Blg. 7.* Lunsod Quezon: Palimbagan ng Lahi.

Sabino, M. T. (n.d.). *Kasaysayan ng langit kapangyarihan laban sa kasamaan.* n.p.

Sabino, M. T. (1950). *Secreto: Mga lihim na pangalan at lihim na karunungan.* n.p.

Sabino, M. T. (1955). *Karunungan ng Diyos.* n.p.

Sabino, M.T. (1957) *Libro secreto.* n.p.

Salazar, Z. A. (2006). *Ang Pilipinong banua/banwa sa mundong Melano-Polynesiano.* Lunsod Quezon, Pilipinas: Bagong Kasaysayan, Palimbagan ng Lahi.

Salazar, Z. A. (1999). *Ang Kartilya ni Emilio Jacinto at ang diwang Pilipino sa agos ng kasaysayan. Lathalain Blg. 6.* Lunsod Quezon: Palimbagan ng Lahi.

Salazar, Z. A. (1999). *Ang babaylan sa kasaysayan ng Pilipinas. Lathalain Blg. 4.* Lunsod Quezon: Palimbagan ng Lahi.

Santos, V. C. (1978). *First Vicassan's Pilipino-English Dictionary.* Philippines: Philippine Graphic Arts, Inc.

Serrano Laktaw, P. (1914). *Diccionario Tagalog-Hispano* Segunda Parte (Ediciones Cultura Hispanica, 1965). Manila, Islas Filipinas: Imp. y Lit. de Santos y Bernal.

Tiyanak. (2010, August 16) Retrieved from http://en.wikipedia.org/wiki/Ghosts_in_Filipino_culture

Vocabulario de la Lengua Bicol. Lisboa, Marcos de, O.P., Manila: Establecimiento Tipografico del Colegio de Santo Tomas, 1865, 88 in Lorenzo-Abrera 135.

Wada, M. T. (1987, March 16). The iglesia sagrada ng lahi, A social movement in the Philippines. Unpublished Manuscript.

Wagan, V. P. (n. d.). Bathalismo, Inc. (Inang Mahiwaga). Tanggapang Pangbansa, Mambangan, San Leonardo, Nueva Ecija, K.P. Manila: Vicente Printing Press.

Wilcox, M. (Ed.). (1900). *Harper's history of war in the Philippines* (New York and London: Harper and Brothers Publishers.

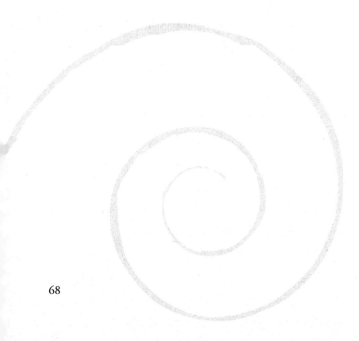

In the Mountain's Womb
Rizalista Practices as
Cultural Memory

Michael Gonzalez

We are a nation of storytellers. No matter how hard the colonial rulers forced us to accept their narratives, we struggled to transform strange languages into our own to speak with our own voices and to tell our own stories.

—NVM Gonzalez, A Story Yet to be Told (1998, video interview)

The presence of Jose Rizal as a revered biography and symbol in the national imaginary continues to be problematic, especially since the Rizal symbol permeates almost every aspect of modern Filipino national culture beginning with the discourse of public education. Jose Rizal, native reformist, physician, author of books, and deemed virtually a "renaissance man," was falsely implicated in an anti-colonial revolutionary plot and executed by the colonial Spanish authorities on December 30, 1896. The revolutionary uprising aimed at overthrowing Spanish colonial rule in the Philippines strategically used his name as a rallying cry to action. With Philippine independence proclaimed on June 12, 1898, then President Emilio Aguinaldo declared Rizal's death anniversary a public holiday. When the Americans took over the Philippines in 1902, they promoted Rizal as the ideal icon for the new Philippines (Constantino, 1991). Rizal's standing as "National Hero" was institutionalized and his works promulgated throughout the school system. The body of works about Rizal is a special collection in most Philippine libraries and labeled as *Rizaliana*. Every town plaza has a Rizal statue depicted as holding a book or wearing an overcoat. Every college student has to take, by law, a course on Jose Rizal (Republic Act 1425). To this day, publishers continue to churn out Rizal biographies and hagiographies and public officials pay lip service to his greatness. Much has been written about the "official" Rizal (Almonte, 2009; Constantino, 1991; Cruz & Chua, 1991; Ocampo, 1996,

2011). In fact, it seems there is nothing of his personal life that has not been unearthed. This is the Rizal story as represented *to* others and narrated *by* others—the public, the national elite, overseas Filipinos—as a national biography, honoring the "official" Rizal.

But there is another Rizal story told by peasants, laborers, and lower middle class Filipinos. Unlike most Filipinos who honor the "official" Rizal, they are known as *Rizalistas*, a conglomeration of various groups (or sects) scattered all over the Philippines that see Rizal and the events surrounding his life as distinctly spiritual, sacred, and personal (Gonzalez, 1985). Among the registered *Rizalista* associations are the *Sagrada Familia, Watawat ng Lahi, Tres Persona Solo Dios, and the Kataastaasang Kapatiran Ng Litaw Na Katalinuhan.* These groups have inconspicuous small churches and sanctuaries that dot the rural landscape along Laguna and Quezon (Aurora) Provinces. I wanted to know about this other Rizal. Inspired by the debates about non-Western ontologies as a means to counter the bias of Western (mostly American) social science perspectives (Montepio, 1978), I was led to investigate these two stories of Rizal for a thesis project. My research took me to the hinterlands of the Southern Tagalog provinces (where there was a concentration of the *Rizalista* groups) to discover, much to my enlightenment, a vastly different biography of Rizal—a biography that, to one schooled in formal historiography and narrative theory, contradicts widely available accepted biographies of the national hero. Because this story was incongruous with the "official" Rizal story, in the minds of many educated Filipinos, the *Rizalistas'* versions were often dismissed as "deluded" owing either to poverty or lack of education, or both.

In actuality, the *Rizalistas* were constructing a different world of existence for themselves and their hero, and had a different vision and narrative of what constituted a "nation" and the notion of a national "soul". As such the Western and classical methods of historiography and evidentiary protocols are only helpful in terms of setting the necessary chronology of national history (Bhabha, 1994). Time itself, in the context of the *Rizalistas*, has no correspondence to time as understood by most modernized Filipinos—a linear and finite progression of events (Alaras, 1988; Pambid, 2000). Thus, while the official records show that Rizal was executed on December 30, 1896, *Rizalistas,* while admitting to the event, do not believe Rizal was actually killed and buried. For example, in 2010, during a visit to the University of the Philippines campus in Diliman, I had an interesting exchange with an herbolario who had come to my mother's campus home to investigate reports of spirits in disquiet. I asked Mang Ed, the herbolario if he gathered his herbs from Mt. Banahaw, the epicenter of indigenous religious groups in the Southern Tagalog provinces. "*Yes, most of the time*", he answered. Did he know any of the *Rizalista's* there? I asked, knowing the area well enough. Mang Ed nodded, "Yes." He then added, "*Hindi pa po patay si Rizal, kaya lang nasa ilalim siya ng dagat*". Rizal is not dead but in the depths of the sea. And with that he proceeded to give me a *bendisyon* (benediction) to ward off any potentially harmful spirits. This conversation occurred in 2010, a year before Rizal's 150th official birthday, in an urban and academic neighborhood.

To comprehend this alternative imaginary, we start by understanding the religious and cultural practices of the *Rizalista* communities, in particular, for the purposes of this paper, the associations known as *Sagrada Familia* of Calamba (Figure 1, 2) and the *Kapatiran*[1] *ng Litaw na Katalinuhan* or KALK (Association of Revealed Knowledge) of Quezon both in the provinces of Southern Luzon (Figure 3, 4). Both have distinct organizational features, the Sagrada is a small community of households who migrated from Pangasinan in Northern Luzon onto the shores of Calamba, Laguna, the birth place of Jose Rizal, in fulfillment of a prophecy. Their religious practices center on the ritual prayers and songs that culminate with a *ganap* (spiritual event) or spirit possession of their leader, Gloria. A typical ceremony occurs in the chapel called a *daungan* (landing/anchorage) built with bamboo and sawali (woven bamboo strips) like most rural homes in the area. The altar consists of two chairs arranged along the altar that is adorned with candles and picture of Rizal, their religious founder Ignacio Coronado and Inang Adarna (Adarna is a magical songbird in Philippine mythology). When a *ganap* occurs, Gloria will take the chair that identifies the spirit and changes her voice accordingly. In this state, the spirit, speaking through Gloria may evoke the spirit of their founder Ignacio Coronado, Gloria's older brother Danny, or Jose Rizal himself. This presence is further identified by the nature of the spirits commands (*utos*) or *payo* (counsel). Gloria herself is a frail looking woman but displays a quiet intensity. My first encounter with her was propitious. As is customary, my companions and I had to share a meal with her family. The meal was a simple soup of squash flowers and fresh water clams. Although I was severely allergic to clams, I felt obligated to participate and honor this act of commensuality. All the time I sensed Gloria's intense gaze upon me. The meal was consumed and we ended our visit without any on toward allergic episode, a surprising condition that my wife reminded me of as we left the compound.

Figure 1. The *Sagrada Familia* settlement in Calamba, Laguna in Southern Luzon (with Rizal statue in background).

---

[1] *Kapatiran*, is best translated as sibling-hood. Tagalog does not differentiate gender in its term for siblings-*kapatid*. The commonly used equivalent term, brotherhood, misconstrues the strong participation of women in this organization.

Figure 2. Ate Gloria-*Sagrada Familia* of Calamba
in Southern Luzon.

The KALK on the other hand has a more formal organization and ritual practice. Their primary ritual is the *misa* (mass) which is concelebrated by three female celebrants or priestesses (*pare*). The mass evokes similarities with the Catholic version but for the choreographic gestures and an altar adorned with statuettes of Rizal and Bonifacio (the other contending figure in the national pantheon of heroes, known as the *Supremo* or Supreme Leader of the Philippine Revolution). Above the altar is a large picture of *Amang Bathala* (God the Father), surrounded by radiating light of wisdom (*katalinuhan*). Like the Sagrada, the group's leader is a woman, fondly addressed as Nanay (mother) Salud by her followers. A former USAFEE (United States Army Forces in the Far East, WWII army) nurse, Nanay Salud had a commanding presence and powerful oratory.

Figure 3. Temple altar of Kapatiran ng Litaw na
Katalinuhan or KALK.

Figure 4. Women priests celebrating mass -Kapatiran ng
Litaw na Katalinuhan or KALK.

Although I spent considerable time with these groups, I also observed other groups that belonged to this *Rizalista* religion complex, in particular, the *Ciudad Mistica de Dios* church on the foothills of Mount Banahaw and other largely women-led associations. Although these groups have unique differences organizationally, they all share a common understanding on the nature of the cosmic order and of Rizal and the hero's role in it (See Figure 5).

Figure 5. An illustration of Rizal's role in the nature of
the cosmic order (Ciudad Mistica de Dios church).

The Mistica priests basically sang me to health with their healing dalit *(psalm/hymns), thereby calming the uneasy spirits that have befallen me.*

These groups are also healing communities whose practices may range from fairly structured healing rituals, spirit divination or herbalism. In fact, while staying with the Mistica community in Mt.Banahaw, I got severely ill with high fever after completing an arduous visit (*pamumuesto*) up and down the crater of Banahaw. The Mistica priests basically sang me to health with their healing *dalit* (psalm/hymns), thereby calming the uneasy spirits that have befallen me.

A description of this cosmic order is evoked in the songs they sing during their rituals. The depiction of this cosmic order is unpacked in Reynaldo Ileto's (1979) excellent exegesis of the *pasyon* (Passion of Christ) as it functioned as a performative re-enactment of the sufferings of the Filipino people under colonial domination; and by several writers on Mount Banahaw spiritual communities (Gorospe, 1992; Marasigan, 1985; Pesigan, 1992) and groups in other places (Alaras, n.d.; Reyes, 1994). In this cosmic view, world order is disturbed by the imperfection of humankind and corrected and put to right by the sacrificial action of spiritual beings (Alaras, 1988; Pambid, 2000). In the *pasyon*, the Biblical Christ becomes the sacrificial being. Among *Rizalistas*, Rizal becomes transliterated as the Tagalog Christ (Gonzalez, 2012). This meta-history is evoked through songs that resonate with images of the Katipunan (the revolutionary society founded by Andres Bonifacio) as a sacred event (translated from the Filipino original "Marangal na Dalit ng Katagalugan).

Long live, long live,
This freedom, this freedom,
Forward Purity and Holiness,
Purity and Holiness;
Banish the Spanish from the Tagalogs
And let us celebrate our peace.

Mabuhay, mabuhay
Mabuhay yaong Kalayaan, Kalayaan
At pasulunging ang puri't kabanalan
Puri't kabanalan
Kastila'y mailing ng Katagalugan
At ngayo'y ipagwagi and kahusayan

The appropriation of this sacred and revolutionary imagery is constructed through a religious song style known as the *dalit* (psalm or hymn) which is characterized by a slow rhythm (usually 60 beats/minute or 60 MM). Thus, when this song style is laid over the melody of the Philippine National Anthem (120MM, march style), the multivocality and clash of ideologies between what is "official" and not, becomes not only audible but also a moment of contradiction that when coupled with other *Rizalista* discourse, constructs its own meta-history.

The aforementioned lyrics evoke imagery that resonate with that of the Sagrada and KALK versions of the Philippine national anthem.

Compare the official version to the Sagrada and KALK songs:

Sagrada Version *	KALK version	National Official Version (1899)***
O our father and mother. We are overjoyed And we praise Your beloved child.	O, Philippines, Land of the East, We are your servants In our love for you.	Beloved land, Pearl of the East, With fervor burning In your breast live;
All our hearts Give thanks to thee. To you Almighty That give him strength	Your flag is The emblem of the land That we must always Defend.	Land of birth. Cradle of noble heroes, Never must you surrender. Seas mountains and breezes
In the brightness of your light You gave Christ to us That we may learn The straight path,	That is why Rizal, Mabini and Bonifacio Died and shed their blood Because of you.	Your sky ever so blue; There's beauty in the poetry And song of our Beloved freedom.
That we might hopefully obtain And adopt a new life That we might hopefully obtain And adopt a new life.	That is why Rizal, Mabini and Bonifacio Died and shed their blood Because of you.	The glitter of your flag Is a brilliant victory The stars and sun Forever shall not dim
[MM=60, dalit style]	It is time now, my countrymen, To unite and be holy, Love and help each other, Do not forget our motherland.	Land of the morn, glory and love, Life is heaven in you arms If there be an oppressor, gladly
	[MM=60, dalit style]	We shall die for you.
		[MM=120, march style]

The Philippine National Anthem is an original music titled *"Marcha Filipina Magdalo"* composed by Julian Felipe (1898) (See Figure 6). Magdalo was Aguinaldo's Katipunan faction. The official version was a march tune originally composed to inaugurate the raising of the Philippine flag of independence from Spain in 1898. The verse that was written expressedly to suit the music was composed in Spanish a year later by Rafael Palma (1899). Under the Americans, an English version was translated by Camilo Osias and A.L. Lane (1920). Successive governments have since remained committed to the anthem as a national symbol. The few modifications of it have centered on translations. Ironically, the official English version preceded the one in Tagalog.

Figure 6. Original broadsheet of the Philippine National Anthem as composed by Julian Felipe in 1898.

The performative context is critical to understanding the significance of such differing musical enactments (Schechner, 2002). In performativity, identity creation is effected through the performance of ritual, deemed a discursive act in itself. Within the *Rizalista* context, performance becomes knowledge. Thus, Sagrada and KALK singing serves to establish a communal identity that is a counter-image to the official ideal. The Sagrada and KALK versions are sung slower than the official one, as indicated by the tape-recorder run time and confirmed by a metronome. In this slow tempo, the fit between tune and verse is poor, leaving the singers to compensate for the shorter endings by resorting to a mellismatic technique, a style noted to be characteristic of the *dalit*, a style common to religious singing (Tamanio, 1978). Historically, the importance of the *dalit* here is made even more significant once we recall that Andres Bonifacio a self-schooled laborer, was Emilio Aguinaldo's rival for the leadership of the Revolution..., had his own anthem, the "Noble *Dalit* of the Tagalogs", written by Julio Nakpil, Bonifacio's brother-in-law and fellow revolutionary. In the case of the Sagrada and KALK, the religious intent of their song versions comes from the substance of the verses and the fact that both sing their anthem within the *ganap* and *misa* ritual context. Although the KALK sing their own and also the official version of the anthem, the latter is performed at public events, or during official commemorative parades.

Apart from the differential tempo for each version, the verses differ in their imagery. In the *Rizalista* versions, the emphasis is on reciprocal obligations. Christ (Sagrada) or Rizal, (KALK) sacrificed their lives and this the faithful must repay by following a "straight path" (Sagrada) or uniting all-Filipinos into a kapatiran (KALK). Holy living, sacrifice, and service are important towards attaining a new life of freedom.

Purity and holiness, however, are not notions espoused in the official anthem of the Aguinaldo faction. In Ileto's (1979) study of the *pasyon* and revolution of 1897-98, he pointed out the difference in the perception of history and social change between the elite and the masses. Bonifacio, who organized the masses, invoked the meaningful elements of the *pasyon* for the revolutionary struggle while Aguinaldo, who represented the interests of the educated and the rural elite, relied on the secular language of "modern" (that is, Western) nationalism.

Ileto (1979) provided us with sufficient basis to suggest that with the shattering of Hispanic hegemony, the ideological development in Tagalog society was being re-articulated along fragments of folk and traditional discursive practices, on the one hand, and an evolving elite-led national(istic) ideology on the other, that competed for hegemonic dominance. The Rizal symbol, the flag, and the anthem were cultural memories competed for—these historical iconographies being repositories or "sacred" sentiments of unquestionable authority.

This bichronic view of the world as having both spiritual and material essence is a common notion held by many who follow the nativist and non-denominational churches and other religious groups that fall under this sociological spectrum (c.f., Alaras, n.d.; Pesigan, 1992; Reyes, n.d.). In this world, the members of these religious associations are aware that they share their environment with spirit beings. Their visibility and presence are communicated either through regular rituals or during spirit possessions. Interestingly, it is only in the past couple of decades that the existence of this world merited the attention of serious scholars and academics bent on decolonizing the Western-dominated epistemologies in the academy using the works of Virgilio Enriquez (1982), Prospero Covar (1991, 1998), and a few enlightened Catholic priest/scholars (Gorospe, 1992; Dagmang, n.d.) and the revelatory scholarship on 19th century relationship between language and christianity by Vicente Rafael (1988) and John D. Blanco (2009).

With the emergence of babaylan studies (www.babaylan.net), the opportunity to re-read my research and attempt to locate the differences within a potently multivocal and polysemic symbol received a new impetus. Indeed Rizal was everyman's hero and every Filipino school child can tell who he was and what he did even while politicians and publishers continue to make an industry of his legacy. Yet, the persistence of a mystical, a-historical Rizal in the imaginary of the religious associations mentioned here, speaks of a different manner of arriving at this knowledge.

In an earlier paper (Gonzalez, 1980), I likened this quest for mystical knowledge as a journey into the womb of the mountain (*bundok*). In this particular case, Mt. Banahaw was the mountain of knowledge. This physical journey entails literally getting into a close encounter with one's spiritual *loob* (inner self) and cultural memory. The mountain, therefore, is not only a repository of medicinal flora, but also an archive of cultural memories that, when subjected to the objective eye of the Western trained academic elides into the materiality of text, or history. What is left is unfortunately, is called folklore, a term that emerged as a distinctive form of knowledge thrown up by modernity. In the Philippine context our cultural memory was complicated by a colonialism that became the very vehicle of modernity, thereby fragmenting the indigenous body of knowledge practices that existed prior to colonization. Thus under the gaze of the colonized academic, these cultural fragments that appeared incoherent as a whole, remained as *mere* folklore. Knowledge practices such as those of the *babaylan* (indigenous healer) were, in the eyes of the Westernized academic, discrete incidents of peasant (folk) behavior that gained historical credence only because they were inscribed in colonial reportage or historical writing.

A different trajectory occurs for the history of Jose Rizal. The official grand narrative of his life need not be repeated here. However, because of the persistence of these indigenous knowledge practices, the reconstruction of the other Rizal within this imaginary is possible but is only sensible to the indigenous practitioners and those who share the same semantic field, while, on the other hand, the colonized modern Filipino only sees Rizal in the light of modern historiographic text and official narratives. This re-creation of Rizal can be illustrated by transposing the semantic field of the babaylan narrative over that of the "folk Rizal". Historical and recent scholarship (McCoy, 1982; Dagmang, n.d.) describes the *babaylan* as in possession of the following:

- healing abilities (divination and/or pharmacological);

- ability to propitiate/communicate with the spirit world either through spirit mediumship or ritual expertise;

- leadership qualities among peers and community (shaman-king/[queen] leader) and repository of cultural practices;

- ability to cultivate magical objects (anting-anting) that make one impervious to harm;

- ability to teletransport; (this skill is considered highest and labeled *dalaganan* in Visayan) (McCoy, 1982)

If, in the context of this *babaylan* semantic field, a re-reading of the other Rizal is made, we see a remarkable resonance. This semantic field is constituted by cultural artifacts that existed as residual "texts" thrown out by colonial modernity, labeled as folklore (superstitions, fish wives tales, anting-anting, etc.), and excluded from critical discourse by a colonialized public education. In my analysis of the Rizal "folklore," a metanarrative can be extrapolated from these stories (Gonzalez, 1985, 2012; Santos, 1973) and re-imagined thus:

- Rizal was born mysteriously, swaddled in clothes marked "Jove Rex Al" [cf. Santos, (1973); http://thetruthaboutjoserizal.blogspot.com/]

- Rizal was separated at a young age from his family to learn languages and be healer [cf. McCoy, (1982): communicative and healing skills]

- Rizal was hounded by enemies when he returned to the Philippines but had powers that protected him from harm [cf. McCoy, (1982): shaman/king (queen) leader figure]

- Rizal was arrested and executed by the Spaniards but people believe it was a look-alike and the gravesite did not reveal a body, but a banana trunk; [McCoy: ability to teletransport]

- Rizal is alive in the bowels of Mt. Banahaw, Mt. Makiling and Mt. Arayat and will return to lead the army of God and redeem the Filipinos

These subordinated constructions, sometimes mistakenly labeled as superstition, began when Hispanization in the 16th century re-organized native society to re-settle in the lowlands (*labak*) placing the church at the center and the resettlement sites *"de bajo de las campanas"* (within the call of church bells). Such practices have been previously perfected in Mexico to bring the Aztec and Mayan cultures within the pale of Catholic orthodoxy. Writing about this period, Diana Taylor (2007) described the conversion method as two fold: "the dismissal of indigenous performance traditions as episteme, and the dismissal of 'content' (religious belief) as bad objects, idolatry" (p. 33). Unlike the harsh conversion that the indigenous Mexicans experienced where temples were dismantled to claim sacred space over which churches were superimposed, the Philippine Indio's response was to accommodate, resist, and retreat (or go underground)—a pattern of response that served native folk well over the centuries, abetted by forested and mountainous terrain. Among the early resisters were Tamblot of Bikol and Bankaw of Leyte, both described by Spanish chroniclers *as babaylans* (Agoncillo & Guerrero, 1990). On the other hand, although the Spanish admired the religious mimicry of those who remained in the lowlands (not without strong suspicions of native duplicity) they failed to prevent the transmutation of Christian knowledge into native knowledge. The Black Nazarene, the *ati-atihan*, the *sinulog*, and

Ironically, as critical scholars attempt to reconstruct indigenous epistemology, the history of the highlanders, the remontados, *religious hermits,* babaylans, *and "outlaws," while fragmented and marginalized in traditional scholarship, are the very same sources whence cultural memory is archived and remains to be retrieved...*

other "idolatrous" behavior were performative expressions of such transmutation, but that the Spanish tolerated as mere "superstitions" as long as they did not alter the economic obligations of their converts in terms of tributes, services, and tithes. Those who retreated from the call-of-the-church-bells were branded as '*salvajes*' (wild) especially those that lived along the whole swath of the mountain ranges that the missionaries failed to penetrate: the Igorottes and other mountain tribes. Christians who retreated became *remontados* (mountain returnees), religious hermits, *babaylans*, and branded literally, as outlaws. Modern Filipino sociology uncritically accepted this dichotomy between the highland and lowland (*bundok at labak*), differentiating, as it were, sources of cultural knowledge and its discriminatory associations that privileged lowland culture because of its Western proximity and adaptation (Gonzalez, 1985). Ironically, as critical scholars attempt to reconstruct indigenous epistemology, the history of the highlanders, the *remontados,* religious hermits, *babaylans,* and "outlaws," while fragmented and marginalized in traditional scholarship, are the very same sources whence cultural memory is archived and remains to be retrieved (Enriquez, 1982). Scholarship has emerged to lay out the linkages between these marginal traditions of the highlands, outside-the-church-bell communities, and *remontados,* at least semantically as resistance or rejection of authority, *herbolarismo,* religious non-conformity, or spiritism, the nexus of which may be found in Mt. Banahaw (Del-Pilar Garcia, n.d.; Gorospe, 1992; Reyes, 1994). No doubt more research will emerge as scholars rethink their epistemological assumptions in these direction. To the degree that devotees are engaged in the same understanding of symbols and sentiments, the performativity of *Rizalista* ritual practices insure that followers of the same tradition remain within the *babaylan* semantic field and other "texts" that might be folded within.

In reflection, when I was first confronted by these alternative fragments of Rizal biography, I did not see such indigenous narratives within the context of *babaylan* semantics, committed as I was, to objectivist historicity. The more recent articulation of *babaylan* scholarship, however, makes it now possible to make these correlations, to open up the canon of what counts for legitimate knowledge in such a way that the multivocal and polysemic respresentations of Rizal as a person of power (leader, healer, immortal) may [now] take their place among these clouds of floating knowledges and cultural memories that had been hidden...for so long but hopefully, no longer.

The official propagation of the Rizal image during the most intense period of national identity building created a distinctively different interpretation of Rizal, one that supposedly advocated slow reform versus revolutionary uprising, and one that, especially, the American colonial administrators and their elite collaborators had hoped would be a solidifying symbol for a modern state (Constantino, 1991). To that extent, as a core symbol of elite politics, Rizal did served as a model for their version of nation-state building, specially since the Rizal symbol carried with it the logical outcomes of nationhood—independence [albeit earned, not forcibly wrested] and progress—twin ideas that were undeniably Rizal's own vision (Pertierra, 2002). Paradoxically, however, the other Rizal became reconstituted into a different symbol among the peasants and the workers, becoming a central symbol during the major social unrests and peasant/labor uprisings of the 1930's, a period whence much of the aforementioned religious associations began their existence and proliferated.

The more recent articulation of babaylan scholarship...makes it now possible... to open up the canon of what counts for legitimate knowledge.... [T]he multivocal and polysemic respresentations of Rizal as a person of power (leader, healer, immortal) may [now] take their place among these clouds of floating knowledges and cultural memories that had been hidden...for so long but hopefully, no longer.

The bulk of the material for this work comes from the lengthy research and fieldwork that I conducted between 1973-1981 (Gonzalez, 1985). While I was at that time satisfied with the outcome and the theoretical perspectives that I took, I was not fully convinced that I gave the material and the *Rizalistas* a compelling location within the pantheon of

Philippine thought, much less in the Filipino imaginary. Although I believed that I have established the validity of honoring the history of the folk and the social dynamics that emerged from it, I feel that their position, the *Rizalistas* and similar associations, remain in a tenuous situation of not having been fully theorized and, as such, easily explained away by agencies who promote the dominant and grand narrative of the Filipino imaginary. As such, if we may paraphrase NVM Gonzalez's observation, no matter how hard the dominant class may force us to accept the grand narratives of Rizal, the folk will speak with their own voices and tell their own stories.

References

Agoncillo, T., & Guerrero, M. (1990). *History of the Filipino people.* Quezon City: Garcia Publishing.

Alaras, C. (n.d.). *Pamathalaan: Ang Pagbubukas sa tipan ng mahal na ina.* Cologne, Germany: Bahay-Saliksikan ng Kasaysayan.

Alaras, C. (n.d.). Pamathalaan. *Series on Filipino Spiritual Culture, 7,* 1-10.

Almonte, N. (2009). *Rizal is my president: 40 leadership tips from Jose Rizal.* Manila, Philippines: OCCI Publications, Knights of Rizal, Advocacy for Patriotic Leadership.

Bhabha, H. (1994). *The location of culture.* New York, NY: Routledge.

Blanco, J. (2009). *Frontier constitutions: Christianity and colonial empire in the nineteenth century Philippines.* Berkeley, CA: University of California Press.

Constantino, R. (1981). Veneration without understanding. In P. Melendez-Cruz & A. Chua (Eds.), *Himalay: Katipunan ng mga pag-aaral kay Jose Rizal.* Manila: Sentrong Pangkultura ng Pilipinas,

Covar, P. (1991). Ang pagtanggap ng samahang milinaryan kay Gat Dr. Jose P. Rizal. In P. Melendez-Cruz & A. Chua (Eds.), *Himalay: Katipunan ng mga pag-aaral kay Jose Rizal.* Manila, Sentrong Pangkultura ng Pilipinas.

Covar, P. (1998). The Filipino, his culture and society. (trans. Romina Santos). National Centennial Commission (1998). *Philippines: Archipelago of smiles.* Preface by N.V.M. Gonzalez. Paris: le cherhe midi editeur S.O.S Incorporated, pp. 119-127.

Melendrez-Cruz, P., & Chua, A. B. (1991). *Himalay: katipunan ng mga pag-aaral kay Jose Rizal.* Manila, Philippines: Sentrong Pangkultura ng Pilipinas.

Dagmang, F. (n.d.). *Babaylanism* reconsidered. *Series on Filipino Culture, 6,* 1-26

Del-Pilar Garcia, M. L. (n.d.). The Tatlong Persona Solo Dios and Inggo La Fuente movements: A cultural heritage in the Philippines (pp. 1-35).

Enriquez, V. (1982). *Decolonizing the Filipino psyche: Philippine psychology in the seventies.* Quezon City: Philippine Psychology Research House.

Ileto, R. (1979). *Pasyon and revolution.* Quezon City: Ateneo de Manila University Press.

Ileto, R. (1983). Rizal and the underside of history. In P. Melendez-Cruz & A. Chua (Eds.), *Himalay: Katipunan ng mga pag-aaral kay Jose Rizal.* Manila: Sentrong Pangkultura ng Pilipinas.

Gonzalez, M. (1908). In the mountain's womb. *Asian Studies, 18*, 58-70.

Gonzalez, M. (1985) Edge of structures: A study of Rizalista ideology and Filipino culture. Master's thesis in Social Anthropology, University of Sydney, Australia.

Gonzalez, M. (2012). Waiting for Rizal: The promise of redemption in Rizalista culture. In E. Lozada (Ed.), *Remembering Jose Rizal: Voices from the diaspora*. San Francisco: Philippine American Writers & Artists Inc.

Gorospe, V. (1992). *Banahaw: Conversations with a pilgrim to the power mountain*. Manila: Bookmark.

Marasigan, V. (1985). *A Banahaw guru: Symbolic deeds of Agapito Illustrisimo*. Quezon City: Ateneo de Manila University Press.

McCoy, A. (1982). Baylan: Animist religion and Philippine peasant ideology. *Philippine Quarterly of Culture & Society, 10*, 141-194.

Montepio, S. (1978, April). Papers of the first national convention of UGAT, UP at Los Banos: *National Convention of UGAT, University of the Philippines, Los Banos, Laguna*, 14-16.

Ocampo, A. (1993). *A calendar of Rizaliana*. Quezon City: University of Santo Thomas Publishing House.

Pambid, N. (2000). *Anting-anting or kung bakit nagtatago sa loob ng bato si Bathala*. Quezon City: University of the Philippines Press.

Pesigan, G. (1992). *Dulang-Buhay ng Bundok Banahaw: Karanasan ng Ciudad Mistica*. Quezon City: University of the Philippines Press.

Pili, J. (2012). The truth about Dr. Jose Rizal. The truth about Dr. Jose Rizal. Retrieved from http://thetruthaboutjoserizal.blogspot.com/2012/05/truth-about-dr-jose-rizal.html

Pertierra, R. (2002). *The work of culture*. Manila: De LaSalle University Press.

Rafael, V. (1988) *Contracting colonialism: Translation and Christian conversion in Tagalog society under early Spanish rule*. Ithaca: NY: Cornell University Press, 1988.

Reyes, S. (1994). Kontemplatibong Pananalanging Pilipino. *Series on Filipino Culture, 8*, 1-55.

Santos, A. (1973). *Rizal miracle tales*. Manila: National Book Store.

Taylor, D. (2007). *The archive and the repertoire: Performing cultural memory in the Americas*. Durham, NC: Duke University Press.

Schechner, R. (2002). *Performance studies: An introduction*. New York, NY: Routledge.

Filipino Tattoos

Pigment as Spirit

Lane Wilcken

Filipino Tattoos: Pigment as Spirit

Figure 1. A fully tattooed "Pintado" of the Visayas,
an illustration from Ignacio Francisco Alcina's book,
Historia de las Islas e Indios de Bisayas – 1668.

Tattooing in western society is a growing trend that has a popular and even celebrity following. Not a few years ago, the art form was considered poor taste and was stigmatized by the West because it was considered the mark of rebellion against mainstream society. However, in the present, tattooing has become more socially acceptable with many different styles emerging, including the so-called "tribal tattoo." The majority of "tribal" tattoos incorporate heavy blackwork designs based off of tattooing traditions of Austronesian speaking peoples of the Pacific Ocean. Austronesian speaking peoples include the islands of Indonesia, the Philippines, Micronesia, Melanesia, Polynesia, Madagascar and Taiwan. Most of these peoples practiced tattooing at one time or another. It is from these cultures that the modern tribal tattoo has been extrapolated. While this style of body ornamentation has rapidly grown in popularity over the last two decades, the designs are usually out of context and very little of the nature of these symbols are understood. As traditional tattooing in much Austronesia has largely waned or become extinct due to westernization, the modern "tribal" tattoo now has come full circle and is worn by the descendants of the very peoples who originally inspired the modern art from the Philippines all the way to Rapa Nui (Easter Island).

As a Filipino heir of this tradition, and wearer of traditional tattoos, I would like to provide some insight into the symbolic and spiritual nature of the tattooing traditions of the Philippines from a holistic paradigm. Because of the abundance of tattooing in the Philippines, there were many commonalities in the customs regarding its practice. What I will discuss are these practices shared in common and as viewed from a reconstructed cultural context. I hope to discuss these sacred designs and motifs in a manner pleasing to my ancestors and to invite the readers to apply these principles in the process of recovering their own indigenous paradigms.

When the first Spanish explorers arrived in our islands with Ferdinand Magellan in 1521, they originally called the archipelago, "*Las Islas de los Pintados,*" which means "The Islands of the Painted Ones" because of the abundance of tattooing they saw. According to the late William H. Scott (in Garcia, 1979), a leading researcher in pre-Hispanic Philippine history, the majority of the peoples of the Philippines tattooed. It was known that the Tagalog people and others who converted to Islam in the southern portion of the archipelago did not practice tattooing at the time of the Spanish advent (Garcia, 1979, p. 334). Still, the word "to mark, stamp or print" in Tagalog is "*tatak,*" which is very similar to its Polynesian counterpart, "*tatau,*" from which comes the modern word for tattoo.

As mentioned earlier, presently many people are interested in tattooing, indigenous or otherwise. Generally most people in Westernized countries look at gaining a tattoo as a symbol of individuality, rebellion, self-expression or identification with some particular subculture or movement. In the western context the individual is the one who decides when they will be tattooed and what is tattooed on them. In the ancient Austronesian past the perspective towards tattooing was very different. Rather than a symbol of individuality, exclusion or separation, tattooing in ancient Austronesian cultures was a symbol of conformity to cultural expectations, spiritual beliefs, and communal responsibility. The recipient does not decide when they will be tattooed or what will be tattooed upon them. Those choices are the prerogative of the community and the tattoo practitioner, not the individual. The marks of tattooing in the Philippines were called *patik*,

Because of the deep symbolism and metaphoric nature of tattoos, the full context of tattoos cannot be understood by simple identification. Nothing in traditional tattooing can be taken at face value.

batek, *batuk*, *batok*, *fatok* or *burik* in the various languages. They were the outward symbols of a commitment to uphold community responsibilities, both spiritual and physical.

Typically our tattooing culture is analyzed by western scholars on a very superficial level. Because of the deep symbolism and metaphoric nature of tattoos, the full context of tattoos cannot be understood by simple identification. Nothing in traditional tattooing can be taken at face value. A holistic understanding of the ancient culture is necessary to fully comprehend the significance and context of tattoo designs and motifs. Some people searching for a "tribal" tattoo mistakenly believe that tattoo motifs are like Japanese kanji where a symbol means a certain word or meaning like "strength" or "bravery." But the practice is much more complex than that. Even though a particular design may convey "bravery," for example, the specific context may be "bravery in the face of an enemy" or "bravery in childbirth." Moreover, the design portrays the underlying *reason* the person earned the inscribed trait, such as bravery. These symbols are typically representative of a value or trait already exhibited by the individual, especially in the case of males. For example, a male wearing a chest tattoo called, *bikking*, *binibikking* or *chak-lag*, (depending on the community), will show both how many victories he has achieved and the spiritual guidance that led him to his success. In addition, certain motifs within the chest tattoo display the fertility his actions produced in the community and constantly remind him of his responsibility to uphold the inscribed values. These motifs and designs conveyed entire concepts, which had many interrelated meanings.

For the modern Filipino, tattooing is difficult to decipher because through westernization we have forgotten old cosmological and spiritual concepts, and their associated metaphors, euphemisms, and figures of speech used in the past that played a role in associated tattooing beliefs. To illustrate this point, let us briefly examine one creation tradition of the Philippines taken from an early Spanish account in 1590.

In the beginning there was only the ocean and the sky. Between the two was a kite or bird of prey which flew on and on with nowhere to rest. Growing weary the kite resolved to create land through stratagem. It incited a battle between the ocean and the sky in which the ocean rose up against the sky. The sky rose higher into the heavens but the ocean continued its rise. So the sky responded by casting down stones to weigh down the ocean and consequently made the islands of the sea. On one of these islands the land breeze and the sea breeze were married, and their union produced a bamboo plant which grew up, broke off, and floated upon the waters. In the meantime the kite made its home on one of the islands. While walking along the beach, the waves washed up the bamboo and hit the bird in the leg. The bird ran to another part of the beach but the bamboo followed it. Irritated by this constant bumping, the kite pecked open the bamboo from which came a man and a woman, *Ka-laki* and *Ka-baye*, the progenitors of the Filipino people (Cole, 1916, p. 187; Garcia, 1979, pp. 315-316).

Now to the Western mind this looks like the pathetic attempt by savages to explain how they came to be. This is why these stories are condescendingly called "myths." To the western mind, there is no possible way these events could be real; they seem too fantastic. But if understood in their original contexts, such stories begin to signify differently. In the particular story just recounted, we have a description in mythological language of the account of our ancestors' migration to the islands, with nearly identical creation traditions in the Pacific Islands where these same metaphors are still understood. In a similar way understanding the use of metaphor plays an important role in the application of the tattoo. "Stones falling from the sky" is a figure of speech from the past describing celestial navigation across the ocean to locate islands. Figuratively, the sky produced an island. The bamboo following the kite is another old reference illustrating what the ancient navigators did when close to an island but outside the line of sight. Certain birds nest on shore at night and are *followed* by navigators at dusk to islands (Thomas, 1997, p. 80). These oceanic birds also flee back to their nests on shore when storms approach, or, in other words, when the *"sky and the sea are fighting."* This poetic way of describing inclement weather as *fighting stars* [i.e. heavens] is still used among the navigators of the Caroline Islands in Micronesia (Thomas, 1997, p. 38). The man and woman being born from bamboo is another old figure of speech meaning that a person arrived by outrigger canoe. The *katig* or outriggers of our canoes are made out of bamboo.

Figure 2. A bangka outrigger canoe of the Philippines with
its characteristic bamboo outrigger floats.

In like manner our tattooing is similarly shrouded to those who do not understand the full context of our ancient culture. I have noticed that many anthropologists tend to single out specific aspects of a culture for study or examine a particular culture without comparing it to related cultures. I recognized that this flawed approach is part of the western mindset's desire to compartmentalize and categorize things in order to rank them. Combined with innate ethnocentrism, the western paradigm is based on a condescending view of superiority over the "primitive" cultures it seeks to rank in relationship to its own. A culture picked apart and understood out of context is easy to explain as "primitive," or in other words, "inferior." Thus only the superficial aspects of tattooing are usually addressed. Typically written about are these superficial aspects of the practice:

- Rites of Passage

- Personal Enhancement / Beautification

- Marks of Identity / Status / Rank / Prestige

Were all of these things aspects of tattooing? Of course they were and other scholars such as Lars Krutak (2009) and Analyn Salvador-Amores (2000, 2004) have written about these aspects of our tattooing. But the greater symbolic and spiritual aspects of the practice are usually not addressed or are only condescendingly described as simply being "magical." What are not typically discussed are these deeper concepts and explanations as to *why* these symbols are powerful or "magical" when used in the proper way. To engage in this kind of deeper analysis, I need to first describe the old beliefs regarding spirits in the Philippines.

Our spiritual world was made up of different spiritual entities. Above all, there was usually a supreme being called by various names such as, Bathala, Laon, Apo Namarsua, Kabunian, Manama, etc. Below this being were lesser gods or disembodied spirits made up of ancestral spirits who had been deified. These are generally called *anito* throughout the Philippines. There were humans who were embodied spirits, and then there were selfish or malevolent non-human spirits called, *mangmangkik* that I came to know about through my grandmother Catalina Coloma Rivera who was a *mangngilut* or midwife and healer. The last groups of spirits are the spirits of animals, plants, rocks, and the natural world. Other authors have confirmed my grandmother's knowledge such as Albert Jenks, author of the *Bontoc Igorot* (1905) and Virgil Mayor Apostol, author of *Way of the Ancient Healer* (2011). All these entities played a role in the everyday lives of people. Generally, the spirits you wanted to interact with were the *anito* because they were family who cared for their posterity and so shared a vested interest in your success. But just like families today, you can have benevolent members as well as selfish members in a family. These disembodied spirits still felt emotions such as love, compassion, anger, and even jealousy. So care was exercised when interacting with these spirits. In certain ceremonies *anitos* were encouraged to care for their posterity and were appeased with sacrifices and offerings. Children were named after ancestors to invoke their blessings (Jenks, 1970, p. 197). The *anito* were able to communicate either directly with their posterity in the form of inspiration, warm feelings, feeling a sudden chill, impressions, dreams, spiritual manifestations, or sometimes, by forceful possession. Such was the frequent experience of my great-great grandmother Honorata Esmerelda Eslabra, a spirit medium called a *mangnganito* in Ilokano. Ancestral spirits could also communicate indirectly through influencing the actions of the natural world, such as the behaviors of animals such as birds, snakes, insects, etc. Many times, specific animals were identified as the physical avatars or representatives of *anitos*. Most common were birds, snakes, crocodiles, centipedes, and lizards, animals commonly reflected in tattoo designs (Krutak, 2009). Killing snakes, for example, was avoided in the Bontoc region for fear of accidentally harming one of their own ancestors (Jenks, 1970, p. 197). In the Visayan region, pythons accompanying men on sea-raids were good fortune in that it indicated the *anito*'s participation with them (Scott, 1995, p. 81). In short, when the *anitos* felt amiable towards their family or descendants, they inspired and guided them on how best to succeed, or simply blessed their lives in general.

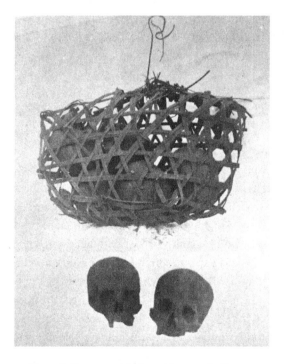

Figure 3. These soot blackened human skulls were photographed in Bontoc ca. 1905 by Albert Jenks. Note the minmináta woven design of the basket representing the "many eyes" of the ancestors.

Among many peoples of the Philippines, the majority of men's tattoos had to be earned through displays of courage in battle and the taking of lives or heads (Salvador-Amores, 2002, p. 110; Scott, 1995, p. 20). These particular tattoos on specific parts of

The anito were able to communicate either directly with their posterity in the form of inspiration, warm feelings, feeling a sudden chill, impressions, dreams, spiritual manifestations, or sometimes, by forceful possession.

the body were the outward marks of valor, courage, manhood, martial prowess, and spiritual communication.

The act of taking a human life is a difficult concept to stomach from our modern paradigms. In order to understand this now foreign concept I offer these brief explanations. Among ancient Filipinos the head was considered the seat of the soul. The top of the head was the nexus or conduit of communication with the ancestors. Procuring a head as a sacrifice was the greatest of gifts one could offer to the spirits. Heads were generally taken from enemy villages. Sometimes these villages could be as close as the first settlement past one's neighboring village. Despite considering their victims enemies, some groups like the Kalinga held elaborate feasts called *cañao* to honor not just the head taker, but also the spirit of the victim. Among many groups in the Philippines, those who suffered death by violence were accepted into a type of

[handwritten: Also true for Hawaiian culture iirc]

paradise that was greater than the afterlife of those who died natural deaths. Among the Bontoc people, those who lost their heads received a head of flames in this heavenly realm where they enjoyed life as before. The flame headed *pin-teng* also became a type of avenging angel upon all those who murdered small children and infants (Jenks, 1970, p. 199). Taking a head was also a way to appease angry *anitos* who would show their displeasure by causing any number of calamities, death or just bad luck upon the family or community. Sometimes a recently deceased person's spirit would be angry because of its own death and seek vengeance. By taking the life of someone else outside of the community, the *anito's* desire for vengeance at the loss of their own life is appeased. This potential vengeful aspect of the *anito* is the basis for why modern Filipinos sometimes place aside food offerings for the dead. This food offering is called *atang* among Ilokanos and is accompanied by a ritual chant addressing the *anitos*, inviting them to come and share in the feast. Often in the *atang* chant there are phrases asking for the *anitos* not to harm the people but to give a blessing instead. Among the Ilongot people, taking heads was a form of retaliation against insults, injuries and death. Renato Rosaldo, in his book *Ilongot Headhunting, 1883-1974: A Study in History and Society* (1980), describes how Ilongots took heads in an effort to "lighten" or "throw away" their grief at the death of a family member. Despite this seeming difference in motivation for head-taking, Rosaldo still describes a similar context in which "the men were pent up with 'anger' as a result of the grief they had not yet 'thrown away' over deaths suffered in their families..." (Rosaldo, 1980, p. 157). So headhunting in the Ilongot cultural context was a way of dispelling anger as well as a means of retaliation for death, injury and grievances.

Another perspective on headhunting is offered by Robert McKinley:

> Robert McKinley (1979), noting that headhunting was continuous across Southeast Asia and Oceania 'prior to the formation of the state,' focuses on headhunting as a ritual to manage 'existential limits of the social world' (McKinley 1979: 95-96). Headhunting is not war waged for territorial reasons, but rather a ritual of community cohesiveness mediating contradictions between life and death, the familiar and the foreign, and human and non-human. He argues that other ethnic groups are perceived as not quite human, as they live across the mountains, a natural realm associated with the spirits, but yet speak. What is important is that headhunters bring the head back to the village, speak to it, give it food offerings, and offer it friendship. The head is central because of the face, which makes it a personal social relationship. Headhunting rituals thus internalize the enemy as a friend and humanize him, which McKinley contrasts to 'our' anonymous modern warfare that 'allow(s) us to forget that our enemies have faces and names' (McKinley 1979: 125-126). (As cited in Scott, 2012).

In many places the successful headhunt assured the fertility of animals, crops and people for the village (Jenks, 1970, p. 174). In some Philippine societies a human sacrifice (i.e. headhunting) secured the spiritual power for a village by honoring the spirit of the victim through a feast celebration called *cañao* in Luzon in which the spirit became a helpful entity towards the village. In other places only the spiritual power of the head was ceremonially distributed among the members of the village (Salvador-Amores, 2002, p. 118). Other times, the sacrifice was to appease the spirit of an actual *anito* who was malevolent due to some offense or to prevent such spirits from becoming incensed and causing misfortune. These are some of the motivations behind the practice of headhunting in the Philippines. With this in mind let us briefly examine the exercise of the headhunting tradition and its relationship to tattooing using the following example.

Suppose a man were to go to an enemy village to procure a head needed for a sacrifice. As this man went out on his journey, imagine that along the way he sees a snake (or any other animal representative of the *anito*) cross his path. His obligation was to observe the snake, see which direction it traveled, which could be an indication of a good or bad omen. Perhaps, the snake is simply in the path, in which case, he pauses, speaks to the snake and meditates on the meaning of the omen event. Once he has done this, he receives inspiration on what he should do at that point of his journey (Garcia, 1979, p. 348). This counsel would come as impressions or thoughts to his mind. Maybe the counsel was to go back home, go a different route, check his weapons for problems, or simply delay his journey. Any type of inspiration may occur at this moment, although generally these omens were thought to be brought on in regard to the expedition at hand. In some traditions witnessing an omen event like a bird flying in the opposite direction of the man's travel was enough of a sign to turn around and go home (Cole, 1916, p. 143). Listening for certain types of bird calls also were warnings for the traveler to be especially attuned to both the spirit world and the environment. A man going on a headhunting raid or war expedition would often pursue his prey with the utmost stealth. While approaching an enemy, the warrior reads a spooked bird as a clue to where his enemy lay. Even if he was the one who startled the bird, the bird would not intentionally fly towards another human. So the direction of the bird's flight could make him aware of the enemy's whereabouts. If the warrior was not the one who frightened the bird, but it came flying towards him in spite of his presence that may have indicated that a larger group of enemy warriors were concealed ahead. Certain birds make specific types of chirps or calls when danger is near to warn each other. Hearing and understanding these different calls gave our ancestors another form of awareness outside of their own senses. It could be considered a type of natural early warning system or surveillance. Paying attention to the calls and actions of animals was practical in nature as well as an excellent reminder to be attuned spiritually.

Generally omen events take the following sequence:

- The omen event occurs.

- Recipient enters into communication through prayer or spiritual attunement.

- Counsel is given from the spirit world.

- Omen recipient is given opportunity to obey the counsel given.

As a warrior obeyed the counsel of the spirit world with guidance from beings that could see farther than mortal eyes could, his ancestral spirits invest in ensuring his welfare. Consequently, he achieved success—a joint victory with those unseen beings that cared for their living descendant. When he returned victorious from his endeavor, with the evidence (in the form of a head) of his successful guidance from the spirit world, he was subsequently tattooed with the marks of this venture. When viewed in this context, the prestigious tattoos of the old headhunters of the Cordillera are a composition of the inter-related symbols based on his successful joint-venture with these spirits. The tattoos symbolize the animal representatives of his ancestral spirits that guided his path as well as the gift of fertility and prosperity his actions provided. As this man went through life, each time he saw his tattoos, he was reminded to conduct himself in accordance with the prestige he had earned. More importantly, it was a constant reminder to him, and to others as they saw his tattoos, to remain spiritually aware and open to the guidance from the spirit world. A man so tattooed was considered to be of the highest character, strong, brave, a servant of the community and most importantly, blessed with awareness and guidance from the spiritual world.

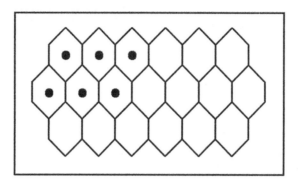

Figure 4. The inufu-ufug / minmináta hexagonal tattoos shown with a few dots placed inside to show the representation as eyes and anthropomorphic figures.

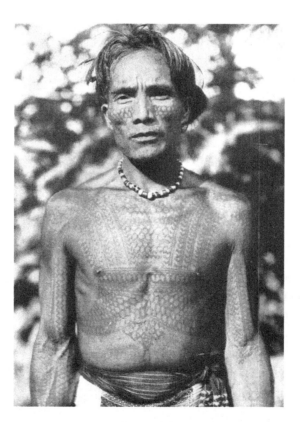

Figure 5. A Kalinga Maingor (warrior) with inufu-ufug hexagonal snake patterns on his chest and upper abdomen.

Although there are many different tattoo motifs, let us examine one particular design that reflects these concepts: the *inufu-ufug* tattoo of the Kalinga. Erroneously thought of as honeycomb patterns, generally the Kalinga people state that the hexagon tattoos represents a woven mat. It is called, *inufu-ufug* or simply *ufug* by the Kalinga people (Salvador-Amores, 2002, p. 135). Among the Itneg people, carrying baskets are woven with this type of hexagonal pattern that they call *minmináta*, meaning "many eyes" (Cole, 1922, p. 422-423). In the past woven rectangular fish traps called *bobo* were made out of bamboo strips with this hexagon pattern. Now these types of fish traps are made from chicken-wire which is coincidently also hexagon in form.

The inufu-ufug design is also said to represent the scales of the centipede among the Ilubo Kalinga, and among people of the Benguet region they are the considered to be the scales of the snake or centipede. This stylized design may actually be many human figures interlocked together. A similar tattoo from the island of Roti in Indonesia southwest of Timor that was placed on the thighs, has a dot within each of the hexagons. Nearly identical patterns have been incised into Bontoc tattoos, shields and *fikum.* (large mother of pearl ornaments). Sometimes within each hexagon is a dot, making the design resemble the many eyes as described in the name "minminata." This may imply the eyes of many ancestors watching over a person or additional spiritual awareness due to the seeing eyes of ancestors. The dots also transform the hexagons into simple anthropomorphic stick figures of human beings. This protective tattoo is likened to the multitude of ancestors, family members and children all interlocked or woven together through the past, present, and into the future. In much of Luzon and other parts of the Philippines, snakes, lizards, crocodiles and other reptiles were also thought to be avatars of the ancestral spirits (anito). So again from this perspective the snake scale design calls to mind the multitude of help from one's ancestors. To illustrate this point, in the ancient mindset, all disease was caused by the malicious actions of evil spirits. During the 19th century there was a severe outbreak of cholera and malaria. The snake-like patterns were said to have protected the wearers from contracting the diseases. The tattoo was thought to be an effective protection from all disease (Salvador-Amores, 2002, p. 125). The reason is clear: if all disease reflects spiritual influence, then all protection from disease requires spirit (*anito*) intervention.

Unlike men who had to "earn" their tattoos through requisite bravery, character and knowledge, generally women were entitled to their tattoos at puberty. Unlike the societies of the Asian mainland, the women of the Philippines were not necessarily considered subordinate or subservient to men. The roles between genders were different but not considered more important than the other. Both partners in a marriage performed important complementary functions to take care of each other and their family. To illustrate this, both partners in a marriage could divorce at will. A man would sometimes even have to pay fines to his wife's family if she left him. So why were women entitled to their tattoos while men had to earn them? I believe this stems from the ancient perception of women in Austronesia. Women were perceived as powerful and inherently spiritual. They were joint creators of life with the gods.

In the kingdom of Tonga in Polynesia we find evidence of the old Austronesian perception of women. In Tonga, a person calls their mother and all of her sisters *fa'ē* but the paternal aunt is called by the title *mehekitanga*. As mehekitanga she has ultimate rights over her brother and her brother's children to control the paternal line. To demonstrate the influence of the mehekitanga, no person however high their rank, including the king, may be called *eiki* (chief) in the presence of their *mehekitanga*. In ancient Hawai'i women's "mana" or spiritual power was viewed as extremely powerful and had to be protected. Consequently Hawaiians had specific taboos to protect women's mana. Some taboos seen through Western eyes view these prohibitions as restrictive or repressive such as certain food taboos like eating pork or bananas. In actuality these were in place to preserve the health of the woman or her children. For example eating certain bananas during pregnancy and nursing causes thrush in babies (K. Nunes, personal communication, Kahua ka Uhi). Among the Iban of Borneo the women performed important spiritual warfare with evil spirits through their weaving of magical symbols into cloth. These powerful talismans in cloth protected the people of the village as well as the men when they conducted physical warfare. In most places of the Philippines the people

> *A woman's tattoos were consequently a visual affirmation of the strength, procreative power and spiritual receptivity she brought with her into this world.*

capitalized on the inherent spiritual power of women by having them as their liaisons with the spirit world. These women were called *babaylan* or variations of the title such as *baglan* in Ilokano. They interpreted omens and dreams, divined the outcome of events, and communicated with members of the spirit world. In some places the babaylan even led the men to battle and ceremonially threw the first spear! (Krutak, 2009). A woman's tattoos were consequently a visual confirmation of the strength, procreative power, and spiritual receptivity she brought with her into this world.

Women's tattoos are most commonly explained as being for the beautification of the body and to increase attractiveness to the opposite sex, which was a component of her fertility. Also, tattooing was considered an essential form of clothing or a substitute for clothing. When foreigners asked the people to stop tattooing, the response was, "We have to, lest we be naked," or "Why, then, we should be naked!" (Vanoverbergh, 1929, p. 188). The Itneg women, for example, wore strings of beads wrapped tightly? around their forearms. Fine lines were tattooed underneath where the beads were so that when the beads were removed the arms would not appear "naked." These tattoos covered all the area where the beads were normally placed and resembled the tattooing of Southern Kalinga but with more space between the lines (Vanoverbergh ,1929, p. 241).

Figure 6. An Itneg woman with arm tattoos that are normally covered in *tinali* beads ca. 1890.

Some of these tattoos themselves were considered a charm to the opposite sex. Tattoo anthropologist Analyn Ikin Salvador-Amores (2002) recorded that the tattoos were thought to help prevent the skin from sagging as a woman aged. Women's tattoos were often placed on the shoulders, arms, and hands, or even just the hands. Much like the women of Palau, certain Dayak tribes of Borneo, the Marshall Islands, Ponape, and women of Samoa, women's tattoos had finer lines and tattoos were more sparsely placed on the same parts of the body, such as the hands, legs, arms and shoulders. Women of the Philippines often received their tattoos at puberty to proclaim their coming of age as a mature and marriageable woman. Tattoos for women also signified fertility and the bravery and strength needed to endure giving birth. After all, being able to endure someone hammering needles into your flesh would certainly be a strong display of your physical fortitude! According to Salvador-Amores, the Ilubo people of Kalinga said that a woman who refused to be tattooed was barren (2002, p. 123). Tattoo motifs for women included items from their lives and roles as women such as rice mortars, seeds, rice plants and symbols of community. These agricultural symbols extended not only to their work in the fields but also were symbolically and spiritually intertwined (via ancestral spirits) with their own fertility and childbearing.

Among the Kalinga a young woman would have one arm tattooed one day and the other arm the next day when she reached puberty. Salvador-Amores relates that young Kalinga women received small "X" shaped tattoos or dashes similar to an equal sign (=) on the face identified as *Lin-lingao*. These were placed on their cheeks, the tip of the nose, chin and on the forehead.

Figure 7. Caption: Lin-lingao tattoos adorn the forehead of Apo Whang-od of Buscalan, Kalina. She is also one of the last traditional tattoo practitioners in Kalinga and Luzon. Photo courtesy of Keone Nunes.

These lin-lingao tattoos marked them as a marriageable woman. These lin-lingao tattoos were also used to confuse the malicious spirits of vengeful beheaded or killed individuals called *alam-alam*. These spirits exacted revenge by taking away the spirits of children or infants (Salvador-Amores, 2002, p. 113). All illnesses were thought of as spiritual in nature due to the machinations of evil spirits or sorcery. So tattoos invoked the protective nature of ancestral spirits as effective fortification from disease. Tattoos were also applied as a form of medicinal treatment such as on goiter or other swellings to reduce the inflammation. Similar medicinal tattoos have been found on natural mummies found in various parts of the world.

Women's tattoos also served a spiritual function. The Ibanag and the Isneg believed that any woman without tattooed hands, would not be accepted into the underworld for the dead. Among the ancient Visayan and Ibanag women, only the hands were tattooed. According to Father Francisco Colin in the 17th century, women of the Visayan Islands limited their tattooing to one hand and part of the other (As cited by Jose Rizal in Garcia, 1979, p. 291). Ibanag hand tattoos were called *appaku* because of its resemblance to the *paku* fern. These tattoos were likely similar to the *fungana* fern tattoos of the Kalinga, which look like a row of diagonal dashes attached to a single or double line resembling a feather. These designs signified the fertility of the land but symbolically represented the women's fertility as well. These *appaku* tattoos were required to pass into the land of the ancestors in the afterlife (Scott, 1995, p. 264). Other peoples of the Philippines shared similar beliefs, which suggests the importance of tattoos for admittance to the underworld or afterlife.

To understand this concept of the underworld, we must briefly look at the ancient cosmological paradigm of our ancestors. In many Austronesian cultures the underworld is associated with the west, the direction of the setting sun. The east is associated with the earth or heavenly world as all heavenly bodies rise in the east. In the Bontoc language the heavens are called, *chay-ya* or *ad-daya* while the word *daya* in Ilokano means the easterly direction. The celestial bodies rise in the east (heavens) and "die" and are "buried" in the earth in the west. Most Austronesian cultures associate the underworld of the ancestors with the West. Our creation myths speak poetically of our progenitors' migration from elsewhere, an ancestral homeland. As they voyaged away from this homeland, the land mass appeared to sink into the ocean as they traveled away from it because of the curvature of the earth. Sometimes, the underworld of the dead is spoken of as on the flip-side of this world. In terms of the sphere of the earth, distant locations are figuratively upside-down. A location a great distance from a person is still spoken of as being "on the other side of the planet." Thus, death was viewed as a cyclical event, the soul's return trip to where we originated. In many Philippine cultures the souls of the dead in their journey through the underworld must pass over a body of water to reach the land where their ancestors await (Scott, 1995, pp. 92, 238). Thus the *underworld* of the dead could be viewed as a poetic description illustrating travel across the curvature of the earth from another place.

With this in mind the placement of tattoos is nearly as important as the tattoo motifs themselves. In general the upper body (waist up) in many Austronesian cultures was associated with the earth world. A person's head was associated with the heavenly world as the seat of the soul. The lower body (waist down) was associated with the underworld and afterlife where our ancestors dwell. The hands were especial members of the body to be tattooed because they symbolically traveled between the earth and heavenly worlds (upper body) and the underworld (lower body) depending on what task they performed. This was especially significant for women who brought new life into the world through birth. The act of giving birth and bestowing life, which originated from the ancestors in the darkness of the underworld, was symbolized as the darkness of the womb into the earthly and heavenly worlds of light. So just as the hands symbolically transverse from the underworld to the earth world, so do women transverse the underworld to the earth world in the act of childbirth. In addition to having tattoos on the hands and arms needed for passage to the afterlife, Isneg women also had tattoo motifs on thighs called *babalakay* (Vanoverbergh, 1929, p. 203). Split into its components, the word babalakay contains both the roots for the words for woman and man, *babae* (baba) and *lalaki* (lakay). Another possible interpretation is "the honored old man from underneath" derived from *I-baba* (under) and *lakay* (honored old man). This motif likely represented ancestors and allowed newborns to be symbolically greeted by their progenitors as they exited the womb.

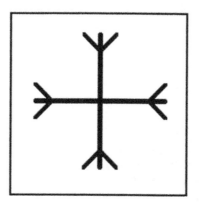

Figure 8. The babalakay tattoo of the Isneg people.

Conversely, parallel to this was a Kalinga male with the *gulot* or head-taker's tattoo on the wrist or hand to show that he had dispatched people from world of the living to the afterlife (Salvador-Amores, 2002, p. 120). In the act of raising the head-ax up and then driving home the beheading stroke, the hand and wrist symbolically travels the breadth of the three realms from the heavens, the earth world and the underworld. Understanding the symbolism of the hand movement becomes especially significant in the observation of traditional dances. Many Bontoc women are tattooed with series of dots or dashes on the back of their hands. Manang Ayeona Langfia, a native of this area, states that these dot patterns represent stars (A. Langfia, personal communication, 2009). Other informants state that these dots are seeds. It is likely that both interpretations are used. A Bontoc woman with seed / star motifs tattooed on her wrists and hands usually sees them below her as she works which reminds her of her role in raising crops, processing rice, etc. But when she dances with her arms stretched out and upwards, these same tattoos now represent the heavenly world (stars) above and the gods who watch her from above. It may be implied that through their blessings her "seeds" or posterity will be multiplied as numerously as the stars in the heavens.

Figure 9. A Bontoc maiden with star /
seed tattoos on her hands ca. 1905

The wearing of tattoos was the outward expression of an enduring and rich spiritual tradition of our indigenous culture. Although only a very small fraction of the tattoo motifs and their spiritual importance are discussed here, I emphasize that it is the knowledge, personal character, and spiritual values that the tattoo represents that are powerful, not the ink in the skin. Especially in the case of males, one had to possess the qualities the tattoos represented prior to wearing them. The internalization of these traits or in other words, the *tattooing of a person's soul* was so important to possess before becoming tattooed. Without it, the marks on the skin are only vain decorations. Those men in the past who were tattooed without earning them were shamefully compared to the halo lizard which is richly patterned yet flighty and cowardly. These ancient tattoos served to reinforce the values of bravery and heroism through spiritual sensitivity, submission to guidance, respect for one's family both living and dead, personal growth, sacrifice, the obligation to know and perpetuate cultural beliefs, protect and serve the community, to be industrious, and to continue one's lineage.

In our modern world fraught with globalization and a vapid departure from indigenous paradigms, many Filipinos have received contemporary tattoos for any number of the contemporary reasons that accompany them. It is my hope that through this writing, many of you, my kindred and family, will be inspired to seek what our culture has already richly practiced for thousands of years. Perhaps in your desire to become tattooed you will seek first to instill those character traits our ancestors valued so highly in the past. Once these have been *tattooed upon your soul*, then will the unseen guidance represented by the tattoos placed on your skin be a shining compass through this world and the next. Your tattoos will serve as an inspiration to all those around you to strive for the qualities that you possess, a modern Filipino fortified by our indigenous heritage.

Figure 10. A Bontoc warrior proudly wearing his chak-lag chest tattoo. Photo by Albert Jenks ca. 1905.

103

References

de Aduarte, D. (1640 Manila – 1962 Madrid). *Historia de la Provincia del Santo Rosario de la Orden de Predicadores en Filipinas, Japon y China*, 1.

Apostol, V. M. (2010). *Way of the ancient healer: Teachings from the Philippine ancestral traditions.* Berkeley, California: North Atlantic Books.

CDIU. (1885 – 1932). Coleccion de Documento indeitos relatives al Descubrimiento, Conquista y Organizacion de las antiguas Posesiones espanoles de Ultramar, 13 volumes. Madrid, Spain.

Cole, F. (1922). The Tinguian, social, religious and economic life of a Philippines tribe. *Field Museum Anthropological Series, XIV*(2).

Cole, M. C. (1916). *Philippine Folk Tales.* Honolulu, HI: University Press of the Pacific

Garcia, M. (Ed.). (1979). *Readings in Philippine Prehistory.* Manila, Philippines: The Filipiniana Book Guild.

Jenks, A. E. (1970). *The Bontoc Igorot. Philippine Islands, Department of the Interior Ethnological Survey Publications, Vol. I* (Reprint of 1905 edition). New York: Johnson Reprint Corporation, Reprint Corporation.

Krutak, L. (2009). *The Last Kalinga Tattoo Artist of the Philippines.* Retrieved from www.larskrutak.com/articles/philippines /

Placencia, F. *Relacion de las Islas Filipinas.* (ca. 1588) (title page missing) fol. 2.

Rosaldo, R. (1980). *Ilongot Headhunting, 1883-1974: A Study in Society and History.* Stanford, California: Stanford University Press.

Salvador, I. (2000, May 2). *The Cordillera's Vanishing Art of Tattooing.* Philippine Daily Inquirer Internet Edition.

Salvador, I. (2004). *Signs on Skin Beauty and Being: Traditional Tattoos and Tooth Blackening Among the Philippine Cordillera.* Ann Arbor, Michigan: University of Michigan.

Salvador-Amores, A. I. (2002). Batek: Traditional Tattoos and Identities. *Contemporary Kalinga, North Luzon, Philippines, 3*(1), 105-142.

Scott, S. (2012, July). Politics and headhunting among the Formosan Sejiq: Ethnohistorical perspectives. *Oceania, 82*(2).

Scott, W. H. (1995). *Barangay: Sixteenth Century Philippine Culture and Society.* Quezon City, Philippines: Ateneo De Manila University Press.

Scott, W. H. (1974). *The Discovery of the Igorots, Spanish Contacts with the Pagan of Northern Luzon.* Quezon City, Philippines: New Day Publishers

Scott, W. H. (1992). *Looking for the Prehispanic Filipino.* Quezon City, Philippines: New Day Publishers.

Swain, T., & Trompf, G. (1995). *The Religions of Oceania.* New York, NY: Routledge.

Thomas, S. (1997). *The Last Navigator.* Blacklick, OH: International Marine.

Vanoverbergh, M. (1929). *Dress and Adornment in the Mountain Province of Luzon, Philippine Islands.* Washington D.C.: Publications of the Catholic Anthropological Conference.

Worchester, D. C. (1912, September). Head-Hunters of Northern Luzon. *National Geographic Magazine, 23*(9). Washington D.C.

* * *

A NOTE ON HEADHUNTING

James W. Perkinson

For most of us as modern readers, indigenous practices of head hunting strike a chord of dissonant ugliness. Reports of such feed into a deep antipathy, produced by a now globalized colonial history, towards all things (seemingly) "barbaric." But this chapter stands forth in all of its stark matter-of-factness as a sign of opacity. We are warned by its honesty: "Beware your own bias." By any measure, modern high-tech societies have been more brutally destructive of human beings and other life forms than any other social form our species has evolved. Looking in the mirror of this writing, our first conclusion must be recognition. We are history's head hunters par excellence. Indeed, we do not really even fit on the same ledger, for our taking of life is now either grossly instrumental or blatantly gratuitous. We kill—and do so with great wastefulness—not with a sense of profound honor and grief, but merely to eat, to boast, to expand, and to leverage fat cat lifestyles whose appetites for "more and more and more" know no bounds (those of us in the U.S. currently pay taxes to drone-bomb increasing hundreds of "other folk" elsewhere in large measure because we want unrestricted access to their oil to pour into our gas-guzzling SUVS to drive to the mall to buy the latest GMOs to feed our increasingly obese bellies. Not to mention all the Iraqis and Afghanis put six feet under since 9/11 for the sake of the same appetite, or the 250-plus invasions of sovereign space elsewhere on the planet over the course of the history of the republic to secure cheap resources and captive labor forces. And very few of us are either withholding our tax dollars in protest or demonstrating in the streets to demand a different way of living).

Indigenous practices of head hunting ritualized the endeavor, lamented the loss, honored the victims (often by adopting them as family members), and typically restricted the practice to an internecine form of exchange (not wholesale war unleashed on others denigrated as less than human). Certainly the practice itself begs reflection as an early form of (largely) male-on-male violence, serving male-on-male initiation rites that verified "honorable masculinity" as only possible at the far end of having risked death in taking the male head of a peer member of an outside clan. Why arrival at manhood should demand such is a worthy question, behind which is an even deeper question of the real function and necessity of ferocity as an admirable quality of being alive. That "spiritedness in living"—comporting oneself with a dignified bearing that is at once gently respectful, exquisitely sensitive to beauty, and yet robustly vital and even forceful when necessary—is a mode of "being human" that indigenous cultures exemplify with far greater finesse than anything the modern world has to offer, is overwhelmingly evident for any who care to look. Perhaps in its deepest evolutionary root, such a capacity for a resistive and violent mobilization of energy has entered our DNA from millennia upon millennia of facing big game in the hunt. Anarcho-primitivist scholar Paul Shepherd has argued that encounter with the wooly mammoth or saber-toothed tiger or great bear of the forest is what fierce feeling is "for" from a deep-history point of view. As the species has altered its modes of living into social forms more and more "contained" within hierarchical structures of power and more and more wantonly aggressive towards their ecological habitats, it is not surprising that some of that violent upsurge of testosterone would find expression in rituals of coming of age. But from our vantage point as "soft modern human beings" sitting behind metal doors, terrified even of spiders and bees, much less bears and wolves, but quite willing to pay others ("soldiers") to do our killing for us, so we can eat with forks while watching TV and pretend that we are non-violent—the encounter with indigenous practices of head-hunting demands deep self-examination. Are we able to appreciate a dignity and ferocity at work that—however much it may trouble us with its violent demand—nonetheless pales before our own lifestyle "demand" for violent support (taking the resources of others through the distant ventures of transnational corporations backed by state-of-the-art militaries) and far outshines our own benumbed sensibility about the worth of others?

As Healer's Dance
A Processual View of Panay Bukidnon's Babaylan in Motion

Maria Christine Muyco

INTRODUCTION

Indigenous healers in the Panay Highlands of Western Visayas, Philippines heal the sick, and themselves as well. They do so through ritual, including ritualized movements that engage and connect them with those they treat as well as with healing and afflicting spirits. As a trained ethnomusicologist, I first encountered this linkage between healing, movement and spiritual interplay when I went to the Panay highlands to conduct immersive research investigating the ideological roots and framing of the dance practice called *binanog* during 2003 and 2004. *Binanog* is a dance that draws its inspiration from the local hawk-eagle called *banog*. The dance, as well as stories about the *banog*, plays central roles in cultural practices of the Panay Bukidnon,[1] the indigenous people that populate the highlands.

---

[1] The Panay Bukidnon are the mountain people of Panay. The name does not refer to any place in particular, as it does in the case of "Bukidnon" in Southern Philippines. F. Landa Jocano (1968) calls these people "Sulod" referring to those living in the interior parts of the mountainous areas of the island. However, during a consultation of the Tapaz local government with the people (which I also attended with anthropologist Alicia Magos), the people claimed that it was the *tagabanwa* (townspeople) who call them as "Sulod," which means, "insiders;" however, they call themselves *Bukidnon*, or the mountain people of Panay. Given this opportunity to speak for themselves, most researchers now call them "Panay Bukidnon."

I start my experiential account of my encounter with this indigenous dance tradition through my story about Violeta Damas, a frail woman in her 50's who sustains herself by eating root crops, grains, and wild greens. When I met Violeta in 2004, her frailty made me wonder, "How she can possibly dance and move in kinetic response to the music of a gong and drum which is so vibrant and energetic?" In my years of learning about *binanog*, dancers usually demonstrate their dancing skills in relation to courtship, or simply for the purpose of entertainment. However, Violeta introduced me to a different realm of experience:

> In Barangay Taganhin, people gathered outside the house of Violeta and set-up a native mat she could sit on. Food offerings such as sticky rice in banana bowls called "simat" were placed around her and sick people sat by her side. She went through phases of possessions as her body shivered; also, her feet repeatedly pounded alternately on the ground — a "kibang," so they called it. Her physical strength built up and she chanted in a different voice, which the people recognized as their ancestor or an ancient spirit possessor. Then the "agung" (hanging bossed gong) was played. As the music was played, she took the simat and held each one on each of her outstretched hands, a gesture called, "ginalaglag" (literally meaning, "Dropping food to the spirits."). This was an act of offering to appease any offended spirit or to request succor and relief from various ailments. The gong music and body/feet movements that she showed were familiar to me; these were units of sound and motion that were part of binanog. The main difference was in the use of arms to offer food and the function of this event for healing. But more than that was the people's deeper intention to continue connecting with spirits who were part of their *kalibutan* (surrounding; cosmic-world; consciousness) (Field notes, May 2004).

In unpacking this experience of healing and dance processes, I inquire into the dynamic of reciprocity and mutually reinforcing forces operating between dancing and curing, and how the synchronizations between them fulfill a healer's intention of bringing harmony to the *kalibutan*, or body-spirit universe. Bringing about this harmony not only heals the afflicted; among the Panay Bukidon, it heals and cleanses the dancer, and appeases the related spirits involved. That is, the definition of healing is more multidimensional and systemic. Through the dance a gestalt emerges and this completeness carries deep meaning for the participants and the community at large.

Through Violeta's expressive and medico-spiritual performance, I realized that some dancers are healers. Interestingly, not all such healers are known as dancers, since they do not regularly join communal dancing nor do they publicly demonstrate their dance skills in and of themselves, or outside of healing rituals. Some healers are also chanters. The connection to the chants is important for at least two reasons: first, because the chants describe various entities involved with sickness and healing, and, secondly, because the movements follow language patterns called "mnemonics." Mnemonics serve to organize, synchronize, and connect musical rhythms and dance steps between dancers and musicians, as well as create a link between these performers and the spirit realm.

I find the body—a communicative body—in rituals interesting as the expressivity of the medium (or the healer) is holistically one with her/his *tubuan* (body), *limog* (voice) as carried out through chant, and even the *kuyapyaw* (eyes) that look up to build rapport with spiritual entities. I watched numerous healing rituals, talked with various kinds of healers (I will describe the distinctions below), and learned more about healing as it appears in myths and chants. In this paper I query the local processes of bridging body-and-spiritual constituents. The particular processes at work draw my attention to the structural and performance praxis of healers. Furthermore, I query

I find the body—a communicative body—in rituals interesting, as the expressivity of the medium (or the healer) is holistically one with her/his tubuan *(body),* limog *(voice) as carried out through chant, and even the* kuyapyaw *(eyes) that look up to build rapport with spiritual entities.*

the motivation behind the act of healing and the employment of certain musical and movement structures that produce a path or system by which a kind of transcendence emerges through and within the ritual. This transcendence is a form of *tayuyon*, or flow, where dancers feel they are in a higher form of consciousness when they connect with the spirits through felt sound and movements. This connection in healing extends my earlier work, which looks at the Panay Bukidnon's ideology called *sibod* within the structural and praxis-oriented frames of *binanog* to enable courtship and communality (Muyco, 2008).

In her analysis of Tongan dances, Kaeppler (1993) uses the term "kinemic" to mean morphemes, or organized units of motions. This kinemic material serves to interpret poetry and form various poetic meanings. For instance, the Tongans dance using hand gestures and symbols that articulate the text in the poetry. My work here takes a similar tack in that I illuminate linkages between the ways Panay Bukidnons see parts of the body being involved in communicating with the spirit world in order to heal. The movements, particularly some elements of the *ginalaglag* that also appear in the *binanog*, employ mnemonic phrases in speech and physical enunciations.

Throughout my inquiry, I have employed the experiential mode of inquiry. I base my work on participant-observation methods and research approaches inspired by Philippine indigenous methodologies proposed by Santiago and Enriquez (1976)[2] and Rogelia Pe-Pua (1985).[3] Furthermore, as a kinesthetic learner, I physicalized my immersion experience by taking lessons from elders and master artists in dancing, performing the accompanying music, and actively participating in healing rituals. Beyond academic grounding, I put indigenous methods and resources to work by using a Panay Bukidnon methodology called *sugid*. Although it literally means, "telling" (Magos, 1996), this method takes different forms of communication such as chanting, the use of poetic words/metaphors, gesture, and storytelling to explain a phenomenon. When one needs more explaining, particularly if a Panay Bukidnon uses archaic, unintelligible words, one could request him/her to *badbad*, literally meaning "to disentangle," or in direct terms, to explain as clearly as possible. I find that *sugid* and *badbad* are complementary methods of learning among the Panay Bukidnon and these can be extended into more rarified forms of speech, such as listening and sharing exchanges around traditional expressive forms such as chanting or storytelling. Because of the rich storytelling tradition and oral teaching of the Panay Bukidnon, I saw *sugid* as an especially effective tool for gathering and understanding information, since it remains closely connected to the culture and its various expressions. The process gives priority to the master practitioners who often drove the inquiry into directions I could not have imagined a priori.

---

[2] Filipino anthropologists Enriquez and Santiago (1976) espouse a culturally grounded method of fieldwork in the Philippines that employed scales of field inquiry:

ISKALA 1 (Simple hanggang kumplikadong paraan): Pagmamasid; pakikiramdam; pagtatanung-tanong; pagsubok; pagdalaw-dalaw; pagmamatyag; pagsusubaybay (ang tatlo sa hulian ay mas nangngangailangan ng partisipasyon galing sa mananaliksik).

SCALE 1 (Simple to complex process): Looking; sensing/feeling; asking questions (around neighborhood); trying; visiting; instinctive feeling; follow-up (the third to the last items would need the researcher's participation).

ISKALA 2 (Batayan sa kalidad ng nakuhang dayta): Sa kategoriya ng Ibang tao (Outsider)— pakikitungo; pakikisalamuha; pakikilahok; pakikibagay; pakikisama.

SCALE 2 (According to the quality of gathered data): In the category of other people or outsider— getting along; mixing with their interests/activities; joining; matching with their preferences; forging camaraderie.

Enriquez and Santiago drew up these procedures with the objective, among other things, to build a situated research methodology rooted in a realistic Filipino setting. They pointed out that there should be "… *daloy ng ugnayan at pagkasunusununod-sunusunod na hakbang ay batayan o paraan sa pagkamit ng pagtitiwala sa mananaliksik-kaugnay* (a continuum among the mentioned processes following procedures step-by-step to build trust between researcher and participant).

[3] Pe-Pua (1985) introduces a Filipino methodology called *pagtatanong-tanong* (asking questions or asking around). Instead of an interview, this method serves as a dialogic approach to engaging participants to verify research questions and to fully validate information.

DEFINING A HEALER

Unlike doctors who decide on their medical profession, Panay healers do not become healers at will; rather powerful spirits or forces select them. I met Menchie Diaz-Caspillo, a young healer in Barangay Tacayan of Tapaz (Capiz). At the age of 20, she was already initiated in the world of spiritual possession and eventually tasked with the mission to mediate between the worlds of the physical and the spiritual. Prior to knowing about her healing obligation, she was sick for a long time and barely had the appetite to eat. Later, she realized that her sickness was part of becoming a healer and she felt the presence of an intruding force coming inside her body. Other symptoms followed: she would feel cold, and in effect, she would shiver and would *kibang* (forcefully pound the ground with her feet in rhythmic motion). If she resisted the task, she would feel the constriction of her heart, an inexplicable pain. Each healer, she shared, must go through ritual phases, initiations, and learning experiences with an older or seasoned guide healer. It was when she finally accepted the healing task that her health improved.

In the Panay highlands, there are many kinds of traditional healers—the *serruano*, the *dalungdungan*, the *babaylans*. I met Noning Lopez of Barangay Cabatangan in Lambunao (Iloilo) in July of 2004. She was a practicing *serruano* in their community and she told me that before I arrived in their place, she already saw a reflection of me in a bottle. She described what she saw: the clothes I was wearing and the color of my pants. She also knew about my plans of going to a remote hinterland and that the spirits had advised her to tell me not to push through. According to her, the spirits were not ready for my visit. I met her after I slipped through a mud, fell down into a pit, and fractured a bone in my left foot. Alas, the warning she gave was too late for my unexpected accident.

As believed, a Panay Bukidnon *serruano* heals with guidance from a *saragudun*, or spirit. The term *saragudun* may mean a being that is fed or supplied with food. Similarly in the healing practice of a *serruano*, offering food[4] is one of the ways to appease the elemental spirits who have been angered for some reason or another. Typical cases would include stepping over a spirit or its territory.[5] Since certain spirits are believed to live on or below the ground, on trees, or under water, they are hurt when they are stepped on or their spaces are occupied without permission. Thus, it is prudent for a Panay Bukidnon to inform the spirits that he or she will trespass a possibly spiritually occupied space, or for a person to ask the spirits to give way for him/her by saying "*panabi-tabi*" (please allow us to pass by). As a precaution, this word is said preemptively as the person cannot see the spirits that may inhabit a place. Observance of respect is a way of preventing danger as the aggrieved spirits can bring on sickness upon those who caused their anger. Also, in a deeper sense, this continually connects them to the spirit world.

---

[4] The kind of food to be offered is usually dictated by the spirits.

[5] For instance, a person who has stepped on a mound of earth said to be occupied by enchanted beings is punished. The beings have the power to make the person sick.

Figure 1. Violeta Damas, a healer in a rite in
Barangay Taganhin, May 2004.

Earlier, I mentioned Violeta Damas from Barangay Taganhin. When I arrived in the
area where she lived, it was time for a fishing harvest. This was also the time when fishermen
called to the water spirits to give them a good catch. Land spirits abound as this month was
like springtime in their place, a lot of flowers bloomed and vegetation was lush. Memories
of the hot days in April were washed away by the showers of May. I met Violeta through
her brother Aurelio Damas who knew the preparation for the food and liquor offering. In
the time of growth after the wilting month of April, he gathered the ingredients for rice
cakes and rice wine. Aurelio told me that his sister Violeta is a *dalungdungan*, a type of
healer who has a *dalungdung*, or a spirit-guide. She has regular spirit-visitors (about seven)
who inhabit her body and they assist her in healing the sick. In particular, she referred to
Pagsandan, the mythical hero of the Panay cosmology, as the leader of all these spirits.
In the Panay Bukidnon community, a *dalungdungan* is tasked to take back the *dungan*
(soul) from a spirit theft, usually of the evil kind. Also a good detector of the presence of
the *maranhig* or *aswang* (witch) and the *ituman* or *malain ginhawa* (dark or evil spirits/
breath), the *dalungdungan* counters their bad intentions against humans. He or she also
uses medicinal herbs and a healing oil called the "*dalungdong*" (incidentally, the same term
for a spirit-guide).

In Barangay Tacayan (Tapaz, Capiz), Menchie Diaz-Caspillo told me about the
babaylan whose power is to call on the presence of the *diwata*, or spirit guide by tinkling a
ceramic bowl or plate. The high-pitched sound produced by a ceramic bowl or plate when
struck by a metal beater is ideally the sound believed to reach the ears of the *diwata* who
dwells in the upper level of the cosmos, or *kalibutan*. In Barangay Badas (Tapaz, Capiz),
Alunsia Castor showed me another way by which a *babaylan* would call the spirits by using
a *tebongbong*, or a bamboo tube. Tapping on the opening hole of this tube, a *babaylan*

creates a series of continuous beats that is followed with a chant to clearly convey the message to the spirits. The chant is a sung dialogue between the healer (a mediator of the guide spirits) and the community or relatives of the sick represented by another chanter.

A *babaylan* has several *hilimuon*, or tasks. One of these is saving the lives of infants or babies from evil spirits. The *kinamnan*, or the soul of an infant, should be retrieved back from the spirit world and returned to his/her physical body. The *kinamnam* is considered one's "double," a necessary unit of life that completes and animates the physical body. Thus, a ritual is undertaken for this retrieval and it is called, *pagsagda*. It entails offering food, particularly to spirits who took the *kinamnan*, playing rhythms through a *tebongbong* (bamboo tube), and chanting or calling the involved spirits. A *babaylan* can also assist a dead man's soul to move towards the spirit world without being harmed by the evil ones. The process is called *pagbilog* (forming), that is, to help the soul solidify instead of liquefying; the latter being a form that can be devoured by the *aswang*. Evil beings can take advantage of a body and transform it into a banana trunk or a jackfruit to deceive the *babaylan*.

In Barangay Daan Sur (Tapaz, Capiz), I interviewed Alfred Castor who knows of a family whose seven adult siblings were all *babaylans*.[6] They performed their healing tasks individually, but they agreed to work together in case they had to help someone with acute or serious illness. One time, a ritual was held that needed the forces of not just one *babaylan*, but more than five as the ailment was so gravely serious and the spirits that needed to be dealt with were powerful ones. The patient, Florinda Castor, was suffering from a ballooning stomach. A hospital in Iloilo deemed her condition incurable so her family decided to seek the *babaylans'* help instead. Alfred Castor wanted to witness the ritual; but as he entered the house where the rite was held, he and other spectators were informed that no one was allowed to leave that place (even if it took days) until the ritual culminated. Castor described the event:

> ...When the seven healers altogether did a *kibang*, it was scary. The whole house shook; their *kibang* was so powerful that they seemed to produce an earthquake effect (Direct translation from *Kiniray-a* to English, Field Notes, January 2004).

However, even if it was scary, Alfred said spectators had to abide by the rules not to leave the healing event, or else something might happen to them. Depending on individual healers, particular rules are mandated. They are made part of an over-all program of a ritual or healing event that somehow assists in the efficacy of healing.

I once witnessed a ritual in Barangay Taganhin (Tapaz, Capiz). As the spirits were supplicated, I was informed that no one should laugh at the performed tasks of a *babaylan*

---

[6] This example refers to the Catamin family. Specific first names were withheld upon requests of the family.

or else "live coals" used in the ritual would attack and burn those who would laugh. The spirits, or *saragudon* that occupy the body of a *babaylan*, would feel insulted and disturbed if there are skeptics and cynics among the spectators.

Other than healing, some Panay Bukidnons have extraordinary capabilities to help their fellowmen. The *dalagangan* (gifted helper) is known to perform unusual feats like running around on the roof of a house and jumping from the ground to a rooftop. The *dalagangan* would do this in order to help those who are in immediate need. According to Aurelio Damas of Barangay Taganhin (Tapaz, Capiz), his deceased mother was a *dalagangan* and she helped those who sought remedy to their ailments. The *dalagangan* can also supplicate certain spirits to provide rain or sun. It is interesting to note that among the lowlanders, or the city dwellers of Panay, the term *dalagangan* has become part of their language to mean—someone to run to for problems, or who can respond quickly in providing help.

Panay Bukidnons believe that the "spiritual and the physical" health are inextricably linked. When sickness occurs, both the spirit and the body are affected. A person with physical manifestations of poor health may have consciously caused his/her spirit's affliction; in some cases, he or she may indirectly be responsible for becoming ill by unknowingly inflicting harm on another being. Thus, healing involves performance rituals to cure an illness, which may be physical or spiritual, or both. These include the offering of food, chanting, and dancing as food is presented to the spirits.

Healers need to take care of their health even while taking care of others. Violeta Damas explained to me that her spirit guides her on what food she should take so that her body would be ready for spiritual habitation. Thus, most healers I met have certain preferences in their diet. They largely eat vegetables, fish, poultry and white meat, e.g. chicken. They avoid red meat or food from larger beasts, e.g. pig, cow, carabao, or dog. Usually they do not eat *sapat*, or insects, and the reptiles of the forest, like the *halo* and the *ibid,* both of the monitor lizard family. Healers supplicate certain spirits and their aides (usually assisting ancestral spirits). There are also physical preparations using medicinal herbs or commercially bought medicines to treat the body.

SUPPLICATING THE SPIRITS

Certain ailments entail petitioning certain spirits for help and intercession. According to Violeta Damas, spirits fall into two main categories: the *putian* (white) and the *ituman* (black) spirits. The *putian* (white) are good spirits and the *ituman* (black) are evil. The *sirangans* I met in different barangays discussed this binary difference. *Sirangans* are those who can see the other dimensions of beings normally invisible to the human eye. I also learned about the *putian* and the *ituman* from those who experienced healing brought about by a *putian's* assistance, or, on the contrary, those who got sick because of the cruelty of an *ituman.*

The Panay Bukidnon acknowledge the existence of various beings generally referred to as *tamawo* (strange beings who look like men, but without an upper lip canal), *enkanto* (the enchanted), *dwende* (tiny beings), and other unseen life forms. These beings can either be a type of *putian*, particularly if they are kind and helpful; or *ituman* if they are harmful and violent.

There are different ways of identifying a *putian* from an *ituman*. An *ituman* is devoid of light. It is usually nighttime when the presence of these entities is determined. Against darkness, a *putian* is visible as it takes a form of a human being but without flesh; its body is filled with light. However, the *ituman* is seen at nighttime as well. But how can one tell if it's *ituman* when it has no light, meaning that it is invisible? Violeta Damas explained:

> When *lati*, or the light of the moon becomes full or in a capacity to fill the night with some degree of visibility, you can see things around; that's when you can see the *ituman*. They have black human form, but with face outlined like a wild cat with whiskers (Directly translated in field notes during interview, September 2003).

The moonlight provides a pitch-black night with a particular clearness, and against this, the *ituman* gains a visible or identifiable form. The contrast of light against dark makes the *ituman* visible. *Itumans* are also called *malaing ginhawa* (bad spirit or breath).

There are exceptions to the binary concepts of white and black. Even as there are general ways of perceiving meanings, there are specific differences noted due to experiences that are not the same as what has been generalized. For instance, a few mountains away from the place where I interviewed healers believing in the *putian* and *ituman* are *serruanos* like Noning Lopez of Barangay Cabatangan (Lambunao (Iloilo) who attested to seeing the *pulahan* (the red ones). These spirits punish people who, in a way, disturb their state of peace and order. Specific cases of such a disturbance would include situations where a person would cut a tree the *pulahan* occupies, or when an individual desecrates the land these beings respect. The *pulahan* may cause an inflictor's skin to turn red. As Noning Lopez would put it, the skin looks like *ga-banog na panit*, or swollen skin.

This tells us that not all cultural communities limit their beliefs to pure opposites, but within the culture itself, there may exist variations and differences nuancing the general cosmology.

THE BODY IN MOTION

In a Panay Bukidnon healing ritual, food and rice wine are not the only components used to appease the spirits. A gong should be present to provide music for the healer when he or she dances *ginalaglag*, a form of expressivity in offering food to the spirits:

Figure 2. Author's sketch of a healer-dancer in a "ginalaglag" during a ritual in Barangay Taganhin (Tapaz, Capiz), 2004.

The movements and footwork of *ginalaglag* are taken from the *binanog*, the hawk-eagle dance of the Panay Bukidnon. This dance, and the accompanying music, utilizes mnemonics, or linguistic memory devices, which become the basis for dancers in the articulation of words while dancing. Referred to as *ta-ta*, dancers' lips move to the syllabic rhythm of the mnemonics, even though the words are not uttered aloud. They take their cue from the gong player who is similarly guided by the same mnemonics. An example of a linguistic memory device is this phrase: "patakdanga guribal." For some Panay Bukidnons, it does not mean anything; to others, however, it's a kind of command for someone to make the steps of "guribal," a rhythmic mode that requires stomping three times on the ground. These three time-stomps synchronize with the accented syllables of "tak-da-nga" or "gu-ri-bal" based on the mentioned phrase, "patakdanga guribal." There are, however, gradations as to the heaviness of the stomping; sometimes some of the healers just execute their steps based on the speech-rhythm of the words, not really stomping hard so as to avoid spilling the food offering on the ground.

In a Panay Bukidnon healing ritual, food and rice wine are not the only components used to appease the spirits. A gong should be present to provide music for the healer when he or she dances ginalaglag, *a form of expressivity in offering food to the spirits.*

I learned the steps from the *binanog* used for the *ginalaglag* from the Panay Bukidnon elders. But aside from the translations of syllables into movements, I was taught about the relationship of arm movements and the directions of these movements, as well as physical posture, and footwork directed to/identified with certain spirits that inhabit specific layers of the cosmic world. Circumscribed within the dance while synchronizing with the gong music is one's deeper motivation to be in sync with forces from different realms. For the Panay Bukidnon, the different parts of the body are involved in acts of linking. First, are the eyes. Most elders of the community, I observed, danced with their eyes looking up. They do this even in the middle of a healing ritual. Secondly, the dancers' arms are flapped like wings; these arms are level with the shoulder. Romulo "Amang Baoy" Caballero explained that the use of the arms implies an earthly play. Dancers in this position relate to earth spirits particularly with the *dutan-on* (earth entities) and the *tubignon* (water entities). *Dutan-on* occupy trees, flowers, and others that grow from earth, while the *tubignon* occupy rivers, lakes, waterfalls, and other bodies of waters. Dancers are conscious of the earth and aware of its breadth and space as they move around their ritual space, and, eventually, around the sick person and the people who are involved in the healing process.

A dancer's feet are also important vehicles for sending messages to the underground spirits, or the *idalmunon*. Through a dancer's steps, Romulo Caballero said, the spirits below the ground are said to be touched, or *tandug*. Perhaps this is the reason why the people translate the rhythms of syllables of certain words into footwork patterns. The *idalmunon* are believed to be keen on sounds created by the feet. This auditory sense of communication is interesting in understanding motion and sound, as well as the effect, or the reception of certain messages, from the spirit entities that hear rather than see.

> *The* idalmunon *[underground spirits] are believed to be keen on sounds created by the feet. This auditory sense of communication... understand[s] motion and sound, as well as the effect on...the spirit entities that hear rather than see.*

IDEOLOGICAL ASPECTS IN PANAY HEALING

For every ritual or form of expression such as dancing and chanting, Panay Bukidnons believe that their acts should achieve *sibod*—a mastery of structures and synchronizations that produces effectiveness, connectedness, and even transcendence. This sense of value is significant as this determines whether an intention or objective is fulfilled by the very expression of an act. For instance, when *sibod* is obtained, one is seen mastering a dance step, or a body seems to flow in harmony with the music. In connection with *ginalaglag*, a dance/healing act is in *sibod* if the sick person is cured of his or her ailment.

Figure 3. Violeta Damas offers food with outstretched arms,
a *ginalaglag* position. Aurelio Damas at the extreme left hands
over the next food offering in line.

When *sibod* happens in the *ginalaglag,* the whole atmosphere is charged with positive and ecstatic energies. The involvement of the people in a healing ritual—the gong player, the family of the sick person, and most of all, the healer—produces an energy that circulates and touches the upper, middle, and lower dimensions of life. Romulo Caballero previously noted this "touching" imagery: *kun sa aton pa, daw natandug bala ang balatyagon ka iba* (it is as if the emotions/sentiments of others have been touched). This image of "touching" relates to *sibod* as a form of synchronization particularly between "music and dance," "music-dance and the healer," the sick person and the other participants of a healing event, and on a larger scale, between the community and the cosmos. Dancing for the Panay Bukidnon means touching the sentiment of the spirits. It means establishing a whole network of interconnected linkages that forms a system or whole/wholeness.

Ginalaglag is similar to the *binanog* in that there are stances that relate to the outstretched wings of the *banog.* A creature that can traverse the space between earth and sky, this messenger is believed to send the prayers of the healer to the ears of the recipient spirits. Myths, fables, and other folklore tell about the genesis of healers in the natural and spirit world of Panay. In particular, Menchie Diaz of Barangay Tacayan (Tapaz, Capiz) tells that:

> In the olden times, when human beings have not yet inhabited the earth, a creature named Pagsandan toured the world, which was located between the sky and the land. He had planned this tour since he was a child. Before he left, he planted a tanglad (lemon grass plant) on the ground to mark the spot where he was supposed to return. When he got back, he

met a beautiful woman named Ginharunan who was sifting through rice grains called lampunaya. Pagsandan ate the grains and he fell in love with Ginharunan. He wanted to marry her, but she said he had to pass the test that her father Bunturami gave to all her suitors. Bunturami, a huge creature, had a seven-foot wide chest. Pagsandan passed all the almost nearly impossible feats as he had supernatural powers like Bunturami and Ginharunan. Impressed that Pagsandan had proven that he was more powerful than him, Bunturamie then allowed the relationship between Pagsandan and Ginharunan to prosper. Pagsandan today is a spirit who helps healers cure the sick. He is also a mediator between humans and the other unseen forces of the world (Translation from interview notes, April 2004).

In this story, Menchie provided information about an old *kalibutan;* this is a world where creatures used to occupy the land and the air, or space between the sky and the land. Creatures in this story can walk on land and on air (or perhaps fly). This made me think of a possible parallel between these capacities and the *binanog* dancers' doing the *bayhunan* (leisure walk), which is followed by other dance steps that simulate flying. The *binanog* unfolds on two levels: on the land and the air. Filipino cultural historian Zeus Salazar (2006) relates a story from Philippine mythology that reflects some of these same themes (p. 27):

"....*galing ang lupa (mga pulo't kapuluan) sa langit na inihagis nito sa dagat nang inudyok ng lawin na magalit ito (dagat) at makipag-away sa kalangitan*"

"...land [archipelago and islands] came from the heavens thrown into the sea when the eagle provoked the sea to be angry and have a row with the heavens."

According to Salazar, "*iisa ang langit at lupa* (the heavens and land are one). How does the *binanog* fit into this scheme? I thought of Menchie's narrative and how in the passing of time, Panay Bukidnons would commemorate, through the *binanog*, what perhaps has been lost into the present world. To dance and look up, the *binanog* dancer establishes a reconnection with his/her *kalibutan*, momentarily commemorating and unifying a sundered world.

According to Menchie, Pagsandan became a powerful spirit who would aid the sick by occupying the body of healers. She attested to the fact that Pagsandan is one of seven spirits that possesses her when she heals. Like other healers, she would conjure him from the *ispirituhanon*, or the spiritual realm (upper space).

Dance has healing efficacy, especially when a *babaylan* (healer) offers food to call for the spirits' aid via the *ginalaglag*, with each hand holding a platter of food as the feet dance the *binanog* steps. In the discussion of spiritual linkage, we see that *sibod* as a *diretso*, or a flow, becomes a vehicle to transport or link the Panay Bukidnon's offering of the *binanog* music and dance to various forms of existence.

CONCLUSION

Earlier in the introduction of this paper, I posed the theme of indigenous ways for bridging body-and-spiritual constituents. The particular processes at work in the healing culture of the Panay Bukidnons drew my attention to the synchronizations between healing and dancing and how each can realize a healer's intention of bringing harmony to the *kalibutan* or body-spirit universe. Magos (1992) notes that the *maaram*, or healer, plays a distinct role in society since she/he mediates between the ancestral spirits, various ancient and elemental spirits (such as those in the water or a tree), and the day-to-day affairs of life. The healer performs such functions through the ways they encounter, and are affected by, these spirit beings. Magos observes that repetitive instrumental music plays a central role in this mediation by serving as a hypnotizing force, bringing the healer to a different plane of consciousness in order to commune with the spirits. More generally, Villaruz and Obusan (n.d.) posit that through instrumental music, chanting, and dancing, traditional Filipinos enact spiritual rites, closely attuning them to nature and to the spirits that keep or sustain both them and their environment. These rites "serve as a popular medium of dramatic expression and entertainment that reflects the people's nature, culture and aspirations" (Villaruz & Obusan, n.d.). However in the Panay Bukidnon epistemology, a shared existence, rather than mere self-existence, is necessary for life and the environment to thrive. This shared existence is defined by the people's deep and rooted awareness of presences around their *kalibutan*—understood to refer to the perceived world, surroundings, and, at times, one's consciousness, awareness, and knowing of these elements. For instance, my teachers would say: "*Ano kalibutan na sa gakahitabu?*" or "What does s/he know about what happened?" In the *kalibutan*, the *ginalaglag*, using the *binanog* music and dance, presents to healers and other individuals ways of seeking aid from, and making gift offerings to, the spirits. In the dance, every part of the body communicates certain messages in this effort. This goes far beyond simple dramatic expression and entertainment: offering food and bodily expression to a spirit is a fundamentally serious matter since it functions to realize connectivity with said spirit. Perhaps that is the reason why Panay Bukidnon elders would reprimand their young ones to be mindful of their actions by saying: "*Di mag-basal ka lacoy-lacoy.*" ("Do not play the instrument half-seriously"). A similar caution in regard to dance is made by admonishing youths not to dance half-heartedly or for "being only half present." The elders believe that focus and full attention to developing and expressing skills are part of enhancing one's consciousness and communing with powerful forces at work in the world.

In Feld's (1990) observation about the rainforest people of Papua New Guinea called "Kaluli," he notes that "... ultimately ecology—birds, waterfalls, forest presences—is the domain of the natural that Kaluli culturalize, while dance, song, costume, and poetics are domains of the cultural that Kaluli naturalize" (p. 14). This "homology" takes the form of two types of enunciations-one from the natural environment and another from cultural expressions-but these enunciations are actually integrated in the formal patterns of a music/dance performance. By the same token, the Panay Bukidnon see themselves located in the wholeness of their *kalibutan*, which includes their natural environment; however, the natural environment is part of the cultural expression in dancing as they link the structural levels of the upper, middle, and lower parts of their kalibutan in relation to their bodies. Furthermore, the pursuit of *sibod* is a much deeper motivation to accomplish the objective of healing.

In involving dance, music, and other aspects of performativity (e.g. chanting), a healer is directed to synchronize his or her movements with the music and with the offering of food for the purpose of establishing connection between the various parts of the *kalibutan*. The simultaneous enactment of healing and dancing realizes *sibod*, and this syncing up, in turn, serves to link the people with the spiritual forces of the *kalibutan*. They would say: *pasibudon,* or facilitating workability between people and spirits, in concert with the said healing act. Note that this act of linking is not unidirectional. The interaction between the spirits and human beings established through dance and healing is, in a sense, social (Buenconsejo, 2000), forming an overlapping network of connections and conjunctions. Healers are involved in a sociable conversation with the spirits, and the spirits, in turn, are known to respond, not in the form of direct speech, but via a medium. The response is "felt" as a form of energy. Performer/healers sensitize themselves to these energy pulses/ fluctuations as they make their music and dance *sibod* continuously; dancing and music-making produce the attraction or gravity between people who are involved in a healing event and other forces at work. This *sibod* brings a frame or network into being that serves as a powerful support and channel to the healer's mediating function and, taken together, this moves the ritual participants toward the furtherance of a working activity.

Thus, *sibod* is a form of linkage that is substantiated through the dancers' physical, acoustic, and affective manifestations in order to: 1) awaken or make the spirits aware of their ongoing social relationships with humans; 2) call on spirits to facilitate healing and provide aid in the community's and individuals' well being; 3) bring the spirits to one's physicality so that dancing and music-making could be more enriched and enriching; and 4) create balance and harmony in the cosmos, including the physical-spiritual world. This balance is crucial to the effectiveness of healing. It enforces order on one's consciousness—a vital core to a healer's state of health and well being as s/he continues to function with expressivity in the healing process.

Coming into contact with healers has added a rich new dimension to my ongoing cultural work with the Panay Bukidnon, particularly in extending my study about *sibod*. With my deeper and deepening understanding and experience of this indigenous tradition, I am guided in regard to the ways I can apply insights from cultural study to community engagement and advocacy. This application encompasses various specific actions, one of which is helping create space for the voices of indigenous peoples to be heard more widely and clearly so their culture may continue to *sibod*, that is, continue to flourish. Honoring indigenous ways of healing also underlies the work I do with and through *Balay Patawili, Inc.*, a non-governmental organization I founded to help support "Schools of Living Tradition"[7] projects in highland communities and workshops. Commitment to supporting indigenous practices also extends to fundraising efforts: funds to help indigenous artists continue to celebrate their traditions and expressions through chant, dance, embroidery, and now, healing rituals, among other expressions. As I work with researchers, volunteer cultural workers, government and private organizations, I myself have begun to express the ideal of *sibod*—and through it, a kind of healing and mediation work—so as to bring the objectives of cultural revitalization into the very core of the self and the community. Healing, after all, as I mentioned in the beginning of this paper, also happens with the healer, not just the ailing patient.

---

[7] The School of Living Tradition (SLT) is a project funded by the National Commission for Culture and the Arts (NCCA) of the Philippines to encourage cultural transmission among generations and individuals among a given group of traditional people. My support for Panay Bukidnons takes the form of organizing master elders and coordinators to propose grants, and also to train young professionals to conduct workshops among themselves.

References

Alejandro, R. G. (1985). Bird imagery in Philippine dance. In Betty True Jones (Ed.), *Dance as a cultural heritage, Dance research II*, 78-82. U.S.A: CORD Inc. Annual XV.

Amilbangsa, L. F. (1983). *Panagalay: Traditional dances and related folk artistic expressions.* Makati: Filipinas Foundation, Inc.

Buenconsejo, J. S. (2000). *Songs and gifts at the frontier: Person and exchange in the Agusan Manobo possession ritual.* U.S.A.: University of Pennsylvania.

Feld, S. (1982). *Sound and sentiment: Birds, weeping, poetics, and song in Kaluli expression* (2nd ed.). U.S.A: University of Pennsylvania Press.

Feld, S. (1986). Sound as a symbolic system. In C. J. Frisbie (Ed.), *Explorations in ethnomusicology: Essays in honor of David McAllester*, 9. U.S.A.: Information Coordinators.

Enriquez, V. (Ed.). (1990). *Indigenous psychology: A book of readings.* Philippines: New Horizons Press.

Jocano, F. L. (1968). *Sulod: A Study in the kinship system and social organization of mountain people of Central Panay.* Quezon City: University of the Philippines.

Kaeppler, A. L. (1993). *Poetry in motion: Studies of Tongan dance* (1st ed.). Tonga: Vava'u Press.

Magos, A. (1992). *The enduring Ma-aram tradition: An ethnography of a Kiniray-a village in Antique.* Quezon City Philippines: New Day Publishers.

Magos, A. (1996, January-June). The sugidanon of Central Panay. *Edukasyon—UP-ERP* Monograph Series 2, 117-123. Philippines: University of the Philippines, Education Research Program, Center for Integrative and Development Studies.

Muyco, M. C. (2008). *Sibod in binanog: Understanding the binanog tradition of the Panay Bukidnon in Western Visayas, Philippines.* (Unpublished doctoral dissertation). University of the Philippines, College of Arts and Letters, Philippines.

Pe-Pua, R. (1985). Pagtatanong-tanong: Katutubong metodo ng mananaliksik. *New directions in indigenous psychology*, 416-430. Manila: National Bookstore.

Salazar, Z. (2006). *Ang Pilipinong Banua/Banwa sa Mundong Melano-Poynesiano.* Quezon City, Philippines: Bagong Kasaysayan.

Salazar, Z. (2004). *Liktao at epiko: Ang takip ng tapayang libingan ng libmanan, Camarines Sur.* Quezon City, Philippines: Paglimbagan ng Lahi.

Santiago, C. E., & Enriquez, V. (1976). Tungo sa makapilipinong pananaliksik. *Sikolohiyang Pilipino*: *Ulat at balita, 19,* 3-10. Quezon City: Philippine Psychology Research House.

Villaruz, B. E., & R. Obusan (n.d.). *The Ethnic tradition in Philippine dance.* Retrieved from http://nlpdl.nlp.gov.ph:9000/shares/finders/CC01/NLP00VM052mcd/v6/v2.pdf

---

Research Participants

Alfred Castor, Barangay Daan Sur (Tapaz, Capiz), research period: 2003-2004

Romulo Caballero, Barangay Masaroy (Calinog, Iloilo), research period: 2002-2006

Violeta Damas, Barangay Taganhin (Tapaz, Capiz), research period: 2004

Menchie Diaz-Caspillo, Barangay Tacayan (Tapaz, Capiz), research period: 2003-2004

Noning Lopez, Barangay Cabatangan (Lambunao, Iloilo), research period: 2004

PART II

INDIGENOUS SOUNDINGS IN CONTEMPORARY PRACTICES

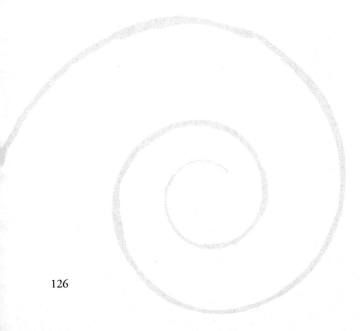

The Death of Maria Clara and the Resurrection of Babaylan

Reclaiming the Filipina American Body

Jane J. Alfonso

I'm sitting in the back of my family's Ford LTD station wagon....suddenly aware of how our car moves through space and time....I notice the nothingness left in our car's wake—how space and time rush in to swallow up where our car has been, every second of its motion is devoured, leaving not one trace. We're traveling but there's no sign of our having been on the road at all; our presence is erased as soon as it is made. Somehow, I connect this sense of motion and simultaneous erasure to my family's history—how we operate in the very American 'perpetual present', eschewing our link to our Filipino past....I learn to distance myself from my history....so this is the American Dream— living in the perpetual present, moving through life without a past, swallowed whole, invisible, but unable to deny the lingering ache of absence....

(de Jesus, 2005, p. 2)

I fed you, burped you, changed your diaper, made sure you were not sleepy. I tried to entertain you, and still you cried. You were a good kid, but a crybaby. I did not know what you needed

(my mother, 2006).

INTRODUCTION

As I remember listening to my mother share with me what I was like as a child, seeing her furrowed brow, an annoyed, distracted and puzzled air about her, I feel again a sense of collapse and contraction, becoming hard and still on the outside, my muscles bound with the effort to not betray what I was feeling. Inside, my heart was sinking, shriveling into a cold, dense pit so deep within me that it was almost inaccessible. *Almost*. I could sense the first stirrings of anger in my stomach and I tightened my core to lock down the burning sensation, tightened the muscles around my eyes to keep from crying. The words that burned and waited on my lips and in my throat (by now, an uncomfortable lump), but which I did not dare say to her, were: what I needed from you was to really *look* at me, really *hold* me. *Pay attention*. I took several breaths, feeling my belly rise and fall as I allowed those evocative unsaid words to move through me. The tightness and immobility slowly subsided and once again I was able to feel all of me, first, a prickly, then flowing, warmth, pulsing and spreading throughout my body, painful yet relieving all at once.

The journey from unconscious and chronic immobility to conscious awareness and freedom of movement is the journey of embodiment and the goal of body-oriented psychotherapy. Rather than distinguishing the body as separate from and a lesser entity than the soul—as a Cartesian, dualistic philosophy has informed notions of the body, it is the central premise of body-oriented psychotherapy that psyche and soma are indivisible, and that attention to bodily experience and processes in the forms of sensate experience, sensorimotor development, gesture, posture, verbal tics, patterns of chronic immobility and tension, patterns of breathing, and changes in energy levels, is critical to emotional and mental well-being.

Indeed, from the somatic perspective, emotional and cognitive content inform somatic "organization" (Keleman, 1979) and vice versa. "Organization," or the shaping of self in response to the inner and outer environment, is largely unconscious. To the extent that the organization is painful or no longer useful, it is a maladaptive response. Change occurs when maladaptive emotional and cognitive beliefs are consciously "disorganized" through exploration of the somatic embodiment of those beliefs. For example, in my somatic response to my mother's story, I organized myself into a shape whose belief was "I am not sad or angry" by tightening the muscles around my eyes and in my stomach. I disorganized this belief by relaxing my muscles, allowing the sensations of sadness and anger to be present. In moving through this continuum of experience—stretching, contracting, expanding, pulsating, shaping and reshaping—the range of possibilities becomes more expansive and flexible, and adaptive responses are developed as a result. The body has a language of its of own which is meaningful when "read" and "interpreted" accurately, which is why developing the capacity to accurately "track" the body is critical for any body-oriented therapist. Within somatic psychotherapy, the non-verbal "moment-to-moment external manifestations of present-time internal experience" (Fisher, 2002, p. 32) are privileged as much as verbal content, both manifest and hidden.

But what does it mean to have a "Filipina American body"? In other words, what is the relationship between ethnic identity (specifically Filipina American) and somatic theory? What are the particular cultural forces that help shape the body? Revilla (1997) argued that the development of ethnic identity is critical because it "affects the maintenance and expression of traditional culture, helps individuals enhance their self-concept and self-esteem, and enables individuals to have a sense of belonging" (p. 96). The need for specific research on Filipino American identity has been identified as an issue of primary importance (Revilla, 1997) especially because there are several factors that differentiate Filipino Americans from other Asian Americans. First, because of the Philippines' fairly recent historical relationship with the United States, Filipino immigrants have relative ease with the English language (in fact, English is one of the official languages of the Philippines). Second, the predominant religion of the Philippines is Catholicism, not Buddhism or Confucianism. Third, the Philippines is the only Asian country to have a sustained, direct, and recent colonial history (Tuason, Taylor, Rollings, Harris, & Martin, 2007).

These factors would seem to indicate that Filipino immigrants and their children would have an easier time acculturating to American life, but research suggests otherwise. Filipino American adolescents have one of the highest rates of suicidal ideation and attempts in the country (President's Advisory Commission on Asian Americans and Pacific Islanders, 2001). Some studies (e.g., Heras & Revilla, 1994) show that second-generation Filipino Americans have decreased college attendance, increased mental health concerns (Wolff, 2004) and lower self-esteem than other Asian Americans (Heras & Revilla, 1994). Filipino Americans have depression rates that are significantly higher than the rates of the general U.S. population (Tompar-Tiu & Sostento-Seneriches, 1995). In addition, there are alarming statistics about the growing rates of other health issues within the Filipino American community such as HIV/AIDS, unintended pregnancy, eating disorders, sexually transmitted diseases, and drug use (Nadal, 2000). Given that there is a health crisis in the Filipino American community and the fact that mental health services are largely underutilized (Ying & Hu, 1994, as cited in Abe-Kim, Gong, and Takeuchi, 2004), it is crucial that further research and education be done.

Although Filipino Americans make up the second largest Asian population in the United States after Chinese Americans, and the largest Asian subgroup within California (2.9% of the population) (David & Okazaki, 2006), they are among the least understood and studied ethnic minority groups (Cimmarusti, 1996; dela Cruz & Agbayani-Siewart, 2003; Kitano, 1980; Sue & Morishima, 1982; Wagner, 1973; Yu, 1980). The dearth of information is striking, but part of this can be attributed to the fact that research on Asian Americans largely does not account for differences among different ethnic groups. For instance, one of the two most widely used models for ethnic identity development, the Suinn-Lew Asian Self-Identity Scale, was based on research on Asian American college students that does not distinguish between ethnicities (David & Okazaki, 2006).

In addition to insufficient research methodology, however, the social and cultural invisibility of Filipino Americans can also be attributed to the oppressive and traumatic colonial history of the Philippines, a phenomena that manifests within and outside the Filipino American community. Cimmarusti (1996) and Cordova (1983) speak of Filipino Americans as the "invisible minorities" and "forgotten Asian Americans."

In the process of writing this paper, it became clear to me that I could not discuss my journey of embodiment without speaking of my ethnic heritage, but what exactly that heritage is has been a mystery to me and a source of anxiety. Being a child of immigrants, I have had to hold the tension of having a double "hyphenated" identity: "first-generation" and "Filipina-American." I have often felt pulled between two worlds, at home in neither, restless in seeking a place of contact. Whether it has been the clash of competing cultural values, constantly mediating the expectations of both and having a constant feeling of dislocation as a result, or the alienation I have felt as a person of color, finding relationship with this identity has been difficult. For example, as one of the few women of color in counseling psychology, and particularly in somatics, I am continually faced with the reality that there are not many people who share my experience. Indeed, it would seem that my experience would be altogether dismissed by well-meaning people who tell me, "I do not notice that you are Filipina[1]; I just see a person," which is just as disingenuous as saying that they do not notice that I am a woman.

As much as it has been painful to feel rejected and not seen for my Filipina body, the internalized hatred of that body by trying to shape it into something it is not, in effect erasing the traces of my ethnic self, has been equally insidious. I come from a culture where the pressure to look white is so compelling that it has just become a "naturally" presumed, deeply entrenched and anxious desire. The pain of this disembodiment and the "misshapen" forms I have taken on result from what I propose is the fracturing of Filipina American identity. Drawing upon feminist and postcolonial scholarship, trauma theory and personal experience, I will also utilize one of the most important contributions of the somatic field, character structure, to examine how cultural forces have fragmented the Filipina American body. Specifically, I will be looking at the figure of *Maria Clara*, the devoted, suffering, self-sacrificial and self-denying mother archetype and the epitome of feminine perfection in Filipino culture, and how she has been shaped by the legacy of colonialism as well as her embodiment in the Filipina American as an intergenerational trauma. Just as my mother was shaped into a woman who did not know what she needed (and therefore, could not know what I needed), I would grow up to "take her shape," patterning myself after her. For this Filipina American, my relationships to mother, Mother Country and the Great Mother (Woodman, 1982) are intimately intertwined and impossible to separate.

---

[1] That is, when I am not confused or mistaken for another ethnicity, an experience common to Filipinos.

It is my recommendation that the healing of this fractured identity include not only somatic work, but also a re-grounding in indigenous psychology (Strobel, 2005) and a decolonized consciousness (Strobel, 1997). Finally, I propose that the fragmented Filipina American body can be made whole through the resurrection of another, more primal feminine archetype in Philippine culture, that of the *babaylan*, the forgotten healer priestess who embodies the principle of equilibrium and offers "an alternative of transcendent humanity infused with spirituality" (Suzara, 2002, para. 9). The *babaylan* has a wholeness and integrity that can hold polarity and duality: chastity or sexual pleasure, domesticity or wildness, body or spirit, feminine or masculine, Filipino or American, self or other. The *babaylan* embraces and integrates elements of all. Just as the mythical Egyptian goddess Isis searched for and reassembled the pieces of her lover, Osiris, the *babaylan* remembers the past, holds it whole in her hands.

This paper is an offering to the *babaylan* spirit, an act of memory that is bittersweet, for recovering the pieces of a lost history despite the pressure to forget is a slow, painstaking process.

My search for who I am, where I came from, and what I need—as a Filipina American, as a woman, as a spiritual seeker—began with that ache borne of discontent, estrangement, and longing for grounding in the root of the root of myself.

As postcolonial theorist Homi Bhabha (1994) states: "Remembering is never a quiet act of introspection or retrospection. It is a painful remembering, a putting together of the dismembered past to make sense of the trauma of the present". (1994, p. 90). Bringing consciousness to this traumatic past, I am no longer able to deny the "lingering ache of absence" that Peminist[2] scholar Melinda de Jesus (2005, p. 2) so eloquently describes. My search for who I am, where I came from, and what I need—as a Filipina American, as a woman, as a spiritual seeker—began with that ache borne of discontent, estrangement and longing for grounding in the root of the root of myself. As a "misfit", I have learned to let go to find my own way, self-defined and self-formed, a process that goes on. I have come

---

[2] This is not a spelling mistake. The use of "peminist", meaning "Pilipina" or "pinay" feminist, is a political choice underscoring the resistance to the colonizer's *f* (a sound that is not in the Tagalog language) by using the native *p* instead. "The *p* over *f* choice may appear to be pedantically semantic" (de Jesus, 2005, p.14), but it is a topic of much discussion within P/Filipino academics. For the purposes of this paper, I will be using the non-native *f*. So shoot me.

back to myself. To tell the story of how this came to be is to say how my search found a home here, in the rhythm and pulse of my own flesh. I am moving forward with the memory and understanding of what was left behind.

COLONIAL THEORY

Although internalized oppression—defined as a condition in which oppressed individuals and groups come to believe that they are inferior to those in power—has been studied at length, the study of the psychological effects of colonialism has not been as extensive in ethnic minority psychology (David & Okazaki, 2006). However, the colonial model is invoked as a theoretical framework for understanding the impact of oppression. The classical colonial model includes four phases of colonization (Fanon, 1965): 1) the forced entry of a foreign group into a geographic territory with the intention of exploiting the native people's natural resources, 2) the establishment of a colonial society that is characterized by cultural imposition, cultural disintegration, and cultural re-creation of the native's indigenous culture (all of which are intended to further create a contrast between the purportedly superior colonizer and the inferior colonized), 3) the portrayal of the colonized as wild and savage peoples that the colonizer has to police and tame, "in essence putting oppression and domination into practice" (David & Okazaki, 2006), and 4) the establishment of a race-based societal system in which the political, social, and economic institutions in a the colony are designed to benefit the colonizer and subjugate the colonized. Fanon (1965) summarized the process and effect of colonialism, thus: "Colonialism is not satisfied merely with holding a people in its grip and emptying the native's brain of all form and content. By a kind of perverted logic, it turns to the past of the people, and distorts, disfigures and destroys it" (p. 210).

In his work with colonized peoples in Algeria, Fanon (1965) argued that colonialism's systematic denigration of the colonized person and the continuous denial of the colonized person's humanity often lead to self doubt, identity confusion, or feelings of inferiority. Memmi (1965) contributed to Fanon's arguments, adding that the colonized person may eventually come to believe in the colonizer's stereotyped perceptions. Freire (1970) further contended that because of the inferior connotations attached to their cultural and ethnic characteristics, the colonized person may develop the intense desire to distance himself or herself from these stereotypical and inferior identities and try to become like the colonizer as much as possible. Needless to say, the traumatic psychological effects of colonialism are as numerous as they are complex.

COLONIALISM IN THE PHILIPPINES: HISTORY AND LEGACY

"No history, no self; know history, know self." (Mel Orpilla, n.d., as cited in Revilla, 1997, p. 98)

Spanish involvement in the Philippines began in 1521 when the explorer Ferdinand Magellan claimed the islands for King Phillip II. Miguel Lopez de Legazpi established the first Spanish settlements in 1565, beginning colonization in *Las Islas Filipinas* that would last for more than 300 years (Agoncillo, 1974). Spain's colonial influence would extend far beyond that in the form of cultural transformations: political organization, customs, language, and religion. Informed by a colonial consciousness that rationalized the conquest of non-Christian peoples, and motivated by *hidalguismo*, the "obsessive pursuit of status and honor" (Rimonte, 1997, p. 42), the Spanish *hidalgo* (translated as "son of God") "was born to life with the certainty of already being what he ought to be; the rest was a matter of time and confidence" (Castro, 1970, p. 191). He would "naturally" regard the animist Filipino as inferior to his God-given superiority and nobility. Rebellions by the native Filipinos were violently subdued while those compliant with colonial rule would be rewarded with land and titles, their descendants eventually becoming the cultural elite. Thus, in line with Fanon's (1965) colonial model, the culture of a native people was forcefully taken over, erased and replaced by the colonizer's "superior" one. In the name of "civilization," native names were replaced by Spanish ones (still evident among many modern-day Filipinos), matriarchy was replaced by patriarchy, the native writing system *alibata* was replaced by the Roman alphabet, and perhaps most significantly, animist and shamanic beliefs were replaced by Catholicism. Written records of the Filipino indigenous history were destroyed (Rimonte, 1997).

The history and legacy of colonialism in the Philippines are central to Filipino ethnic studies (de Jesus, 2005; Rimonte, 1997; Root, 1997; Strobel, 1997, 2005) and increasingly, to psychological research (Nadal, 2004; David & Okazaki, 2004). Rimonte (1997), in her scathing indictment of Spain's colonial legacy, challenges the characterizations by historians, educators and culture critics that Spain's colonization of the Philippines was "benevolent in intent and beneficial in effect" (p. 39); arguing instead that Filipinos were "victimized on several fronts: by the

Rebellions by the native Filipinos were violently subdued while those compliant with colonial rule would be rewarded with land and titles, their descendants eventually becoming the cultural elite.

133

assumptions and presumptions of colonial ideology, by the very act of cultural invasion itself, by coercive cultural transformation, and by the complicit collaboration of leaders and elders who perpetuated the violence of historical distortions" (Rimonte, 1997, p. 41).

Several scholars write about the effects of this victimization. E. San Juan (1994) writes about how it has "created the predicament and crisis of dislocation, fragmentation, uprooting, loss of traditions, exclusions and alienation" (p. 206) in modern Filipino Americans. Campomanes (1995) argues that the crisis of Filipino American identity is rooted in an "imperial rationality" which demands the forgetting of colonization. Filipino Americans are transcribed by and within "powerful acts of forgetting and impressions of formlessness" (1995, para. 37, 24-26). Indeed, colonization's inclusion in Nadal's (2004) Pilipino American Identity Development Model indicates that it is a powerful shaper of identity, contrary to what some research (e.g., Tuason et al., 2007) has suggested. Young and Erickson (1988) concur: to the extent that ethnic identity is conflicted and compounded by trauma, isolation, and disenfranchisement, shame can result (as cited in Gusman, Stewart, Young, Riney, Abueg and Blake, 1996).

It must be said that it was with great resistance that I chose this topic for my research project, precisely for the reasons that San Juan (1994) and Campomanes (1995) give: feelings of shame, alienation, and powerlessness. I did not want to believe that I have been oppressed, and I felt ashamed that I should feel like a victim in any way. I also feared that I would not be able to find much information about Filipino history, or at least, history that did not automatically champion the Spanish and American colonial cause(s), let alone find psychological or academic research about my people. My discovery that there is, in fact, critical information out there (albeit in small areas of academia) has been a powerful affirmation to me. However, I also know that my search for meaningful and substantial writing could have easily ended in surrender, which I recognize comes out of the frustration and despair that I have experienced in trying to find a version of Filipino-ness that is not always already informed by Eurocentric ideas and ideals.

I did not want to believe that I have been oppressed, and I felt ashamed that I should feel like a victim in any way.

Rimonte (1997) contends that as a result of internal oppression, Filipinos under Spanish rule developed a "colonial debt", characterized by a deferential attitude toward Western culture and the tendency to accept maltreatment by the Spanish as the cost for civilization. She speaks of the "Golden Legend" still held by many modern-day Filipinos and Filipino Americans, the belief that pre-Hispanic Filipinos were uncivilized savages who were gifted culture and religion by the Spanish, and later, by the Americans. "So pervasive and persistent is this golden legend that anyone growing up in the Philippines breathes it in with the air itself"

(Rimonte, 1997, p. 40). I remember the discussions I would have with my cousins whose families knew Spanish, and how they thought this made them "more Filipino" somehow. I remember, too, the peculiar pride with which my mother and others in her family held the ability to speak English. Rather than viewing it as being the result of American imperialism, my mother seemed to think that this ability makes her better than other minorities who do not.

The question of language being a colonial tool is an interesting and particularly charged issue because to be able to speak the language of the Other does accord one a power unavailable to someone who does not. For example, being a native speaker of English and having been an English major for my undergraduate studies has allowed me to navigate the world more confidently and excel in graduate school. I enjoy a certain level of privilege because I can speak and write in the language. However, the power of knowing English is an ambivalent one because I learned to speak it at the expense of learning Tagalog, the Filipino dialect spoken by my parents. Having been told by my preschool teacher that teaching me Tagalog would interfere with my learning English, my parents did not speak it with me. It is unfortunate that neither my teacher nor parents knew that young children can easily learn and be fluent in multiple languages, and I am still angry that my parents did not teach me our native tongue. When I meet other, older Filipinos, often the first question they ask is: do you speak Tagalog? I have to tell them that I do not, much to my regret (although I do understand conversational Tagalog). It is difficult to discern: is my feeling that I am not Filipino enough coming from them, or is it a judgment I have about myself? Either way, I sense a distance between me and them.

Jose Rizal, the Philippine national hero who was executed by the Spanish for rebellion and sedition during the Filipino revolution of the late 1800's, would write about the effects of colonialism under Spain nearly 80 years before Fanon (1965) would theorize about it:

> Then began a new era for the Filipinos; little by little they lost their old traditions, the mementos of their past; they gave up their writing, their songs, their poems, their laws, in order to learn by rote other doctrines which they did not understand, another morality, another aesthetics different from those inspired by their climate and their manner of thinking. Then they declined, degrading themselves in their own eyes; they became ashamed of what was their own; they began to admire and praise whatever was foreign and incomprehensible; their spirit was dismayed and it surrendered [to]…this disgust of themselves. (Rizal, 1889, pgs. 130-131)

The denial of this past as articulated by Melinda de Jesus (2005) and Jose Rizal (1889) is the source of a "crippling confusion" about Filipino identity (Rimonte, 1997, p. 41). The self-hatred that can manifest because of the colonial mentality and the shame and longing to be like the Other, i.e., the "superior" colonizer, creates an "acute, destabilizing [and] discomfiting self-awareness" (Rimonte, 1997, p. 41) —a phenomenon familiar to oppressed people as many have attested (Memmi, 1965; Fanon, 1965; Freire, 1970). The self is split. "It is a peculiar sensation," W.E.B. DuBois (1903/1961) wrote:

> this double-consciousness, the sense of always looking at one's self through the eyes of others, of measuring one's soul by the tape of a world that looks on in amused contempt and pity. One ever feels his twoness… two warring souls, two thoughts, two unreconciled strivings; two warring ideals in one dark body, whose dogged strength alone keeps it from being torn asunder." (DuBois, 1903/1961, pp. 16-17)

The Philippines, ironically, would undergo another period of colonization just when Spain's control was effectively challenged and subverted by a nationwide Filipino revolutionary uprising toward the end of the 19th century. In a face-saving attempt to avoid surrendering to what it deemed "mere Indios," Spain struck up a deal with the United States in the now infamous 1898 Treaty of Paris ceding control of the Philippines in exchange for 20 million dollars (Espiritu, 2003; Pido, 1997). For nearly 50 years thereafter, the Philippines would become U.S. territory until "granted" independence in 1946 after World War II. Espiritu (2003) argues that the United States became convinced that "education, instead of outright military suppression, was the more effective means to pacify the Filipinos" (p. 26). In addition to teaching the English language, the Thomasites (teachers who came to the Philippines on the U.S. army vessel St. Thomas in 1901) were said to have been responsible for "inculcating Pilipinos with American values" (Pido, 1997, p. 26) as well as reshaping the Filipino worldview with American political ideas (Go, 2003). The Thomasites were said to have portrayed the United States as a land of endless opportunity and wealth—the "land of milk and honey" (Pido, 1997, p. 24), the consequence of which was that Filipinos developed a glorified view of life in the United States, while internalizing a negative or mediocre attitude toward anything Filipino (Tompar-Tiu and Sutento-Seneriches, 1995). This tendency was similar to how Filipinos were taught to believe that Spanish culture was superior to their own. The significant U.S. political and military presence in the Philippines likewise served to reinforce the belief in American superiority (Espiritu, 2003; Karnow, 1989). Once again, Filipinos would look through the eyes of the Other and found themselves lacking.

THE VIRGIN MARY, MARIA CLARA, AND THE CREATION OF THE FEMININE IDEAL

The role of Catholicism in the colonization of the Philippines deserves special discussion as it is perhaps the most pervasive cultural legacy left by Spain. Nearly 83% of Filipinos identify as Catholic (Sustento-Seneriches, 1997), making the Philippines officially the only Christian nation in Asia. Rimonte (1997) implicates the Catholic Church in endorsing the Golden Legend during colonial rule by promoting the idea that Filipinos who did not change, "Hispanicize," or "civilize" themselves are deemed to have "strayed from the prescribed Catholic path of righteousness" (Rimonte, 1997, p. 59).

In addition to the constraining effects that Catholicism would have as a tool of colonialism, its prescribed taboos against the expression and discussion of female sexuality and agency would also limit ideas about what is acceptably female. The introduction of the Virgin Mary into the culture, with her qualities of purity, chastity, and sacrifice would create a new ideal for the Filipina, eventually finding embodiment in the figure of Maria Clara. The heroine of Jose Rizal's novels, *Noli Me Tangere* (1887) and its sequel *El Filibusterismo* (1891), Maria Clara, is the exquisitely beautiful *mestiza* daughter of a Filipina and a Spanish priest (Rizal, 1887). A demure, self-effacing "pure soul," she is said to have lepers tearfully kiss the ground she walks on. All are enchanted by her presence. As an unspoiled soul, she begs her father to confine her in a convent after she learns (mistakenly) that her loved one has been killed and is betrothed to a man she does not love, threatening to commit suicide if her father does not agree.

Death or the nunnery, these were the choices afforded Maria Clara. As fate would have it, she would end up dead *in* the nunnery in Rizal's second novel, her lover unable to "rescue" her before they could consummate their love. Thus, she died pure and untouched. As an icon, she remains the ideal Filipina woman, beautiful, devoted, loyal and chaste. Her character inspired the names of the national costume of the Philippines as well as a collection of traditional folk dances. In many ways, she has come to represent the Mother Country (Joaquin, 1977). That Rizal wrote his two novels, *Noli* and *Fili* (as they are nicknamed) as satirical critiques of the corrupt Spanish friars and government as well as the obsequious Filipinos who would court Spanish favor is ironic given her present status as a role model. As several critics have pointed out (Joaquin, 1977; S.P. Lopez, 1968) why would Rizal, a national hero, pick a "simpering ninny", a subservient "half-Spanish bastard child", to represent the perfect Filipina woman if not to caricaturize the colonizers' ideals of what Filipina women should be? Rizal himself was said to have a high regard for Filipinas' determination and strength of will and character (Joaquin, 1977), traits noticeably absent in his heroine, requiring a likely ironic treatment of the Maria Clara character rather than a straightforward literal reading of her as a virtuous heroine.

> *Death or the nunnery, these were the choices afforded Maria Clara. As fate would have it, she would end up dead in the nunnery in Rizal's second novel, her lover unable to "rescue" her before they could consummate their love.*

> *To take refuge in Maria Clara is the spiritual bypass of the traumatized, but to be her is to attempt to attain an impossible ideal: virginal, pure, selfless, endlessly devoted, and half-European.*

Stripped of any ironic or satirical reading of what Maria Clara represents, or even an alternative view of her being a spiritually strong woman who consciously chose a contemplative nun's life instead of an arranged marriage as some critics have argued (e.g., Joaquin, n.d.), the development of her iconic status among Filipinos has resulted, I assert, from an internalized sense of oppression. Forced or coerced into Catholicism, the "dark" body of the Filipina denigrated, the privileging of disembodied spiritual perfection over an embodied humanity is unconsciously chosen. Strobel (2005) argues: "By preaching sin and hell, churches appeal to the fatalistic and frightened consciousness of the oppressed. The promise of heaven becomes a relief for their existential fatigue" (p. 26). To take refuge in Maria Clara is the spiritual bypass of the traumatized, but to be her is to attempt to attain an impossible ideal: virginal, pure, selfless, endlessly devoted, and half-European. Maria Clara becomes the epitome of selflessness whose focus is always on the Other, European or otherwise, rather than on herself. Consequently, she labors no end fulfilling others' needs and expectations of her.

In this way, Maria Clara embodies the shadow side of the Virgin archetype, as Marion Woodman (1982), the feminist Jungian analyst, describes:

> The negative aspect of the virgin can perhaps best be seen in a paralyzing demand for perfection. In this paralytic condition she assumes the demonic guise of the negative mother or witch. Cut off from the wisdom of the body, the virgin is frozen. For the perfectionist who has trained herself *to do*, simply *being* sounds like a euphemism for nothingness, or ceasing to exist." (Woodman, 1982, p. 84).

This "addiction to perfection" is construed by Woodman (1982) as being a split between body (*matter*) and spirit (*mater*). The body is rejected, a consequence of the alienation from the Great Mother (Woodman, 1982) who is grounded in the instinctual, creative force of her body and always aware of her own needs. For the mother who is fragmented and not in touch with her own body, what results is that "the child cannot root itself in its own body, and no matter how hard it tries to find security through the mind, it is always, on some level, dependent on others and therefore in fear of abandonment" (Woodman, 1982, p. 86). The worth of the self is determined by others, and in the seeking of perfection through compulsive labor, discipline, duty, and efficiency, the self is lost because the body is abandoned. Creativity is lost because the receptivity required for creative life is not allowed to happen, and indeed, feared (Woodman, 1982, p. 85).

The disembodiment that results from the impossible standard that Maria Clara imposes can also be seen in Stephen Johnson's (1994) analysis of the oral character structure, also known as the "abandoned child." Based on the idea that psychological defenses are manifested somatically through particular habitual muscular patterns as well as energetically, cognitively and behaviorally, character structure is one of the most cogent theories to develop out of somatic psychotherapy.[3] Orality, or the denial of need, is the central element in the self-negation process of the oral character. It develops when an infant is "essentially wanted and an attachment is initially or weakly formed but where nurturing becomes erratic, producing repeated emotional abandonment, or where the primary attachment figure is literally lost and never adequately replaced" (Johnson, 1994, p. 100). Chronically ill, depressed or alcoholic caretakers are among the "prime creators" of the oral person (Johnson, 1994, p. 101). External circumstances can also contribute to the quality of early nurturance and the development of orality; denial of self and denial of need take place within a broader cultural context. A mother who may have been "good enough" for one child with the support of a husband and/or extended family may be inadequate with two or more children, as a single parent, or when isolated from extended family. Johnson (1994) posits that the vulnerability of the nuclear family in our highly mobile, industrialized, and I would add, disconnected and isolated, society is what is responsible for the preponderance of schizoid (another character type) and oral issues. Essentially:

> the oral character develops when the longing for the mother is denied before the oral needs are satisfied. The unconscious conflict, then, is between need on the one hand and the fear of repeating that awful disappointment on the other. (Johnson, 1994, p. 110)

Seen in this light, Maria Clara does not know what she needs because she is defended against having them. "If I do not need anything," the oral person thinks, "then I cannot be abandoned."

Not having had them met as a developing child, her needs are projected onto others. Within relationships, she may lose herself in hopes that the "paradise lost" of childhood is regained in symbiosis with another person. If the oral person attends to others' needs instead, then again, she cannot be abandoned, unless and until the other person grows tired or resentful of the oral's suffocating or clinging behavior. Thus, the abandonment that the oral person fears gets triggered. This fear of abandonment and loneliness may cause the premature rushing into inappropriate relationships, as well as fuel problems of jealousy or panic attacks if the threat of abandonment is perceived. It may also explain the oral person's propensity to abandon others before she gets abandoned. She may compensate by being extremely self-reliant, taking on more responsibility and independent action than

---

[3] Although there are different maps or schemas of character types among different schools of somatic psychotherapy, most share a common understanding of the nature and function of character (Cornell, 2002).

can be healthily sustained. "I do not need anyone" becomes the oral person's sad and defiant refrain, when in fact, "needing too much" is also an underlying fear. "If I need too much, I will be despised and abandoned" (Johnson, 1994, p. 117). The hatred toward the mother is turned toward the self; need is denied at all costs.

The young infant, however, is "oblivious to these [psychological] insights. He only knows that he hurts, physically or emotionally, and that the hurt is not being relieved" (Johnson, 1994, p. 102). On an energetic and somatic level, the expression of need will be contained. The oral person will constrict those muscles that will restrain natural and spontaneous self-expression, similar to what I described in the opening paragraphs of this paper: tension around the eyes, jaw and lower abdominal region to inhibit crying, restriction of breathing to suppress feelings, such as rage at being abandoned and unfulfilled, the eventual despair that brings about, and the fear of losing again. Chronic tension in the shoulder girdle and in the upper back and arms may be present, demonstrating the oral person's inability to reach out, as well as a suppression of an angry impulse to strike out.

Psychotherapeutic work with an oral person, then, would primarily involve the identification of and expression of needs that have been denied and suppressed. Working through the resistance to the expression of these needs through somatic work and cognitive behavioral interventions will be a crucial part of working with the oral person (Johnson, 1994). For example, as fear and anger at having had those needs unmet inevitably arise in the client, the therapist can help normalize these natural reactions. The therapist can also help the client develop insight about how she had prematurely contracted against her own need and developed a compensatory "false self", offering to others what she has not received. The internal scripts that say, "I do not need. I have to do it alone. If I need, then I will be despised and abandoned" can be worked through, as well as the cycle of rejection and abandonment that the oral person creates by the unrealistic demanding of unconditional, total acceptance and love.

To recognize how I have patterned and shaped myself into the oral, self-denying Maria Clara, and how I came to be estranged from mother, Mother Country and the Great Mother and ultimately reunited with them is the focus of the next section of my paper.

HEALING THROUGH HERSTORY: DESCENT INTO THE BODY

> *I wanted to stop this,*
> *this life flattened against the wall,*
> *mute and devoid of colour,*
> *built of pure light,*
> *this life of vision only, split*
> *and remote, a lucid impasse.*
> *I confess: this is not a mirror,*
> *it is a door*
> *I am trapped behind.*

> Margaret Atwood (1976), from "Tricks with Mirrors"

> *"When did your Mom get this way? She didn't use to be so hard."*

> my mother's brother (2004)

My mother, who crossed over an ocean—alone—to search for a better life. My mother, who left her beloved family—to live in a foreign land with only a straw suitcase in hand (which broke open promptly upon arriving). And though she speaks the language, she speaks it with an accent that marks her as different and Other.

What did she want for her future? I want to know and understand. She arrived and she created children, and I have known her as an idol, the immovable statue, an unreachable, untouchable idea and ideal. I can only guess at the constellation of events that would eventually conspire against her, and harden her.

I remember wanting to be held in her embrace, only to find in her a stony silence, unyielding. I shrink back in remembrance. How I wanted to warm her! But I could not. Her grief had hardened into despair. My mother, the despairing saint.

But she is no saint.

To say that both my parents sacrificed much to give me the life I have now is an understatement. In answer to my uncle's question, I replied bitterly that I rarely experience my mother any other way, and that living the American Dream comes at a high price. Was it worth it, though? The "dream" meant that I had parents who were under an incredible amount of stress, barely present to take care of more than our bare, physical needs. They often speak about how they started out with nothing, how hard they have worked, and how proud they are to have sent all their children to college, bought us cars and houses, etc. (which in the San Francisco Bay Area is no easy feat). They have always striven to make better lives than the ones they had left in the Philippines, and they have accomplished this beyond their wildest expectations. I have had an incredibly privileged life, and I do not remember their presence much before the age of five.

I have often wondered why my parents are together, for they have been miserable for as long as I can remember (yet another reason why I think that my nurturance was less than adequate). In researching my early childhood, the reason became clear: my parents did not know each other well when they married, but since they were acquainted from being from the same town, they got together more out of hope than love, I think now (that, and the fact that my mother's work visa was about to expire, and my father was already a U.S. citizen). I imagine my twenty-something year old mother and father, seven thousand miles away from everything they knew, shocked out of their minds and bodies, lonely and hopeful in a new country where they were the Other, where they did not know many people, had few friends and lacked support, and I feel a mixture of sadness and a sense of resignation. I was born one year after they got married, two years after their arrival.

I felt secondary to their establishing themselves in this country, "the land of milk and honey." As they endlessly toiled (for that is how it felt—endless), I would wander the house or sit quietly, wondering to myself what I did wrong that my parents did not love me. I heard them say it, but I did not *feel* it. I remember being in my room, crying silently because I did not want anyone to hear me; I felt ashamed that anyone should hear my need. I remember the silence reverberating with the energy of a slammed door, wanting to scream into it and being afraid to do so because I thought it would destroy me, or them. I did not want a brusque inquiry into how I was because I could feel the inevitable dismissal. Silence prevented such, and indeed, I was rewarded for it: I remember growing up and hearing stories about myself, sitting quietly in a corner until my parents or babysitter woke up, not making a noise, which made all the adults very happy. Although I do not remember protesting that I needed something from them, I remember the despair of not getting my needs met, the void that I felt, and I remember finally giving up.

At an unconscious level, I gave up these needs because I felt that my parents' needs were greater than my own. I did not want to be a burden any more than I felt I already was. I did not want to be an additional reason for their haggardness or short tempers. I wanted to be a "good girl" because I witnessed how much my parents, especially my mother, gave up to raise us. My mother worked the graveyard shift in order to be able to take us to school and pick us up. Without fail, she would be there, at least in body. In her bleary eyes and tired voice, I could sense how she was *not* there. I can remember the few times that she would be late, the wild terror of feeling that I had been forgotten, so upset that I could not speak. "What? What? *What?*" went her voice, irked at being put-upon. How could I answer that, especially said in that tone? I felt tremendous guilt that I should want more than what they had to give me. "We do everything for you....Look how hard we work....It is all for you." I began to equate having material belongings with love, but because I knew how hard my parents worked to give me those belongings, I could never really receive them without guilt. Love=material belongings=guilt. It is no wonder that I felt ambivalent, or still find it so difficult to accept and receive what anyone gives me, even when it is freely given.

Although this process of not having my needs met began at an early age, it would come to a head when I reached thirteen years old. Having grown up in Daly City with other working class Filipino families, I was shocked when I moved to a mostly white, upper middle class neighborhood in South San Francisco. In reality, the distance between the two cities is not so great, but the gap between the two cultures was enormous, and to me at that age, unfathomable.

I entered the brutal years of junior high school without friends, being one of the few Filipina Americans there. I felt like an outcast. I would look at my classmates' long blond hair and limbs, wishing I could look like them and have their ease, hating the fact that I did not. I wished I had paid more attention to my mother's and grandmother's admonitions to "stay out of the sun! You'll get too dark!" I did not feel like I could bring this up with my parents, however, because we had moved to a "better" neighborhood. How could I dare to complain?

Besides, they were deep in conflict about their own faltering marriage. When I found out that my father was having an affair with a blond-haired, blue-eyed, white woman (a woman whose last name was "White", no less), my hatred for my brown body grew. Out came the bleach to dye my skin and hair, an attempt to erase myself and look white, an attempt to be someone that I was not. Although I outwardly blamed my father, inside I wondered what my mother had done wrong. As twisted as it is to me now, I believed on some level that she was not white enough, and therefore, beautiful and worthy enough for my father—a bitter irony since she had always prided herself in having the skin color of a *mestiza*. Of course, I now understand as an adult that human relationships are far more

I began to equate having material belongings with love, but because I knew how hard my parents worked to give me those belongings, I could never really receive them without guilt.

complicated than they appear, but I did not and could not know that then; I could only see that my family was being torn apart.

In wanting to help my family somehow, I aligned myself with my mother whose love and acceptance I had longed for, becoming her confidante. I became the parentified child at fourteen years old, listening to her because I thought that I could relieve her pain. When it came to my own needs, though, I felt that I had to bear them alone. I attempted suicide at the age of fourteen, no one finding out about it until my school counselor advised my parents to get counseling for the family because teachers had noticed my depression. In that one and only session, I cried out to them how the silence about the reality of us not being a happy, perfect family was killing me inside, how I had swallowed a bottle of pills, only to throw it up. I was again met with silence. Nothing. A void. I don't remember anything that the counselor said; I only know that my parents said nothing. To this day, they have said nothing.

This blessedly failed act of self-negation served to propel me as far away from myself as possible. I became estranged from any sense of feeling Filipino. I rejected any notion of God, for what kind of God would give me parents who constantly abandoned me with their silence? I became an atheist and took refuge in my studies, continuing the splits between my mind, body and spirit. When I would stay up late into the night, reading to keep the anxiety and depression at bay, I would override my tiredness in my pursuit of being the "perfect student." If I would not be noticed for my pain or need, I decided unconsciously, then I would at least be acknowledged as a highly achieving scholar. This would serve me well within my family and in the educational and professional worlds, but it would take many years to undo the belief that I am not what I produce or achieve in my professional or personal life, and that I deserve recognition as a human being, simply for being myself, failures and weaknesses included.

For a long time, it has been far easier and safer to notice and attend to the needs of others. For almost as long as I can remember, I have identified myself as the caretaker, the nurturer, the one who does not bother anyone and who instead, does her best to make sure everybody else is taken care of first and will not rest until that is done. The energy that I do feel tends to move out towards others, keeping little of it for myself. Seemingly paradoxically, I also feel that I tend to receive others' energy in an uncontained way, a "sponge" for other people, waiting to be filled. To use Keleman's (1979) language, I am overbounded against my own needs, and underbounded to others' needs. In other words, I am constantly filling myself with other people's needs, a substitution for my own.

I tend to move slowly and carefully; I feel guarded. I strain to scan my environment and the moods and emotional tones of the people who surround me, and feel hyper-aware of what is going on around me at all times. I am more comfortable being an observer and careful to not draw attention to myself. I feel that I am preparing for getting hurt by others, so I will seek out safety and protection in self-reliance. I have the idea that I need no one but myself, which is typical of the oral compensated character. The defense is so firmly in place that it appears that I am totally self-sufficient. "When the oral character is well-compensated or defended, you will see a superficially effective person whose basic needs are not being met" (Johnson, 1994, p. 114). I walked and talked early, prematurely asserting an independence that I did not really have.

Eventually, the enormous guilt that I felt for needing either gave way, or got subsumed by the belief that I did not need anything. A key word for the oral character is *inhibition*. My jaw and neck are chronically tense from holding back anger, frustration and expression of need. My face looks and feels like a mask at times, smooth and lifeless—all in service of hiding my inner life. It used to feel like a betrayal of self to show anything on my face (when in fact it is a betrayal of the *false* self that does not need). Underneath the defense of the detached façade, there is still pain. My arms tend to lay stiffly at my sides, largely unexpressive. "Reaching out" is a difficult movement to make, which in therapy I have noticed elicits a couple of reactions: 1) I have the urge to push away, which gives me a feeling of strength, but my need for contact goes unmet, or 2) I feel shamed, threatened and helpless, which also makes it difficult to receive contact. I notice that I would much rather keep my arms still and by my sides because that feels less vulnerable, but the cost of controlling myself is that I have a lot of tension in my shoulders, neck and abdomen, made worse by breathing shallowly.

For my chosen relationships (i.e., relationships with people outside of my family), I "picked projects", not people, which Johnson (1994) speaks of poignantly as follows:. "[The oral character] will tend to *identify* with the other melancholy babies of this world, and take care of them" (Johnson, 1994, p.114). My "friendships" were remarkable for their one-sidedness, with me being stuck in the role of "therapist," endlessly listening to their problems and concerns, forgoing my own. Although I was nurturing and generous on the surface, underneath was my contempt, resentment and rage that they needed "so much", a projection of my own neediness (Johnson, 1994). It was cold comfort believing that they needed me more than I needed them.

For my first intimate relationship, I chose someone who I felt would always need more than me, for which I was grateful because I could focus all my attention on him and not on myself. He was Irish Norwegian, bipolar, from an abusive family that had a history of mental illness, probably schizoid. I thought that I loved him, but now I think that I loved the idea of saving him even more. I knew on my wedding day that I was making a mistake, but I had such a fear of being abandoned that I stayed with him, believing that I would never get another chance and would never have another choice. I was only twenty-three years old. I clung to him for seven years, terrified that he would leave, paranoid that there were other women. Johnson's (1994) description of these "tendencies toward desperate clinging, fear of being alone or abandoned, and poor self-care juxtaposed with a reluctance to express [] need or ask for help, an overnurturing of others" (p. 101) is an understatement. My stomach was in knots all the time. I was starting to have digestion problems and no amount of medicine or trips to the doctor seemed to work. I felt helpless.

When he left me, I could not believe it. "Everything I do, I do for you", I told him, an echo familiar from my childhood. I lost myself in a flurry of activity: working too many long hours, and deriving satisfaction from being a needed, though much abused, perfectionist paralegal, spending too much money, not sleeping enough. I set out to prove that I did not need him; that I did not need any man. I filled the emptiness inside me with everything but true nurturance. I cycled between an "independent grandiosity in elated or manic periods" where I worked all day and partied all night, and dark depression (Johnson, 1994, p. 101). When I hit bottom, lost, exhausted, fearful of the future, my stomach problems getting increasingly more painful, I called a therapist.

I withdrew the energy that I had been investing in things outside myself and focused on me, although initially I felt guilty for "needing so much." I sought out alternative forms of healing, and resumed my yoga and martial arts practice. I eventually quit my job in corporate litigation, getting into bodywork instead (and was at first perplexed with the emphasis on self-care). I called back my soul from its hiding place, my inhibited body, and in so doing, also reconnected with my sense of spirituality. I especially remember the struggle to feel the sensations and muscles of my face, how it is alive, how every part of me is alive, if I allow myself to feel it. To what extent can I let myself move and reshape my body, "shapeshift" if you will, and still feel like myself, has been my exploration. The deeper my awareness of myself grows as an incarnate spirit, the more possibilities exist.

Yet being one of the few Filipinas in my graduate program has wakened me to the necessity of this questioning and overcoming, for on some level, how can I be an embodied being if people do not acknowledge the body I am in?

To explore this shapeshifting, however, is to also confront the anger and feelings of betrayal that arise when I question where I have come from. Can I let go of this identity as Maria Clara, step out from behind the mirror that Atwood (1976) speaks of and still feel connected to my mother and country? Can I overcome the cultural prescriptions to keep silent about private family matters and tell my story? My initial reaction was that I could not, not without feeling disloyal and ashamed of my history. Yet being one of the few Filipinas in my graduate program has wakened me to the necessity of this questioning and overcoming, for on some level, how can I be an embodied being if people do not acknowledge the body I am in? Too many times I have been told that the color of my skin does not matter, that I am seen as "just" a person, that race and ethnicity are unimportant. To say these issues are not important and do not matter is the privilege of the non-oppressed. I have been judged not just for the color of my skin, but for its shade as well: light enough for some Filipinos who admire my *mestiza* appearance, and not white enough for others who have looked down upon my brownness. I have been ashamed to be dark skinned, bleaching my skin until it burned and I felt erased and "improved." I have felt degraded when a white man told me many years ago as I was sitting in my car, "I guess I am the only human being around here," looking straight at me (or through me, I am not sure). I know that I have been found lacking when I hear that my Chinese friend has been disowned from her family because she fell in love with a Filipino man. That I am constantly told that it does not matter that I am Filipino, and thus erased and effectively made invisible despite the diversity and cross cultural awareness trainings that we have received as students is a continual source of anger, despair, and frustration.

Yet I persist in raising awareness as my own therapeutic process of decolonization. Proposed by Strobel (1997) as a way to develop a critical consciousness that can articulate the silence and invisibility of the Filipino, "decolonization is a psychological and physical process that enables the colonized to understand and overcome the depths of alienation and marginalization caused by colonization" (Strobel, 1997, p. 64). To decolonize is to be able to name internalized oppression, shame, and inferiority, to understand the need to recover one's cultural and personal memory, to ask: where do I go from here? To decolonize is to reclaim the body. These are but a few of the tasks set out in the decolonization process.[4] Far from just being the purview of feminist and postcolonial scholars, therapists must also be aware of decolonization as a therapeutic goal. This would require the gaining of knowledge of Filipino culture and history, as many texts on cross-cultural counseling recommend (e.g., Sue, D.W. & Sue, D., 1998). It entails as well the developing of the capacity to contain the anger and despair that can be evoked by a client undergoing the decolonization process.

To decolonize is to also reflect on the relationship to religion and spirituality as it has been informed by colonial ideology. In my rejection of the Church, I was also rejecting the notion of the disempowered female as embodied by Maria Clara and my mother, and the idea that my religion could be satisfactorily represented by saints with Caucasian features, as so many religious figures are depicted. This rejection would temporarily cut me off from feeling connected to a deeper spirituality; again the feeling that I have betrayed my culture or mother by not being Catholic would arise. I would struggle with the question: am I Filipino "enough" if I do not believe in the church, a central gathering place for Filipinos? In some very important ways, to not believe is to be removed from the community.

I yearned for another model of womanhood and spirituality, one that honors a powerful female agency that does not depend on martyrdom. My need for this would remain

---

[4] Please see Table 1 for a complete description of Strobel's (1997) Decolonization Framework.

I yearned for another model of womanhood and spirituality, one that honors a powerful female agency that does not depend on martyrdom.

underground in the form of dreams: the ruptured street that my grandparents' lived on revealing a swift-running river underneath, the house that I grew up in being deconstructed, stripped down to the studs, the Egyptian queen with the huge headdress of a serpent reaching her hand out to me, the Druid priestess tilting my head back to pour a potion down my throat that set my body afire. Through these dreams, I felt called to transform my understanding of what I was raised to believe a Filipina woman should be.

That my soul and sense of self were changing on a core level would be confirmed to me when I went to the Philippines the summer before starting graduate school. While visiting my mother's childhood home, I would find written on the entrance gate, *sakura*. *Sakura*, translated as "cherry blossom", the icon of Japanese culture, *sakura*, the tattoo that I got on my back five years previous to my trip as a reminder and promise to myself that I would live an authentic life. To see this symbol that was so intimately familiar, yet foreign in a very real way (something which I have questioned myself about—why did I, a Filipina, choose an iconic Japanese figure to symbolize my commitment to authenticity?) was an epiphany: it is as if the inscription of the Other on the gate of my mother's house and on my back were the entrance into a new understanding of "home."

I felt called to come closer to what I had rejected, to search for something below, behind, within. "One must not discount the influence of indigeneity at the unconscious level, for even though, on the one hand, the colonization of Filipinos seems to be total, there remains an unarticulated/intuited sense of primordiality in their sense of self, something deeply rooted…" (Strobel, 2005, p. 26). I would start to research Filipino psychology (not knowing at first that there was such a thing), and discover indigenous values such as *loob* (the core of being), *kapwa* (the shared inner self), and *diwa* (psyche), words that felt foreign on my lips yet I resonated with on a body and soul level. Just saying them made me feel happy, these words of interiority and wholeness, so different from the values I grew up knowing and resenting, for they seemed to privilege the other at the expense of self: *hiya* (shame), *utang na loob* (indebtedness) and *pakikisama* (smooth interpersonal relationship). Here were words for Self and self in relation to others that I did not know existed (Jocano, 1997).

In my persistent search for a new model of feminine spirituality, I would finally unearth the healing counterpart to Maria Clara, the *babaylan*, indigenous healer priestess. Largely hidden from the view of modern Filipinos, historical knowledge about the *babaylan* is sparse and limited mostly to the academic world. What is known is that prior to Spanish colonization, wealthy and prestigious women called *babaylan* served as community leaders and healers. She functioned as a "folk therapist, wisdom-keeper and philosopher," provided stability to the community's social structure; accessed the spirit realm and other states of consciousness and trafficked easily in and out of these worlds (Strobel, 2004, para. 2). She was sexually liberated, not limited by Christian ideals of virginity before marriage and wifely fidelity, at least among the non-elite (Brewer, 2004). In confirmation of my disquieting and hopeful sense that there must exist or have existed a different view of women within Filipino culture, Brewer (2004) describes how these powerful women's roles were devalued, reviled and usurped, their lands taken away from them by the Church. They would become known as *bruja* (witches) and be replaced by the "cult" of the Virgin Mary, which would become a "fulcrum for the conversion project" (Andaya, 2002, p. 2). Maria Clara would be born; the *babaylan* forgotten.

It would be too easy, though, to dismiss Maria Clara as a colonial figure of contempt or pity. Rather, I hold her as the dark side of the Virgin archetype whose counterpart can be found in the original meaning of the word virgin. As examined by Esther Harding (1965), the virgin is "one-in-herself:" self-sufficient because she is pregnant with possibility and not dependent on any man or god, divine in her own right. Woodman (1982) asserts:

> When the virgin, understood in this way as the feminine ego or identity,
> is firmly planted in her own wisdom—which is traditionally imaged as
> the lap or throne of the Great Mother—the authentic woman emerges
> out of her own biological, cultural and spiritual heritage (pp. 83-84).

Babaylan is the "pregnant virgin" because she transcends the duality and polarity that would fragment her body: she mediates between the worlds of spirit and of earth, holds *loob* as important as *pakikisama*, is neither angel nor whore. She rejects no one, embodies beauty and ugliness, life and death. She is complex, living on the border of extremes—whole and complete. She holds her broken sister, daughter, mother in her strong arms.

> *I look in the mirror, seeing shadows of her face; I hear my name, so similar to her own, and I balk, breath pulling in. I look at her, and I wonder what is mine and what is hers. I see the similarities between us, the scar on our foreheads, the round-shouldered stoop of the burdened, the same almond-shaped eyes, and I resent them sometimes. I wonder what I can align myself with in her. Her image is like a ghost in me, something I have grasped at and feared.*
>
> *Do I want her? What do I desire? Am I chasing her, or is she reaching out to me? I oscillate between the two possibilities, the vibration coursing through me, quickening. This sense of self that I carry within me—the pregnant virgin who is pregnant with possibility—moves as elusively as my mother.*
>
> *I sense a wildness creeping beneath my skin and hers, wanting to break through. And I want to hold her in my arms and tell her, "I love you still."*

CONCLUSION: THE GIFT AND TASK OF THE FILIPINA AMERICAN

As economic pressure and lack of opportunity compel 11 million Filipinos to live and work abroad (about 11% of the Philippine population) (Espiritu, 2003), the notions of "home" and "homeland" remain important areas of inquiry. How the "enforced homelessness" (Espiritu, 2003, p. 2) of the modern Filipino affects rootedness in ethnic identity is another rich topic yet to be fully explored in psychological research. In addition, it has been suggested (e.g., de Jesus, 2005) that diaspora consciousness, used as a framework for understanding African American experience (e.g., Jimoh, 2004), can be applied to the Filipino and Filipina American experience as well. This experience is something that de Jesus (2005) writes, "we have yet to claim" (p. 12). As articulated by Jimoh (2004):

> *Diaspora consciousness is a profound recognition of being part of an immense and harrowing breaking away…a mass psychological, perhaps even corporeal, desiderata for recovery of the missing parts. A New World state of mind, an Old World forgetting—to disremember, to be disremembered… dismembered—yes. And the blood…It is not about the blood; it is not solely in the blood. It is beyond the political, cultural, or biological hybrid. Yet it is not simply in the mind either.*

Diaspora consciousness exceeds the binary; the double located in the one dark body, abandons the singular and personal struggle between self and power—empire, imperialism, colonialism, supremacy… instead diaspora consciousness seeks to reconstruct the disparate parts in order to revise, though refusing to forget, the old narrative that was inscribed upon the minds, scattered, and yes, scarred minds. Diaspora consciousness gives precedence to that embattled part of the divide—the sundered part within each dark body that is striving for its existence and against domination—and seeks to occlude the breach that separates the one dark body from others similarly besieged—divided, severed, ruptured, dispersed, though connected. (A. Yemisi Jimoh, 2004, as cited in de Jesus, 2005, pp. 11-12).

For many in the diaspora, there is no going back home, whether for political, economic or sociological reasons. As the notion of home is expanded and redefined as being beyond the boundaries of geography, a new paradigm of home as located within the body must be developed, the body that is "striving for its existence and against domination" (Jimoh, 2004). To the extent that its existence is threatened or dominated, it is the political work of those who would remember the body to hold this in consciousness. The modern *babaylan*, who embodies the capacity for self-determination because she has confronted the internal barriers to her freedom can, and will, mobilize herself and others in pursuit of recognition and justice. In other words, she is free to act in differing capacities and in various spheres. Whether through art, activism, teaching, healing, or other modalities of service, she inspires her community to act with integrity for she is at home within herself.

And who would not fight to protect home?

References

Abe-Kim, J. & Gong, F., Takeuchi, D. (2004). Religiosity, spirituality, and help-seeking among

Filipino Americans: Religious clergy or mental health professionals? *Journal of Community Psychology, 32*(6), 675-689.

Agoncillo, T.A. (1974). *Introduction to Filipino History*. Quezon City, Philippines: Garotech.

Alfonso, Jean (2006). Personal communication.

Andaya, B.W. (2002). Review of *Holy confrontation: Religion, gender and sexuality in the Philippines, 1521-1685* (2001).

Atwood, M. (1976). Tricks with mirrors. Retrieved January 1, 2008, from http://www.cs.rice.edu/~ssiyer/minstrels/poems/1363.html http://www.cs.rice.edu/~ssiyer/minstrels/poems/1363.html

Bhabha, H.K. (1994). *The location of culture*. New York, NY: Routledge.

Brewer, C. (2004). *Shamanism, Catholicism and gender relations in colonial Philippines,*

1521-1685. Ashgate Publishing. Campomanes, O. (1995). The new empire's forgetful and forgotten citizens: Unrepresentability

and unassimilability in Filipino American postcolonialities. *Hitting Critical Mass: A Journal of Asian American Cultural Criticism, 2,* 145-200.

Castro, A. (1970). The Spanish sense of nobility. In H.B. Johnson (Ed.), *From reconquest to empire* (pp. 189-208). New York: NY: Knopf.

Cimmarusti, R.A. (1996). Exploring aspects of Filipino-American families. *Journal of Marital And Family Therapy, 22,* 205-217.

Cornell, W.F. (2002). "Body-centered psychotherapy." Unpublished.

Cordova, F. (1973). The Filipino American: There's always an identity crisis. In S. Sue & N. Wagner (Eds.), *Asian Americans: Psychological perspectives* (pp. 136-139). Palo Alto, CA: Science and Behavior Books.

Cordova, F. (1983). *Filipinos: Forgotten Asian Americans*. Dubuque, IA: Kendall/Hunt.

David, E.J.R., & Okazaki, S. (2006). Colonial mentality: A review and recommendation for

Filipino American psychology. *Cultural Diversity and Ethnic Minority Psychology, 12*(2), 1-16.

de Jesus, M.L. (2005). *Pinay power: Peminist critical theory*. New York, NY: Routledge.

dela Cruz, M., & Agbayani-Siewert, P. (2003). Filipinos. In E. Lai & D. Arguelles (Eds.). *The new face of Asia Pacific America: Numbers, diversity and change in the 21st century* (pp. 45-50). Los Angeles, CA: Asian Week, UCLA Asian American Studies Center, and the Coalition for Asian Pacific American Community Development.

DuBois, W.E.B (1961). *The souls of black folk*. New York, NY: Fawcett. (Original work published 1903).

Espiritu, Y.L. (2003). *Home bound: Filipino American lives across cultures, communities, and countries*. Los Angeles, CA: Temple University Press.

Fanon, F. (1965). *The wretched of the earth*. New York, NY: Grove.

Fisher, Rob (2002). *Experiential psychotherapy for couples: A guide for the creative pragmatist*. Phoenix, AZ: Zeig, Tucker & Thiesen, Inc.

Freire, P. (1970). *The pedagogy of the oppressed*. New York, NY: Continuum.

Go, J. (2003). The chains of empire: State building and "political education" in Puerto Rico and the Philippines. In J. Go & A.L. Foster (Eds.), *The American colonial state in the Philippines: Global perspectives* (pp. 182-216). Duke University Press.

Gusman, F.D., Stewart, J., Young. B.H., Riney, S.J., Abueg, F.R., Blake, D.D. (1996). A multicultural developmental approach for treating trauma. In A.J. Marsella, M. J. Friedman, E.T. Gerrity, R.M. Scurfield (Eds.), *Ethnocultural Aspects of posttraumatic stress disorder: Issues, research, and clinical applications (pp. 439-457). Washington, DC: American Psychological Association.*

Harding, Esther. (1965). *The I and the not-I*. (Bollingen Series LXXIX). Princeton, NJ: Princeton University Press.

Heras, P. & Revilla, L. (1994). Acculturation, generational status and family environment of Filipino Americans: A study in cultural adaptation. *Family Therapy, 21*, 129-136.

Jimoh, A. Y. (2004). Address at Plenary Panel, MELUS (Society for the Study of Multiethnic

Literatures of the United States), University of Texas-San Antonio. In M. de Jesus (Ed.), *Pinay power: Peminist critical theory* (1st ed., pp. 1-15). New York, NY: Routledge.

Joaquin, N. (n.d.). The trouble with Nick. Retrieved December 15, 2007, from http://www.bulatlat. com/news/4-13/4-13-nick.html

Joaquin, N. (1977). Anatomy of the anti-hero: Jose Rizal: July 19, 1861 - December 30, 1896. In N. Joaquin (Ed.), *A Question of heroes: Essays in criticism on ten key figures of Philippine history* (pp. 50-74). Makati, Philippines: DBI Printing Services.

Jocano, F.L. (1997). *Filipino value system: A cultural definition.* M. Manila, PI: Punlad Research House.

Johnson, S.M. (1994). *Character styles.* New York, NY: W.W. Norton & Company.

Jolindon, Wilfredo. (2004). Personal communication.

Karnow, S. (1989). *In our image: America's empire in the Philippines.* New York, NY: Random House.

Keleman, S. (1979). *Somatic reality: Bodily experience and emotional truth.* Berkeley, CA: Center Press.

Kitano, H. (1980). *Race relations.* Englewood Cliffs, NJ: Prentice Hall.

Lopez, S.P. (1968). Maria Clara—paragon or caricature? In P. Araoy and D. Feria (Eds.), *Rizal: Contrary essays* (pp. 81-84). Quezon City, Philippines: Guro Books.

Memmi, A. (1965). *The colonizer and the colonized.* Boston, MA: Beacon.

Nadal, K.L. (2000). F/Pilipino American substance abuse: Sociocultural factors and methods of treatment. *Journal of Alcohol and Drug Education, 46,* 26-36.

Nadal, K.L. (2004). Pilipino American Identity Development Model. *Journal of Multicultural Counseling and Development, 32,* 45-62.

Orpilla, Mel (n.d.). As cited in Revilla (1997), Filipino American identity: Transcending the crisis. In M.P.P. Root (Ed.), *Filipino Americans: Transformation and identity* (1st ed., pp. 95-111). Thousand Oaks, CA: Sage Publications.

Pido, A.J.A. (1997). Macro/micro dimensions of Pilipino immigration to the United States. In

M/P.P. Root (Ed.), *Filipino Americans: Transformation and identity* (pp. 21-38). Thousand Oaks, CA: Sage Publications.

Pierce, L.M. (2005). Not just my closet: exposing familial, cultural, and imperial skeletons. In M. de Jesus (Ed.), *Pinay power: Peminist critical theory* (1st ed., pp. 31-44). New York, NY: Routledge.

President's Advisory Commission on Asian Americans and Pacific Islanders (2001). *Asian Americans and Pacific Islanders: A people looking forward.* Retrieved December 10, 2007, from http://aapi.gov/

Revilla, L. (1997). Filipino American identity: transcending the crisis. In M.P.P. Root

(Ed.), *Filipino Americans: Transformation and identity* (1ˢᵗ ed., pp. 95-111). Thousand Oaks, CA: Sage Publications.

Rimonte, N.(1997). Colonialism's legacy: The inferiorizing of the Filipino. In M.P.P. Root

(Ed.), *Filipino Americans: Transformation and identity* (1ˢᵗ ed., pp. 39-61). Thousand Oaks, CA: Sage Publications.

Rizal, J. (1972). The Philippines a century hence. In National Historical Commission (Ed.), *Political and historical writings* (Vol. 7, pp. 130-163). Manila: National Historical Commission. (Original work published 1889).

Root, M.P.P. (1997). *Filipino Americans: Transformation and identity.* Thousand Oaks, CA: Sage Publications.

San Juan, E. (1994). The predicament of Filipinos in the United States: "Where are you from? When are you going back?" In K. Aguilar & E. San Juan (Eds.), *The state of Asian America: Activism and resistance in the 1990s* (pp. 205-218). Boston, MA: South End.

Strobel, L.M. (1997). Coming full circle: narratives of decolonization among post-1965 Filipino Americans. In M.P.P. Root (Ed.), *Filipino Americans: Transformation and identity* (1ˢᵗ ed., pp. 62-79). Thousand Oaks, CA: Sage Publications.

Strobel, L.M. (2004). Babaylan. Retrieved January 16, 2008, from http://en.wikipedia.org/wiki/Babaylan

Strobel, L.M. (2005). A personal story: On becoming a split Filipina subject. In M. de Jesus (Ed.), *Pinay power: Peminist critical theory* (1ˢᵗ ed., pp. 19-30). New York, NY: Routledge.

Sue, S. & Morishima, J. (1982). *The mental health of Asian Americans.* San Francisco, CA: Jossey-Bass.

Sue, D.W. & Sue, D. (1998). *Counseling the culturally different.* New York, NY: Wiley.

Sustento-Seneriches, J. (1997). Filipino American families. In E. Lee (Ed.), *Working with Asian Americans: A guide for clinicians* (pp. 101-113). New York, NY: Guilford Press.

Suzara, A. (2002). *Babaylan rising.* Retrieved January 16, 2008, from the Pusod web site: http://www.pusod-us.org/CallofNature/2001/babaylan.html

Tompar-Tiu, A. & Sustento-Seneriches, J. (1995). *Depression and other mental health issues: The Filipino American experience.* San Francisco, CA: Jossey-Bass.

Tuason, T.G., Taylor, A.R., Rollings, L., Harris, T., & Martin, C. (2007). On both sides of the hyphen: Exploring the Filipino-American identity. *Journal of Counseling Psychology, 54*(4), 362-372.

Wagner, N. (1973). Filipinos: A minority within a minority. In S. Sue & N. Wagner (Eds.), *Asian American psychological perspectives* (pp.295-298). Palo Alto, CA: Science and Behavior Books.

Woodman, M. (1982). *Addiction to perfection: The still unravished bride*. Toronto, Canada: Inner City Books.

Wolff, E. (2004, July 6). 2nd-generation Filipinos in U.S. falling behind. *The New York Sun*, p. 2.

Ying, Y.W. & Hu, L.T. (1994). Public outpatient mental health services: Use and outcome among Asian Americans. *American Journal of Orthopsychiatry, 64*(3), 448-455.

Young, M.B. & Erickson C.A. (1988). Cultural impediments to recovery: PTSD in contemporary America. *Journal of Traumatic Stress, 1*(4), 431-443.

Yu, E. (1980). Filipino migration and community organization in the United States. *California Sociologist*, 3, 76-109.

Table 1

Leny Mendoza Strobel's (1997) Framework of Decolonization

Naming:

- To decolonize is to be able to name internalized oppression, shame, inferiority, confusion, anger.
- To decolonize is to acquire cognitive knowledge about Filipino culture and history.
- To decolonize is to understand the meaning of "loss of cultural memory" and its consequences.
- To decolonize is to understand how the loss of language affects Filipino identity.
- To decolonize is to heal the self, heal the culture.
- To decolonize is to name the oppressor and the oppressive social structures.
- To decolonize is to recognize the orality of the Filipino culture.

Reflection:

- To decolonize is to develop the ability to questions one's reality as constructed by colonial narratives.
- To decolonize is to develop critical consciousness than can understand the consequences of silence and invisibility.
- To decolonize is to understand the need to recover one's cultural and personal memory.
- To decolonize is to understand the generational gap as being constituted by historical realities that shape each generation's experiences.
- To decolonize is to understand ideological struggles within a multicultural context and the relationships of power within these struggles.
- To decolonize is to understand the need for connection with the parent culture.
- To decolonize is to ask: Where do I go from here?

Action:

- To decolonize is to decide to give back to the Filipino American community.
- To decolonize is to learn to question.
- To decolonize is to support and become involved in developing community institutions.
- To decolonize is to take leadership positions in moving the Filipino American community toward visibility and empowerment.
- To decolonize is to tell and write one's story, that in the telling and writing, others may be encouraged to tell their own.

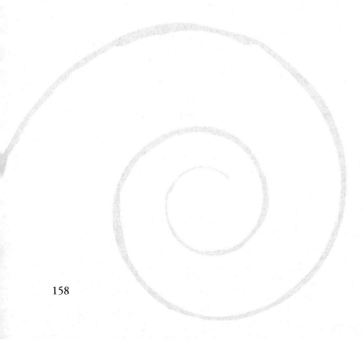

Glimpses into the Indigenous Cultural Portals and Ethnic Identity Development among Second Generation Filipino Americans

Maria J. Ferrera

INTRODUCTION

> *At the age of six, I had, for the first time, a friend from school over for a play date. At that time, my family and I were living in a suburban town that was predominantly white. My playmate, Linda, was white. As it is customary, my mom provided us with a snack. Instead of crackers and juice or cookies and milk, she decided to put out a plate of rice and pork chop adobo. I was mortified. As Linda stared at the plate seemingly confused, I protested to mom, "She does not eat rice!"*

The image of us sitting at the table is still vivid and the mortification is still palpable in my memory. As a child I did not want to appear different from others. It did not occur to me until many years later in my adulthood that I was born into an environment that reinforced assimilation, and, perhaps, unintentionally, shame in my own culture. In the following years of my childhood, I spent much of my energy trying to *accommodate* and *blend in* – at school, in the neighborhood, among my white friends. It did not matter if I felt conflicted, inferior, or invisible. I was a minority. I did not question. There was no sharing of culture or framing for ethnic pride. Consciously and unconsciously, I developed a competence to conform.

But, at what cost?

This question led me to my research area as a Filipina American social worker, and continues to plague me as an academic engaged in issues of social justice. Not unlike my own struggle as a doctoral student in a prestigious university, I continue now as a faculty member trying to prove my worth on a tenure-track line. This struggle is intimately intertwined with my reluctance to claim my own *spiritual authority*, as Trisha Agbulos Cabeje puts it (in Strobel, 2010). With her story and those of others, I am inspired to share my work and research, to dialogue with others in a critical way, as well as share how my own personal experience as a second -generation Filipina American informs this work.

In the story that opens this essay, a number of questions arose for me: *How many of us, Filipino Americans, feel this sense of shame? Why does the dominant white culture have so much power over our psyches as individuals and as a community? If an alternative framework for cultural understanding is not cultivated, to what extent is our own emotional and spiritual health compromised? How much is our own history masked or concealed from us? Who and what contributes to our loss or lack of heritage, history, and cultural pride? Who creates "knowledge"? And how are we interpreting received knowledge as a community? What does it mean to liberate ourselves from colonial mentality? To what extent do I contribute to the maintenance of colonial narratives in my own work? To what extent does my own set of privileges cloud my ability to see the realities of others' experiences and struggles within my own community?*

Many of these questions have been wrestled with in the discourses of high theory within the academy but the deep insights all too rarely percolate down to the level of popular understanding among our communities. It is for this reason that the process of identifying these questions and why they are important to ask has become central to my own work. These questions serve as the nexus of my own journey to engage the Babaylan spirit that for me codifies an alternative cultural memory important to freeing up an abjected subjectivity that has kept many of our communities down.

In the following paragraphs, I discuss why we need to be conscious of the challenges among second generation Filipino Americans (SGFAs); and how scholars have conceptualized colonial mentality and ethnic identity development. I will then discuss my research study in which I utilize an indigenous perspective in understanding the experiences of SGFAs, and how decolonization education and perspectives seem to be particularly warranted within this group. What I have learned that is particularly compelling in the narratives of the participants is that they resist internalizing inferiority in multiple ways. Despite a long history of colonization, SGFAs long to understand what it means to be Filipino. In their active pursuit to understand their own culture, they are able to transcend the negative messages of their colonial heritage about who they are. They challenge how they have been socialized and educated as children of immigrant parents, and gradually find ways to liberate themselves from the ramifications of a colonial mentality that has been transmitted over generations and time. In their struggle to decolonize, they acquire glimpses of their culture as well as their adopted "home" in the U.S. and this transforms them. In this slow and gradual liberation, bit by bit, they discover themselves. The indigenous perspective has helped me document their narratives, and honor their voices and their experiences of transformation as sacred.

HISTORICAL BACKGROUND WHY WE SHOULD BE CONCERNED

Although Filipino Americans are one of the largest and oldest Asian Pacific ethnic groups in the United States, we know relatively little about their mental well-being (Agbayani-Siewert, 1994; Araneta, 1993; Espiritu & Wolf, 2001; Mossakowski, 2003; Uba, 1994; Ying, 2005). The notion of an "immigrant paradox" is based on recent studies that reveal how "more highly acculturated immigrant youth display less academic excellence and/or more risky behaviors than their less acculturated peers" (Garcia-Coll & Marks, 2012, p. 4). This counter-intuitive data highlights the need to examine why second generation children of immigrants may have special challenges and more negative outcomes than those of their first generation parents. Suarez-Orozco (2000) identifies the growing psychological problems of ethnic minority youth using a 1998 large-scale study conducted by the National Research Council that found that "the longer immigrant youths are in the United States, the poorer their overall physical and psychological health" (p. 15). Furthermore, the more "Americanized" they become – defined as more fluent in English and increasingly adopting American values and behaviors – the more likely they are to engage in risky behaviors such as substance abuse, unprotected sex, and delinquency (Suarez-Orozco, 2000). These findings are alarming, particularly as Rumbaut (1999) found that middle-class Filipino immigrant youth are the most "Americanized" of contemporary Asian-origin groups and also the most socio-economically advantaged. Rumbaut found that this group of immigrant children exhibits higher rates of suicidal ideation and attempts than most other immigrant, ethnic minority youth groups.

Discussion about how a colonial mentality is commonly adopted among Filipino Americans and how this leads to a loss of a sense of heritage or "rootedness" and weakened (Filipino) ethnic identity continues to grow (Adefuin, 2001; Espiritu, 1994; Nadal, 2004 & 2011; Rimonte, 1997; Strobel, 2000). Further, Mossakowski's research with Filipino Americans (2003) suggests that a weak ethnic identity is associated with higher depressive symptoms. Given such, it is critical to wrestle with what we know about postcolonial psychology and ethnic identity development, and find ways to examine, identify, and address mental health struggles, and how we might overcome these struggles as a community.

The factors that contribute to the successful cultural adaptation of second generation Filipino-American youth within the United States—as individuals embedded in highly contextualized environments—demand treatment that is at once sociological, historical, political, and psychological. This critical consideration of the broader context warrants the use of an ecological systems framework that outlines the complex patterns of social and institutional relationships, developmental processes and the complex, systemic factors that influence SGFAs over their life span (Adams, 2001; Brofenbrenner, 1979 & 1986; Coleman et. al., 2003; Carter & McGoldrick, 1999; Suarez-Orozco, 2000). Within this framework, what must be considered are the effects of racial categories, notions of essentialism, racialized social structures, multi-systemic forces, human agency, as well as the dynamic nature of individual identity development over time (Garcia-Coll, 1996; Samuels, 2009). What then becomes salient involves highly complex processes including: the dynamics of discrimination and differential power relationships between the Filipino American community and the dominant (white and patriarchal) society (Rafael, 2000); enculturation as a process of cultural and racial socialization within the family; racial bias that is perpetuated on the individual, community, and societal level; and the way all of these dynamics are internalized and negotiated (consciously and unconsciously) by second generation Filipino Americans as they develop their individual and ethnic identities.

COLONIAL MENTALITY AND POSTCOLONIAL PSYCHOLOGY

A brief examination of the history of relations between the U.S. and the Philippines is warranted to understand the impact of colonization and historical trauma on the Filipino American community. After 350 years of Spanish rule, the Philippines was "purchased" from Spain by the U.S. in a superpower agreement that undercut the triumph just beginning to be enjoyed by the Philippine Independence Movement at the conclusion of its two-year (1896-1898) countrywide revolutionary uprising against Spanish rule. The agreement marked the inception of US invasion of the islands, flexing its overseas muscle for the first time as a newly militant imperialist power. It triggered what became known as the Philippine-American War (1899-1902) which resulted in the massacre of an estimated half a million to a million Filipinos and imposed a new colonial "master" on the archipelago.

Karnow (1989) highlights that this is the first time U.S. soldiers fought overseas and acquired territory beyond the country's shores – "the former colony itself becoming colonialist" (p. 79). Thus, U.S. expansionism began by identifying Asia as its "new frontier," where civilizing the Filipino "savages" took on the heroic narrative of the "White Man's Burden" to justify conquest of the newly-liberated islands (Ignacio et. al., 2004).

Over 400 years of such colonial imposition on Filipinos by both European and American governments makes the Filipino immigrant experience unique, and worthy of ongoing analysis as it relates to the way Filipino Americans view themselves today. Juanita Tamayo-Lott (1976) articulates the phenomenon of a colonial mentality (CM) among Filipino Americans as a result of this history of colonization. Studies contend that CM continues to exist and has profound, psychological implications for the health and well-being of Filipino Americans (Rimonte, 1997; Tompar-Tiu & Sustento-Seneriches, 1995; Root, 1997; Strobel, 2000). Colonial mentality, as evident in minoritized populations, is often associated with an "outsider" perspective (Ogbu, 1978) that involves a pervasive attitude of neither belonging nor "fitting in." It is a phenomenon that has been paralleled to W. E. B. DuBois' (1903/1961) notion of a "double consciousness," the sense of always "looking at one's self through the eyes of others, of measuring one's soul by the tape of a world that looks on in amused contempt and pity" (p. 16). Strobel (2000) defines colonial mentality and internalized oppression as the process whereby an individual consciously or subconsciously, accommodates the ideals, values, and behaviors of the colonizer. The works of Freire (1970), Fanon (1963), Nandy (1983), and Memmi (1965), who argue that the colonized experience is shared among dominated groups, whether Nigerians, Algerians, or Native Americans, provide a rich resource for this discussion. Colonial mentality, or internalized oppression, carries with it an ingrained norm of cultural hierarchy. Therefore, it is expected that Filipinos and Filipino Americans would develop a sense of *internalized inferiority* in response to a perceived superior, dominant colonial culture. Freire's (1970) discussion on colonial mentality involves an analysis of colonialism's severe impact on the individual, noting that the colonial process

> …begins with dehumanizing cultural invasion. First, the invader deprives the invaded of her freedom, then he inscribes himself on the victim, whom he regards as no more than part of the environment. Cut off from her cultural memories, yet not entirely de-racinated, the victim becomes *detribalized or inauthentic* (p. 50).

David and Okazaki (2006a and 2006b) developed a scale specifically designed to test for colonial mentality among Filipino Americans. In their study of Filipino Americans, a significant number of whom were second generation, David and Okazaki (2006b) found that persons who manifested CM reported lower personal self-esteem and higher depression levels than those who did not exhibit traces of CM. The authors make distinctions between OMCM (Overt Manifestations of Colonial Mentality) and CMCM (Covert Manifestations of Colonial Mentality). OMCM refers to the open, behavioral display of colonial mentality where the individual acts to distance him or herself from what is perceived as inferior traits of the colonized culture. Examples of this include trying to look white, or more European, such as trying to pinch one's nose so that the nose becomes narrower, or acting discriminatorily towards newer immigrants (e.g., calling them "fresh off the boat", or "FOBs"). CMCM refers to the internalization of inferiority by the individual, who feels shame, embarrassment, and resentment about being a person of a colonized culture. Colonial Debt (Rimonte, 1997), considered a third aspect of CM, refers to the perception that the colonizer is not only considered superior but perceived as "well-intentioned, civilizing, liberating or noble heroes" (David & Okazaki, 2006b). As a result, the colonized forgives the colonizer for the history of oppression as they perceive this as the price necessary to pay for "civilizing" their people. The notion of Colonial Debt as conceptualized by David & Okazaki does not necessarily involve the sense of "owing" America (as the name of the construct may easily suggest), but a *tolerance* for historical oppression and violence that is regarded as the price that had to be paid for "progress," or for inclusion in the dominant group. These distinctions are important when considering the impact CM may have on the mental health of SGFAs.

RELEVANCE OF INDIGENOUS KNOWLEDGE
THE BABAYLAN AS INDIGENOUS PSYCHOLOGIST

According to Enriquez (1993), the Babaylan was the first Filipino psychologist. As a priestess, she was also the guardian of Filipino sacred knowledge. Within Filipino psychology, or *Sikolohiyang Pilipino*, Enriquez emphasizes the importance of this sacred knowledge as the foundation of Filipino consciousness, defining "the *totality* of the Filipino – both his [or her] material and spiritual aspects" (p. 3). Thus, an understanding of indigenous Filipino beliefs and values, including Filipinos' communal culture, shared history, and collective memory that has developed a community psyche, or *kamalayan* (p. 34) must be part of our paradigm as we examine issues of mental and emotional health among our Filipino immigrant communities. Referred to as a liberation psychology, *Sikolohiyang Pilipino* strives to provide insight into the psychology of individuals and peoples who have suffered the violence of colonization. Within this paradigm, we are encouraged not to reject wholesale, but to consider the knowledge gained from, western theories of development and psychology with a critical eye, as only one among many. In line with decolonization perspectives, *Sikolohiyang Pilipino* urges Filipinos to raise awareness on issues of social justice that impact Filipino and Filipino American communities. It is within these considerations that I'd like to discuss western-based psychological concepts and theoretical perspectives as well as those developed by Filipinos and Filipino Americans tailored for the community and how they may (or may not) be applied to the experiences of second- generation Filipino Americans.

ETHNIC IDENTITY DEVELOPMENT
CONCEPTS AND MODELS

A fundamental task of development among adolescents and young adults in their movement toward independence is that of achieving a secure identity. As part of their identity formation, immigrant children and adolescents have the salient task of developing a strong ethnic identity (Garcia Coll & Magnuson, 1997). The specific relationship between minority ethnic identity development and mental health among immigrant children has been examined to some extent. Studies have shown the positive effect of ethnic pride on overall adjustment among immigrant youth within various ethnic groups (Phinney et al., 1990; Phinney, 1993). Mossakowski (2003), for example, found that higher levels of Filipino ethnic identification are significantly associated with lower levels of depressive symptoms. The experience of *uprootedness* among Native Americans who have been stripped of both land and culture has been proven to have a negative impact on the mental health of Native American youth, with studies on this population revealing outcomes of depression, antisocial behavior, and poor self-image (Phinney, 1990). In the same vein, immigrant children who accept mainstream society's negative stereotypes of their race experience alienation, which is predictive of poor mental health outcomes (Phinney et. al., 1990). Internalization of inferiority has been found to also lead to feelings of alienation, marginality, and loss of identity (Berry & Kim, 1988). Although these studies do not specifically examine second-generation Filipino American youth, they suggest that having a sense of ethnic pride (pride in one's culture of origin), involvement in ethnic practices, positive attributions toward one's culture, and cultural commitment to one's racial/ethnic group is directly beneficial for the mental health of Filipino Americans. Thus, there is evidence that developing a strong ethnic identity may serve as a stress buffer to help SGFAs cope with perceived discrimination from mainstream society and attain a strong sense of self-worth and individuality among other ethnic groups.

In the research on ethnic identity development, there is tension among those who endorse stage models of ethnic identity development and those who advocate a focus on core processes in development. Before I discuss this tension, it is worth summarizing the core principles of each paradigm.

There are two stage models that are of particular relevance to Filipino Americans. Atkinson, Morten, and Sue (1989) developed a 5-stage, Minority Identity Development Model (MIDM) with particular relevance to the experience of identity development of immigrant children and children of immigrants. Nadal (2004) has also posed a "non-linear," 6-stage model that is specific to Filipino Americans. The stage models seek to codify the process through which individual minority youth try to understand themselves, their minority culture, and the relationship between the minority and dominant cultures (Uba, 1994). The MIDM identifies *conformity* as the first stage. Here, the individual seeks to assimilate to the dominant culture, predominantly identifying with members of the dominant group. The second stage, *dissonance*, represents the ambivalence experienced by the minority youth when the values and beliefs of the dominant culture are not commensurate with that of his or her minority culture of origin. The third stage, *resistance and immersion*, occurs when the minority youth embraces his or her minority culture, and rejects that of the dominant group. The fourth stage, *introspection*, represents the process through which minority youth begin to form a sense of security in his or her identity and recognizes the negative and positive aspects of both the minority and dominant cultures. The fifth and last stage, known as the *synergetic articulation and awareness stage,* represents a period in which the minority youth would have attained some sense of self-worth and individuality. At this final stage, the minority youth has a consciousness of the values and beliefs he or she accepts and rejects about both the minority and dominant culture. In this stage, the ethnic minority youth may gain insight that there does not have to exist a hierarchy in cultures. Furthermore, a reciprocal process may reinforce this awareness stage, where members of the dominant culture may abandon attitudes of white superiority and earn the trust of the minority youth. This notion that the relationship between the minority individual and individuals of the dominant culture is dynamic is an elaboration of the MIDM by Sue and Sue (2003), who name this final stage the *integrative awareness* stage in their racial/cultural identity model. In their model, the fourth and fifth stages of *introspection* and *integrative awareness,* respectively, require that the individual have some understanding or sense of his or her own cultural history and heritage in the diaspora, in addition to the rituals, traditions, cultural legacies, attitudes and behaviors prominent within his or her culture of origin. This understanding is considered critical to ethnic identity development. Minority groups who are embedded in a receiving culture that is more idealized and dominant than their culture of origin, may have more proclivity toward understanding the cultural history, rituals, traditions, attitudes and beliefs of the dominant culture than their own. As a result, it becomes more difficult for minority individuals to achieve *introspection* and *awareness* in the absence of cultural validation from their school, family and society.

Building on the MIDM developed by Atkinson et al. (1989), Nadal (2004) poses a nonlinear, 6-stage ethnic identity development model that is specific to Filipino Americans. Nadal posits that among Asian American and Pacific Islander Americans, there are more than 30 different national originations. Furthermore, even when only considering peoples from the Philippines one must still account for the variance among 65 or more distinct ethnic groups and cultural minorities within the country alone (Bautista, 1998). As such, Nadal argues that to homogenize identity development of individuals into one model is illogical. In addition to the stages parallel to the Minority Identity Model previously outlined, he outlines the sixth, additional stage that he considers to be the "highest form of identity evolution" (p. 59): the *incorporation stage.* At this stage, the first- or second-generation Filipino American has come to an understanding and acceptance of both the positive and negative aspects of his or her Filipino identity, in relation to American, Asian American and other ethnic minority cultures. At this stage, the individual Filipino American would have attained a sense of Filipino American ethnic pride, and a sense of his or her own "personal or collective identity" (p. 59) – where he or she may be more compelled to "advocate for himself or herself, his or her F/Pilipino community, and for social justice as a whole [for all ethnic and racial groups]."

Identity development models such as the MIDM are essentially based on foundational Black identity models (Cross, 1985; Jackson, 1976). They build on an explicit understanding of power relations and power structures which are understood to impact all people of color, often leaving them oppressed and marginalized through racial discrimination, social dislocation, and the de-valuation of non-western behaviors, attitudes and values. On the other hand, rather than focusing on stages of ethnic identity development, Adams (2001) proposes looking at the *core generic processes* involved in racial identity development that are shared by diverse minority groups. In this alternative framework, the first two core processes involve a *transformed consciousness* and a *redefinition* of one's perspective toward his or her own culture of origin vis-à-vis that of the dominant society. These generic processes parallel the stages of *conformity, dissonance, resistance and introspection* within the Minority Developmental Model. However, Adams' third process, *parallel developmental tasks*, in particular, focuses on the task that dominant groups, for their part, must undergo in their own identity development, namely, coming to a deeper awareness of their (white) privilege and adopting more "non-racist" attitudes. Adams also distinguishes between ethnic identity development and ego identity development under a core process she describes as *interactions between racial and ego identity functions*. The core developmental processes posed by Adams thereby give a more generic background to the identity development of all ethnic groups, whereas the stages or processes proposed by Atkinson et al.(1989), and further elaborated by Sue and Sue (2003), outline what may be more nuanced processes experienced among minority groups, namely, the process of conscious negotiation between the positives and negatives of both the minority and dominant culture, a process not discussed in detail by Adams.

There is benefit to endorsing both the stage models and pan-racial process models. Both paradigms allow for a critical consideration of the unique experiences of each group of individuals as they undergo the process of cultural adaptation. Whatever their limitations, each framework clearly demonstrates that ethnic identity development is always *dynamic*, never static, and that the stages are *processes* that are not fixed ideal stages or "fixed entities" (Sue & Sue, p. 232). Thus, the incorporation of an ecological systems perspective allows us to "move beyond linear explanations of human behavior" (Coleman et. al., 2003, p. 40).

Given the detrimental effects of essentialist perspectives (that take psychological phenomena as fixed inherent characteristics rather than historically and socially constructed), ethnic identity cannot be discussed apart from the individual's own narrative of how he or she makes meaning or constructs his

In the case of Filipino Americans, in particular, it is critical to understand the role history plays in their process of identity development and, more importantly, the ways in which they interpret and make sense of that history.

or her own reality as well as the political and sociological context in which the individual is embedded (Espiritu, 1994). In the case of Filipino Americans, in particular, it is critical to understand the role history plays in their process of identity development and, more importantly, the ways in which they interpret and make sense of that history. Many recent academic and literary works (Araneta, 1993; Bonus, 2000; Espiritu, 1994 & 2003; Igloria, 2003; Ignacio, 2000; Okamura, 1998; Posadas, 1999; Revilla, 1997; Rimonte, 1997; Root, 1997; San Juan, 1998; Strobel, 1996 & 2000) have tried to grapple with these acts of inheritance, repletion and interpretation by Filipino Americans. Pervasive in these works is the conclusion that ethnic identity, however fragmented and amorphous in nature, is profoundly impacted by colonial history.

ETHNIC IDENTITY DEVELOPMENT AMONG SECOND GENERATION FILIPINO AMERICANS

In the years between 2006 and 2008, I conducted a study on the experiences of 30 second generation Filipino American (SGFAs) young adults between the ages of 18 and 22 years in the Chicago area in order to understand if and how such factors as family socialization, colonial mentality, and ethnic identity formation might play a role in the high rates of depression noted among this population (Harker, 2001; Kuo, 1984; Rumbaut, 1999; Tompar-Tiu & Sustento-Seneriches, 1995; Willgerodt & Thompson, 2006). Some of the questions that drove this research study included the following: *What might account for the high rates of depression among Filipino American youth? What unique challenges do they face as Filipino Americans? What factors affect their mental health and emotional well-being?* This study incorporated an indigenous perspective and life story narrative approach to examine these questions. The indigenous paradigm encourages and empowers indigenous people to bring to light the traumas of colonization (Denzin, 2005), while the life story narrative is a qualitative research method that provides the means for individuals to express how they see their own experiences, lives and interactions with others over time (Atkinson, 2002). For this study, I also found the research paradigm of Smith (1999) helpful. Smith calls for a *decolonization* of research methods for colonized ethnic groups like Filipinos and Filipino Americans who have been disconnected from their original culture and history, marginalized, and "Othered" (p.6) through colonization. For Filipino Americans and other ethnic groups, their knowledge or account of their own history and cultural heritage may be censored, filtered, or altered by dominant groups who have had control over how knowledge is produced, researched, and taught over time. Among unsuspecting scholars, there is also the inclination to adopt dominant theories and worldview perspectives as a result of being trained by an educational system that is based on a "white world view" only (Cauce et. al., 1998, p. 324). A decolonization framework was used in order to help address these ethical problems in research arising from the power differences between dominant and non-dominant populations (Cauce, et. al., 1998; Kelman, 1972). For SGFAs in particular, it was important to consider the backdrop of Philippine-American colonial relations given the fact that they now live in the country of their past colonizer. Within the indigenous perspective, the participants are seen as the experts of their own experience, and furthermore, they are encouraged to confront the knowledges and perspectives of the colonizer, and to become aware of the extent to which such might impact their community. This indigenous perspective thus incorporates a learning-teaching component within the interview process (Finn & Jacobson, 2008; Freire, 1970). In this approach, the individual participants' strengths and areas of resilience are foregrounded during the interpretation and analysis of data. Given that individual and community empowerment is an integral part of this approach, this researcher has committed to the ongoing responsibility of sharing knowledge and initiating dialogue with members of the Filipino and Filipino American community, who, in turn, are invited to participate in the process and presentation of the research and findings.

It is clear from the research findings that SGFAs in this study have had experiences similar to other ethnic minority youth. They have experienced and must continually negotiate: intergenerational family conflict, individualist and collectivist cultural scripts, differing styles of parenting, the pursuit of independence and autonomy, and the idealization of western or American culture. SGFAs also seem to contend with a remarkably profound sense of indebtedness to family that at times has led to feelings of being emotionally overburdened (Ferrera, 2011). What was found unique in the experiences of the SGFAs in this study was their longing for cultural knowledge and access to Filipino culture and history. In their narratives, participants talked about how they were socialized and how their first generation parents seemed to undervalue the retention of Filipino culture within their homes. *Cultural portals*, a concept that has emerged from the findings of this study, is used here to refer to points of access that provide exposure to, and an understanding of, Filipino history and culture. The experience of cultural portals (that may include but are not limited to: immersion trips to the Philippines, active learning of Filipino language and history, engaging in Filipino organizations, exposure to Filipino cultural events, etc.) became transformative for many of the participants. The highlights of their experiences with particular cultural portals are the focus of the discussion that follows.

It is generally recognized that in a non-dominating context, ethnic minority children typically undergo a process of *enculturation* or normative cultural socialization within their ethnic families and community (Knight, 1993). These enculturative experiences lead to the development of living skills, values, behavior competencies, as well as to the constitution of a cultural identity (Knight, p. 106) relevant to that individual or child's culture of origin. In the case of first generation Filipino parents, considerations of survival and social and financial stability dictate that they invest in their children's ability to do well in school. More often than not, this means the assumption of assimilating well. It seems, however, that the energy required to "make it in America" and succeed socioeconomically (Borjas, 2006) comes at the cost of valuing and retaining Filipino culture among some Filipino American families, thus constraining the process of enculturation (or transmission of the culture of origin by first generation parents). As a result of this *constrained enculturation* (Ferrera, 2011), SGFAs have a more difficult time internalizing what it means to be Filipino. There is evidence of this from this study. According to participant narratives, their identities are often more "American" than "Filipino." Twenty out of the 30 participants expressed that they identify more with mainstream American culture than with Filipino culture. Edward, an 18-year old SGFA stated that he identifies himself as more "American" and assimilated, echoing a common sentiment within the narratives. As Edward responds to the question, "what makes it easy for you and your generation to assimilate?" He states, "We don't see it [Filipino culture] as much. We are born here... this is the only place we know really. We experience this world everyday versus a history which is only relevant when you hear it, it seems." Here Edward seems to touch upon the lived reality that may be true for many other SGFAs—that "American" (i.e., mainstream, white) ways and culture are more valued and readily accessible to him than Filipino culture. Thus, more "American" cultural scripts have influenced his attitudes, beliefs, values and behaviors.

Of particular interest and importance is the dynamics involved with *racial socialization*, or the way in which parents' attitudes and behaviors transmit worldviews about race and ethnicity to their children (Hughes, 2003). With constrained enculturation, it can be argued that SGFAs tend to experience negatively biased racial socialization. Several participants talked about their parents wanting them to look more European or have lighter skin by telling them to use an umbrella, stay out of the sun or continually pinch their nose. Adopting a more assimilationist trajectory seems to have created some difficulties for participants, particularly when questioned about what their race, in addition to their ethnicity, meant to them on an individual, personal level. In this study, 15 participants out of 30 reported growing up feeling like an "outsider." Nine of these 15 grew up in predominantly white neighborhoods. In addition to living in these neighborhoods, socialization by their first generation parents regarding their racial appearance also worked to reinforce these marginalized experiences. Six out of the 30 participants described experiences where at least one of their parents continually pinched their nose as they grew up so that their noses would look narrower. Five out of the 30 discussed how they received the message from their parents that lighter skin is more beautiful and valued. As May, a 20 year old participant stated, "My mom did not want to get dark —she was [always] carrying an umbrella. My parents always tell us not to get dark, not to be in the sun that long." Six of 30 participants agreed with the statement embedded within the colonial mentality scale: *I find persons with lighter skin-tones to be more attractive than persons with dark skin-tones.* Despite this type of socialization from their parents, four-fifths (24 of 30) of the participants rejected OMCM (Overt Manifestations of Colonial Mentality related to phenotypical appearance, which involves the idealization of "white" associated with a Eurocentric perspective (David & Okazaki, 2006b). Some SGFAs, for instance, expressed "wanting to look tan" and seemed to embrace their darker skin tones. Although "getting a tan" might typically suggest—among whites—a consciousness of class and a valuing of a more lavish lifestyle (as in sunning on the beach), the responses indicated that this desire for a darker complexion on the part of these SGFAs had more to do with a conscious embrace of the external markings of ethnicity as a brown-skinned Filipino.

Still and all, manifestations of colonial mentality were layered among this group. There is the idealized view that "American" culture is superior to Filipino culture. Some participants reveal a sentiment that is in line with a sense of thankfulness to the U. S. (and tolerance of U.S. intervention) despite the history of U.S. colonial domination of the Philippines. In their responses to the portion of the colonial mentality scale developed by David & Okazaki (2006b) that is within the dimension of Colonial Debt, more than half (19 out of 30) of the SGFA participants in this study agreed with the statement: *In general, Filipino Americans should be thankful and feel fortunate for being in the United States.* There was also evidence of some degree of denigration of Filipino culture by expressing negative attitudes toward new immigrants and not identifying and affiliating with "Fresh off the Boat" immigrants. Responses from the colonial mentality scale developed by David & Okazaki revealed that 14 out of the 30 SGFA participants agreed with the statement, *I tend to divide Filipinos in America into two types: the FOBs (newly arrived immigrants) and the Filipino Americans.* Six participants (or one fifth of the sample) agreed with the statement that *newly arrived immigrant Filipinos (FOBs) are backward, have accents, and act weird.* Six participants also agreed with the statement that they (the new immigrants) *should become Americanized as quickly as possible.*

Compounded by attitudes toward new immigrants and the idealization of Eurocentric appearance, the lack of language retention within participant families should also be noted, as it arguably reinforces colonial mentality. Colonial mentality and idealization of mainstream American culture plays out in language acquisition. In this study, seven out of 30 participants, reported being bilingual (can speak both Tagalog and English fluently). Nine indicated that they can understand a little bit of Tagalog, but often will speak back to their parents in English (without protest from parents for not speaking back in Tagalog), while almost half (14) state that they cannot speak Tagalog at all. According to some participants, the rationalization for not teaching their children their native tongue is that they did not want their children to struggle in school and risk being discriminated against because of their accents.

Espiritu (2003) shows that even in the Philippines, there is some level of social capital in speaking English well, because since World War II, English was the "language of aspiration, prestige, and power" in the country (p. 72). Tagalog was thus reserved for use by those in the provinces and the hired help within the homes. Despite efforts to have Tagalog used as a primary language in the country, English remains the preferred and valued language within the nation's still Americanized school system and within most of the Philippines' urban centers. English language primacy is then maintained and reinforced as families migrate. As Portes and Rumbaut (2001) state, "Losing a language is also losing part of one's self" (p. 144), and it can therefore be argued that a catalyst for the loss of Filipino culture is the loss of Tagalog and other indigenous languages as valued languages. The effects of losing the linguistic translation of culture and valuing the English language over Tagalog and all other languages cannot be underestimated (Phillipson, 1992).

In response to experiencing constrained enculturation in their home, school and community, participants expressed a desire to learn about Filipino culture and history. Among this SGFA sample, 21 out of 30 participants stated that they felt their parents had not made it a point to teach them about Filipino *history* (they either responded "not very true" or "not true at all" to the statement: "My parents make it a point to teach me about Filipino history"). Five participants revealed that their parents have made strong, conscious efforts to impart the culture to them (by teaching them about Filipino history, through Tagalog classes, by exposing them to other Filipino groups or organizations, or by facilitating multiple visits to the Philippines). Less than half (14) of the sample of 30 had knowledge of the history of colonization in the Philippines, and 12 participants had no knowledge of the Colonial Mentality concept.

Despite the evidence of constrained enculturation and strong inclinations to assimilate and adopt a more mainstream American or Eurocentric identity, 19 out of 30 SGFA participants expressed a desire to better understand his or her own cultural heritage and history. All 30 participants expressed the belief that it is important that he or she understand Filipino history and culture. Participant narratives supported this quantitative data, affirming that some felt that their parents were not proactive in helping them to learn about Filipino culture and/or history. As a result of this constrained enculturation, participants felt that what they were taught or were exposed to was incomplete, or severely inadequate. Ann, a 22-year old participant, for example, talked about the sense of not knowing about Filipino history and culture growing up thus: "Shamefully, I am ignorant on a lot of Filipino history and culture. Or, like, I am not entirely sure <pause> of what it entails …because I never really got any of that when I was growing up. So [the] majority of what I know is through [the name of the Filipino club at her school]. Amy, an 18-year old participant, when asked whether or not her parents encouraged her to learn about Filipino history and culture, responded, "No not really. They never taught us the language. And I didn't know much about it until I came here [to college] and then I joined [the name of Filipino organization in her school]." This lack of knowledge and lack of opportunities to learn about culture and history within the home was often coupled with the desire for cultural knowledge.

Findings from this study reveal the importance of *cultural portals*, or experiences that provide access to the history or culture of the Philippines for SGFAs. The desire to learn more about their culture often prompted the experiences of cultural portals, enabling SGFAs to explore their own ethnic identities and thus challenge the endorsement of a colonial mentality. This was fairly common among the participants notwithstanding their experience of constrained enculturation and their resulting ambiguous ethnic identity status. Twenty-seven of the study's 30 participants were able to point to some type of cultural portal and/or report finding opportunities to challenge CM. Some of the Cultural Portals they identified were made possible through association with other Filipinos and Filipino Americans and through performing a reversal of racialized stereotypes, i.e., by attempting to look darker, trying to learn Tagalog, going to identity workshops, participating in a Filipino club or organization, and/or visiting the Philippines. These experiences were often initiated by the participants themselves. Following these experiences, SGFA participants displayed the ability to challenge how they were socialized, reflect or think critically about how their race and ethnicity impacts them, reject colonial thinking that encourages a sense of shame and internalized inferiority, and have positive experiences associated with Filipino culture. In what follows, I discuss how Cultural Portals appear to serve as a protective factor for SGFAs vulnerable to CM and the detrimental effects of constrained enculturation, assimilation, and negatively biased racial socialization.

The desire to learn more about their culture often prompted the experiences of cultural portals, enabling SGFAs to explore their own ethnic identities and thus challenge the endorsement of a colonial mentality.

The narrative experiences of Carolyn, a 21-year old SGFA participant, exemplified the inclination to assimilate and "internalize whiteness." She talked about growing up with a desire to be "American" (i.e., white). When asked what her experience was like growing up in a relatively homogenous community on Chicago's northwest side, she responded, "Ummm… I guess just because I really didn't know much about the Philippines or being Filipino… so its kinda like… 'cause everyone else was white… and I wanted to be like them and they had traditional dinners and stuff and …. Yeah….[I wanted to be] like basic American." She then went on to say, "I didn't really blend in… didn't fit in." She revealed that her parents did not particularly talk to her about Filipino culture, and sent messages that having lighter skin was more attractive. Carolyn herself did not feel attractive, and did not feel like she fit in because she looked different than most of her peers at school. She verbalized wanting to look more Irish or Hispanic—essentially, lighter-skinned. She referred to a strong desire to fit in, and the idea that she needed to adopt American ways in order to do so. This experience speaks to a subtle, yet very real experience of marginalization and internalized inferiority. It suggests a challenge that may be a relatively common experience for SGFAs as they find themselves in contexts where they may look different phenotypically.

In the interview, Carolyn shared that she felt like an outsider as a Filipino American growing up in a predominantly white neighborhood. Toward the end, however, she talked about her transformative trip to the Philippines at the age of 19, one that enabled her to gain a different perspective about her culture of origin and her own ethnic (and racial) identity. She discussed how this trip helped her appreciate for the first time her unique ethnic background and its difference from the white American norm she had formerly idealized. Referring to how her Filipino identity now impacts her individual identity, Carolyn states, "I think in a more positive way [about] it… it just makes [pause]… life more rich."

SGFAs apparently find multiple opportunities to reject OMCM and embrace their "Filipino-ness" by attempting to look darker, trying to learn the language, going to identity workshops, participating in a Filipino club, and/or visiting the Philippines. May, a 20-year old SGFA, experienced all of these opportunities that served as cultural portals for her. She was one of the leaders of the Filipino organization of her university, and participated in an identity workshop sponsored by her school. She spoke about the influence of the media in defining what is considered an ideal concept of beauty within the Filipino community thus:

> We are all having these new actors and actresses on TFC [Filipino channel in the U.S.], but a lot of them are half Filipino or half Australian or half whatever. They are not embracing the one hundred percent Filipino celebrity or Filipino beauty because a lot of the Filipino actresses are not always pure Filipino — they are half German or half Australian.

In other words, in terms of media representations, the *mestizo* or *mestiza* (a native with mixed European ancestry) is still held up as the ideal. She added that in the Philippines, there's a prevalence of skin-whitening soaps and that her cousins are among those who want to get lighter skin. But she reports that through the identity workshop she attended, she has begun to experience a shift in desire, embracing her brown-hued skin more, and no longer wanting to pass for white. Like the other participants, she began finding ways to question negative messages regarding her ethnic background and is now more able to detect bias in media representations and its negative impact on communities of color such as that of Filipino Americans.

Similar to the foregoing participant responses, when asked to talk about Filipino culture and what about it they like, most participants in this study responded with more general themes that may be common among immigrant and collectivist–oriented families. These themes include the value of togetherness as a tight-knit family, getting a good education, and respect for elders or other people in general. Many of the SGFAs in this study often are unable to distinguish what is uniquely Filipino from what is mainstream American. They often have a good idea of what it means to be "white" or "American," but often have, at best, vague ideas of what being Filipino means outside the culture of families and group orientation. What may be notable here is not only that participants feel they do not have enough knowledge to adequately describe what Filipino culture and history involves, but perhaps how intangible this knowledge may be even to their community and their first generation parents. During his interview, one of the participants, Ben, hinted at the profound impact of more than 400 years of colonization may have had, as he ponders the question, *what does being Filipino mean?* He reflected, "*… what is Filipino culture then [if] it is under that mentality that it has been lost through the colonization? ….I guess the* real Filipinos you would have to interview would be up in the mountains like the natives, the real Filipinos." Ben laughs as he makes this statement, but it is noteworthy because he touches upon what may be a common quandary among the participants – *what does it mean to be Filipino?* His reference to the "natives" that can be found "in the mountains" seems to suggest that the answer may be in what is regarded as the more indigenous (those still living on the land), or in his words, "real" Filipinos, who may have been least penetrated by centuries of both Spanish and American colonization. This may be regarded as another aspect of the concept of constrained enculturation. Cultural and historical knowledge of the Philippines may have been limited or incomplete not only because of a colonial mentality among first generation parents and within the Filipino American community, but also because centuries of Spanish and American cultural domination have effectively erased much of the indigenous culture in the first place, including the memory of the Filipino peoples' struggle to throw off the yoke of colonial oppression. Thus, there are layered and complex reasons why knowledge of Filipino history and culture may be elusive and enculturation constrained among this group. The reasons might well include the fictional ascription of authenticity or purity to the concept of "Filipino" such as is implied in Ben's remark about the "real" Filipino as perhaps only existing in remote mountain areas.

DISCUSSION AND REFLECTION

A growing number of scholars assert that *biculturalism*, or a multicultural, *integrative* model is the optimal strategy of cultural adaptation (Berry, 1997; Birman, 1994; LaFramboise et. al., 1993; Phinney et. al., 2001; & Ward, 2001). In other words, individuals who have the ability to alternate effectively among culturally appropriate behaviors are known to exhibit relatively higher cognitive functioning and optimal mental health than people who are culturally assimilated, separated, or merely marginalized. The multicultural, integrative strategy supposes that SGFA youth can alter behavior to fit a particular social context, and assumes that it is possible for the youth to have a sense of belonging in two (or more) cultures without compromising his or her sense of cultural identity. Because participants in this study revealed a stronger inclination to assimilate and identify with mainstream American culture, their sense of belonging in Filipino culture may be compromised and an integrative strategy of adaptation that enables bicultural competence may be more difficult to attain for SGFAs.

This seeming limitation notwithstanding, the narratives of second generation Filipino Americans manifest an overall desire to know more about their Filipino cultural heritage and, in the process, learn to embrace more the Filipino aspect(s) of their identity. At the time of the interview, most of these participants were experiencing college life. These "odyssey" years of young adulthood (Brooks, 2007), are considered a developmentally appropriate time to explore and question the multiple facets of their identity. As many of these participants experience life away from the constraints of home (and daily parental monitoring and protection) for the first time (e.g. in college dorms, within the context of university life) they find more freedom to reflect on the type of subjects they want to study, the career they want to pursue, the relationships they want to develop, and the person they internalize themselves to be. Also, academic environments that at least pay lip service to the value of diversity and multiculturalism may allow some space for questioning the received knowledge around race, normative identities, and the power structures that constitute such knowledge. Consequently, in the experiences of these SGFAs, there appeared to be a growing awareness of the social meanings of the color of their skin, their home culture, their country of origin, and the implications of such for the position they find themselves in within the country's racial hierarchy. What is revealed in the narratives of this study is that the strains of Colonial Mentality and the (often unconscious) negative racial socialization that originated from their first generation parents, does not have to determine their reality. As they experience physical independence, these young adults also seem to discover a measure of emotional and cognitive independence in pursuit of the goal and necessity of self-discovery.

It appears that as participants actively explored their own sense of self and individuality, they also began to acquire conceptual tools with which to understand differently the familiar messages they have received during their childhood socialization. In the process, they gained capacity to create more liberating narratives for themselves separate from the negative ones that only tend to perpetuate a legacy of oppression and trauma. The desire to experience their Filipino-ness in this sample of SGFAs creates an opening for undoing Colonial Mentality through the process of decolonization as discussed by Strobel (2000). It is a process that requires wrestling with the reality of the oppressive historical relationship between the Philippines and the U.S., and the power dynamics that continue to manifest in both covert and overt forms of Colonial Mentality. As second generation Filipino Americans gain more exposure and knowledge of this history through various Cultural Portals, they may yet strengthen their ability to critically navigate both mainstream American and Filipino cultures, as well as develop their bicultural competence.

In many ways, the lives of second-generation Filipino Americans are complicated by the erasure from memory of the colonial relationship between the Philippines and the U.S. through their parents' buying—wittingly or unwittingly—into the notion that their success, and maybe even their very survival, is contingent on their ability to assimilate to mainstream American culture. Constrained enculturation within the family and the resulting lack of cultural and historical knowledge appears to lead to a fragmented development of ethnic identity in contrast to a healthier process requiring access to or knowledge of one's ethnic history and culture (Phinney, 1993; Atkinson et. al., 1989; Nadal, 2004).

Within the Minority Identity Development Model (MIDM) (Atkinson, et. al., 1989), the second stage, called the *dissonance stage*, represents the ambivalence experienced by the minority youth when the values and beliefs of the dominant culture clash with that of his or her minority culture of origin. For some of the SGFAs in this study, one would think that the lack of cultural knowledge growing up may not provide enough occasion for experiencing cultural dissonance, with unquestioning assimilation being the typical response. However, experiences of discrimination, negative racial socialization, and feeling different or like an outsider, all serve as critical encounters that trigger the experience of dissonance. The same is true with the *resistance and immersion stage*, where it is assumed that the minority youth begins to embrace his or her minority culture and reject the dominant culture. However, if ethnic pride in Filipino culture is not necessarily encouraged within the home and community, resistance to a dominant culture may be a process that remains dormant throughout childhood, and perhaps even through young to late adulthood.

In the study, Cultural Portals, or various experiences of Filipino culture and history appeared to serve as sources of resilience for SGFA participants who struggled with constrained enculturation and negatively biased racial socialization. Notably, it was the participants themselves who initiated these experiences. Cultural portals can involve: visits to the Philippines, having Filipino friends or mentors, participating in ethnic identity workshops, attending Filipino or Tagalog language courses, joining Filipino organizations and interfacing with other Filipinos and Filipino Americans. SGFA participants counter messages of Colonial Mentality, as they display an active desire to learn about their culture, question their enculturation, and seek ways to access their culture through these various portals. Some narratives revealed a transformation or adjustment in their perception about Filipino culture and the personal meaning it may have for them. Following these experiences, SGFA participants in this study displayed the ability to think critically about how their race and ethnicity impacts them, reject components and notions of CM that involve a sense of shame and internalized inferiority. Thus, they developed positive associations with Filipino culture. These experiences seemed to have led to a stronger appreciation of their own Filipino culture, more respect for Filipinos as individuals or new immigrants, an appreciation for family and the hardship their immigrant parents may have endured to get to where they are, and a more positive, enriched sense of self. Cultural Portals thus serve as protective in that they enable SGFAs to gain access to their cultural heritage, and furthermore, to integrate multiple parts of who they are, including a sense of cultural heritage that they may yet fully understand. In this sense, the experience of cultural portals serves to initiate, expand, or enhance the process of ethnic identity exploration and development for second- generation Filipino American youth.

In a sense, SGFAs display a sense of nostalgia for their homeland. It is a nostalgia that involves a longing for culture and familiarity with a heritage that they may not yet know.

The collective psyche of most Filipino American communities is often marked by a history of oppression as well as vulnerability toward internalizing a sense of inferiority. However, SGFA narratives in this study offer evidence that our *Kamalayan* (consciousness) continues to evolve and break ground toward new, complex, and hybrid identities. Second generationers arguably display the capacity to challenge Colonial Mentality in their search for self-actualization and authentication. In a sense, SGFAs display a sense of *nostalgia* for their homeland. It is a nostalgia that involves a longing for culture and familiarity with a heritage that they may not yet know. But they do know with certainty that being Filipino, however amorphous and ambiguous it may be at this point in their lives, is a part of themselves that they cannot deny. The reconciliation of this longing requires the interrogation and unraveling of oppressive messages and negative racial socialization through enlightened awareness of our community's oppressed history. It can be argued here that cultural portals provide glimpses into our indigenous inheritance that can incite legitimate longing for a much longer, older history than that often acknowledged in the adopted country. As a community, we continue to be in diaspora, as scattered seeds that experience "Otherness," shame, uprootedness, and disconnection in constant and variant ways. It is this experience of dissonance around clashing values and culture, identity, shame, and the sense of not "fitting in," that compel us to find ways to constructively wrestle with the ongoing dis-ease. By questioning, challenging and resisting, we form our own unique sources of resilience. We continue to evolve, reinvent ourselves as individuals, and as a community. Accordingly, the face of our *Kamalayan* changes in color and form. Collectively, the shades of our skin and our identities begin to signify to us differently—as no longer markers of abjection but as signs of grace and beauty harkening back to a long history of struggle, resilience, and thriving of a once oppressed people. It is a good time to keep writing our stories.

References

Adams, M. (2001). Core processes of racial identity development. In Wijeyeysinghe, C.L. & Jackson, B.W. (Eds.), *New perspectives on racial identity development: a theoretical and practical anthology.* New York: New York University Press.

Adefuin, J. Y. (2001). *Ethnic identity formation among Filipino/a American youth: A study of Filipina American high school girls.* Unpublished Dissertation. University of California, Los Angeles.

Agbayani-Siewart. (2004). Assumptions of Asian American Similarity: The Case of Filipino and Chinese American Students. *Social Work, 49.*

Araneta, Jr. E. G. (1993). Psychiatric care of Pilipino Americans. *In culture, ethnicity, and mental illness,* Albert C. Gaw, MD, Editor. Washington D.C.: American Psychiatric Press, Inc.

Atkinson, D., Morten, G., & Sue, Derald W. (1989). A minority identity development model. In Donald Atkinson, George Morten, & Derald W. Sue (Eds.), *Counseling American minorities* (pp. 35-52). Dubuque, IA: William C. Brown.

Atkinson, R. (2002). The life story interview. In J. F. Gubrium & J.A. Holstein (Eds.) *Handbook of interview research: context and method.* Thousand Oaks, CA: Sage.

Bautista, V. (1998). *The Filipino Americans: from 1763 to the present.* Farmington Hills, MI: Bookhaus.

Berry, J.W. (1997). Immigration, acculturation, and adaptation. *Applied Psychology: International Review,* 46(1), 5-34.

Berry, J.W. & Kim, U. (1988). Acculturation and mental health. In P. Dasen, J.W. Berry, & N. Sartorius (Eds.), *Health and cross-cultural psychology* (pp 207-236). Newbury Park, CA: Sage Publications.

Birman, D. (1994). Acculturation and human diversity in a multicultural society. In Trickett, E.J., Watts, R.J. & Birman, D. (Eds.) *Human diversity: perspectives on people in context.* San Francisco: Jossey-Bass Publishers.

Bonus, R. (2000). *Locating Filipino Americans: ethnicity and the cultural politics of space.* Philadelphia: Temple University Press.

Borjas, G.J. (2006). *Making it in America: Social Mobility in the Immigrant Population.* Working paper 12088 for NBER (National Bureau of Economic Research). Cambridge, MA. Retrieved July 16, 2009 from NBER http://www.nber.org/papers/w12088.

Boyce, James K. (1993). *The Philippines: The political economy of growth and impoverishment in the marcos era.* Honolulu, Hawaii: The Macmillin Press, LTD.

Brofenbrenner, U. (1986). Ecology of the family as a context for human development: research perspectives. *Developmental Psychology, 22(6),* 723-742.

Brofenbrenner, U. (1979). *The ecology of human development: experiments by nature and design.* Cambridge, MA: Harvard University Press.

Brooks, D. (2007, October). The Odyssey Years. *New York Times.* Retrieved from http://www.nytimes.com/2007/10/09/opinion/09brooks.html?emc=eta1

Cabeje, T.A. (2010). Accessing my Filipina spiritual authority. In L.M. Strobel (Ed.), *Babaylan: Filipinos and the call of the indigenous.* Philippines: Ateneo de Davao University Research and Publications Office.

Carter, B. & McGoldrick, M. (1999). *The expanded family life cycle: individual, family and social Perspectives (3rd Edition).* Allyn & Bacon.

Cauce, A.M., Coronado, N., & Watson, J. (1998). Conceptual, methodological, and statistical issues in culturally competent research. In M. Hernandez & M. R. Isaacs (Eds.), *Conceptual, methodological, and statistical issues in culturally competent research.* New Jersey: Brookes.

Coleman, H. L. K., Norton, R. A., Miranda, G. E., & McCubbin, L. (2003). An ecological perspective on cultural identity development. In D. B. Pope-Davis, H. L. K. Coleman, W. M. Liu & R. L. Toporek (Eds.), *Handbook of multicultural competencies in counseling & psychology* (pp. 38-35). Thousand Oaks: Sage Publications.

Cross, W.E. (1985). Black identity: rediscovering the distinction between personal identity and reference group orientation. In M.B. Spencer, Lonner, W.J., & Trimble, J.E. (Eds.), *Beginnings: the social and affective development of black children.* Hillsdale, N.J.: Lawrence Erlbaum.

David, E.J.R. and Okazaki. (2006a). Colonial mentality: a review and recommendation for Filipino American psychology. *Cultural Diversity and Ethnic Minority Psychology, 12(*1), 1-16.

David, E.J.R. and Okazaki. (2006b). The colonial mentality scale (CMS) for Filipino Americans: scale construction and psychological implications. *Journal of Counseling Psychology, 53(2),* 241-252.

Denzin, N.K. (2005). Emancipatory discourses and the ethics and politics of interpretation. In N. K. Denzin and Y.S. Lincoln (Eds.) *The sage handbook of qualitative research, third Edition.* Sage: Thousand Oaks, CA.

DuBois, W.E.B. (1903/1994). *The souls of black folk.* New York: Dover Publications, Inc.

Enriquez, Virgilio. (1993*). From colonial to liberation psychology. The Philippines experience.* Quezon City, Philippines: University of the Philippines Press.

Espiritu, Y.L. (1994). The intersection of race, ethnicity, and class: The multiple identities of second-generation Filipinos. *Identities, 1*(2-3), 249-273.

Espiritu, Y.L. (2003). *Homebound: Filipino American lives across cultures, communities, and countries.* Berkeley: University of California Press.

Espiritu, Y.L. and Wolf, D.L. (2001). The paradox of assimilation: Children of Filipino immigrants in San Diego. In R.G. Rumbaut & A. Portes (Eds.), *Ethnicities: Children of immigrants in America.* Berkeley: University of California Press.

Fanon, F. (1963). *The wretched of the earth.* New York: Grove Press, Inc.

Ferrera, M. J. (2011). The intersection of colonial mentality, family socialization, and ethnic identity formation among second generation Filipino American youth. *Dissertation Abstracts International, 72* (05), April. (UMI No. 3445022).

Finn, J.L. & Jacobson, M. (2008). *Just practice: A social justice approach to social work.* Peoria, IA: Eddie Bowers Publishing Co., Inc.

Freire, P. (1970). *The pedagogy of the oppressed.* New York: Continuum International Publishing Group, Inc.

Garcia-Coll, C. & Marks, AK. (2012). *The immigrant paradox in children and adolescents: Is becoming American a developmental risk?* Washington D.C.: American Psychological Association.

Garcia Coll, C. and Magnusson, K. (1997). The psychological experience of immigration: A developmental perspective. In Booth A., Crouter, A.C., and Lawndale, N.S. (Eds.). *Immigration and the family: Research and policy on U.S. immigration.* Mahwah, NJ: Laurence Erlbaum Associates.

Garcia Coll, C., Lamberty, G., Jenkins, R. McAdoo, J.P., Crnic, K., Wasik, B.H., Garcia, H.V. (1996). An integrative model for the study of developmental competencies in minority children. *Child Development, 67,* 1891-1914.

Harker, K. (2001). Immigrant generation, assimilation, and adolescent psychological well-being. *Social Forces, 79*(3), 969–1011.

Hughes, D. (2003). Correlates of African American and Latino parents' messages to children about ethnicity and race: A comparative study of racial socialization. *American Journal of Community Psychology, 31*(1/2), 15-33.

Igloria, L. A. (2003). Writing from the Filipino diaspora. In Luisa A. Igloria (Ed.) *Not home, but here: Writing from the Filipino diaspora.* Manila, Philippines: Anvil Publishing, Inc.

Ignacio, A., De La Cruz, E., Emmanuel, J., Taribio, H. (2004). *The forbidden book*. San Francisco, CA: T-Boli Publishing & Distribution.

Ignacio, E. N. (2000). Ain't I a Filipino (woman)?: An analysis of authorship/authority through the construction of "Filipina" on the net. *The Sociological Quarterly, 41*(4), 551-572.

Jackson, B.W. (1975). Black identity development. In Golubchick, L.H. & Persky, B. (Eds.), *Urban, social, and educational Issues*. Iowa: Kendall/Hunt.

Karnow, S. (1989). *In our image: America's empire in the Philippines*. New York: Ballantine Books.

Kelman, H.C. (1972). The rights of the subject in social research: An analysis in terms of relative power and legitimacy. *American Psychologist, 27*(11), 989-1015.

Knight, P., Bernal, M.E., Cota, M., Garza, C.A., Ocampo, K.A. (1993). Family socialization and Mexican identity and behavior. In Bernal, M.E. & Knight, G. (Eds), *Ethnic identity: Formation and transmission among Hispanics and other minorities (SUNY Series, United States Hispanic Studies)*. Albany, NY: State University of New York Press

Kuo, W. (1984). Prevalence of depression among Asian –Americans. *Journal of Nervous Mental Disorder*, 172 (8), 449-456

LaFromboise, T., Coleman, H., and Gerton, J. (1993). Psychological impact of biculturalism: Evidence and theory. *Psychological Bulletin* 114: p. 395-412.

Lott, J.T. (1980). Migration of a mentality: The Pilipino community. *Migration Today*, 2:6.

Memmi, A. (1965). *The colonizer and the colonized*. Boston: Beacon Press.

Mossakowski, K. N. (2003). Coping with perceived discrimination: does ethnic identity protect mental health? *Journal of Health and Social Behavior*, 44:318-331.

Nadal, K. L. (2004). Pilipino American Identity Development Model. *Journal of Multicultural Counseling and Development, 32*, 45-63.

Nadal, K. L. (2011). *Filipino American psychology: A handbook of theory research and clinical practice*. Hoboken, NJ: John Wiley & Sons

Nandy, A. (1983). *The intimate enemy: Loss and recovery of self under colonialism*. Delhi: Oxford University Press.

Ogbu, J.U. (1978). *Minority education and caste: The American system in cross-cultural perspective*. San Diego, CA: Academic Press.

Okamura, J. Y. (1998). *Imagining the Filipino American diaspora: Transnational relations, identities, and communities.* New York: Garland Publishing, Inc.

Phillipson, R. (1992). *Linguistic imperialism.* Oxford: Oxford University Press.

Phinney, J. S.(1993). A three-stage model of ethnic identity development in adolescents. In M.E. Bernal & G.P. Knight (Eds.), *Ethnic identity: Formation and transmission among Hispanic and other minorities (pp. 61-80).* Albany NY: State University of New York Press.

Phinney, J. S. (1990). Ethnic identity in adolescents and adults: Review of research. *Journal of Early Adolescence, 9, 34-49.*

Phinney, J.S., Lochner, B.T., & Murphy, R. (1990). Ethnic identity development and psychological adjustment in adolescence. In A.R. Stiffman & L.E. Davis (Eds.), *Ethnic issues in adolescent mental health* (pp. 53-72). Newbury Park, CA: Sage Publications.

Phinney, J. S., Horenczyk, G., Karmela, L. and Vedder, Paul. (2001). Ethnic identity, immigration, and well-being: An interactional perspective. *Journal of Social Issues, 57*(3): p. 493-510.

Portes, A. and Rumbaut, R.G. (2001). *Legacies: The story of the immigrant second generation.* Berkeley: University of California Press.

Posadas, B. (1999). *The Filipino Americans.* Connecticut: Greenwood Press.

Rafael, V.L. (2000). *White love and other events in Filipino history.* Durhan & London: Duke University Press.

Revilla, L.A. (1997). Filipino American identity: Transcending the crisis. In M. Root (Ed.) *Filipino americans: Transformation and identity.* California: Sage Publications

Rimonte, N. (1997). Colonialism's legacy: The inferiorizing of the Filipino. In M. Root (Ed.) *Filipino Americans: Transformation and identity.* California: Sage Publications.

Root, M. P. (1997). Contemporary mixed-heritage Filipino Americans: Fighting colonized identities. In M. Root (Ed.) *Filipino Americans: Transformation and identity.* California: Sage Publications.

Rumbaut, R. G. (1999). Assimilation and its discontents: Ironies and paradoxes. *The handbook of international migration: The American experience.* C. Hirschman, Kasinitz, Philip, DeWind, Josh. New York, Russell Sage Foundation: 172-195.

Samuels, G.M. (2009). Using the extended case method to explore identity in a multiracial context. *Ethnic and Racial Studies,* pp. 1 - 20.

San Juan, E. (1998). *From exile to diaspora: Versions of the Filipino experience in the United States.* Boulder: Westview Press.

Smith, L. Tuhiwai. (1999). *Decolonizing methodologies: Research and indigenous peoples.* New York: St. Martin's Press, LLC.

Strobel, L.M. (2010). *Babaylan: Filipinos and the call of the indigenous.* Philippines: Ateneo de Davao University Research and Publications Office.

Strobel, L.M. (1996). "Born again Filipino": Filipino American identity and asian panethnicity. *Amerasia Journal, 22*(2).

Strobel, L. M. (2000). *Coming Full Circle: The process of decolonization among post-1965 Filipino Americans.* Quezon City, Philippines: Giraffe Books.

Suarez-Orozco, M.M. (2000). Everything you ever wanted to know about assimilation but were afraid to ask. *DAEDALUS: Journal of the American Academy of Arts and Sciences.*

Sue, D. W. & Sue, D. (2003). *Counseling the culturally diverse: Theory and practice, 4th edition.* New York: John Wiley & Sons, Inc.

Tompar-Tiu, A. & Sustento-Seneriches. (1995). *Depression and other mental health issues: The Filipino American experience.* San Francisco: Jossey-Bass Publishers

Uba, L.. (1994). *Asian Americans: Personality patterns, identity, and mental health.* New York: Guilford Press.

Ward, C. (2001). The a, b, c's of acculturation, in D. Matsumoto (Ed.) *The handbook of culture and psychology.* University Press: Oxford. p. 411-445.

Ying, Y. (2007). The effect of intergenerational conflict and school-based racial discrimination on depression and academic achievement in Filipino American adolescents. *Journal of Immigrant & Refugee Studies, 4*(1).

Willgerodt, M.A. & Thompson, E.A. (2006). Ethnic and generational influences on emotional distress and risk behaviors among Chinese and Filipino American adolescents. *Research in Nursing & Health, 29*, 311-324.

Towards a "Kapwa" Theory of Art

Working towards Wholeness in Contemporary Practice[1]

Margarita Certeza Garcia

WORKING TOWARDS WHOLENESS

Situating an art practice within a theoretical framework can be challenging. For someone perceived by dominant modalities of race, gender or culture as "Other", it can be a particularly difficult and even perilous attempt. It's hard to even talk about, as the discussion itself triggers assumptions about identity, acceptable artistic expression and "authenticity;" as if "who I am" should directly affect "what I make" and how "real" that creative expression is. Using the language of academe runs the risk of being considered a parrot or sellout by those who think that true art comes from having a certain "street" credibility and "keeping it too real" often results in being dismissed or tokenized by those who guard the doors of the art world from the "uneducated" masses. Yet both the street and the academy are parts of my "real" voice and they refuse to be silenced in my work, even when it would make things simpler in a world that likes easy categories. At one point in my life, trying to create while balancing the dichotomies of life in the United States literally wore my body down. By day, I was a "good" immigrants' daughter; a highly paid executive and card carrying member of the digerati who launched dot.coms in Times Square, with an Ivy League degree on the wall that didn't stop my colleagues from occasionally asking me for their take-out

---

[1] Adapted from the text of *Finding Homeland*, a MFA thesis completed under the guidance of Professors Liz Bachhuber, Boris Buden and Lisa Glauer at the Bauhaus University in Weimar, Germany and revised with significant input from Professors S. Lily Mendoza and Leny Strobel.

food deliveries. By night I was an editor of progressive work, a hip-hop photojournalist, art student, mural painter, and activist who made banners and t-shirts for rallies. The year I tried to manage 24 simultaneous websites for IBM while editing two books and going to night school I cracked three ribs, broke my ankle, tore my meniscus and ripped both anterior cruciate ligaments in half. I tried to keep going for a while, hobbling around in an obvious metaphor for my disjointed life, but after a second surgery, I took time off from my day job. I was inspired by the organizers of *Ugnayan* (a grassroots organization of Filipino youth) and *Damayan* (an organization for Filipino im/migrant workers rights led by domestic workers), to apply for a Fulbright to make art in the Philippines.

This was a leap into the unknown for me, as I had been raised in a mostly academic environment, with little contact with my roots, other than visits to my extensive family in the Philippines. As my sister pointed out, I spoke French, Portuguese and Spanish much better than Filipino and had lived longer in Brazil than in the Philippines. I was comfortable with my origins, but in my joyous exploration of the world, I took them a little bit for granted. When I won a Fulbright, something in my planned life broke loose – perhaps all the bone breaks set something free – and I started to operate without a plan. Spinning a map, I pointed to Batanes, the typhoon-isolated northernmost islands, and decided to visit, and then stay. Community arts classes blossomed into an Indigenous youth arts organization, the *Yaru nu Artes Ivatan* and an offer to work as the executive director of the Pacita Abad Center for the Arts. The Center mushroomed due to the talent and dedication of the indigenous Ivatan artists and the support of the local community. I never went back to my old life in NYC and one year turned into several. The youth, some of whom had never left the island before, presented their work in Manila, sold work online abroad, taught basic art to 90% of the community, painted a series of murals—the ceiling of the local chapel and the altars of the churches—and were even chosen to have their work included in the permanent collection of the United Nations.

During this time, I was honored and blessed to meet with countless artists, healers, community workers and traditional leaders who, although extremely talented, were incredibly open; allowing me to stay in their homes and learn how to put my pieces into something resembling a whole. Without my conscious awareness of it, they were demonstrating *Kapwa* to me – a way of "being-at-home-in-the-world" (De Guia, 2005, p. 8) that forms the central theme of this essay. One of these humble community workers (who introduced himself to me as my driver when he was actually the local director of a health project) became my life partner and our journey has taken us to Europe where I now work in Public Art and attempt to put the lessons of *Kapwa* into practice.

This essay is divided into four parts – my personal context and rationale above, a theoretical section that examines problems with inclusivity in the mainstream contemporary art world, a reflection on my personal experiences of *Kapwa* in the Philippines and a concluding practical exploration of the implications of *Kapwa* for my artistic practice. None of these explorations are meant to create an authoritative theory of "*Kapwa* Art", or to privilege my own experiences as definitive, but merely to serve as a signpost of the possibilities in *Kapwa* and a marker of my own journey towards the artistic territory I would like to inhabit.

THE UNWANTED FRAMEWORK OR THE "OTHER" (AGAIN?!)

While numerous examples of successful artists of every denomination abound, particularly in the past three decades which have seen global lip service paid to the virtues of multiculturalism, pluralism and integration, the fact remains that the category of "Artist," while universal in theory, has for the mainstream art world, been anchored in a norm that is "more often than not, straight, white, male and middle class" (Kester, 2004, p. 4). Despite tokenizing attempts towards inclusivity, the answer to the questions: "Who gets to make art; who even gets to imagine that they might become an artist? And who gets to have their story told through art?" is, more often than not, "Someone in a relative position of privilege" (Moore, 1998, p. 52).

Although the boundaries of privilege and perceptions of the "Other" can shift with the temporal and cultural context of the practitioner, it's important to note that artists seen as the "Other," who are, more often than not, either-or/and Queer, visible minorities, female identified and/or working class, are often presented with an almost binary choice, stifling in its repetitive monotony. Either one is seen as the "Other Artist" – an artist defined by national origin, race, gender, class or sexuality (whether this choice is self-identified or imposed from without) or one can state that it doesn't matter and try to define oneself as a "pure" artist, making "Art" solely for art's sake, or within a previously established art practice or genre.

Setting aside for the moment Kantian questions of purity or universality in art, which have been thoroughly interrogated by post-modernist movements, (cf. Risatti, 1990, pp. 1-11) the Faustian choice to identify as an artist of "X" or claim neutrality under the umbrella of "Art" is almost ridiculous in its reductive implications. On the one hand, attempting to define a universal aesthetic or art practice and thus posit a neutral "Artist" is riddled with pitfalls, including the denial of the specificity of place, culture and experience of the individual. On the other hand, the desire for simplification and easy categorization can render recognition of an artist's specificities problematic by reducing them to ambassadors of an often tokenized culture and/or expecting them to only represent the "Other" in their person, theory, and practice.

What, then, is the large percentage of the population of the world—who could be categorized as "Other"—to do when attempting to enter the bastions of the formal art world, other than, at least for women who might be perceived as desirable, take off their clothes, as the Guerilla Girls sardonically suggested in a series of posters placed in the

Can the Filipino concept of Kapwa *(shared being) help to create a coherent practice that acknowledges the multiple possibilities and hybrid and shifting positions of contemporary life?*

New York City arts scene in the 1980s (Hess, 1995, p. 320)? That question, sans the mocking response, (which is both humorous and painful in its stark reality), forms the crux of this problem. Are there additional ways for artists from a non-dominant modality to position themselves and their work? Can the Filipino concept of *Kapwa* (shared being) help to create a coherent practice that acknowledges the multiple possibilities and hybrid and shifting positions of contemporary life? Where do I, as a hybrid Filipino American artist working in Europe stand in relation to this debate?

Because I like beating things into the ground – it is unfortunately necessary to re-interrogate the categorization of the "Other." The current recycled public discourse is nauseatingly predictable, yet again resurrecting the specter of the immigrant "Other" in order to avoid addressing the real issues brought about by unbridled capitalism and globalization. In this discourse, the trope of the immigrant "Other" posits an unwashed, uneducated horde that is uninterested in working, greedily feasting on the welfare smorgasbord and taking advantage of "special" handouts at the expense of hard-working ordinary citizens, despite countless studies that show nothing could be further from the truth (cf. Miller, 2012; Hinojosa-Ojeda, 2010; Zavodny, 2011). As philosopher/artist Adrian Piper (1998) puts it:

> If we are ever going to move towards a resolution of the problem of racism… internationally, we've got to overcome the divisive illusion of otherness, the illusion that each of us is defined not just by our individual uniqueness but by our racial uniqueness. The ideology of otherness is a pernicious symptom of the inability to gain self-worth except by differentiating oneself from others implicitly viewed as inferior. It's a false ideology, based on invalid inductive generalizations with a low probability of truth. (As quoted in Berger, 1998, p. 217)

Even when the essentialist racial reduction of the sum of experiences of another human being to the idea of "race" is intended as benign, as art theorist Cynthia Freeland notes in her examination of the mainstream art world's search for the "primitive," "exotic," and the "authentic," such attitudes are inseparable from a long line of colonial stances that reduce encounters with the "Other" to touristic snapshots for posting on Facebook – the contemporary equivalent of a big-game hunter's trophy room (Freeland, 2001, p. 66). As artist and cultural critic Coco Fusco (1998) eloquently notes:

Identification with the generically oppressed…Other has been the favored proof of a first world artists/intellectual's political correctness… More often than not, the avant-garde has balanced its fascination with foreign Others with miserly tokenism and/or disavowal of the black and third-world artists within proximity…The fetishization of rarity in the avant-garde art world detracts from an inquiry into the reasons for the relativity of that rarity in the first place. (pp. 69-70)

As is clear from a purely statistical point of view, those who cannot be positioned as the "Other" makeup a fairly small proportion of the world. Thus, the fact that labels such as "exotic" even exist underscores inequalities in who gets exhibited, who gets funded and who even gets to conceive that they might become a part of the mainstream art world. Particularly in terms of proportion, since contrary to assertions by neoconservative politicians/media, the essential reality is that artists identified in any way with non-dominant modalities have a more difficult time being taken seriously, if in fact they are noticed at all by art institutions and the media. Even more disturbing is the sense that the discussion of subjectivity, objectivity, race, gender, class and politics is somehow passé and the art world is somewhat "relieved to get back to the "real business" of art making" (Kester, 2004, p. 7).

Such "calls for a return to the object and somatic forms of knowledge" can be seen as part of "a more general art world backlash against the twin specters of multiculturalism and theory" (Kester, 2004, p. 14). The idea that art can be "pure" and an artist unaffected by the sum of their experiences is as disturbing as the assumption that a "pure" art is by definition one that has nothing to do with anything experienced by an "Other." In one particularly contentious review of a multicultural/activist art show at the Whitney Museum of American Art in New York, critics accused the curators of having "sacrificed aesthetics in favor of collective political self interest," a statement that, when closely examined, shows the use of "a century old Kantian trump card of aesthetic value" (Wright, 1998, p. 80) to deflect the discussion from the discomfort raised by the show itself.

Often, calls for aesthetic value are "expressed through the manufacture of a highly coded commentary, in turns wry and ironic," that serve to exclude all discourse that is direct and understandable to any but a select group of insiders, who usually "just happen" to be the elite (Kester, 2004, p. 9). This is a particularly insidious form of subtle racism, in which the culture, mores, and aesthetic tastes of one group of peoples is identified as normative –quietly relegating all else to the abnormal and impure. As Darrell Moore (1998) discusses in his analysis of multiculturalism's pitfalls, this allows "whiteness to function at a level of invisibility such that … it appears to posses no specific qualities at all. Identified as one among many, power and domination are ignored" (p. 54). As Professor Cornell West (2001) puts it: "What is distinctive about the role of the classical aesthetic and cultural norms at the advent of modernity is that they provided an acceptable authority for the idea of white supremacy" (p. 98). This concept is so embedded that cultural borrowing if done by Western artists (such as in the case of Picasso or Giacometti) is hailed as genius (and the entire source culture ignored) but if done by non-Western artists, denigrated as imitative and derivative (cf. Ogbechie, 2008, pp. 166-183).

BEYOND ESSENTIALISM: EXPERIENCING KAPWA

Having rejected both essentialist identity formulations and "pure" aesthetic possibilities as similarly stifling, where does that leave my understanding of my own position in relation to my art? After all, it's always easier to define what one does not wish to do, or be identified with, than articulate what one may desire. The previous discussion borrowed from many different analytical frameworks in many different cultural contexts– not due to a lack of awareness of particularity but rather to emphasize the limitations of current analyses and the need to find possibilities for connection and collaboration beyond essentialist categorizations. The persistence of identity-based structures of power rendered the previous analysis necessary if only to identify the patterns of colonial, post-colonial and neo-colonial structure that I wish to avoid. But what then? As multicultural professor Leny Strobel (2005) asks, "What then becomes of us when we are emptied of colonial projections?" (p. 182). Following the advice of radical feminist bell hooks (1984), I've chosen to move the discussion from the margin to center – from the outside to the inside – and take a look at Indigenous Filipino knowledge, as defined by Strobel (2005):

> I use the term Indigenous to refer to the self that has found its place, its home in the world. Emptied of projections of "inferiority," "third world," "undeveloped," "uncivilized," "exotic and primitive," and "modernizing," it is the self capable of conjuring one's place and growing roots through the work of imagination, re-framing history, and re-telling the Filipino story that centers our history of resistance, survival, and re-generation. (p. 182)

In my own work, I have always been pulled towards questioning essentialist categorizations (much of my early photography was on the intersections of identity and interrogations of race, gender, and class stereotypes) and more and more towards collaborative practices, sometimes interspersed with re-enacted/re-imagined rituals. Interestingly, the emerging discourse on Filipino Indigenous Knowledge Systems and Practices (IKSP) supports this practice – implicitly recognizing and prioritizing concepts of the communal over the individual. In particular, the concept of *Kapwa*, partially expressed in English as "the shared self," a sense of "fellow being" or "the unity of the self with the other" is an especially productive one (cf. De Guia, 2005; Enriquez, 1986). This concept is divergent from Western notions of both individuality and unity as it expresses a meta-relationship in which an inclusive sense of shared identity is constantly expressed in an ever-changing, poly-synchronous concert of diverse improvisations. *Kapwa* is a being-together-with that is not the mere adding up of various individualities but exists as the result of a fluid dance of intertwined energies. Those who practice it can be described as "at-home-in-the-world" (De Guia, 2005, p. 8). As described below by Ho, Peng, Cheng-Lai and Chan (2001) *Kapwa* differs from notions of western individuality as follows:

> Unlike the English word 'Other,' *Kapwa* is not used in opposition to the self and does not recognize the self as a separate identity. Rather, *Kapwa* is the unity of self and others, and hence implies a shared identity or inner self. From this arises the sense of fellow being that underlies Filipino social interaction (p. 69).

Interestingly, during my time in the Philippines, I felt calmer and more connected than I ever had before, not only because I seemed to physically blend in (it's difficult to realize how tiresome it is to be asked to explain your presence every time you step outside until you simply don't have to anymore) but also because of the way this sense of fellow being was tangible.

A discussion of my direct experiences in the Philippines may help in grappling with the tricky concept of *Kapwa*; however it's necessary to contextualize my own position in doing so. A journey to one's ancestral roots can be an artistic cliché, especially when combined with a problematic and ultimately racist/colonialist/imperialist tendency to romanticize Indigenous peoples… as if "indigenous" were a single global entity frozen in time, *sans* cultural and individual variation that functions as a fetishized token for the stresses and losses (real or imagined) of contemporary life. Thus, it is important to acknowledge my relative position of privilege in this discussion (inclusive of my feelings of loss of "homeland") as a non-indigenous person of Filipino ancestry, born and raised in the United States as well as my fortune in being blessed to actually have had first-hand experiences of indigenous cultures through direct interaction with indigenous peoples. (Both my husband and I are adopted Ivatans who have worked and studied for years around the world, often with indigenous peoples.) It is this personal context that frames my attempts to engage the elusive, beckoning concept of *Kapwa*, in the hope that my stories are helpful to its embodiment and potential as an artistic practice.

One of the first things that struck me when I arrived on the windswept islands of Batanes (200 miles north of Manila and geographically and culturally isolated by typhoons and rough seas for much of the past four centuries) was the absolute lack of pretension of the people. While I found Filipino cultural traits (such as a reluctance to talk about one's self and an avoidance of titles other than familial and generational terms of respect) to be a refreshing change from the rat race of New York City, the people of Batanes seemed to take it to another level. When my plane touched down on the bumpy runway inches from the semi-dormant volcano that overlooked the provincial capital of Basco that I would later learn was the only place flat enough in this mountainous island to land, my group struck up a conversation with a kindly, dignified, yet unassuming, man as we waited. He casually invited us to dinner "later" before collecting his suitcase and walking away. To our surprise, we were hosted by the Governor that evening, the highest official in the province. That afternoon, as our group toured the 32-kilometer island, I was struck by the beauty of the lighthouse on the island's tip with crashing waves below and exclaimed, "I want to live here!" Later that evening, as we sang karaoke, Governor Gato told me I reminded him of a favorite niece and asked if I needed the lighthouse key right away, since it still needed to be cleaned. I burst into delighted laughter and instinctively decided to come back and stay for a few weeks, but due to a never-ending stream of similar "coincidences," which in retrospect were all products of both *Kapwa* interactions and tacit ways of working, I ended up as the unofficial lighthouse keeper for several years. This sense of shared self that characterizes *Kapwa* was palpable in the unceasing generosity of the local Ivatan people, from the smallest child I encountered, one of whom was sent by her mother with cooked yams on my second evening in the lighthouse in case I was hungry or lonely, to the highest officials such as the Governor and Congresswoman who lent their support to the trickle of kids who dropped by to see what the lighthouse painter was doing, turning the place into a virtual flood of artists and art.

It's telling that I started with an individualistic plan of completing my painting portfolio in romantic isolation and ended up instead running a youth-focused community art center and working on murals with 300+ children at a time. *Kapwa* infused the way we worked, finding a way to harmonize diverse styles of painting into collective murals literally nourished by the community, with delicious home-cooked meals often consisting of fresh bounty from the sea caught by local fishermen. (In a true *Kapwa* relational web, the painters, fishers, and cooks were sometimes all one and the same persons; as many Ivatan fishermen could both paint and cook, and so could their children.) Dina and Butch Abad, a local couple who supported this project, turned out to be two of the most influential people in Philippine politics (they have both been members of Congress and Butch, in addition, is a former Secretary of Education, and of Agrarian Reform, now serving as Secretary of the National Budget), yet they also exemplified *Kapwa* as they were completely approachable and gave unreservedly of their time, resources, and talents. They let us use their vehicles (which at the time were some of the only cars on the island) to drive kids to and from community workshops—a generosity that must have personally inconvenienced them as I can attest that the uphill, unpaved private road to their house is no joke to navigate. Butch even designed and built a classroom complete with hardwood artist stools and easels for us to work in once the classes grew too large, first for the space in the lighthouse, then, in their personal home. I also have to recognize the posthumous influence of Pacita Abad, whose studio home we lived and worked in and whose foundation—the Pacita Abad Center for the Arts –run by her dedicated husband, Jack Garrity, eventually funded my work. Pacita and Jack had built an expansive studio/home on the cliffs by the ocean, which we used for classes and sponsored painting competitions and workshops on the islands before her death. Although Pacita passed away from cancer before my arrival, her influence permeated our work—from the riotous blend of colors and exuberant circles we used in painting to the half-joking calls for her spiritual intervention during logistical and financial challenges. She always came through, and, at times, when we called her, the wind would blow or the lights flicker and usually, a solution to our problems was then on the way. I learned that *Kapwa* suggests that those who have come before us are as much a part of our relational web as any other and from the number of times Pacita has answered, I would be remiss not to acknowledge her profound influence on my life and that of many others who were similarly inspired by her work and example.

Pacita was also an important role model for me, as a powerful artist who, like many of the Filipino women I met (such as Congresswoman Dina), seemed to operate outside the dynamics of gender oppression. I was raised in the U.S. and currently live in Germany, both places with dismal records of gender equality, yet rife with fantasy projections of purportedly submissive and "even more oppressed" Asian women—a legacy of colonialism, the Vietnam War, and mail-order bride catalogues. Although sexism certainly exists in the Philippines, according to the World Economic Forum's 2012 Gender Gap report, it is also the 8th best country globally to be a born female in terms of education, life expectancy, and economic and social parity. Thirty five percent of business directors and executive board members are female, in stark contrast to much of the rest of the world (cf. World Economic Forum, 2012, p. 293.) In contrast, the U.S. in the same report ranked 31st overall and Germany 13th due to education, but also 31st in terms of gender economic participation. Personally, it was amazing to work in a relatively egalitarian environment (much like the sudden shock of living without being differentiated by ethnicity). Although the need to make executive decisions was rare when operating in the context of a *Kapwa*-centered team, when I needed to, I was rarely questioned or second-guessed in a way I was as a woman in a leadership position in NYC. My presence at traditionally male activities such as fishing and *inuman,* (traditional hangout sessions involving snacks and drinking) was laughingly accepted. Batanes is also one of the few places I have seen where women would routinely gather for their own *inuman,* where much of the day's official business was often unofficially (and speedily) concluded. Whether or not this is directly attributable to *Kapwa,* an underlying belief in the equality of human potential clearly does not hurt gender relations. As art historian and critic Gao Minglu (2008) points out, gender roles have been more fluid in some Asian contexts as the multi-synchronous nature of development resulted in a "female consciousness [that] overlapped or shared with the contemporary consciousness of men within the same context" (pp. 136-137).

Another significant feature that contributed to my feeling of connectedness in Batanes was the ease of making friends, who, after a very short while, would attempt to integrate me into their kinship networks by addressing me with a familial title (e.g., *Anak,* "my child" or *Ate,* older sister) and my nickname, Mar. This was prevalent throughout the society and unless it was a very formal occasion, I learned to address the District School Supervisor as "Auntie" and expected, in turn, to be called *Anak*. My students and colleagues called me *Ate* as a sign of affection and respect. Similar customs exist in the rest of the Philippines and persist in the Filipino American community I grew up in. In a funny example, my Japanese American cousin, whose parents were informally adopted by my grandparents 25 years ago, was recently shocked to realize that he was not actually genetically related to us since our family had surrounded him from the moment of his birth. Despite having a Japanese name and a set of parents who maintained their culture, language, and food traditions even while joining us at gatherings, once he realized we weren't really blood relatives, he exclaimed, "What do you mean we're not Filipino?!"

A Tagalog word, *kinakapatid,* literally means someone made into a sibling – which is what happened among the people I worked with in Batanes. As more kids kept turning up for art classes, an art family grew around me, forming into the *Yaru nu Artes Ivatan* whose core members, Olan Gonzales, Xavier Abelador, Jaypee Portez and Javier Ponce are all talented artists with diverse approaches to both art and life, yet we managed to work together to teach (for which they volunteered out of *Kapwa*-inspired community service) and create murals and exhibits, at times arguing passionately. Outside of work, my adopted siblings took our relationship quite seriously, making sure I was never alone and was always taken care of, both physically and emotionally. As I was used to having a certain amount of solitude having been raised in the US, this took some getting used to. One time I thought I had gone for a solitary swim on an empty beach and returned to find one of my students sitting by my things and a text on my phone that read, "This is your *Kuya* (elder brother) Byron. You can't swim alone, the current here is very dangerous!" When I texted back to ask him how he knew, he laughingly replied that he had eyes in the sky, which, as I got to know, was actually true, since the funny thing about an almost uninhabited island is that the inhabitants know absolutely everything about each other as the *Kapwa* network of relationships is so tightly intertwined. I even began attending church, to my own mother's delighted shock after the Bishop mildly asked where I was on Sunday mornings. I even managed to get there on time after one priest greeted my late arrival from the pulpit. My family was all the more amused when I was chosen as the model for Mary Magdalene in a Pieta mural that "Uncle Butch" commissioned for the beautiful chapel he designed in the picturesque village of Tukon after I left.

On one of my trips to connect with other indigenous art collectives, another *pinsan* or cousin, Howie Severino, who happens to be an award winning journalist and documentary filmmaker suggested that I visit musician and artist Datu Waway Saway of the Talaandig tribe. As it wasn't the first time someone said, "Go see Waway," during my trip I decided to listen to my instincts and try and find him. Although I had arrived without any warning from a long journey from Batanes to the capital city of Manila to a connecting flight to Mindanao on a dusty local *jeepney*, a literal chicken in tow, Waway greeted me like an expected family member. We were both a bit too shy to talk much that evening, deciding just to draw and play music together. But after showing me the incredible work of the Talaandig community in building an art and music center that functions as an island of peace in a part of the Philippines often riven by religious conflict, Waway quietly told me that he had dreamt I was coming and that I was one of his sisters. When he visited me in Batanes to share his music and art, he definitely treated me as one, not acting aloof at all, as one might imagine someone would whose recent engagements include playing Grammy-nominated music with Dave Eggar at the Lincoln Center for the Performing Arts in New York and teaching soil painting in Paris at the Quai Branly Museum. He hung out with my self-nominated brothers, playing practical jokes on me with sly wit and often making *me* breakfast despite staying up late laughing, he being an early riser who was always ready to pull out his bamboo flute and play for a local child. Even after he went home, the connection persisted, as we kept running into each other. To my great honor, when he found out on Facebook that I was pregnant, he immediately sent a message stating that he was my child's *ninong* or godfather and that my son Kai was part of an indigenous tribe that was waiting to welcome him.

The *Kapwa* relationship network and emphasis on egalitarian relations is supported by ethnographic studies of the cognatic societies of South East Asia, which hold matrilineal and patrilineal lineage to be equally important. These investigations frequently remark upon the difference this makes in concepts of personal history in the way less emphasis is placed on genetic or ethnic origin and more on the present family and communal figures, whether or not related by blood. Kinship knowledge stretches outwards into degrees of relatedness rather than simply backwards to lineal predecessors—a horizontal, rather than a vertical, line of connection. A theory put forward to explain such a phenomenon credits the high degree of migration between islands in South East Asia as a possible precipitant for this type of kinship to the degree that travel renders it "crucial… to create kinship through the formation of new ties…Newcomers are transformed into kin through hospitality…marriage and…children." (Connerton, 2011, p. 37)

In the way I experienced *Kapwa*, I found that people would seek acknowledgement of a shared bond by trying to find a connection that ultimately widened the sphere of the self. Yet interestingly, this network rarely left me feeling oppressed (or claustrophobic) despite years of indoctrination in concepts of privacy, individualism, and individual liberty. I don't mean to paint a rosy picture of indigenous peoples and rural life; the people I met were not the idealized "Other" often encapsulated in the racist stereotype of the "noble savage," but real human beings subject to the same possibilities—good and bad—as the rest of the contemporary world. On my journey, I encountered

In the way I experienced Kapwa, *I found that people would seek acknowledgement of a shared bond by trying to find a connection that ultimately widened the sphere of the self.*

people who wanted absolutely nothing to do with me after getting to know me (or not), and despite my efforts not to offend, I'm sure my blunders and mistakes irritated many of the people I met, indigenous or not. Yet overall, I was struck by the *Kapwa* sensibility of most of the people I encountered as they attempted to connect with me in empathetic reciprocal exchange marked by a generosity of spirit and open and trusting dialogue. It led me to conclude that the linguistic concept of *Kapwa* carries with it an inherent ethical obligation to treat others as part of one's self, with equal regard and respect.

KAPWA POSSIBILITIES FOR PRACTICE FROM MARGIN TO CENTER

To return to the original question of this paper, what would art inspired by the notion of *Kapwa* be like? As I conceive of it, a *Kapwa* approach helps me accept the often seemingly contradictory parts of my own existence and creative process. Such an orientation pushes me to reach beyond the boundaries of the (privatized) self. The focus is no longer on individualistic self-expression; rather, in keeping with my degree in Public Art, art is performed for—and with—the community. In this creative state there is no inside/outside, there is no us/them, there are only equals who are interconnected in an intricate web of relationships where the norm is respect and careful tending. Contemporary philosopher Jürgen Habermas proposes a possibility that can meet the criteria of *Kapwa* art, suggesting that art could be used to find "beautiful ways of harmonizing interests rather than sublime ways of detaching oneself for others' interests" (as cited in Gablik, 1993, p. 37). De Guia (2005) describes Kapwa-motivated art practices as generally:

> "inspired by ancestral traditions like functional art, trance dance, audience participation, ephemeral installations and unstructured music...Artworks tend to be contemplative, commemorative and ceremonial. Culture bearer artists treat their pieces frequently as an offering, which means those works might be sacrificed or destroyed...[The works are] often functional, instructional or aiding the community-building process, including activities that bring people together, rouse awareness and awaken collective memories. Such art is usually presented for free, given away or bartered" (p. 37).

De Guia goes on to provide an extremely helpful survey of artists working in *Kapwa* traditions, one to which I hope to add someday in a longer essay that properly acknowledges my many sources of wisdom and inspiration, both in the Philippines and globally. However as this essay is focused on my own fumbling attempts towards coherence, I'd like to now turn to a few examples from my own practice. This brief survey of some of my work pulls from many traditions that can be seen as extending the network of relations found in *Kapwa*.

A critique of such borrowing, particularly when elements of indigenous cultures are used, could be that it constitutes a form of "cultural appropriation" that calls into question its authenticity. However, one of the things I learned while living with actual indigenous peoples is that the very idea of "authenticity" can be a romanticized one and rooted in colonial essentialism. Indigenous cultures and peoples innovate all the time and their practices are as available for change as any other. Hence, thinking of them as fixed, static, and incapable of connection with contemporary life is a form of racism. While I dislike it when people with privilege copy traditional cultural forms without adding any work of their own for commercial gain, it is different when synthesis and syncretism are used with intent. Art historian Sylvester Okwunodu Ogbechie (2008) points out that challenging ideas of essentialism can be liberating. If, instead of thinking in terms of fixed boundaries, one imagines "cultures as open systems where individual actors negotiate access to and traffic in symbolic elements which have no fixed meaning," then mediating possibilities exist, with artists functioning as nodal points in a global system that connects cultures (p. 183). While such a notion can easily lend itself to exploitative (or ludic) appropriation, when nuanced by the ethic of *Kapwa*, it allows for the fluidity of experience and the possibility of communal interconnection. Anthropologist Arndt Schneider (2003) adds more depth to the usual understanding of artistic appropriation, pointing out that when enacted by non-dominant narrators, it allows for "the non-west" to become "the active historical agent in an 'alterative' encounter, one that subverts and deconstructs the ideological terrain of its present and former colonial masters" (see extended discussion in pp. 215-299). As I also believe that public art should be created in service of the public (as opposed to some contemporary practitioners who seem to enjoy making insider jokes for the elite with public funds), I am also quite clear about the political subtext to my work which has a clear intention of both accessibility to the public through participatory processes and rousing historical awareness to challenge essentialism. In order to illustrate these themes, I've chosen three examples to discuss.

NURTURING THE SPIRIT: AN EXPLORATION OF FOOD, RITUAL, AND HEALING

Sarap sa Puso was a ritual performance piece designed with input from Kay Ulanday Barrett for the First International Babaylan Conference in 2010 held at Sonoma State University in California and performed with the help of Karen Muktayani 'Muki' Villanueva and Mia Villanueva.

Figure 1. Flyer for "Kamayan: With These Hands"
a community fundraiser dinner.

Although I had not specifically intended to follow De Guia's guidelines, this performative artwork was participative, ephemeral, and designed to awaken collective memories. It was literally eaten by the participants as they were offered a tasting of 7 courses in an interactive performance set with ritual intention and served on handmade vessels. Each offering was presented ceremonially and designed to provoke indigenous knowledge that had survived the assaults of colonization and migration in the seemingly unthreatening feminized space of the kitchen. Offered flavors included items to both delight and challenge. One course was *tapsilog* and *longsilog*, traditionally a breakfast of fried meat (*tapa* or *longganisa*), fried rice (*sinangag*), topped with fried egg (*itlog*). For the performance, miniature pieces of art were created – different IKSP quotes were written on the inside of emptied and painted eggshells and fried rice was placed inside with a slice of meat and a fried quail egg on top. The participants were allowed to keep their eggshells with inscriptions of embryonic messages that they had literally digested. Other courses included slices of *ampalaya,* a very bitter melon often eaten to stimulate the heart, edible clay and *salabat,* a ginger tea, to evoke the bitterness of imperialism, root participants to the earth, and stimulate traditional healing. The participants were enthusiastic, taking three hours to share individual memories triggered by the offerings. This piece was so successful that it was presented again in New York in modified form with the help of Riya Ortiz, Analiza Caballes and Allison Faelnar for members of *Damayan,* a grassroots im/migrant workers association led by domestic workers and I plan to present it again this year in Germany.

Figure 2. Horst Hoheisel & Andreas Knitz. *Monument to a Monument*, 1995.
Stainless Steel, Buchenwald with Offerings *from Human Human Memorial*
by Margarita Garcia and Yuequn Zhang, 2012. Photo by Gao-Yu.

HUMAN HUMAN MEMORIAL

This work led to a performative art piece that also meets De Guia's guidelines for
Kapwa-based work at the Buchenwald Memorial, a former Nazi concentration camp
located directly above Weimar, the city in Germany where I recently completed my Master
in Fine Arts. This site of trauma, where human beings suffered and more than 50,000 died
due to racist ideologies taken to the extreme, literally hung over the charming classical
town that I lived and worked in. It was very hard to know how to respond, both as an
outsider and an artist, yet the site required a response as silence seemed like collusion
with the past. After two years, I attempted what is known as a "small gesture" of a public
art piece that operates quietly, without fanfare. In the resulting action, performed with
colleague Yuequn Zhang, a meditation and ritual offering took place on Horst Hoheisel &
Andreas Knitz's monument, *Memorial to a Memorial in Buchenwald, 1995.* The monument
consists of a steel plate set in the ground and kept at body temperature, inscribed with the
nationalities of those interned. One of the striking things about this list is that so many
different backgrounds were represented, suggesting how diverse Germany was before the
Holocaust and how easy it was once it began, to position almost anyone as the "Other."
Although people of Jewish heritage bore the primary brunt of Nazi aggression, LGBT
people, Roma/Sinti, religious leaders, women, people of diverse origins and people in
many other categories also suffered. As Vietnam was listed and I felt that these victims
might not be as well known, it felt appropriate to include offerings of incense, Vietnamese

heaven and earth cakes, "bahn day" and green tea. Buddhist belief suggests that unfed spirits become "hungry ghosts" doomed to wander the earth, thus descendants must feed their ancestors as well as make offerings to unmourned ghosts who have been forgotten or who died violently. A quote from a Buchenwald survivor that I had seen on an earlier visit to the museum also emphasized the constant gnawing hunger of the prisoners. The action took place on November 1, traditionally "All Hallows Day" where in Catholic belief, the dead can visit the earth in spirit form. In the Philippines, families gather at the graves of their loved ones (much like in Mexico's celebration of Dia de los Muertos or Day of the Dead) and picnic, even spending the night.

Figure 3. Margarita Garcia & Yuequn Zhang. *Human Human Memorial,*
Buchenwald, 2012. Photos by Gao-Yu.

During the action, we walked slowly across the parade grounds where prisoners were forced to stand at attention in all weather for hours as a form of torture, activating the space with our offerings. We then sat in meditation on the memorial. This simple action, (which I had not expected anyone to notice as I had not asked for official permission or publicized it) drew a large impromptu audience who fell instantly silent and seemed to join in our meditation without any instruction. After 20 minutes, we left our offerings on the memorial, including a handmade bamboo plate inscribed "the *Babaylan* [indigenous healer] exists in the moments of courage when we refuse to be pacified into conformity." When I later sent documentation and an explanation to the memorial coordinators (apologizing for not asking first) I was honored to receive a positive response from Daniel Gaede, the Director of Education, who plans to use the piece in educational materials.

White Wash / In Memoriam

In 2012-2013 I worked on a series of historical re-enactments in Germany that challenged ideas of home and homeland by creating mini-performances in historic locales that disrupted and interrogated what has been commemorated from the past. The performances used humor and satire to address serious issues of exclusion by positing alternative realities, such as Goethe and Schiller, two classical icons, kissing in front of their famous statue, portrayed by a Cuban/Turkish couple.

Figure 4. White Wash / In Memoriam

Figure 5. A Cuban/Turkish couple portraying
Goethe and Schiller.

. . .[I]n this Kapwa-generated flow, I'm at last able to bring together the seeming contradictions of my hybrid life, allow them to balance and work together, and find a home in the practice of community-oriented Public Art.

I reshot a photo of the Bauhaus Masters, many of whom became famous artists using the female staff of the Art Department, with a lone male professor in a dress to represent the lone woman on staff in 1926. On an empty pedestal that once held an equestrian statue of Grand Duke Carl Alexander, I convinced an Iranian friend to mount a hobby-horse dressed in a Superman costume in a sardonic send-up of militarism and masculinity. Feminist pre-cursor, Grand Duchess Anna Amalia (who was included in Judy Chicago's *The Dinner Party,* in 1977) was re-imagined by an Israeli American friend as a ruler and a mother who also breastfed. I then memorialized these performances in a series of postcards that the public could fill out and mail free of charge, literally sneaking my re-inscriptions of a more inclusive past into nearly every district of the country as they became so popular among Weimar's visitors that the end distribution blanketed the country. These pieces were intended to expand the ways in which people can be at-home-in-the-world and open public spaces for alternative re-narrations.

I then built an installation of white laundry in the attic of my home and projected a black and white slideshow of these images, as well as other serious evocations of exclusion that had rendered it necessary to create these challenges to the status quo, onto the laundry. The result, to quote my mentors, was compelling. The images I had shot, which had seemed innocuous in isolation, when juxtaposed against the appalling historical record of genocide, slavery, colonization, and sexism were revealed to be radical and poignant.

Images included original drawings of tattooed indigenous peoples from the "discovery" of the Philippines, a self-portrait sent by contemporary filmmaker Auraeus Solito at the burial ground of his Palawan ancestors, and images from World War II and the Philippine American War. Even the small children who entered the space couldn't help but watch the entire 20-minute series as images flickered over the gently waving laundry, shifting and changing as they moved over the different layers. The work hoped to evoke tacit ways of knowing, acknowledge the traumas of the past, and envision alternative possibilities.

Figure 6. Selected images from the slideshow projected onto *WhiteWash /
In Memoriam.* Margarita Garcia, 2012. Images from a variety of sources.

CONCLUSION

In conclusion, contemporary life, riven by the dislocations of migration and the general
detachment caused by isolation and dependence on electronic gadgetry often makes any type
of cohesion challenging, let alone a theory for a community-oriented public art practice.
Yet *Kapwa*, with its focus on connection and its ability to transcend divisions by honoring
particularities while emphasizing relationships, can help forge coherence. To put it in the
vernacular, *Kapwa* helps me get in the flow – a strange thing to try to explain in today's
rationalist world. But as almost everyone I've talked to who creates reports: when it's working,
the world goes quiet. Something takes over and your hands seem to move of their own

accord – maybe you hear instructions inside your head (from yourself, or your ancestors) and maybe you just "know" what to do, but either way it *works*. I have always thought of my work as being "Ni Ha, Ni Ho", neither here nor there, as Kidlat Tahimik, the father of Philippine independent cinema, puts it, but in this *Kapwa*-generated *flow*, I'm at last able to bring together the seeming contradictions of my hybrid life, allow them to balance and work together, and find a home in the practice of community-oriented Public Art.

References

Berger, M. (1998). Interview with Adrian Piper. In G. Kester (Ed.), *Art, activism & oppositionality: Essays from afterimage* (pp. 215-231). Durham and London: Duke University Press.

Connerton, P. (2011). *The spirit of mourning: History, memory and the body.* Cambridge: Cambridge University Press.

De Guia, K. (2005). *Kapwa: The self in the other: Worldviews and lifestyles of Filipino culture-bearers.* Pasig City: Anvil Publishers.

Enriquez, V. G. (1986). Kapwa: A core concept in Filipino social psychology. In V. G. Enriquez (Ed.), *Philippine world-view* (pp. 6-17). Pasir Panjang, Singapore: Institute of Southeast Asian Studies.

Freeland, C. (2001). *But is it art? An introduction to art theory.* Oxford: Oxford University Press.

Fusco, C. (1998). Fantasies of oppositionality. In G. Kester (Ed.), *Art, activism & oppositionality: Essays from afterimage* (pp. 60-75). Durham and London: Duke University Press.

Hinojosa-Ojeda, R. (2010). *Raising the floor for American workers: The economic benefits of comprehensive immigration reform.* Washington, DC: Center for American Progress, Immigration Policy Center.

Hess, E. (1995). Guerilla girl power: Why the art world needs a conscience. In N. Felshin (Ed.), *But is it art? The spirit of art as activism.* Seattle, WA: Bay Press.

Ho, D. Y. F., Peng, S.-q., Cheng Lai, A. & Chan, S.-f. F. (2001). Indigenization and beyond: Methodological relationalism in the study of personality across cultural traditions. *Journal of Personality, 69,* 925–953.

Hooks, B. (1984). *Feminist theory: From margin to center.* London: Pluto Press.

Kester, G. H. (2004). *Conversation pieces: Community and communication in modern art.* Berkley, CA: Duke University Press.

Miller, A. P. (2012). *From immigrants to activists: Immigration, nativism, welfare reform, and the mobilization of immigrant voters in the late nineteenth and late twentieth centuries.* (Unpublished doctoral dissertation). The University of North Carolina at Greensboro (UNCG), Greensboro, NC.

Minglu, G. (2008). Particular time, specific space, my truth. In T. Smith, O. Enwezor, & N. Condee (Eds.), *Antinomies: Modernity, postmodernity, and contemporaneity.* (pp. 133-164). Durham and London: Duke University Press.

Moore, D. H. (1998). White men can't program: The contradictions of multiculturalism. In G. Kester (Ed.), *Art, activism & oppositionality: Essays from afterimage* (pp. 51-59). Durham and London: Duke University Press.

Ogbechie, S. O. (2008). The perils of unilateral power. In T. Smith, O. Enwezor, & N. Condee (Eds.), *Antinomies: Modernity, postmodernity, and contemporaneity* (pp. 165-186). Durham and London: Duke University Press.

Risatti, H. (1990). Art and aesthetics: Late modernism and the formalist debate. In H. Risatti (Ed.), *Postmodern perspectives: Issues in Contemporary Art.* Englewood Cliffs, NJ: Prentice Hall.

Schneider, A. (2003). On "appropriation." A critical reappraisal of the concept and its application in global art practices. *Social Anthropology, 11*(2), 215–229.

Strobel, L. M. (2005). *A book of her own: Words and images to honor the babaylan.* Tiboli Publishing.

West, C. A. (2001) A genealogy of modern racism. In P. Essed & D. T. Goldberg (Eds.), *Race critical theories: Text and context* (pp. 90-112). Oxford: Blackwell Publishers.

World Economic Forum. (2012). *The global gender gap report 2012.* Geneva: World Economic Forum.

Wright, C. A. Jr. (1998). The mythology of difference: Vulgar identity politics at the Whitney. In G. Kester (Ed.), *Art, activism & oppositionality: Essays from afterimage* (pp. 76-93). Durham and London: Duke University Press.

Zavodny, M. (2011). *Immigration and American Jobs.* Washington, DC: American Enterprise Institute for Public Policy Research, Partnership for a New American Economy.

DJ Qbert as Cyber-Maniac Shaman

What Does Hip-Hop Tricksterism Have To Do With Traditional Babaylanism?

James W. Perkinson

POETIC INTROIT

Filipino-American DJ Qbert emerged in the early 1990s as hip-hop's premier turntablist—someone not merely playing backup to an MC send-up of significance, but grabbing the ozone by way of scratch-tones, and beat-loans, and digitalized, mixer-synthesized, cyber-moans, that pulled the bones of history from the loam of urban ecology like a warrior drone of sonic insanity signaling the arrival of a new incarnation of rhyme-spitting dexterity in a cyborg-mode of selectivity transforming calamity into levity and depravity into beauty and new vision.

THE SITUATION

We have a problem today. We inhabit a planet now on the edge of radical upheaval. Climate is changing in such unpredictable ways that the US Defense Department is already busily planning for massive waves of climate-refugees as a national security assault that will make 9/11 and the wars in Iraq and Afghanistan seem like kindergarten by comparison. Cheap oil availability is "peaking"—threatening to upend our car-culture addiction and oil-driven food production in levels of social violence and war exceeding anything this country, or perhaps even this world, has ever witnessed. Extinction rates of other species have so catastrophically increased as to render uncertain our own species survival (if the bees really do disappear, humans have about four years to live according to Einstein). What can be euphemistically called "population overshoot" is turning increasing sectors of the globe into ever-burning garbage heaps hosting the new ecology of slum cities that will soon "house" nearly one-half of the world's urban population whose sole vision is simply securing the next meal (Davis, 2006, p. 151). These four "horsemen of the apocalypse," as they might be called, force to the surface a fundamental question that, for me anymore, frames every spiritual consideration I entertain, whether by way of private musing, or in public commentary such as this essay represents.

And that question is simply this. What are we doing here on this planet? What is a human being? A human society? A sustainable future? As a participant in a shared dialogue on spirituality—if I am going to think healing in the key of *babaylan* feeling and vision (as I will in what follows), in service of what kind of future am I doing such? Is our fascination in this dialogue—whether homeland practitioner, diaspora laborer, or merely repentant Euro-colonizer such as myself—simply a matter of giving a bit of indigenous flavor to an otherwise upwardly-mobile-aspiring, middle-class-dreaming, contentedly-consumerist-buying, iPhone-scheming participation in contemporary globalization, hoping the War on Terror and the foreclosure bailiff stay out of our front yard?

The challenge for me arising out of any consideration of indigenous practice is profoundly polemical. Whatever else I take away from the engagement, I take it for granted that the basic issue at stake is lifestyle itself—an entire belief and practice system that I have been socialized into, privileging growth and technology, consumer goods and Hollywood, accumulation of gadgets and rights to comfort, flush toilets and private closets full of Saks labels or Target imitations, police forces keeping the criminalized poor away from my door and a military operating on my tax dollars invading other "places" on average of once every 14 months to secure the resources that I am trained by corporate advertising to covet, to kill for (by way of mercenary surrogates and patriot acts), and finally to consume and so feel like "I am somebody"! The issue in examining *babaylanism* is, for me, a question about an entire way of life, not just spirituality. And finally it is about ecology—about my life as a human in relationship to all of the other human beings and life forms I am utterly dependent upon, but have no knowledge about or appreciation of, because I now live inside a gated country protected by war-on-terror legality and encased inside cement and silicon, wood and steel and plastic to such a degree, I no longer even recognize the kinship and living vitality of relationship that I have lost. Human beings and life forms which I nonetheless prey upon like the most rapacious and callous of slave masters or development engineers that ever lived! I live as beneficiary of a global system of utter pillage and depredation. I am content to have chickens live their entire lives bent over in a mesh cage so crammed with other chickens none of them ever get to raise their heads entirely—so long as I get my "healthy choice" chicken Caesar salad! And content, as well, to let darker-toned Third World "others" of my own species extract the raw materials and pick the fruit and stitch the clothing and process the garbage that leverages my own air-conditioned comfort.

So just what is it that I think I am doing in exploring Filipino *babaylanism*? One more act of pillage to add to my collection of little practices and fetishized insights, after which I merrily head off to the mall? The "voice" that this tradition of homeland healing codifies is ultimately a voice of archetypal Abel, "disappeared" by Cain-the- agribusiness-city-builder of biblical fame, an Abel-of-the-outback whose *bedouin* blood cries from the ground on which he was slain, according to the Genesis text that remembers him (Gen. 4:1-17). *Babaylanism is* the Filipino sounding out of that bloodied ground, whatever else it signifies and rounds out. It echoes through a cold colonial history that has always had economic plunder as its rationale and that has never ceased its predatory conquest up to the present—even if today it goes by the name of "free trade." That subaltern voice of the crushed and disappeared indigenous—named *bedouin* "Abel" in the desert of the ancient Mid East or *babaylan* "indio" in the beautiful archipelago of the South China Sea—demands full hearing if it is to be countenanced at all. And the full demand of that hearing is what we must courageously outline in our attentions in this place—even if it cuts against our own consumerist habits and desire.

My contribution is minor, but evocative. I speak to the topic by way of sufferance—a white male North American, unwitting beneficiary of the entire history of colonial relations between my ancestors and the Philippine Islands since 1898, granting my people access to Asian markets at the expense of a million Filipino lives lost in resisting the invasion; and more lately benefiting from Filipino labor never paid its full due over decades of working these shores as farm hands or domestics, nurses or clerks, or more distantly as call center imitators of my region's dialect, or masseuses for my tired bones, when I visit "the homeland" in company of my *Kapampangan* wife.

Whatever insights I bring to the table derive from my peculiar history of a quarter century lived in the inner city. An eastside Detroit community of activist Christians, pooling assets and making life-decisions together on a poverty-level budget, provided the base from which to engage a hard-rocking urban tract of African American struggle up against the fate race and class decreed as their state of existence. Gradually over a

DJ Qbert as Cyber-Maniac Shaman

first decade in that "underclass" neighborhood, I unlearned some of my privilege, had scales fall from color blind eyes to see the deep effects of white supremacy on a dark-toned community, but just as provocatively, learned the subtleties of the cultural judo that community performed on its incarceration in a depraved stereotype (when not behind actual steel bars). Over time, debrided by black humor and anger, schooled in call/response antiphony and the polyphony of a jazz sensibility—crosscut with hip-hop antipathy towards all things "unreal"—I emerged in a new sense of identity and possibility, the joy and task of being more than simply "white." As spoken word poet, earning a living as adjunct professor of things spiritual in an urban college, I took in the angular pulse of rhythm with which my students of color and co-residents on the block probed life choices and broke down opposition. The ability regularly to re-figure reality under the beat of syncopation, making desperation yield beauty in spite of itself, hipped me to what I later came to call the gift of shamanic percussivity.

Black culture—in West African origins, on slave plantations and southern reincarnations of the community after slavery, and in northern cities after the two wars and despite more recent postindustrial deprivation—has innovated consistently and thoroughly with rhythmic patterns of creativity. It has done so in dance, in music, in walk like Richard Pryor and talk like Tupac and thought like Toni Morrison's, in sartorial combat with the skin stereotype, in all manner of political organizing and cultural struggle to survive an impossible circumstance. The ability to take in energy from the environment, run it through a breeder-reactor core of the culture, giving out even more than was taken it, in a "stepped down" fashion—thus conserving anguish as an incubator of vitality—became a cipher for me for how an entire community elaborated pain into power in a shamanistic vein of visionary transformation. Part of that skill is a matter of bending words into new vibratory potency, stringing together an impossible riff of sound that elaborates the angst of rejection into an eloquence of off-timed[1] celebration, creating an alternative "body" of sonic freedom for the compacted life locked down by white society inside the oppressed black body. All of that became a school house for me—teaching me beyond the import of mere words, of the living possibilities of energy, once they are given a new communal texture of expression. It is out of that experience that I offer my comments on a new mode of sonic improvisation going by the name of "scratching"—emerging in the last quarter century as shamanistic probe of the hard surface of postindustrial urban life—that in someone such as DJ Qbert, may even warrant examination as a diasporic echo of *babaylan* power.

---

[1] Cf. the article on "off-timing" as a survival skill for a mid-twentieth century generation of African Americans, using various modes of jazz-like "syncopation" to side-step oppressive incursions on the community (Lattany, 1994, p. 172).

SCRATCHING THE SPIRITS

Filipino-American DJ Qbert emerged in the early 1990s as hip-hop's premier turntablist—someone not merely playing backup to an MC send-up of significance, but grabbing the mike with a cyborg strike of vocabulary coming straight from the future. With his posse of *Invisibl Skratch Piklz,* Qbert blazed a sonic trail into the inner ether by melding human hand and vinyl disc into a mestizo mix of tricks, doing judo on the diasporic clash of cultures defining California's coast at the millennial crossover. Today, he is both ancestor and cipher for an entire posse of wobble-fingered masters, whose demographic profile is disproportionately populated by vinyl-wonks of Filipino descent, ranging in DJ name from Babu (Chris Oroc) to Eddie Edul, Marlino to Manila Ice, Geometrix to Jester the Filipino Fist, Kuttin Kandi to the Icey Ice man of LA's 93.5 FM—among others! DJing in the manner of Qbert and company embodies a different ethic than the "beef culture" resulting from MC battles and "diss" rap. In a subtle divergence from the "playa" impulse to get over at all costs, reproducing capitalist competition in vernacular form, turntablists regularly share techniques, and make new scratch products available to each other in a constant search for elevating the practice collectively, in a communal ethic of reciprocity. Qbert himself is vegan, careful about keeping his body in balance and aware that limitation is a necessary part of vitality: he will voice in interviews, for instance, that over-laboring the tables is unhealthy. The issue is rather using the new vocabularies of sound to create a rhythmic probe of silence, to suggest, to open the world to an emergent form of intelligence that does not immediately submit to old conventions or expressive logics controlled by the status quo.

Scratch is here a technique of conjure, divining below the surface of machine-culture, probing the possibilities of sensation released when substances newly minted by industrial design are brought aggressively together in rhythmic incantation. Vinyl groves meeting steel needles under a beat yield an ecological significance not yet decipherable in conventional human language. Strangely, the result is rather visionary—a "seeing," by way of sound, through a portal without a tongue to convey the import. Like Amazonian *yagé*-drinking shamans silently orchestrating the undulating landscapes of color experienced by their "*yagé*-tripping" clients, as we shall see below, sight and

With his posse of Invisibl Skratch Piklz, Qbert blazed a sonic trail into the inner ether by melding human hand and vinyl disc into a mestizo mix of tricks, doing judo on the diasporic clash of cultures defining California's coast at the millennial crossover.

211

Like Amazonian yagé-drinking shamans silently orchestrating the undulating landscapes of color experienced by their "yagé-tripping" clients . . . sight and sound are here pulled apart and put together outside grammatical structure, letting the world be reassembled as if in genesis again.

sound are here pulled apart and put together outside grammatical structure, letting the world be reassembled as if in genesis again. This is perhaps the essence of healing, unlocking energies of meaning from entropic logics of pain and repetitive modes of self-destruction and rendering them available for recreation.

In this sense, shamanism is work with the elementary particles of living reality, traversing unseen underworld and overworld potencies of both spirit and matter, probing the strange and fantastic grammar of serpentine information embedded in all life forms, common to vine and humankind, jaguar spots and clots of bacterial colonization in the colon, the primal coiling and uncoiling of ever-proliferating DNA, dancing in ceaseless antiphonies of the body like a micro-frequency of the galaxy, living imitation of the interstellar overtones and undertones of pulsating space, heard by Pythagoras, or the dark matter and dark energy of modern physics, whose mysterious absence grants to light its very possibility of speed and fecundity. Scholars today are re-investigating the shamanic imagination with a vengeance, recognizing, in a late epiphany, remarkable "ecocentric epistemologies" of both botany and biology encoded in shamanic logics of metaphor and vision, song and rhythm, that may hold keys to our species' ability to survive the catastrophe we seem rapidly to be precipitating.

It is no accident that the term has also been drafted to describe the effects—if not the intent—of hip-hop wizardry working rhymes and beats into an epiphany of postindustrial delirium. In using fractal methods of sound-creation opportunistically to seize a product designed by a corporation for consumption and profit (the vinyl record) and use it against its intended use to release levity and vision from within the electronic interior of de-industrialized ecology, scratching could be said to be articulating a new sonic vocabulary for the boiling up of human enlightenment. At least such will be the tack taken here. I am not so much interested in lionizing Qbert as camping out on the creativity he signals and reading it shamanistically. Transcoded across lines of gender and age for a changed historical situation, we might even say scratch innovation channels a fractured mode of postcolonial *babaylanism*. Rightly grasping the nature of that fractured impulse, however, requires asking the deepest possible question about the intention of the pre-colonial practice. And at core that question is, "What really is a 'human?'"

SHAMANIC "HUMANISM"

I do not pretend to be more than a distant learner in relationship to the deep impulses of historic *babaylanism,* as indeed in relationship to indigeneity in various forms around the globe. I do think today, in the face of the crisis whose physiognomy I outlined above, sitting down before indigenous vision and struggling to learn its wisdom and challenge to a supposedly "civilized" world fast careening off the cliff edge of self-destruction, is an imperative of the species, if we hope to survive this century in any form other than that of a Mad Max movie or a Cormack McCarthy road-walker, laboring across a post-apocalyptic landscape of horrors. But rather than underscore *babaylan* vision here—since there are others far more appropriately equipped to do so than me—I want briefly to visit another culture's mode of shamanic healing to open perspective on the scratching virtuosity just enumerated. I have already alluded to its eloquence in the reference to rainforest dwellers using a plant extract known as *yagé* (or *ayahuasca*) to galvanize healing.

The particular culture whose skills and tradition highlight turntablist practice are the Shipibo of the Peruvian Amazon, one of some 72 *ayahuasca*-using cultures in Western Amazonia (Luna, 1986, p. 57; Narby, 1998, p. 41). The psychotropic tea that for millennia has animated shamanic ritual explorations of affliction in the rainforest is a carefully brewed mix of plants combining the alkaloid properties of the hallucinogenic *di-methyl-tryptomine* (which is also produced inside the human brain) and a *monoamine oxidase* inhibitor that inactivates the human stomach enzyme that would otherwise render the hallucinogen ineffective (Narby, 1998, pp. 10-11). After centuries of European colonial suppression of the practices, recent medical analyzes of *ayahuasca* have clarified its long-term harmlessness and its therapeutic benefits, legalizing its use, even in Westernized urban centers such as Rio de Janero, in Brazil. But it is not primarily the empirically validated effects of the combinatory brew that are of interest here, but rather the ecological understanding of the practice when it is pursued in a shamanically supervised gathering, in its natural environs of the rain-forest.

The indigenous comprehension of the kaleidoscopic visions that result from drinking the tea emphasize the experience as one of being "taught by the plants." The idea that plants might communicate has been a great stumbling block for Western scientific, and now commercial, interests, whose attentions have been provoked in recent decades by *yagé's* verified benefits and well-studied

Transcoded across lines of gender and age for a changed historical situation, we might even say scratch innovation channels a fractured mode of postcolonial babaylanism.

efficacy. But as anthropologist Jeremy Narby has detailed in his own years-long initiation into its use, and the gradual disabuse of his own disbelief, the sophistication of the plant combination necessary for the tea to work belies discovery by merely trial and error. The natives' own explanation—that the plants themselves have taught their own use—can so far not be easily gainsaid (Narby, 1998, pp. 42-43, 51, 109-110, 127-131, 177). But it is not just that the plants "teach" through the brewing up of their own bodies, but what and how they teach that gives pause for my project. They invariably work their holistic potency in a multi-media ensemble of song and vision.

Indeed, among the Shipibo, seeing and hearing represent a synesthetic reciprocity that may well be a shared cultural trait. At the heart of Shipibo spirituality lies a responsiveness to a non-manifest and ineffable world rooted in the rainforest that is evoked and invoked in the human world by way of creative design-patterns constituted simultaneously of sound and sight (Charing, 2008). Their weave is patterned into textiles, embroidery, and artisan craft, for instance, by women initiated into the practice when Piripi berry juice was squeezed into their eyes as young girls (Charing, 2008). The seeing supposedly lasts a lifetime and is understood to represent the vibratory potency of the Cosmic Serpent, *Ronin Kene,* the great Anaconda of Being, Mother-Creator of all that exists, whose skin radiates in an electric reverb of color, generating all possible patterns—past, present, and future—in ever-new, inimitable fusions that permeate the world with form, light, and sound. These patterns can be invoked in songs that immediately generate corresponding visions, or grasped in a geometric gestalt of seeing that issues in song. What artistic production materializes before the eye is just as readily invoked through sound. The undulating iridescent snake-hallucinations that shamanic ritual regularly provokes in its clientele by way of *ayahuasca*-induced trance is accompanied by shamanic singing that itself generates, intensifies and moves the visions.

In either case, the geometrics caught in the art-form or the mental apparition induced hallucinogenically are understood to be co-extensive with the entire universe, not bound inside their respective "media" (whether textile, painting, chant, or visual field of imagination). For shamans, reportedly, the filaments of the *ayahuasca*-vision "drift" towards the shaman's lips and assemble in the mouth as an *icaro* or chant-form that when sung, penetrates the patient's body and harmonizes the energies there with the larger canvas of creation (Gebhart-Sayer, 1986, p. 196; Charing, 2008). Bodies—sonic, aural, visual, liquid, and solid—resonate in a precise vibrational harmony visible to the shamanic eye when the patient's physical and psycho-spiritual energies have "unknotted" over multiple sessions into a restored consonance and become clearly embedded in the body as a durable *Arkana* or pattern of protection for the spirit. The reported experience is one of being "saturated by design," a kind of cosmic tune-up in the key of interpenetrating frequencies, presided over by someone prescient in the operative synesthesia (Charing, 2008). Here lies a living "visual music," as one scholar intones, that refuses the Western scientific modality of disclosure by way of autopsy or its epistemology of "the rational gaze, that separates before thinking" (Gebhart-Sayer, 1986, p. 196; Narby, 1998, pp. 67-68, 179). And it is just here that this rainforest modality of shamanic inquiry and healing offers silently suggestive commentary on the likes of a DJ Qbert and company.

KOSMIC SKRATCHING

DJ Qbert, in this essay, stands in for the entire enterprise of improvising a new sonic vocabulary in crosscutting the established technologies of sound with a syncopated rip of hard stuttered melody going by the name of "scratch." In industrial music production and popular culture consumption up to the 1970s, turntables dutifully spun discs of vinyl under phonographic needles to generate pre-recorded "legitimacies" of hearing pleasure— jazz, chamber, pop, etc.— from the spiraling grooves. When Grand Wizard Theodore accidentally bumped a needle across the face of a still turning record in his room as a young teenage DJ in New York in the 1970s, however, his "hip-hop-headed" mindset heard something more than "noise." Why had no one else ever caught this drift? Undoubtedly, millions of needles had scratched millions of records under countless errant hands in the previous half-century. But Theodore's ear framed the sound as cipher and meaning. And quickly the emergent DJ movement of the blighted Bronx of the 70s "imbricated" the vibe with its necessary surround. Scratching became the aural invocation of urban desolation, giving a metalico-harsh tongue to a mode of experience rendered absurd by the postindustrial politics of abandonment. Burps of dissonance, purposely tattooed across heavily structured rhythmic intervals, established a whole new sonic currency.

In turntablism's growing finesse with the result, a new electro-digitalized cyber-language emerges. Throbs of earth-groan ground into the body by way of drums and base are suddenly irradiated with a meteoric burst of galactic laughter. The effect is ineffable. A crossroads of cyber-possession, techno-riffs of trance mounting the beat like an *orisha* climbing into the head of a devotee of Santeria when the *babalawo* starts singing. Are spirits limited to bodies of blood? Can a machine-matrix be mounted by an astral energy? A whole zone of new questions opens here.

In West African traditions of trance possession, the *orisha-lwa* known as Ogou presides over the entirety of modernity and all of its post-modern, post-industrial, post-colonial temporal offspring (Cosentino, 1997; Barnes, 1997). Ogou *in situ* is patron of blacksmithing, at work anywhere human and planetary energies manage to pull hot minerals from their underworld forges of molten manufacture onto the earth's surface for new possibilities of hard-edged employment (Armstrong, 1997, p. 29). Ogou, in this understanding, is also simultaneously guarantor of political authority and animator of political rebellion, cutting open the community with explosions of uncontainable vitality when order waxes brutal and locks down creativity or puts the poor in early graves, such as in the 1791 Haitian Revolution of slaves or the LA Uprising of 1992 responding to the Rodney King

Scratch riffs beg hearing under this code as prophetic omen—a language of the telluric womb singing ecstasy and foreboding in the key of a shamanic cyborgism.

verdict or generalized oppression in South Central (Brown, 1997, pp. 70-82; Cosentino, 1997, p. 293; Baker, 1993, p. 45). These are understood by aficionados of the tradition as "Ogou events." While depth-analysis of this particular coding of human perception and experience is beyond what can be pursued in this writing, suffice it here to note that, for initiates of this complex of practices (Santeria, Candomblé, Vodou, Umbanda, etc., in all of their African and diasporic expressions), Ogou hovers surly and insurgent over all innovations of metallic provenience—railroads, cars, planes, radio wires, computer chips, steel girders, fiber-optic cables, and indeed, turntables—the entire menagerie of mineral cacophony that goes by the name of modern technology. For the eye thus trained to see, Qbert and crew host a visitation characteristic of an entire age, spirit ghosting metal, boasting rage, toasting technique with a brown patina of organic warning, threatening to roast every gesture of high-tech repression in the fires of a rebellious explosion of flesh and earth.[2] Scratch riffs beg hearing under this code as prophetic omen—a language of the telluric womb singing ecstasy and foreboding in the key of a shamanic cyborgism.

But Qbert's emergence offers food for thought along another line of inquiry as well. Graham Townsley notes, in his treatment of Amazonian shamanism, not only the interweaving of song and vision, but the arcane strangeness of shamanic verbalization, seeking in human tongue to emulate the spirits of nature (Narby, 1998, pp. 97-98; Townsley, 2003, pp. 459-460). Rather than direct address, shamans speak in the "abstrusest metaphoric circumlocutions." Night becomes, for instance, "swift tapirs"; the forest itself is designated as "cultivated peanuts;" jaguars are "baskets" and anacondas "hammocks," etc. In shamanic parlance such wild indirection is *tsai yoshto-yoshto*, or "language-twisting-twisting" (Narby, 1998, p. 98; Townsley, 2003, p. 453). As one practitioner told the anthropologist:

> With my *koshuiti* [spirit-songs] I want to see—singing, I carefully examine things—twisted language brings me close but not too close—with normal words I would crash into things—with twisted ones I circle around them—I can see them clearly (Narby, 1998, p. 98-99).

Townsley (2003) extrapolates to say that all shamanic relations with the spirits are "deliberately constructed in an elliptical and multi-referential fashion so as to mirror the

---

[2] Cf for instance, the thought experiment I offered in a 2009 publication reading Tupac Shakur as a manifestation of Ogou (Perkinson, 2009, p. 63-65).

refractory nature of the beings who are their objects"—beings both "'like and not like' the things they animate" (p. 465). Metaphor then is not merely a manner of speaking *about* spirits, it *is* the mode of relationship with them.

Juxtapose to this the arcane vocabulary of witty-fingered record-warpers at the heart of turntablism's emergent tradition: beat juggling whose moves now include chirps and transforms, scribbles and tears, military scratches and flares, and all manner of cutting going by the name of uzis and tweaks, lasers and crabs, chops and skronks and squalls and strobes (O'Conner & Tremayn, 2000). But the words are mere circumlocutions for the sounds that themselves erupt in the head of a DJ like Qbert as "chopped up shapes" he cannot define. Mistakes and accidents continue to birth the ambient squiggles that become slight rips in the fabric of silence through which pops a glimpse of infinity (O'Conner & Tremayn, 2000). The DJs regularly reflect that they "see" far beyond what they can produce. We might easily ad lib that these are sounds simultaneously "like and unlike the technology they animate." Again, the issue here is whether mineral artifact can be made to host spirit animation. But for the artists in question this is undoubtedly a post-modern equation of access to other dimensions of reality, a bending or breaking into alternative planes of being through a "neuromancing"[3] of the machine, synching up nerve passages with cosmic frequencies and optic auras of digitized ineffability. The sounds thus found indeed circle round a resonance that can't be named without being crashed and distorted. But here is nonetheless a need to read the development in its historical traces for a time of mounting apocalypse.

SCRATCHING FOR SOIL

So far so good in my own burst of scratch-work, you might say, but what does this have to do with *babaylanism?* To the degree *babaylansim* can be grasped as an upwelling of animate energy, particular to the island ecologies of the Philippines, ventriloquizing spirit-divinity through a human body and sensibility for the purposes of maturing the species and keeping it in balance, some of the intersection with what I have laid out should be suggestive and obvious. Qbert, as icon of a broadly shared capacity, could be embraced as Filipino-American ventriloquist of island currents of vital memory, channeling ancestral wisdom and *babaylan* vision in the key of a diasporic logic of "mixture," combining a *kapwa* sensibility with a cyborg propensity to make turntables and synthesizers yield healing and community in an impossible circumstance of capitalist accumulation, American delusions of world-mastery, and neo-liberal commodification of everything everywhere. But if so, the channeling must be recognized as partial and the ventriloquism fractured, as already

---

[3] This is a reference to William Gibson's 1984 Cyberpunk classic, *Neuromancer,* exploring the cyborg revolution engulfing the social order and slicing human being into the globalizing machine-matrix that is rapidly inverting the relationship between flesh and technology (p. 243-244).

noted. The issue is not only celebration of what has survived the ocean-crossing, but even more crucially right reading of the creative upsurge. To what does it point? And here the various local shamanisms already solicited converge. Whatever their particular means of practice—whether plant ingestion or danced possession, *anting-anting* invocation or *agong* percussion—they point towards a vital economy of reciprocal exchange with their local ecologies. And this is the hard truth of our time. The question already underscored of whether machine can be ghosted with spirit belies a deeper and more radical urgency. Indigenous shamanisms are quintessentially rooted in communicative intercourse with indigenous species of flourishing biota and function as a schoolhouse for the human spirit in the necessities of sustainable relations with life-forms far older and (ever-more conspicuously evident today) wiser in long term survival than our own yet admits of being.

Taking diaspora fascinations with spirit animation seriously—whether in the form of more traditional modes of *babaylan* practice or in the techno-trance version I have been exploring in scratch creativity—demands asking what life is ultimately about. The energies of invocation of ancestral spirits or postmodern circuits of sonic vitality require for their realization, healthy "bodies" of practice. Imagined with full shamanistic integrity, those bodies must be asserted as not merely human and individual, but as locally existing *eco-communities* of co-constituting plants and animals that nowhere today are surviving inside the market pretensions of globalizing capital. Everywhere the basic material conditions for a *babaylan* visioning of spiritual life are being ruthlessly dismembered. The litmus test for that vision of life, even in the Philippines itself today, must be the few remaining communities of indigenous—invaded and "uprooted" and under assault even as we speak, like the *Aeta* of Pinatubo—whose memory of how to live in symbiotic concert with their native ecology is being shredded as pitilessly as the ecology itself. Reading the impulse in *babaylanism's* core message in actual historical context means giving up a dream of attaching the practice like an ethereal appendage to an otherwise upwardly mobile lifestyle committed to pillaging the planet in search of consumerist bliss and walling off humanity in gated-community supremacy from all other kindred beings. *Babaylan* singing and scratch-riffing alike point towards recovery of a bigger body of human being than that found inside a Gucci suit or an SUV. The songs and vibes cry for exiting commodity culture, and re-learning the language of nurture and correction from the python and parrot, the squirrel and ferret, the coyote and salmon and ant, the cactus and banyan and *caapi* vine plant. And from the few remaining members of our own species who yet know the names of the spirit-shrines and cosmic-designs capable of initiating us into our own true vocation in this world.

Reading Filipino fast-fingered scratching requires a tricky flipping of the script: we might say,

this is scratch finesse as channeling
a faint haint of the *babaylan* colonial fate of
being fed to crocodiles by missionaries
afraid of shamanic wiles and being resurrected
inside diaspora communities as a form of
kapwa-immunity to the harsh insanity of
consumerist inanity and capitalist criminality
in seeking to put the entire planet up for sale!

It is we well-fed Westerners who are read by the probe of sound Qbert and crew spew and it is *babaylan* history that stands forth in *Aeta*-faced mystery as trickster-healer of the calamity modern humanity is precipitating in insisting on its specious superiority. And it is indigenous notions and animal motions and plant potions that offer the living script that requires our response of translation and transfiguration. Will we learn to dance like an *Igorot* echo of the gecko crawling up hauntingly inside all of our dreams? Or simply insure the coming of the impending collapse by eagerly returning to our shopping once we've finished reading the book?

References

Armstrong, R. G. (1997) The etymology of the word "Ogun." In Sandra T. Barnes (Ed.), *Africa's Ogun: Old world and new* (pp. 29-38). Bloomington: Indiana University Press.

Baker, H. (1993). Scene . . . not heard. In R. Gooding-Williams (Ed.), *Reading Rodney King, reading urban uprising* (pp. 38-50). New York: Routledge.

Barnes, S. T. (1997). Africa's Ogun transformed: Introduction to the second edition. In Sandra T. Barnes (Ed.), *Africa's Ogun: Old world and new* (pp. xiii-xxi). Bloomington: Indiana University Press.

Brown, K. M. (1997). Systematic remembering, systematic forgetting: Ogou in Haiti. In Sandra T. Barnes (Ed.), *Africa's Ogun: Old world and new* (pp. 65-89). Bloomington: Indiana University Press.

Charing, H. G. (2008). Communion with the infinite: The visual music of the Shipibo tribe of the Amazon. Retrieved from http://www.ayahuasca.com/spirit/primordial-and-traditional-culture/communion-with-the-infinite-the-visual-music-of-the-shipibo-tribe-of-the-amazon/

Cosentino, D. J. (1997). Repossession: Ogun in folklore and literature. In Sandra T. Barnes (Ed.), *Africa's Ogun: Old world and new* (pp. 290-314). Bloomington: Indiana University Press.

Davis, M. (2006). *Planet of slums.* New York: Verso.

Gebhart-Sayer, A. (1986). Una terapia estética: Los diseños visionarios del ayahuasca entre los Shipibo-Conibo. *América Indígena, 46*(1), 189-218.

Gibson, W. (1984). *Neuromancer.* New York: Ace Books.

Lattany, K. H. (1994). Off-timing: Stepping to the different drummer. In Gerald Early (Ed.), *Lure and loathing: Essays on race, identity, and the ambivalence of assimilation* (pp. 163-174). New York: Penguin Books.

Luna, L. E. (1986). *Vegetalismo: Shamanism among the mestizo population of the Peruvian Amazon.* Stockholm: Almqvist and Wiksell.

Narby, J. (1998). *The cosmic serpent: DNA and the origins of knowledge.* New York: Jeremy P. Tarcher/Putnam.

O'Conner, B. & Tremayne, J. (2000). Ahead of the curve: For nearly a decade, Invisibl Skratch Piklz have transformed the battle jock arena into a multi-million-dollar industry. Now they map out turntablism's new terrain. *DJ Times Magazine.* Retrieved from http://www.djtimes.com/original/djmag/may00/Piklz.htm

Perkinson, J. W. (2009, March). Tupac Shakur as Ogou Achade: Hip-Hop anger and postcolonial rancor read from the other side. In A. Pinn, & M. Miller (Eds.), *Culture & religion: An interdisciplinary journal* (Special Issue on Hip-Hop and Religion), *10*(1), 63-79.

Townsley, G. (1993). Song oaths: The ways and means of Yaminahua shamanic knowledge. *L'Homme,* 2(4), 126-128, 449-468.

Part III

Babaylan Resurrections
Out of the Crocodile's Belly

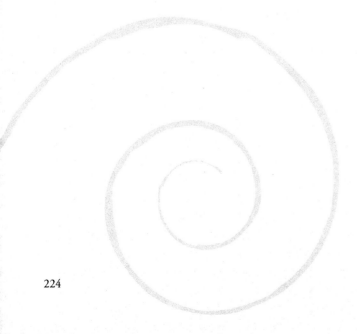

Imperial Remains

Footnotes on an Energy Healer

Tera Maxwell

"A nation which loses awareness of its past gradually loses its self."

(Milan Kundera in Angel Velasco Shaw, 2002, p. ix)

"If loss is known only by what remains of it, then the politics and ethics of mourning lie in the interpretation of what remains—how remains are produced and animated, how they are read and sustained."

(Eng and Kazanjian, 2003, p. ix)

"The loss of stories sharpens the hunger for them. So it is tempting to fill in the gaps and to provide closure where there is none. To create a space for mourning where it is prohibited. To fabricate a witness to a death not much noticed."

(Saidiya Hartman, 2008, p. 8)

My grandmother tells this story about her favorite *lola*. Every night, Gregoria sipped homemade wine from a tiny glass to help her fall asleep. The alcohol caused a skin rash, attracting the attention of a U.S. Health Inspector during a routine visit through her Manila neighborhood.[1] The red patches covering her body looked suspiciously

---

[1] Writing about the medical colonial project, Warwick Anderson (2006) argues that the colonial state took leprous individuals away from their families in the interests of hygiene and "in the interests of medical and civic reformation" (quoted in Stoler, 2006, p. 94). Public health and education were the two tools of American colonialism, cast as benevolent assimilation.

My grandmother's story reveals how U.S. public policy seeps into personal and familial histories and the inextricable link of personal and more public histories.

like leprosy; the inspector ordered Gregoria to be quarantined in the leper unit of San Lazaro's Hospital. It was an exile marking Gregoria's decline, according to my grandmother. Even after she was permitted to leave the hospital several months later, she never cast off the stigma of a leper. She became an outcast in a home where she once enjoyed respect owed to the matriarch. Fearing contagion, her daughter-in-law confined Gregoria to the basement and forbade the grandchildren to eat with her. As a teenager, my grandmother would visit Gregoria in Manila and sit with her in the basement to keep her company. "It was horrible how everyone treated her, especially her daughter-in-law." My *lola* concludes the story with melodramatic flourish: "Gregoria couldn't take it anymore. She took a butcher knife and thrust it into her stomach. She died of a broken heart."

Whenever my *lola* shared this tale, I never comprehended Gregoria's desperate act of suicide and the impact it must have had on the family, including my *lola*, only 16-years-old at the time.[2] Strangely, I felt disaffected from the gravity of this story; it was just one of those impenetrable stories about "back home." It is precisely this troubling disconnection that motivates my scholarly project as I place this feeling—not simply as personal emotive inability—in a larger fabric of incomprehensibility. This affective inability suggests a block or impasse, defying the boundaries of language and logic. The melodrama of the story deluges feeling, leaving in its wake, apathy. My grandmother's story reveals how U.S. public policy seeps into personal and familial histories and the inextricable link of personal and more public histories. By tracing these connections and disconnections, my project places this familial memory within a broader landscape of United States' and Philippines' history to map out an affective history of American Empire in the Philippines.

---

[2] This story always surfaced whenever I had a stye in my eye or pink eye. My lola would recall her lola's remedy for pink eye. One day, my lola Flossie, only a teenager, woke up with pink eye. The nuns at the boarding school in Manila sent her home to her uncle's house. Her parent's home in Bataan was too far away. At her uncle's house she preferred to stay in the basement with her lola. Her lola directed her to pee in a cup. Flossie complained because she did not want to pee in the cup, but her grandmother insisted. After she produced a urine specimen, her lola made her dip her finger in the urine and then on her eye to cure the pink eye. "It worked," my grandmother insisted, "oh, I cried and cried, but it worked." It is only in reference to this story of the cured pink eye that my grandmother invariably tells me the story of her lola's misdiagnosed leprosy and suicide. The story's association with pink eye suggests a theme of not seeing what is so obviously there, a reoccurring theme in this archival project.

The scope of my project is a reading of Filipino and Filipino American cultural productions to show the interconnectedness between seemingly disparate narratives. Sifting through the remains of empire requires sifting through both official and unofficial archives, studying memories, oral histories, art, literature, films, websites, and museums that trace the story of U.S. imperialism as it begins in the Philippines. My research wanders through different time periods—the Philippine-American War, the Japanese Occupation, and recent decades dealing with the challenges of globalization and migration—to highlight the effects of and responses to imperial trauma, both at home in the Philippines and in the United States. This meaning of "remains" as artifact toys with Eng's and Kazanjian's evocation of the term "remains" in this essay's epigraph. My project explores the connections between memory, history, narrative, and archive. What gets included and excluded in the official archive? Gregoria's story calls for a different reading of history that stretches the boundaries of the archive. How might an alternative archive contest dominant versions of history? What are the connections between history, institutions of memory such as museums and historical sites, and trauma? My alternate archive of American empire is idiosyncratic and eclectic, shuttling back and forth from official and unofficial remains to reveal the enmeshment of individual, familial, and political histories. Drawing upon official archives such as the United States Military records in the United States National Archive or the Pacific War Museum in Fredericksburg, Texas as well as the tourist museum at Corregidor Island, I juxtapose familial stories and other testimonies with official history to fill in the silences. I look to medieval legend and oral history about the warrior princess Urduja and its reinterpretation in cyberspace and in art. As a *double entendre*, imperial remains highlight the long-lasting impact of American empire in the Philippines while also evoking a disturbing visual—the decomposing bodies of the dead. My project sifts through these archival remains to pause at the richness of this latter image because it is here where we might find fertile ground for springing forth a new story.

But that is only one story that I tell. I began my sojourn as a word weaver, enchanted with words and books to make sense of my world. As a second-generation Filipino American (born of Filipina mother and Caucasian father), I chose English literature, then ethnic/ Third World studies, then Filipino American cultural studies, delving deeper and deeper into academic specialization as if I could conjure up a key to unlock this puzzle in my soul.

FILIPINO STUDIES

My project introduces a history of the United States' occupation in the Philippines with the story of my great-great grandmother because her death highlights the enmeshment of private and public histories, and speaks to the omissions in more official history. My work adds to scholarship in Filipino Studies writing against the grain of mainstream U.S. history, what has been called "imperial amnesia," the forgotten history of the U.S. occupation of the Philippines. I came to Filipino Studies with early graduate training in postcolonial studies, yet the Philippine question presents a special dilemma, a point Oscar Campomanes makes in his 1995 essay "The New Empire's Forgetful and Forgotten Citizens." Describing the conundrum of postcoloniality for the Filipino and Filipino American as "the categorical unrecognizability of U.S. imperialism," he questions, how can the category of postcoloniality apply when U.S. colonial history was barely even recognized or acknowledged in both the Philippines and the United States? (p. 148). In 2002, Angel Velasco Shaw and Luis Francia's anthology *Vestiges of Empire* captures Filipino Studies' debate with mainstream U.S. history: the elision of the Phillippine-American War and aftereffects of that elision. Particularly, this anthology is rife with the politics of forgetting and the impact of the bloody aftermath of the Philippine-American War, what Shaw calls "betrayal narratives" and the urgency to recover a forgotten history (p. x). In the afterword John Kuo Wei Tchen writes that in the wake of this imperial history, we "improvise with whatever is around" to create an alternate archive of empire (Shaw, 2002, p. 439). My intervention traces an affective history that delves into the incomprehensible, and in so doing my work dives into micro-histories, women's voices, stories, fantasy, the supernatural, even fabricated truth—not easily accessible to history. I want to tease out what would not even be recognized by history and show how even in their unrecognizability, these stories are important to reckon with *as* history. Motivated by a similar urgency to recover these forgotten histories, my work enters this discussion about the politics of forgetting, yet as I will explain later, the very violence of this archive—from the most horrific to the banal—requires unorthodox measures to write an alternative history of American empire.

> *I want to tease out what would not even be recognized by history and show how even in their unrecognizability, these stories are important to reckon with as history.*

Adding to this historical revisionist trend in Filipino Studies, this project is a form of archival recovery. I seek to understand why the overarching story of imperialism requires the intervention of other narratives and the rich play that occurs through such archival performance. I am interested in the shifts created from the juxtaposition of disparate cultural productions, how the Filipino response to an archive of violence is what Strobel (2010) calls a kind of "culling" for truth. She writes, "Out of fragments, culled from sources outside of one's own imaginings, borrowings here and there from other people's languages, I attempt to create a narrative consistent with my intuition and experience" (p. 2). Strobel references Vicente Rafael's use of the fishing metaphor—fishing for truth "out of a barrage of unreadable signs"—to describe how Filipinos constructed meaning out of the words of the Spanish priest, spinning "out discrete narratives that bear no relation to the logic and intent of the priest's discourse" (Rafael, 1993, p. 11). I share affinity with Strobel and Rafael as I foreground my role as storyteller in this archival project in culling a montage of stories, a peculiar archive of empire that serves the discerning of the present.

My strategies of storytelling share similarities with Vicente Rafael and others, whose focus on "episodic histories" rather than epic accounts means paying attention to the details that "do not easily fit into a larger whole" (Rafael, 2003, p. 4). Rafael explains that the usefulness of this writing "lies in its ability to attend to the play of contradictions… thereby dwelling on the tenuous, or might we say ironic, constitution of Philippine history" (2003, p. 4). This irony extends to both Philippine and United States' histories, since each share mutually constitutive constructions of nationalism, a point Sharon Delmendo (2004) makes in *The Star Entangled Banner* (p. 20). I am interested in not only how these episodic stories intervene in histories of Filipino and American nationalism, but also articulate a useful "imagined community" for a Filipino diaspora.[3]

And isn't my work as a storyteller a kind of academic version of the shaman? Working at the construction of truth to make meaning for herself, her family, and her community? My academic project sought healing and recovery through the creation of an archive. But where words failed me, I was to find solace in moving energy, assisting family and friends in healing, and communing with the spirits of my ancestors.

A foray into United States-Philippines relations reveals a story of betrayal. In 1896 the Philippines fought for independence from Spain and agreed to an alliance with the United States. The newfound Republic of the Philippines enjoyed a brief victory, only to have its sovereignty seized by the United States, which saw a foothold in the Philippines a strategic advantage to expanding in the Pacific.[4] In the 1898 Treaty of Paris, in an imperial trading with Spain, the United States purchased the Philippines, Puerto Rico, and Cuba for the sum of twenty million dollars. The Filipinos did not submit to American colonial rule without a fight, however, and the Philippine-American War lasted from 1898-1902, although Filipino guerrilla fighters continued to defy the American military for a decade more.

As a former U.S. colony (and, one might argue, a continuing neocolony) the Philippines suffers from a ravaged economy, decimated natural resources, and high rates of unemployment and poverty. The effects of globalization on a Filipino diaspora haunt many scholars today. For example, in *Servants of Globalization* Rhacel Parrenas (2001) examines how Filipina domestic workers negotiate the "dislocations" caused by everyday effects of global restructuring (p. 3). Likewise, Neferti Tadiar (2004) looks at how the dreaming practices of nation-states and transnational capital delimit the exploited Filipina

---

[3] See Benedict Anderson in Imagined Communities.

[4] In her forthcoming book *Colonial Cosmopolitanism: American Empire and Filipino American Identity*, 1898-1946, Kimberly Alidio argues that the United States seized Filipinos' sovereignty through the guise of the Benevolent Assimilation Proclamation informed by "globalized humanism [;] . . . McKinley implicitly stripped Filipinos of political freedom and will" (pp. 1-2).

domestic worker first and foremost "as a corporeal body" (p. 115).[5] My own work further explores the less tangible effects of globalization, what I call an internal dis-ease, lurking in the collective psyche—what might be characterized as an underlying unsettled feeling. In *Vestiges of Empire* Shaw (2002) discusses that what "haunted" her the most about writing this history of empire was "the effects on the psyche, the aftermath of a bloody war," and especially the subtle violence of war" (p. x). And while I cannot speak for Filipino Americans collectively, I witnessed this subtle unsettling in my own life and the lives of my extended family. It might be traced in chronic depression, procrastination, spending excessively, hoarding clutter to fend off the specter of poverty, or even, refinancing the house (and eventual short sale and loss) to stage American success to other relatives. It could be heard in the toxic gossip, or *chismis*, the endless comparing to other Filipino neighbors and relatives. All the time I felt this nagging uneasiness that there lingered below the surface of academic discourse a *something* that history failed to adequately address. While these symptoms may not be exclusive to Filipino Americans and might be seen as symptomatic of U.S. capitalism, I argue that the specific history of Philippine-United States relations nuances these signs differently. Like salt on an old festering wound, a wound so engrained into the skin of everyday living it hardly registers as pain, the volatility of the U.S. economy and current recession causes double injury, a reminder of the broken promises of an American Dream. My project aims to not only trace these differences in this archive, but also render them more legible.

In Filipino Studies the first scholarly work I read addressing this incomprehensible feeling is Leny Strobel's *Coming Full Circle* (2001). Strobel describes the process of decolonization for the younger generation of Filipino Americans as a process of rethinking "colonial mentality," of being conscious of how we are interpellated as consumerists and materialists as the primary signifier of good citizenship in this country, the U.S.A. Her work draws upon the work of Virgilio Enriquez, dubbed as the Father of Filipino psychology. *Sikolohiyang Pilipino* is a theory that features the core values of Filipino personhood such as *kapwa* (shared identity), *loob* (shared humanity), *damdam* (capacity to feel for another), and *paninindigan* (strength of conviction). Rather than use the terms of western psychology to describe Filipino personhood, this indigenous psychology references an indigenously-reconstructed Filipino worldview. By drawing upon Filipino spirituality and psychology concepts to look at key areas where change occurs, Strobel's study examines how Filipino Americans recover from colonial trauma and how healing is possible. Strobel (2001) writes:

> "The process of reclaiming Filipino history as a counter narrative to the history written by outsiders, becomes a process of reclaiming one's memory: memories that were submerged because they were considered

---

[5] Tadiar proposes that fantasy and dreaming practices of nation-states are limited for Third-World subjects. The West controls or owns "the codes of fantasy" and the Philippines as a nation-state internalizes these codes of desires (p. 12).

unimportant, inconsequential, and memories that were negated because of the internalized self-hatred of the colonial psyche" (p. 98).

In other words, Strobel and other scholars in Filipino studies draw upon Freire's concept of "colonial mentality" to name this psychic aftermath of centuries of Spanish and American colonialism.

The story of betrayal does not start with the United States' colonizing the Philippines, but rather begins with Spanish contact five centuries earlier. The Spanish colonized the Philippines after Magellan's encounter with the islands in 1521. He named the islands after King Felipe and initiated the conversion of the inhabitants to Roman Catholicism. Spain used the Catholic Church to wield colonial power. Friars seized land for the church and subjugated the people through Christianity. Jose Rizal's classic novel *Noli Me Tangere* describes the abuses of the Catholic church in the Philippines and the need for political reform. Their indigenous writings, spiritual practice, and relics were all but destroyed, as Carolyn points out in *Holy Confrontations* (2001). Her work studies the Spanish colonial archive to trace the activities of the *babaylans* or indigenous healers who resisted Spanish colonization and preserved their ways of knowledge despite persecution. The Philippines fought for their independence from Spanish rule only to have their newfound freedom interrupted by American rule.

In Filipino American literature Bienvenidos Santos' short story "The Day the Dancers Came" (1967) addresses this theme of alienation as a product of the history of colonialism. Tony suffers from a strange skin disease in which his skin peels off to reveal a layer of white skin underneath. "I am becoming a white man," he laments (p. 114). The skin affliction accompanies the sharp scraping pain in his intestines, and he knows that he is dying. This story describes the loneliness of the Filipino exile in the United States, nostalgia for the homeland, and a longing for inclusion accompanied by exclusion from that desire. My great-great-grandmother Gregoria's story of alienation from her family, community, and self parallels the self-alienation in Santos' story and provides a counter-reading of the long-term effects of American interventionism. Immersing myself in Filipino Studies, I started to connect this unsettled feeling with centuries of Spanish and American colonial history in the Philippines. My project foregrounds the intangible effects of American imperialism, traced in generational memories of Filipinos and Filipino Americans, even long past recognition as authentic Filipino.

IMPERIAL TRAUMA

Trauma studies provided me with a framework to systematically look at the United States' occupation of the Philippines as a traumatic moment, even though this body of work came out of a different historical context—the Holocaust. With words such as "betrayal," "forgetting," "haunting," or "subtle forms of violence," Filipinists invoke the vocabulary of trauma yet do not fully engage with this discourse. Trauma studies provides a

With words such as "betrayal," "forgetting," "haunting," or "subtle forms of violence," Filipinists invoke the vocabulary of trauma yet do not fully engage with this discourse.

vocabulary to understand these private and familial traumas within a larger history of Philippine-United States relations, and even the earlier history of Spanish colonialism.

To illustrate this point, I recount the story my grandfather Amado Lopez tells about his emigration to America and his career as an enlisted man in the U.S. Navy. He came to the United States through joining the U.S. Navy shortly after World War II. With only a fourth-grade education, he struggled to pass the tests requisite for promotion. As a Filipino, he served as a steward, a racialized position designated for African Americans and Filipinos, and worked in the kitchen. His story is intended as a narrative of success, of overcoming the odds and racism to eventually become a Master Chief Petty Officer, the highest rank for an enlisted man, and chef of a mess hall serving ambassadors and admirals. In this putative success story he tells how he dreaded the test. Although he studied, his lack of formal education and lack of confidence in absorbing the material made passing the test an impossible feat. Every time, he chokes up in tears at this point in the narrative. To his grandchildren, the tears are incomprehensible in this normally cheerful man, yet his affect marks a charged history beyond the individual and familial. Even though the rhetoric and structure of his narrative reveals that he subscribes to the myth of the American Dream, his tears tell another story. Beyond words, his affective expression points to a history of U.S. immigration policies, of a war-ravaged country as a result of the U.S. occupation of the Philippines, of poverty that prompted my grandfather to join the U.S. military, and of promised citizenship in exchange for indentured military service. Storytelling along with trauma theory helps elucidate the conundrum of Philippine history in compelling ways. It also honors private, individual memory as part of collective memory, while challenging dominant versions of U.S. history.

Trauma discourse gave me a critical framework to ask questions about something that seemed troubling, just beneath the surface. Certainly, the beginnings of the American occupation in the Philippines constituted a form of trauma: the widespread violence during the Philippine-American War, the betrayal of an American promise including the sexual atrocities committed by American soldiers against Filipino women that I write about in "Resisting the Footnote: During the Philippine-American War" (in Maxwell, 2011, pp. 53-104)[6] Imperial trauma encompasses the material, psychic, and spiritual repercussions

---

[6] For photographs of this violence displaying Filipino dead bodies heaped in trenches see Paul Kramer (2006, April).

on the colonized that might start at the point of colonial contact but extends beyond the life of an empire. In other words, imperial trauma begins with the physical point of contact but may be transmitted generationally, so that it becomes a generational memory, lingering in the subconscious, a kind of energetic ripple in the DNA. Imperial trauma points to a generational pattern, a cluster of beliefs and affects that started at the point of imperial contact but continue to influence, even when the traumatic memory is forgotten. Here, I borrow Ron Eyerman's (2001) definition of cultural trauma as trauma—not necessarily experienced first-hand—that becomes part of collective memory and shapes a communal identity (p. 15). My work focuses on the layered nature of trauma, as a sedimentation of private struggles and public memory, of tangible and intangible effects, woven into transgenerational memories. Even the story of my grandfather's heritage reveals the layered nature of a trauma so banal, it hardly registers as trauma. Whenever I heard the story of my lolo's childhood, his Spanish heritage was always emphasized: his father was a jeweler born in Spain. My *lola* described his tall stature (5' 11"), "not typically Filipino" and "guapo (comely) Spanish looks." Though born of a well-to-do family, he was orphaned at a young age and all the inheritance went to his uncle. While his uncle sent his own children to school in the states, my grandfather and his siblings were beaten and treated as servants, yet my grandfather never harbored any bitterness towards his uncle or about the neglect he received as a child. At his eulogy I described his generosity and service to others in Christian terms—he was the most saintly person I knew. My *lolo* turned over his monthly military pension to my grandmother, but reserved his entire social security check for giving—to relatives or strangers in need. A typical visit from *lolo* meant he spent the day scrubbing the kitchen clean or polishing my car. But it wasn't until reading Katrin de Guia's *Kapwa: the Self in the Other* (2005) that I recognized the admirable qualities my grandfather possessed as part of his Filipino heritage. De Guia describes the "Filipino culture-bearer," as "the contemporary mythic man" who "draws from the heart-blood of surviving ancestral traditions." (pp. 10-11). According to de Guia, Filipino culture bearers cultivate "an air of openness," "build instant friendships," and share their lives and possessions freely (p. 11). The story of my grandfather's childhood reveals the violence of alienation from his Filipino heritage while idolizing his Spanish heritage. Even his good qualities were not identified as Filipino, but rather, Christian. Imperial trauma covers the more "diffuse" kinds of trauma, beginning

Imperial trauma points to a generational pattern, a cluster of beliefs and affects that started at the point of imperial contact but continue to influence, even when the traumatic memory is forgotten.

with national trauma, war trauma, and more public kinds of trauma, but also the private traumas in the intimate spaces of our hearts, our kitchens and beds, and our minds. Imperial trauma insists on acknowledging the violence of imperial contact, often physical, even sexual, as I discuss in my work on rape during the Philippine-American War, but then covers less easily categorized forms of violence.

As I write this academic prose, I feel bound by the limitations of language to convey my truth. What started out as a scholarly obsession with imperial trauma—the long-lasting impact of the United States' occupation of the Philippines and its resonance today—metamorphosed into a calling as an energy worker as I learned that many limiting beliefs and affects can simply be cleared from the subconscious.

CULTURAL MEMORY AND MELANCHOLIA

As a kind of placeholder, imperial trauma describes a pattern of storytelling about Filipino and Filipino American experience, yet my focus is on its underlying "constellation of affects," fuelled by imperial melancholia (Kazanjian, 2003). My concept of imperial melancholia is drawn from David Eng and Shinhee Han's (2000) theory of racial melancholia. In "A Dialogue on Racial Melancholia" David Eng and Shinhee Han interpreted the phenomenon of depression in Asian American college students, not as a cultural, but rather as a political issue. In other words, Eng and Han report that these students experienced not simply clinical depression, but racial melancholia, a fractured psyche from failing to be fully assimilated into "regimes of whiteness" (p. 350). Racial melancholia is a permanent longing for the lost object of assimilation. This essay shows how melancholia is the longing for the unattainable, i.e., whiteness, which signifies assimilation. As a result of this longing, there exists for this marginalized ethnic group "a type of national melancholia, a national haunting, with negative social effects" (p. 347). Also writing about racial melancholia, Anne Cheng (2001) describes how "narratives of joy and sorrow encode the yearning and mourning associated with histories of dispersal and the remembrance of unspoken losses" (p. 23).

Imperial melancholia best captures the Filipino/American experience as a kind of racial melancholia haunted by histories of Spanish and American imperialism. In other words, imperial melancholia does not begin with the story of immigration to the United States, but "back home" in the Philippines with nostalgia for America—even before setting foot in America. In *America is in the Heart* Carlos Bulosan (1943) describes a similar betrayal when he discovered his childhood adoration for the United States and American culture to be blatantly one-sided when he finally arrived in the United States. His fantasy of the U.S. was blighted when he realized how little his race was regarded here. "The mockery of it all is that Filipinos are taught to regard Americans as our equals. . . . The terrible truth in America shatters the Filipinos' dream of fraternity (p. xiii).

In the Philippine context imperial melancholia starts much earlier than American contact, but encompasses centuries of colonial history and longing for a lost past. Imperial melancholia is illustrated in Bienvenidos Santos' (1979) story about the protagonist Tony's physical disease of whiteness when he claims "I am dying inside," suggesting a bodily manifestation of a psychic injury. His psychic injury is the internal manifestation of material conditions—the Filipino immigrant's systematic exclusion from achieving success, as defined by the myth of the American dream. Similarly, the anecdote of my grandfather illustrates imperial melancholia and the inadequacy of psychoanalysis to account for his tears. My reading of my grandfather's tears recalls Eng and Han's work, their refusal to read the depression experienced by Asian American college students as individual pathology but rather as a "depathologized structure of feeling" (p. 344).

Imperial melancholia fuels this project and search for lost histories, alternative histories, forgotten histories, and even fabricated histories. A chapter in my dissertation (Maxwell, 2011), for example, discusses contested figures such as the warrior princess Urduja that marks a place in Philippine medieval history. But although I excavate traditional archival remains, such as museum artifacts and military records, these are simply touchstones for the more elusive, intangible remains that make up my archive: affective remains that span generations and continue to define the present.

As Cheng (2001) points out, "If we are willing to listen, the history of disarticulated grief is still speaking through the living…" (p. 29) Affective remains help us to understand how intergenerational memory works. Sometimes, a memory is just a story passed down from one generation to the next, much like the story of my great-great grandmother's suicide. But other times, there is simply a feeling, belief, or energetic imprint, shared across generations, even when the actual memory is negligible. An example of this intergenerational memory is explained in my work on war atrocities committed during the Philippine-American War, a "memory" of sexual trauma and feeling of outrage passed on generationally, even when there is no story about the atrocity or memory shared (cf. "Resisting the Footnote" in Maxwell, 2011, p. 55).

I never understood this impulse under my skin. These rape stories stirred me, just as the image of the violated girl from Joseph Lacaba's poem haunted me—her figure signaling an unspoken memory in the Filipino imaginary. I knew this story needed to be told. Some people wonder, was I a victim of rape? As a teenager and young adult, I spent hours in front of psychiatrists, therapists, and counselors who all insisted: you have the classic symptoms of a sexual abuse victim. As much as I strained memory, I could never cough up an incident that amounted to sexual abuse, beyond the stepfather who tried to crawl into my bed when my mother worked nightshift as a nurse; after his fumbled attempt, my grandfather promptly changed the locks to my bedroom door. It was not until I started digging into rape stories in the military records housed in the United States National Archive that my grandmother revealed the story about her own mother Conscorcia's rape. It helped me understand a maternal pattern of withholding love. Did the memory of this violation surge through my veins, written on my mestiza body, expressed in my own shame of never enough? But now, awareness deepens. As a decolonizing Filipina, I read centuries of colonialism and pre-colonialism etched in my DNA.[7] I start to piece this postcolonial puzzle together.

Recently, a ghost visited me. It happens more often, as I have come to understand my babaylan roots and realized my own gifts as an energy healer. I saw a shadow hovering in the stairwell in my home, after the children had fallen asleep. She was fourteen-years-old, a Delgado, perhaps a sister of my grandfather's grandmother Isabel. I never knew much about my grandfather's side of the family since he was orphaned at a young age. She would have been a teenager during the Philippine-American War; I calculated. She beckoned me with a message. I felt the urgency of an outrage that happened during the war, of something to clear from my generational line. I suddenly realized that this project had greater implications than I understood, this reckoning with the dead. My recovery of this generational memory, recalls a passage in Ninothka Rosca's State of War (1988) *when on the eve before her wedding, Maya lays with her mother. Her mother's touch transmits the outrage of her deceased grandmother: "Through her mother's flesh, she had met her own grandmother who was still raving against what the Spaniards had done…" [how] "the Spaniards infected them with shame and made them hide their strength beneath layers of petticoats…" (pp. 191-192). This fleeting visitation left me with tears in my eyes as I recognized there were unseen forces, my own ancestors, urging and guiding me in my academic work. I was brushing up against more than some old documents in the United States National Archive.*

And while spirits don't usually appear in western scholarly writing, except as abstract theoretical figures, my haunting experience gestures to the intergenerational memories running through the threads of this chapter and dissertation and through Filipino cultural memory, sometimes as negative imprints that need to be cleared.[8] These Filipinas' stories in my work on sexual atrocities during the Philippine-American War are our stories, even if these women are not our direct ancestors. Their memories are our memories. It wasn't until this ghostly encounter that I recognized the spiritual urgency to reckon with this history as what drives my work on sexual trauma on the Philippine-American War.

---

[7] For a moving analysis of this process of decolonization, read Leny Strobel's *Coming Full Circle: The Process of Decolonization among Post-1965 Filipino Americans* (2001).

[8] In *Ghostly Matters* Avery Gordon (2008) writes that when the "critical vocabularies" failed her, she looked to "ghostly matters" to understand "how social institutions and people are haunted." She writes, "The ghost or the apparition is one form by which something lost, or barely visible, or seemingly not there to our supposedly well-trained eyes, makes itself known or apparent to us...The way of the ghost is haunting, and haunting is a very particular way of knowing what has happened or is happening" (p. 8).

A Babaylan Journey

As often happens with academic work, my intellectual life and personal life are deeply enmeshed. Through the process of raising three children, moving repeatedly for my spouse's job, and writing a dissertation away from the university, I was stuck in liminal space, a kind of dissertation limbo. Desperate, I put aside my skepticism and distaste of "New Age" remedies and accepted a friend's offer "to clear the blocks" getting in the way of my finishing. After experiencing a radical shift, I wanted to learn more about energy healing. Serendipitously, my academic research had already introduced me to an ancient tradition of energy healing in the Philippines as I studied the *babaylan*, an indigenous healing tradition that predated Spanish contact. Here, I found an online community of Filipina women who recuperated the *babaylan* figure in their own lives as cultural healers. Originally, my affinity with the *babaylan* was simply intellectual—with the *babaylan* construction serving as a useful shibboleth for Filipina feminists across the diaspora. But as I studied energy medicine, I grew to understand a different kind of knowing, already familiar to the *babaylans* and the indigenous worldview, but held hostage to those afflicted with modernity consciousness. A personal crisis helped my heart to connect with the *babaylan* figure. In the introduction to the *Babaylan* anthology Strobel (2010) writes about this otherly knowledge found in *babaylan*-inspired work that holds the potential for healing (p. 6). What started out in my research as a focus on imperial trauma and the long-term effects of American imperialism metamorphosed to an interest in the *babaylan* movement as a powerful paradigm for change.

In my family, suicide looms as a generational pattern, a kind of option or fantasy when the going gets tough. As I child, I often heard my mother threaten to kill herself "if it wasn't for you kids." I spent my teens and twenties flirting with death, repeated suicide attempts and hospitalizations until one stint landed me in the ICU with only fifty percent chance of living. My near success frightened me, but that never stopped me from entertaining such dark thoughts. More recently, my 5-year-old daughter invokes the melodramatic threat of ending her life when displeased with parental decisions, and my heart panics, wondering whether this outburst is normal or a perpetuation of a family curse.

Not too long ago, I dedicated an energy healing session to my mother in California. She was afflicted with the dark thoughts of depression and half-heartedly wished her own death. I knew she had some energetic blocks that needed clearing. I use intuition and muscle-testing to "feel into" where I should go in an energy session. When working with a client, I connect with his or her spirit and always ask permission to facilitate this work. As I located the heavy energy and cleared it, I encountered a deeper block, an ancestral pattern that had been passed down, something that would not so easily clear. I felt the presence of an ancestor in the room, a female spirit on the maternal side of her family line. This spirit wanted to release the negative energy surrounding a death. At first, I didn't recognize who this spirit was or understand what she wanted released. I thought perhaps the spirit still grieved a loss when she had been alive. Yet

This story of American empire… is a history that requires unorthodox measures to calculate, by looking in the gaps and silences, the cracks and fissures of official history.

my puzzlement turned to tears when I realized this was Gregoria, my mother's grandmother, and the death she was grieving, her own abrupt ending of her life. Tears welled up, as I understood this affinity for death—a tendency that seemed to run in my family—as a generational pattern, and one that could be released. I acknowledged Gregoria's presence and felt a burden lift as I cleared this block. My mother's energy was also now clearer than before. In a few energy sessions the psychic bondage of "suicidal tendencies" has been released in our family—what years of traditional talk-therapy could never really cure.

ALTERNATIVE HISTORIES AND THE ARCHIVE

This story of American empire begins "over there," shuttling across oceans and time, through generations, and dispersed in memories. It is a history that requires unorthodox measures to calculate, by looking in the gaps and silences, the cracks and fissures of official history. It requires an unusual archive, not just collecting but also interpreting, and requiring unorthodox means, such as visiting cyberspace, recalling strained memory, revisiting official archives, or even acknowledging spirits to capture this troubling under the skin of Filipino memory. Tchen (2002) calls for the need for "secret archives," what he describes as a "process of opening spaces for the voicing of the kinds of secreted experiences" (p. 440). My compass was merely a feeling—what might miss the standard of empirical methods—that something is not quite right. For example, even though there was this unpopular memory of rape during the Philippine-American War, where was this story represented in Philippine literature? Why are Filipino war veterans marginalized at museums memorializing veteran sacrifices during World War II in both Texas and Corregidor? What was the pull of a legendary warrior princess Urduja standing in for Philippines' medieval history in my memory?[9] How do we make the illegible, the invisible, the spiritual and psychic effects of trauma legible and visible? Aiming to make these stories explicit, my archival work is an affective history of American empire. Tchen (2002) argues that "[a]rchives-building embodies a people's reflexive self-creation" (p. 439). My work, in this sense, adds to a body of work in Filipino Studies emerging from what Freire (1970) calls a "culture of silence." Strobel (2001) points out the need for a re-telling

---

[9] I identify stories about warrior princess Urduja in medieval legend and Pangasinan oral history and in cyberspace and art to consider how Filipinos employ her memory to address the legacy of imperial trauma in "Urduja Through the Looking Glass" (pp. 158-219).

of stories: "The re-telling is, therefore, a process of imagining and creating a new story, a useful fiction, so to speak, in order for the story to become a source of empowerment through a new way of looking at history" (p. 69). An affective history is unruly and messy, not easy to tame, categorize or define. To paraphrase Saidiya Hartman's (1997) words, it is a history "predicated on impossibility" (p. 2). It requires paying attention to signs that would be easily dismissed by conventional methods, to feelings that might be considered impolite, inconvenient, or unimportant. My project begins with the difficult remembering of sexual atrocities committed by American soldiers during the Philippine-American War, but ends on a celebratory note examining the *babaylan*-figure as cultural healer and spiritual practice as a way to bridge difference, create community, and effect change.

There was a time when I used to think language about effecting change was just hopeful rhetoric. It sounded good, but I only half-believed it. What I have come to know through energy healing is the power of words, language, and stories to shift energy, and literally, to shift reality. We are only the stories that we tell…The memories that we hold on to… so why not choose empowering stories? It is not so much what happens to us that matters, but the stories we tell about what happened… and the actions that spring forth from our thoughts….

I started this journey as a scholar and a critic, but my understanding of energy healing has shifted the questions I will ask and the words that I will ponder. It may be too soon, but I imagine a time when imperial trauma or decolonization no longer has the power to evoke pain and struggle. It will no longer be forgotten history, but akin to recalling old grief turned to forgiven remembering and ironic gratitude. Strobel (2010) writes about what we can learn from the indigenous worldview. There are rumors, of course not academically verifiable, that we are shifting to the Intuition Age, and leaving behind the age of capitalism and industrialization, ruled by masculinist thinking.

Is it naïve to talk about energy healing or to evoke the babaylan figure in my academic work? By including the backstory to my academic work, I risk a kind of schizophrenic prose, but I juxtapose the footnotes of an energy healer to my work to foreground the possibilities of real change. The story of my great-great grandmother Gregoria comes full circle as she assists me in healing our family line. I felt her anguish, the salty bitterness of her regret, but now, after proper mourning, we bury the past.

> *The story of my great-great grandmother Gregoria comes full circle as she assists me in healing our family line. I felt her anguish, the salty bitterness of her regret, but now, after proper mourning, we bury the past.*

References

Alidio, K. (Forthcoming). *Colonial cosmopolitanism: American empire and Filipino American identity, 1898-1946.* University of Chicago Press.

Anderson, W. (2006). States of hygiene: Race "improvement" and biomedical citizenship in Australia and the colonial Philippines. In A. L. Stoler (Ed.), *Haunted by empire,* 94-115. Durham: Duke University Press.

Brewer, C. (2001). *Holy confrontation: Religion, gender, and sexuality in the Philippines, 1521-1685* (1st ed.). Manila: C. Brewer and the Institute of Women's Studies, St. Scholastica's College.

Bulosan, C. (1943). *America is in the heart.* Seattle: University of Washington Press.

Cheng, A. A. (2001). *The melancholy of race: Psychoanalysis, assimilation, and hidden grief.* NY: Oxford University Press.

De Guia, K. (2005). *Kapwa: the self in the other: Worldviews and lifestyles of Filipino culture-bearers.* Pasig City: Anvil Publishers.

Delmendo, S. (2004). *The star-entangled banner: One hundred years of America in the Philippines.* New Brunswick: Rutgers University Press.

Eng, D. & Han, S. (2003). A dialogue on racial melancholia. In D. Eng & D. Kazanjian (Eds.), *Loss: the politics of mourning* (pp. 343-371). Berkeley: University of California Press.

Eng, D. & Kazanjian, D. (2003). Introduction: Mourning remains. In D. Eng and D. Kazanjian (Eds.), *Loss: the politics of mourning* (pp. 1-25). Berkeley: University of California Press.

Eyerman, R. (2001). *Cultural trauma: Slavery and the formation of African American identity.* Cambridge: Cambridge University Press.

Freire, P. (1970). *Pedagogy of the oppressed.* New York: Herder and Herder.

Gordon, A. (2008). *Ghostly matters: Haunting and the sociological imagination.* Minneapolis, MN: University of Minnesota Press.

Hartman, S. (1997). *Lose your mother: A journey along the Atlantic slave route.* Farrar, Straus, and Giroux.

Hartman, S. (2008, June). Venus in two acts. *Small Axe, 12*(2), 1-14.

Kramer, P. (2006, April). Race-making and colonial violence in the U.S. Empire: the Philippine-American War as race war. *Diplomatic History, 30*(2), 191.

Milan, K. (1980). Afterword: A Talk with the author by Philip Roth. In *The book of laughter andfForgetting* (Michael Henry Heim, Trans.). New York: Penguin.

Maxwell, T. (2011). *Imperial remains: Memories of the United States' occupation in the Philippines.* (Dissertation). University of Texas at Austin.

Parrenas, R. S. (2001). *Servants of globalization: Women, migration, and domestic work.* Stanford: Stanford University Press.

Rafael, V. (1993). *Contracting colonialism.* Durham: Duke University Press.

Rafael, V. (2000). *White love and other events in Filipino history.* Durham: Duke University Press.

Rosca, Ninotchka. (1988). *State of war.* New York: Simon and Schuster.

Santos, Bienvenidos. (1979). *Scent of apples: a collection of stories.* Seattle: University of Washington Press.

Shaw, A. V., & Francia, L. H. (Eds.). (2002). *Vestiges of empire: the Philippine-American War and the aftermath of an imperial dream 1899-1999.* New York: New York University Press.

Stoler, A. L. (Ed.). (2006). *Haunted by empire: geographies of intimacy in North American history.* Durham: Duke University Press.

Strobel, L. M. (2001). *Coming full circle: The process of decolonization among post-1965 Filipino Americans.* Quezon City, Philippines: Giraffe Books.

Strobel, L. M. (Ed.). (2010). *Babaylan: Filipinos and the call of the indigenous.* Davao City: Ateneo de Davao University Research and Publication Office.

Tadiar, N. X. M. (2004). *Fantasy-production: sexual economies and other Philippine consequences for the New World order.* Hong Kong: Hong Kong UP.

Tchen, J. K. W. (2002). Afterword: The secret archives. In A. V. Shaw & L. H. Francia (Eds.), *Vestiges of empire: The Philippine-American War and the aftermath of an imperial dream 1899-1999,* 437-441. New York: New York University Press.

B(e)aring the Babaylan
Body Memory, Colonial Wounding, and Return to Indigenous Wildness

S. Lily Mendoza

This essay tracks my personal journey out of colonial subjection into the healing wholeness of *kapwa* (shared being) and an indigenous sense of being in the world. Where my religious socialization insisted on a denial of the body and the primacy of abstract thought, asceticism, and the disciplining of the flesh, my way through has been via the struggle to recover the sensuous wildness of indigenous being, to embrace the sacred wounding of intimate betrayal, and to rebuild sustainable forms of community. The Filipino *babaylan*, as her archetype in other cultures also suggests, is a Wounded Healer—a mystical figure resonant in my own autobiography. However, mine is still a story in search of the full circle: a calling-in-the-making whose contours and rough outlines I can only grope for vaguely through the cacophonous soundings of insistent questionings having to do with place, giftings, and ecology. Although I often hurry to go beyond the questions to the eureka of definitive answers, it seems that for now the waiting itself is the needed pedagogy. The beginning connections of my own personal story to the Larger Story that is longing to be born and to be woven collectively by us, inheritors of ancient Filipino memory and history, structures this autobiographical narration.

The writing of this essay is tinged with irony on many levels. For one, I do not claim to have intimate knowledge of the indigenous healing tradition exemplified in the figure of the *babaylan* found in many Filipino pre-colonial ethnic communities. That's because like perhaps most modern Filipinos, that tradition has not been part of my spiritual and cultural upbringing; neither has it been specifically a focus in my scholarly study. For

243

another, although my own initiation back to our indigenous culture is powerfully rooted in a first-hand encounter with the artistic creations of Filipino indigenous communities, I find that in seeking to make sense of my homeward itinerary, I tend to draw liberally from various sources and cultural traditions (including those not necessarily Filipino). Most importantly, the writing of this paper comes at a time of a great fallow in my life, of what seems like an interminable impasse—one where the gods appear to have stopped speaking and my own deep desire, romance, and passion, are nowhere to be found. And so, I, too, have come to the gathering of the First Babaylan International Conference (for which this essay was originally written) in need of inspiration and re-energizing, hoping that through the mutual sharing of our stories, I/we may find the thread that connects and thus find a way back to the healing nurture of *kapwa* and community. Who knows, perhaps in the very act of putting pen to paper (or rather, fingers to keyboard), the gods may take pity and start speaking again. As one writer notes,

> The Gods love our poetry, our offering shrines, our beautiful clothing, the complex chirping banter of our village streets, and especially the expansive combination of all our abilities into ritual offerings and ceremonies. The Gods perceive[] us as delicious fruit. They love[] our excesses as long as they [are] beautiful and the Gods got to eat a lot of them. (Prechtel, 1998, p. 200)

EXCESSES

What is this quality of too-muchness, of excess, that the Tzutujil Mayan-trained indigenous writer Martin Prechtel notes the Gods love to be fed with as long as it is beautiful? An anthropologist once remarked that when you ask native peoples a question, chances are, you get a story in reply. It is in keeping with this native tradition that I'd like to respond with a story.

The time was the early 1980s. I still remember the taunt of a renowned anthropology professor and number one purveyor, as he was sometimes charged, of Filipino "cultural chauvinism," as he bumped into me on my way to my bible study cohort at the Philippine Center for Advanced Studies at the University of the Philippines, "My god doesn't look like a missionary today!" There I was in my little spaghetti strap dress, three-inch heel strappy sandals showing off bright red pedicure with matching long painted nails, and my big hair in wild lioness curls framing my exquisitely made up face, bright red lipstick and mascara. I was what they called a technical assistant/writer/researcher at the center's Division of Advanced Projects, but given where much of my energy went, that official job only played second fiddle to my real love—what I considered my vocation of "discipling the intelligentsia for Christ." Indeed, for more than a decade and a half, I was "Mother Lily" to a brood of brilliant doctoral students and upcoming scholars at the Center that

I'd recruited to Christian discipleship. The group included: one who would become the first Filipina medical anthropologist, a sociologist, an Asian Studies scholar, an Islamic Studies specialist, a literary writer, a doctoral student in Philippine public administration, two political science and international studies scholars (who ended up taking diplomatic posts in different countries) and two big, burly brothers, now both having passed on to the next life, one of whom served as a high-ranking administrator in one of the universities in Mindanao, and the other, a beloved community leader in his home province in Isabela in Northeastern Luzon. (The moniker "Mother Lily" was a pun on the figure of Mother Lily Monteverde, prominent Filipino film producer with a knack for discovering and developing young, attractive talent, particularly female, in the movie industry.) I was a cloak-and-dagger missionary to the intelligentsia, my greatest adventure being that of combining intellectual savvy with a particular interpretation of scripture, informed by what I now recognize as only a lighter version of right-wing Christian evangelicalism—a religious ideology that has been so devastating to the culture in the United States and elsewhere. Indeed I saw it my mission to make sure no one fell into perdition but that all would be "saved" through faithful gospel preaching and observance of the holy teachings.

My early spiritual shaping took the form of Sunday school lessons supplemented by my family's close relationship with the American Protestant missionaries who came to serve in the local Methodist church where our family regularly attended. When I think of how unusual it was then to be a Protestant in a predominantly Catholic society, I took pride in noting that my Catholic peers' haphazard catechism was no match for the rigor with which we learned biblical hermeneutics and committed scripture to memory. Funny how to this day, I can recite 1Peter 3:3-6 that says, "Let not yours be the outward adorning with braiding of hair, decoration of gold, and wearing of fine clothing, but let it be the hidden person of the heart with the imperishable jewel of a gentle and quiet spirit, which in God's sight is very precious." I swear "the hidden person of the heart with the imperishable jewel of a gentle and quiet spirit" was certainly there, but alas, try as I might, there was no way I could give up my love for bodily adornment, loud scandalous colors, outrageous fashion, and, oh, did I mention funky footwear? Indeed, to this day, to my own embarrassment, whenever I see photographs of fleeing refugees, the first thing I notice is not their misery or endangerment but their gorgeous hand-woven clothing with all the exotic prints and exquisite colors! Needless to say, my "disobedience" in the bodily department became a nagging source of guilt, a sin calling for repentance, a reproach for being less than modest and austere. My dutiful conscience would constantly accuse me of not walking the talk, but the body seemed to have a mind of its own.

Little did I know that, in fact, my body's rebellion was to be my salvation. A decade or so later, following the trauma of the breakup of my first marriage and identifying with the archetypal figure of Psyche in Jean Houston's *Search for the Beloved: Journey into Sacred Psychology* (1987), I wrote in my journal: "I am Psyche with a quality of "too-muchness"— too much energy, enthusiasm, beauty and joy, 'accused of excessive intelligence or

245

Now looking back, I see that the "excess" that refuses to conform, to be disciplined into submission... is the quality of the natural, undomesticated self, unencumbered by impositions of authority from without, the only authority it knows being that of its own inner guidance forged in relationship to a particular community and ecology.

sensitivity, of too much insight, strength or even grief.' Alas, I have accommodated to the shrunken reality of my world by shrinking."

Such excess, which I have not always appreciated, but oftentimes felt a burden, Prechtel (1988) notes, is in fact "food for the gods" (p. 200). Now looking back, I see that the "excess" that refuses to conform, to be disciplined into submission, in my own experience, is the quality of the natural, undomesticated self, unencumbered by impositions of authority from without, the only authority it knows being that of its own inner guidance forged in relationship to a particular community and ecology. In the words of a Huron Indian, "We are born free…. I am the master of my body, I dispose of myself, I do what I wish, I am the first and the last of my Nation…subject only to the great Spirit" (Brandon in Weatherford, 1988, p. 123). It is no wonder that the over-civilized European explorers, upon recovering from their initial amazement at the guilelessness and almost Edenic quality of life among the native peoples they encountered in the New World and elsewhere, in their next breath, condemn such practice of radical freedom among the indigenous peoples as little more than "promiscuity," "indulgence," a givenness to profligacy and undisciplined passions, especially among the women. Needless to say, the result of such valuing of freedom among native peoples was the wild proliferation of forms and norms, of ways of human *being*, so much so that there was not one dominating standard of beauty (thin, anorexic), one measure of success (wealth accumulation, upward mobility), one "correct" belief (Christian), one form of civic virtue (individualism), one legitimate mode of survival (industrial culture), etc. Just like the wild proliferation of forms, colors, and ways of being in the natural world, for much of the history of human existence on the planet, the defining characteristic of cultures was plenitude and diversity—not imposed uniformity. It is this quality of freedom, the spontaneous, the uncalculated affect, and the joyfulness and generosity of spirit that was lost in the widespread colonization of peoples during the so-called Age of Exploration. Today, it continues to be lost in the institutionalization of hierarchy, elitism, Western monoculture, and the now globalized ideology of consumer citizenship. In the words of Prechtel (1998), one more time speaking of the experience of the indigenous Mayan peoples he became a part of, "It was nature, wildness, this undomesticated spirit that fled when it got enslaved, insulted, maimed, beaten, or scared off" (p. 164) and it is this trespass on one's personal nature or soul that Mayan shamans considered the prime source of illness for humans.

What was to be my own way out of colonial malaise and entry into what I would call the journey "home"? The catalyst for me was a graduate course in the Humanities taught by ethnomusicology professor Felipe de Leon Jr. at the University of the Philippines, titled, "The Image of the Filipino in the Arts." Here, I learned for the first time about the cultures of our indigenous communities least penetrated by colonialism's reach as these were expressed in their various arts and other cultural creations. As I wrote in my journal of that moment:

> Suddenly, something very powerful ignited in the depths of my being. For the first time—there, in the intricate weaving designs, complex polyrhythms, mellifluous singing, graceful dancing, and richly-textured sculpture and untamed artistic sensibilities of the indigenous communities that Prof. Jun de Leon regaled us with—I gained a recognition of a self separate from the self that was always wanting to be other than itself, like a self recognizing itself for the first time, or like looking into a mirror and finding not a degraded creature staring back but someone human. (Journal entry, September 26, 1986.)

Even before my mind could make sense of that fateful moment, it was as if my body knew; it knew this was an encounter with primordial energy as embodied in those works of art, calling for the release of the same in me. My journal entry continued:

> I was like a fool, bawling my heart out as I walked out of every class session, not knowing what it was that hit me from all the innocent aesthetic descriptions of the indigenous communities' art forms and what they expressed in terms of a different way of being. Now I know that that different way of being was the way of being I had always instinctively shared but had repressed; hence, the intense internal contradiction. For the first time, here was an entire people I felt I could belong to and identify with, a legitimate human community not necessarily degraded because different from the invisible white colonial norm.

It would take a few more years before I would theorize the full import of that fateful encounter, but the psychic healing that began in that moment was all the more remarkable given that it was something I've never fully experienced previously despite the Christian teaching of God's unconditional love. And maybe that's because, as the Brazilian educator Paolo Freire once noted in an interview, when all the authoritative representations around

[W]hen all the authoritative representations around you have nothing to do with your own reality, it is like looking into the mirror and finding no one there. This, in a lot of ways, is what colonial education has meant in my experience—an exercise in self-alienation, marginalization, and self-sabotage.

you have nothing to do with your own reality, it is like looking into the mirror and finding no one there. This, in a lot of ways, is what colonial education has meant in my experience—an exercise in self-alienation, marginalization, and self-sabotage.

I would learn later that the psychic power of my encounter with the vibrant arts of our indigenous communities actually had deep roots in a given culture's energetic economy. As anthropologist Michael Taussig (referencing Goethe) notes in his book, *What Color is the Sacred?* (2003):

> "Men [and I would add, women] in a state of nature," wrote Goethe in his book on color, "uncivilized nations and children, have a great fondness for colours in their utmost brightness." The same applied to "uneducated people" and southern Europeans, especially the women with their bright-colored bodices and ribbons…." On the other hand, in northern Europe at the time in which [Goethe] wrote in the nineteenth century, people of refinement had a disinclination to colors, women wearing white, the men, black. And not only in dress. When it came to what he called "pathological colours," Goethe wrote that people of refinement avoid vivid colors in the objects around them and seem inclined to banish vivid colors from their presence altogether. (p. 3).

Taussig likens the encounter between the two to an uneasy encounter between two presences:

> It is as if there are two presences glowering at each other, shifting uncomfortably from one foot to the other. It is as much a body thing, a presence thing…. One "presence" is people of refinement. The other is vivid color. (p. 3)

I still recall that when I was newly arrived in the U.S., I scandalized one of my sisters with my penchant for bright red lipstick and loud screaming colors, at one point, being cruelly teased by her as we headed out to a mall, "I don't know you. You look like a leprechaun." Later, she would hand me a light colored lipstick, "Here," she said, "Use this instead." But today, what began as the occasional breakthrough of the spontaneous self out of its imprisonment in a colonial idiom through guilty bodily transgressions, has become a wholehearted embrace of the re-membered self, a full-fledged permission of the body to be, and one whose ritual honoring, in no small measure, serves as a lifeline to our ancestors' differing subjectivity and memory even while in exile.

WOUNDINGS

Prechtel (1998) puzzles:

> I don't know why people in modern life want to be shamans. There's nothing romantic about it. We just go around capturing monsters, re-sweetening the earth, and making people's memories taste good again. (p. 232)

What he doesn't mention is the obligatory initiation required of those called to the shamanic vocation that would give pause to any enthusiastic aspirant. For to be called to a healing vocation is to undergo woundedness, to be willing to suffer some form of death or even a physical near-death experience—to cross over, as it were, to the other world, and to come back in a miraculous resurrection in the aftermath. While I, by no means, lay claim to any such calling, there is a sense in which one may speak of all woundings as having potential toward sacrality. Indeed there is no transformation and rebirth without death. In Jean Houston's (1987) words, "Wounding involves a painful excursion into pathos, wherein the anguish is enormous and the suffering cracks the boundaries of what you thought you could bear. And yet, the wounding pathos of your own local story may contain the seeds of healing and transformation" (p. 105).

It had been the end of an eight-year long adventure battling crack addiction in my ex-husband. He had been a wonderful, bright, and warm-hearted person that I fell in love with precisely because of his childlikeness and free spirit, a quality I hungered for in myself in those days. Alas, it was that same spirit that I had also

While I, by no means, lay claim to any such [babaylan] calling, there is a sense in which one may speak of all woundings as having potential toward sacrality.

249

unwittingly sought to quash and utterly destroy by my insistence that he fit into a certain mold that in my mind defined a "mature" Christian man. Along with my discovering that he suffered from what they now call in medical parlance as the ACOA syndrome (Adult Child of an Alcoholic parent), when he confessed that he had gotten addicted to crack while I was away on a month-long vacation in the U.S. during the second year of our marriage, my gut instinct told me there was something significant that I was meant to learn from this terrible affliction that had befallen us. Although he was prepared then for me to leave him—what with his occasional smoking enough to launch me on a tirade regarding his "lack of discipline and self-control"—I told him, "No, I will not leave you, we will fight this together." So years of going in and out of detoxification programs, seeking prayer and the laying on of hands in charismatic healing circles, meetings with Narcotics Anon, and reading up on the literature on ACOA, taught me the precious lesson of loving unconditionally and of letting go of all judgment and control, at the same time that I was compelled to acknowledge the futility or limits of the human will.

But adventures grow old and die. When, by the end of eight years of battling addiction and lessons in loving, he still mysteriously wouldn't hit rock bottom and recover for good, I started to get bored. He wasn't getting any worse, but neither was he getting any better, and that plateau, that lack of movement, dissipated all energy from the adventure. On the work front, I had also hit a wall in my professional career where I found burdensome and oppressive my involvement in various projects I really didn't much care for but had no way of extricating myself from. Most significantly, it was also around this time that my reading up on the subject of mysticism, in preparation for possible graduate studies in intercultural communication, began to undermine the foundations of my Christian faith through its questioning of the primacy of reason and rationality in determining Truth (with a capital "T"). This latter unraveling proved to be most devastating, given that up until then my faith (held onto with not a small degree of literalism) had been my ultimate raison d'etre. With this latest disillusionment, I fell into a deep, dark depression and came close to nihilism. I don't recall now which came first—the actual ending of my life's big romances—my marriage, my career, and most of all, my faith—or the body preempting such demise by performing death in the face of the emerging emptiness. All I recall was that I fell ill, subjected to a series of three major surgeries in the span of five months, having five and a half feet of my small intestines cut off, and even then, lay there dying on my hospital bed with tubes going every which way and my digestive system refusing to function. During my month-and-a half stay in the hospital after the very last surgery, the only indication of any remaining will to live was…my appetite for food! About the only thing that gave my attending physicians a glimmer of hope was when I'd perk up at the delicious smell of chicken barbeque with java rice and *achara,* that tangy sweet-sour of pickled papaya, that one of my best friends would pick up from the nearby *Aristocrat* restaurant and take to my *Ma* and *Tang* who faithfully watched over me in those days in the hospital.

My mysterious recovery and pulling back from the brink can be the subject of a whole other story, but recover I did, miraculously. I remember reading in Fritjof Capra's *Uncommon Wisdom: Conversations with Remarkable People* (1988) that illnesses are our body's problem-solving mechanism. And indeed, my brush with death (which actually became a celebrated medical case that led to a convening of physician specialists at the medical teaching school of the country's premier university led by the chancellor, to determine an innovative final solution to prevent further intestinal blockage) freed me, gave me permission, as it were, to break free from what were no longer life-giving priorities and to begin life anew. For sure, the battle with addiction showed me the futility of moralism and willful control in the face of a tortured soul's affliction; the release from my professional obligations saved me from frittering away my time on things that wouldn't have been worthy food for the gods because not coming from a place of deep joy, passion, and desire; and the rending of the boundaries of my faith taught me that the next phase of my life would no longer be about putting up fences and drawing boundaries but about tearing them down and expanding the reach of my communal embrace to exclude no one. More importantly, the letting go of the presumption of one correct modality of belief when it came to matters of ultimate meaning was like an entry into a different world altogether—one full of wondrous mystery, of unexpected joy amidst struggle and uncertainty—albeit now clouded with a sense of foreboding, of talk of end times. No, not the end times of Armageddon or of the Left-Behind right-wing evangelical variety—but of a dying, wounded, planet, groaning under the weight of human folly and excesses of a different kind, of the reaching of natural limits everywhere, of peak oil, of species extinction, and the poisoning of everything in the earth—of land, water, food, and air.

RETURNINGS (OR MORE FITTINGLY, FURTHER DETOURS)

The unraveling of my life in the homeland just at the point of having touched indigenous power (beginning with that life-altering class on our indigenous peoples' arts and their different ways of being) was one more irony in the series. My body's wisdom now serving as my new compass, the newly awakened desire that Frantz Fanon (1963) calls "the passionate search for national culture" (p. 209)—a necessary phase in decolonization but one that he would also ultimately warn against—led me to rethink my plans for graduate studies and to shift to *Sikolohiyang Pilipino* (Filipino Liberation Psychology) as a focus. In search of more of the goodness I had tasted in that class in the humanities, I decided to enroll in a graduate course in Filipino Psychology taught then by *Sikolohiyang Pilipino* pioneer Virgilio "Ver" Enriquez. Sadly, it was to be his last class before succumbing to illness shortly thereafter. Notwithstanding the dire circumstances attending his health, I counted it an honor to be part of that last cohort to sit at the wise elder's feet. There were times when, in the middle of a lecture, we'd have to rush him to the hospital owing to a sudden attack of excruciating pain. It became so that we eventually moved our class meetings to his residence at the Philippine Psychology Research and Training House, cramming ourselves into his tiny bedroom where he was determined to keep teaching down to his very last breath. Refusing to die till he did (I'd be struck by how physically weak and emaciated he had become from when we first started the semester), he would prop himself up on a pillow with much difficulty and with nary a breath left in him, begin speaking with a raspy, barely audible voice, coughing a number of times in mid-sentence to clear his throat, until suddenly, his voice manages to break through, rising to a powerful crescendo and growing ever more urgent, his impatient love for his culture and native land overriding his bodily frailty. In the magic of that moment, I'd find myself transfixed: all the myths of resurrection, as it were, converging in that frail dying body—the Phoenix rising again from the ashes, the burning bush speaking once more, the holy Grail found and the wasteland healed (cf. Houston, 1987, p. 107). Although in time, the great teacher would eventually pass to the Great Beyond, the seed he had planted, along with the work of other mentors like him, Zeus Salazar, Popeng Cover, and Felipe de Leon Jr., took on deep root in my soul. I ended up writing my dissertation on the work of indigenization among scholars in the Philippine academy, and, for another decade and a half, this project became my great new romance and adventure.

Funny how only now with this writing did it occur to me that my adventures seem to run in fifteen-year cycles. Today as I mentioned in the beginning of this paper, I find myself once more in that familiar cocoon of "dead space" where magic seems to have all but faded and fear of not knowing what comes next sometimes filling me with a sense of dread. Activist writer Derrick Jensen (2004) remarks that "transitions by definition involve pain, loss, sorrow, and even death" (p. 175). Perhaps part of the death for me in regard to my romance with indigenization as a nationalist project, at least, in its primary articulation in the academy, is what I often see as its failure to engage the present perilous moment and to ask deep questions about how now to live, to ask probing questions, for example—beyond concerns for self- and community-edification—about living differently in the midst of what is now a globalized empire where rapacious greed and predation have become (if ever not) the name of the game. This imperial nightmare of expanded wars, of corporate takeover of governments, economies, and every inch of public space, and the glorification of unlimited growth leading to cutthroat competition over the planet's fast diminishing resources, now stares us in the face, threatening to bring about a collapse far more devastating than the fall of Rome, and planetary in both scope and proportion. And yet for those of us still with the means to conduct business as usual, such a nightmare, which in fact is already the lived reality of the vast majority of the world's poor, still presents itself to us as a dream, that good old "American dream," in the form of "harmless" ambition, upward mobility, and, whether as individuals or nations, the taken-for granted pursuit of unlimited growth in the name of progress and development.

For me, the urgency of the moment is best exemplified in a warning issued by the Kogi, an indigenous tribe living in the Sierra Nevada de Santa Marta mountains of northern Colombia, in South America who, for the first time in 1990, decided it was time to speak out to the rest of the world. The Kogi believe themselves to be the keepers of the earth, tasked with protecting its heart which they understood to be their territory. They call themselves "the Elder Brother" and us, civilized peoples, "the Younger Brother." For centuries, they had eluded colonization by Spain, managing to survive by keeping themselves isolated in the deep forest hinterlands. But now, a sense of urgency compels them to send a message to the Younger Brother. As noted in a documentary report, "They could see that something was wrong with their mountain, with the heart of the world. The snows had stopped falling and the rivers were not so full. If their mountain was ill then the whole world was in trouble"[1] So they called BBC—don't ask me how they knew to do this—but for the first time, they invited a film crew to enter their sacred territory where no outsiders had ever been allowed before. The message that their shamans gave spoke of the Younger Brother's violation of the demarcation line that they believe God had drawn between them and the Elder Brother. It said,

> Younger brother was permitted in other places, other countries. There was a dividing line, the sea. He said, "Younger Brother that side, Elder Brother this side. You cannot cross it".... But Younger Brother came from another country and immediately saw gold and immediately began to rob, violating the basic foundation of the world's law.... Robbing. Ransacking. Building highways, Extracting petrol, minerals.... The earth feels, they take out petrol, it feels pain there. So the earth sends out sickness. There will be many medicines, drugs, but in the end the drugs will not be of any use. The Mamas [as the shamans were called] say that this tale must be learnt by the Younger Brother.[2]

After the filming by BBC, they warned that this is the last time they will ever speak or make contact with the Younger Brother and warned of the certain destruction that was to come.

It is this cry of the heart of the world that the Kogi warned about that has also now become a personal wounding that I feel deeply in my gut. It has become so that I can no longer do academics or intellectual work as though it were business as usual. Oftentimes, I feel that to do so is very much like the proverbial indictment of Emperor Nero for (supposedly) "fiddling while Rome burns." This urgent, Larger Story has irrupted into my little personal story, seeding it, as were, with a tragic vision—a vision of a war waged by what has now

---

[1] http://documentaryheaven.com/the-kogi-from-the-heart-of-the-world-the-elder-brothers-warning/ (last accessed: August 6, 2013)

[2] http://zentobe.blogspot.com/search?q=kogi (last accessed: August 6, 2013).

Could it be that the hatred ultimately is about that—that in the face of corporate industrial culture's insistence on its own way as best, indeed, as the only way to live, there remain witnesses to a whole other way of being beckoning the disillusioned romantics among us to think that another world, another way of life, is actually possible?

become our collective globalized industrial culture. This corporate monocultural infrastructure upon which we're now utterly dependent for our survival has been waging a war with ever intensifying rapacity in the last 500 years. Its logic of addiction to ease, comfort, domination, wealth accumulation, and control, is a war waged against all that will not submit to its demand—i.e., against all that is wild, raw, untamed, anarchic, and free. And that includes all the wild species now threatened with extinction by the destruction of their habitat, and all that remains of the tribe of the Elder Brother, deemed by this culture as useless, disposable populations because of no direct use to the market and, more importantly, because they happen to sit on top of the last remaining untapped natural resources that really "belong to us" but that just somehow got under their feet. We need those resources—for our cellphones, gadgets, and toys, yes, but also, more fundamentally, to grow our food, build our houses, heat our showers, fuel our cars—how else would we survive and continue to live as we do if we let our concern for the Elder Brother keep us from accessing those precious metals, old growth timber, and fossil fuels?

I've read somewhere of the phenomenon of hatred for hunter-gatherer peoples. At first, I failed to understand why, but one day, it came to me. It is because of their incomprehensible temerity: how dare they—in this great modern techno-age of unprecedented human achievement—how dare they insist defiantly on surviving without, or outside of, it? Could it be that the hatred ultimately is about just that—that in the face of corporate industrial culture's insistence on its own way as best, indeed, as the only way to live, there remain witnesses to a whole other way of being beckoning the disillusioned romantics among us to think that another world, another way of life, is actually possible?

I'm afraid it is here where I must leave my story and content myself for the moment to sit with the lessons of my dark cocoon. Ironically, I now live in Detroit, that old motor city, birthplace of the great industrial revolution, but now a ghost of its former splendor and promise. Like my cocoon, I see it as a place of fruitful gestation. The first post-industrial city in America that some analysts say is the likely future of most cities around the world a decade or so from now, it appears to be birthing a whole other culture, this time no longer the color of rust, steel and iron, but green. Organic life is slowly returning to the city, with its residents knowing the bitterness of betrayal by the false promise of development, unlimited growth, wealth and prosperity. The miracle is that neighbors now are speaking to each other, forming communities, growing gardens and taking care of their poor and homeless. It is no accident that in the year 2010, it was chosen to host the second U.S. Social Forum, a gathering of 15,000-20,000 peace and justice activists looking to learn not only from the problems and challenges the city faces, but from models of humanity there already in practice. This is home now away from home, and my hope is that like those called to be bridge-builders among worlds, I may, in time, learn how to bridge my two clashing worlds—my indigenous world that lives mostly in my gut and body memory and the world of a resurrecting city with all the lessons it has to teach that other, globalizing world: the world of Empire, now, hopefully, in its final throes of decline and demise.

References

Capra, F. (1988). *Uncommon wisdom: Conversations with remarkable people.* London: Fontana Paperbacks.

Fanon, F. (1963). *The wretched of the earth.* New York: Grove Press, Inc..

Houston, J. (1987). *The search for the beloved: Journeys in mythology and sacred psychology.* Los Angeles: Jeremy P. Tarcher.

Jensen, D. (2000/2004). *A language older than words.* White River Junction, Vermont: Chelsea Green.

Prechtel, M. (1998). *Secrets of the talking jaguar: Memoirs from the living heart of a Mayan village.* New York: Jeremy P. Tarcher.

Taussig, M. (2009). *What color is the sacred?* Chicago: The University of Chicago.

Weatherford, J. (1988). "Liberty, anarchism, and the noble savage," In *Indian givers: How the Indians of America transformed the world* (pp. 117-131). New York: Fawcett Columbine.

The East-West Quest

Intergenerational Mythweaving and Cultural Identity

Ethelyn Anguluan-Coger

Ang hindi lumingon sa pinanggalingan ay di makararating sa paroroonan. (One who ignores the past arrives nowhere.)

Filipino proverb.

INTRODUCTION

As a Filipino steeped in the proverbs and folklore of my elders, I have been conscious of the truth that my present life has been one lived in constant transference with the past. This going back and forth, like the perpetual shifting of tides, presents an ocean that is still but is also always moving. Into the waters I take my boat and paddle towards a future that is yet unknown, keenly aware of the wind as it whistles in my ears. It is the same wind that has carried the tales of my elders and the elders before them, as they unfurled their sails and navigated seas that took them to lands beyond the horizon. It is the same wind now singing the song of my life, urging me to go forth and dive into the ocean of meanings. It murmurs: only by sinking to the depths would you know of the ocean that embraces and simultaneously lifts.

Mythweaving is the same act of moving back and forth, of regarding the past not as a fading relic of a bygone era but a dynamic continuum of timeless strands being woven purposively to unfold the now. Thus, the past represents a continuing link to myth, defined as the story emanating from the deepest sanctum of meaning, like the ocean's message of emergence from darkness into light, from uncertainty to clarity. The process of mythweaving is one where I continuously plait and mesh life experiences into an endless creative search for substance and purpose. It is a quest that mirrors those of others, those of my ancestors, and the unfolding of the great beyond.

Carl Jung (1976) asked himself, "What is the myth you are living?" and found that he did not know and so taking it as the "task of tasks," proceeded to "…know what unconscious or preconscious myth was forming me." Jean Houston (1996) referred to the mythic quality of her life as "…the individual version of the pattern taking place among us all: the local stories… bound up with the larger story… of convergence; everybody and everything… woven together into a new world myth." Joseph Campbell (2008) described myth as "…the secret opening through which the inexhaustible energies of the cosmos pour into human cultural manifestations… where… mythology and rite… supply the symbols that carry the human spirit forward…"

I have used these definitions of myth and mythology, whether personal, collective and cosmic to illuminate the mythweaving that I am involved with. It is a mythweaving that is premised on the unceasing metamorphosis of a self interlaced with indigenous cultural symbols from the past. When these symbols were further recreated during meaningful exchanges with elders, they showed a capacity to transform the present which could serve as trajectory into the future.

My parents called a local healer, called makkatta (one who discerns) in the Itawit language, who told us after assessing the diseased condition, that my brother angered an earth spirit with his malicious mischief.

IN THE BEGINNING

Growing up in Tuao, Cagayan a valley community located in Northern Philippines, I remember an instance when my elder brother's face and body filled with sores that my uncle doctor could not cure. My parents called a local healer, called *makkatta* (one who discerns) in the Itawit language, who told us after assessing the diseased condition, that my brother angered an earth spirit with his malicious mischief. She then proceeded to restore ease and hovered over my brother with prayers that I tried to read from her murmuring lips. She held a bottle of liniment that she slowly spread over his sores. After a few days, we were all relieved to see that the sores disappeared. I also remember a cousin whose unexplained illness lingered for days, leaving her spent and pale, almost unmoving on her sick bed. My aunt called another local healer who performed a ritual that was capped with an offering of a chicken to propitiate the displeased spirit. My cousin eventually regained her strength and her health afterwards. There was also an instance during a group prayer for a cousin who just died when a relative suddenly slumped unconscious. One of the elders present strongly urged someone to get "*ya manto, ya manto!*" (the black veil, the black veil!). The veil was then draped over the unconscious relative's head. A few moments later, the latter spoke with a voice not hers but that of the person who passed away. The voice admonished the grieving mother that she, the deceased daughter, was in a good place and that the mother need not worry about her. When she regained consciousness, the relative who served as a medium, could not remember what transpired. It was also quite natural for families in our clan to be visited in the dream state by departed ones, leaving messages that made it clear that the bonds between the living and the dead continued in spite of death.

These and so many other examples filled my childhood years with an awareness of different realms inhabited by ancestral spirits, departed souls, other beings and entities, whose presence paralleled our own. The *makkatta's* healing work left an indelible mark which imbued me with a keen sensitivity to the presence of these beings, and the need for respecting the balance that connected our worlds in a harmonious web of spiritual, supernatural, and human relations. During my forays with cousins into the woods, we would say: "*panalanan nu ikami,*" (please let us pass) and took great care to ask for the consent of these beings, and treat with reverence all the plants, shrubs, trees and creatures that stood along our path.

Our elders' stories also filled our imagination with mythical creatures, benevolent entities and magical animals that served in different capacities as heroes, heroines, animators, tricksters, and guardians of their realms and ours. With the *makkatta* and the elders, I learned that everything was throbbing with life and proceeded in perfect rhythm: ancestors, spirits, humans, nature, and the universe; everything flowed and ebbed, and flowed again, like the great ocean. The sense of self that was not apart from everyone else, as embodied by the *makkatta* or healer who restored balance in one's relations with fellow beings, and the elders whose stories confirmed this essential interconnection, was the identification clearly ingrained in my consciousness.

Such a perception of being an integral part in the whole order of creation was described by De Guia (2005) as *kapwa*. It is a Filipino viewpoint that regarded each person as but part of one family that shares this planet Earth. The roots of *kapwa* according to her, "extend into ancestral memories. The shared Self becomes a shared life…where respect and consideration for the Other is extended to all beings: animals, plants, trees, springs, rocks, the living planet and the spirit worlds" (p. 9).

KAPWA ECLIPSED

The *kapwa* bliss that filled my childhood years abruptly ended when my parents decided to leave our valley home and transferred to Manila. Here, life became a wrenching and wretched experience; our family crammed into a single room like sardines in a tiny tin can, in a squalid city that did not know any silence or order, that never gave us any peace; a city that robbed my parents of their smiles and nurturing touch, turning them into silenced automatons who left early for work and came home at night too exhausted to speak.

Growing up in Manila meant a rejection of everything that I held dear during my early childhood years. The nature spirits and guardians and the sacred web that connected all creation totally disappeared. In their stead rose white skinned heroines like Snow White, Cinderella, and the gods and goddesses from Hollywood. Folklore became fake lore while Western literature was deemed as the truth. Everywhere one turned – in movies, on television, books, billboards, and all media – these white super beings dazzled the brown populace with smiles of flawless beauty.

In public and Catholic schools where I attended, English speaking was imposed. To be caught talking in one's local language meant paying an enforced fine and earning the ire of teachers who threatened erring students with lowered grades. I was constantly taunted and shunned as "Neggie," the Black Other because of my darker skin. My fair complexioned classmates were glorified as pretty mestizas, sought after by male suitors and friends. Gripped by a sense of alienation in my own homeland, I became a lost soul, trudging the streets of Manila, as I went from elementary to high school, grappling with an identity that was painfully split from the stories of my elders and the healing of the *makkatta*.

Filipino author and professor, Randolph David in his foreword to De Guia's (2005) book, *Kapwa: The Self in the Other*, summed such a state:

> Successive crises in the Filipino nation's life have led many thoughtful analysts to suspect that the country's main problem could be the dysfunctionality of the entire educational system. This system, largely borrowed and imposed from without, has failed to spring roots in the soul of the people. Instead of drawing strength from the local milieu, it arrogantly asserts its superiority… In the name of nationhood, it has suppressed native sensibility. It continues to denigrate traditional folkways and wisdom in the name of global cosmopolitanism… (p. iv)

LOVE IN A SEASON OF COCKROACHES

Attending the state university as a college student introduced me to the revolutionary stories behind the fiery flag of Mao Zedung and an activism that vigorously questioned and opposed the benevolent authoritarian manifesto imposed by the dictator Ferdinand Marcos. I joined street demonstrations and witnessed police brutality first hand. I saw how young students, with eyes choked in tear gas, became punching bags that the men in uniform banged furiously, incessantly with their clubs. Crouched behind a building after fleeing the police, I could see the smoke which hovered like a ghost in the aftermath of our protest. Leaflets, broken glass, slippers without pairs, and blood, splattered the pavement. It was incomprehensible how so many of my peers, the youth in their physical and intellectual peaks, described as the country's brightest future, could end up stiff and lifeless in cold coffins, mourned by those of us who were not as brave as they who chose the frontlines. It was even more incomprehensible how so many of my other peers would become rebels lost in mountains that swallowed them forever, leaving parents grappling with shadows and grieving inconsolably for life.

Amidst this chaotic inner and outer backdrop during the first two decades of martial law, a subsequent failed marriage and three young children in tow, life surprised me with a gift. He was the long sought for beloved, the one with eyes that were deep pools of sanctuary and healing. He was "of the stars" he said, and with gentle hands and a soothing voice bathed me in the music of his poems and songs. His love eased the great yearning to be whole again, his heart a bottomless vessel from which poured the most tender affection I have ever known. Once more, I felt that I was exactly where I should be, a shining drop of light in the golden healing ocean of the universe, connected with *kapwa*, the whole of creation.

In time, my brood of three became six and slowly, the stories and mythic images from my childhood reemerged from my consciousness, playfully tumbling and animating my children's imagination. During this period, the influence of Dorothy Heathcote's (1967) drama in education, Paolo Freire's (1970) pedagogy of the oppressed, and Augusto Boal's (1985) theater of the oppressed inspired me to recreate folklore images into contemporary dramatic forms. These enlivened creative expressions led to the building of a community-funded school and a children's theater group composed of my brood and neighboring schoolchildren. We became a touring troupe of

> **Kapwa** *was alive, with all the sharing that connected children, youth, parents, community members, and other elders, enjoying the freedom of coming alive through our stories.*

261

parents and our kids, connecting with schools and communities, sharing our symbols, now transformed into narratives on children's rights. *Kapwa* was alive, with all the sharing that connected children, youth, parents, community members, and other elders, enjoying the freedom of coming alive through our stories. We were a hit and our story was featured in national newspapers and magazines.

I took a master's degree in family life and childhood education to further strengthen my mission to teach but the idyllic life was shattered when my beloved died, leaving me alone to raise a rapidly growing family. By that time in 1992, the dictator Marcos had already been deposed by the bloodless People Revolution and the widow Cory Aquino installed as head of state. Like her assassinated husband, Ninoy, Cory was dedicated to the service of our people. However, dedication alone was not enough to address an entrenched system that oppressed the teeming majority while a minority gripped most of the country's wealth and resources. The key players in this system were the Catholic Church and the imperial American big brother who bought the country from Spain for 20 million dollars in the 1898 Treaty of Paris. They were supported by paid minions in government. This conspiracy between government, the church, and America left the Philippines wholly dependent on foreign trade and aid, and wallowing in debt. Corruption in government and the greed of a few transformed the country into one of the poorest and most corrupt in the world.

I was not spared such poverty, deprivation, or hunger. As a single parent supporting six children, even a master's degree and a teaching position in the university could not feed my children adequately. It was unbearable to see my children's thinning frames and even more difficult to cling to meager wages. We were luckier than most however. Around the nation, more than half of the population ate only one meal a day. I realized that a drastic measure was needed to appease my family's hunger and support my children's dreams to go to college. Thus I was forced, like millions of other Filipinos, to swallow the pain of leaving my children and the homeland for the milk and honey of the US.

GRATING AND INTEGRATING IN AMERICA

In 2000, I arrived in the US completely humbled by the irony of eating the words previously imparted to my college students: "I shall never conspire with the enemy, the White colonizer." I wondered how they would now regard me, considering how passionate I was in condemning the evils of feudalism, capitalism, and imperialism. Surely with disdain, I thought, and shuddered at the idea of being regarded as a "traitor." I tried hard to dispel the idea and steeled my mind instead to survive and live, for the sake of my children. It was the first and only priority. And so I went unflinchingly to face the land and the dreaded colonizer, entering the cultural stew that was Los Angeles, California where I was determined to discover the meanings layered onto a new life in a foreign country.

I kept house and became nanny to my sister's two children. In between my many tasks, I discovered wonderful notes in the music that was America. There were the soaring sounds of my ooh's and aah's for the cultural diversity that I saw in the nearby library. Children, together with my niece and nephew, were all seated on the floor listening to a storyteller. Looking at the back of their heads, I was struck by a never-before-seen kaleidoscope of browns, blacks, blonds, reds, and the in between hair colors bobbing happily together. Equally astounding was the constant roar of cars zooming on the vast expanse of freeways, and the similarly vast expanse of educational opportunities open to everyone, including seniors. And how could I ignore the sweet cacophony of so many different tongues expressing their stories in different languages, lilting in different tunes and tones?

After two months, I went to the Kansas State University for a summer intensive training course in drama therapy. I felt at home in the lush greenery of its campus, but was puzzled at Americans who greeted me with "How are you?" but did not seem to have the time to listen to the answer. I became silent. I saw the friendship on the surface but underneath, I felt that most of them preferred to be left alone. There seemed to be a line I could not cross. I quelled the longing for the warmth of sharing and deep connection that my Filipino culture gave.

Remembering *kapwa,* how could I not miss *kapwa*? But as quickly as I asked, I had to cut the thought and reminded myself that this was America, and with that, further steeled my heart not to feel any emotions. It was all right to keep this resolve during the day while I was busy with classes and assignments. But when night came, I would see the moon from my dorm window and I'd know it was the same moon gazing at my orphaned children back home, then the tears would fall unbidden. It was like putting the heart in a blender and grating it into small pieces. It was like dying a slow, painful death.

After Kansas, I went back to Los Angeles and started my new life as wife to an African American-Native American who petitioned for my children. I also found a job as a social worker for older adults in an adult day health care facility. Everything seemed to flow smoothly. But the domestic bliss did not last long. My husband took once more to drinking and his drunken stupor in the evenings loosened his tongue to rave and rant about people and things I hardly knew. Sometimes, he turned his anger on me, and I would cower in silence not knowing what to do, waiting for his wrath to dissipate. Most of the time, I stayed with the television as an excuse for keeping away from him. "Can you not get yourself out of the victim box?" I would ask him during his sober moments, trying to be a social worker. "You'll never understand what I've been through because you never experienced what I have," he answered simply. I spoke no more. Through his response, I intuitively grasped the truth and connected with the deep suffering of people of color in America, even if during that time, I did not completely understand why.

FROM BLISS TO BLIGHT

The understanding came sooner than expected. We were both on his truck in a busy Los Angeles street when suddenly a booming voice struck our silence. It was a police car and we were asked to pull over to the side. The two policemen appeared sleek in their crisp-looking uniforms but I was not prepared for what they did next. My husband was ordered to get down from the truck, face the wall, put his hands up, and was searched from head to foot as if he was a criminal. Bewildered, I asked the other officer about this abominable behavior that infringed on the human right to dignity. My husband threw me a sharp look that clearly told me to shut up. He was very meek with the officers but was raving and ranting when we rode back on his truck. Arriving home, I had a splitting headache and vomited on the bathroom floor, traumatized by what my husband termed as racial profiling. It was not to be the last. There were more to follow, at other times, when my two sons were riding with him. They too became traumatized like me. The sudden stab of anxiety, the worried look on the face always followed whenever we saw a police car cruise by.

Profiling I found out, was mild compared to actual killing. This killing did not only happen among adults but was also inflicted on children, whose lives were snuffed out like saplings yanked by the storm. There was one 11-year old boy, my husband's cousin, just coming out from Sunday church, who was gunned down by men on a roving, unidentified car. Another was my brother-in-law's 17-year-old son, pursued and shot dead by police in his friend's car. Police claimed that the victims were armed so they shot the boys in defense. I could not ask my brother-in-law for details because after the incident, he went into deep depression. I recalled the same depression that his parents suffered, after their daughter, my husband's only sister, was raped and murdered many years before I became part of their family. Nobody talked about it; they simply washed their concerns away with alcohol. It was frustrating to fill that seemingly bottomless pit of grief as I struggled to communicate to them how much I felt their pain. But just as my husband had told me, it was a futile effort. I knew as he knew as his parents knew that I will never even approximate the depth of their suffering because I was a mere onlooker, an outsider looking in.

Racial conflict apparently did not happen only to Black people. It also happened among Brown people. One day, inspectors from the Department of Aging came to my workplace and did their usual audits. A Filipino inspector looked at my records and deemed me lacking in social work credits. She recommended me for termination from the job and without question, the center owner, my Filipino boss, fired me. I understood that she had to do it as she did not want the health facility's licensing by the department jeopardized. At the end of work day, my breath seemed slashed from my throat. As I sat on the street corner waiting for my bus, I looked up at the sky and beseeched the heavens to help me and my children.

I was hired as an assistant social worker in another health facility a few weeks after on less wages, but I was relieved that I had a job to support my family. I was tasked with opening a health program for Filipino veterans and to integrate them among a large group of mentally ill participants, composed mostly of minority people. The team of female social workers that I belonged to had a White American, a Russian, a Hispanic, and myself. The administrator boss who was Caucasian treated everyone in a perfunctory manner, but openly favored the White American who he later promoted as program director despite her lack of experience. I wondered at the business acumen of my boss and his Caucasian partners who made profit by herding groups of mentally ill people from other facilities and bribing them with money and cigarettes to attend. I also wondered if they cared about the people they herded. Some were catatonic and did not speak at all, while others were constantly bickering or quarreling with one another. It was difficult to relate to everyone because the program could not match the needs of the many mentally ill participants. The Filipino elders, in the meantime, exhibited depressive and anxiety symptoms from acculturation stress. I myself had the same symptoms but struggled to keep my balance and put on a brave and smiling front. Everyone in the center seemed overstressed, participants and staff alike.

It was in this frazzled setting of disjointed racial relations in the workplace, reflecting the same fragmentation in my husband's family and our community, that the Filipino elders and I began storytelling circles once a week.

THE MYTHIC JOURNEY

It was in this frazzled setting of disjointed racial relations in the workplace, reflecting the same fragmentation in my husband's family and our community, that the Filipino elders and I began storytelling circles once a week. We found comfort in each other's narratives and during further sessions, delved into the characters originating from Philippine tales they knew. There was particular resonance with the legend of a Filipino hero, one with superhuman strength, and the journey that led him to seek clarity and fulfillment by confronting the mythical mountain with two clashing rocks within its bowels. Further research revealed that this hero, named Bernardo Carpio, served as the symbol of Filipino revolutionaries in their struggle for emancipation from Spain in the late 1800's.

The elders and I took the hero's message of freedom and journeyed inward where we discovered the strength of our indigenous stories, dipping into their symbols and immersing ourselves into their transcendent meanings. Years later, using the expressive arts therapies that I was specializing in, the elders and I did intergenerational exchanges with university students. To our collective amazement we found the generation gap effectively bridged. Everyone of us – young and old alike - cherished the healing sanctuary that the myth of Bernardo Carpio provided. Becoming Bernardo Carpio ourselves, we mirrored his heroism as we exchanged stories that related how each of us faced the clashing rocks of our Eastern origins and adopted Western home, constantly pushing and pulling us apart. We found a new home listening to each other's heroic tales, depicted in stories of despair and delight, of degradation and deliverance, of retrogression and rebirth. Through our Filipino mythic images, we were able to come home to one another. We have come home to *kapwa* and felt renewed in spirit.

HEALING DENIED

I did further research for my dissertation on the expressive arts therapies and found that cultural identity was a crisis suffered by a majority of Filipino Americans in the diaspora. Armed with the realizations culled from the interchanges with elders, I identified mythweaving as the process that could restore integration and healing, leading to a strengthened cultural identity, as what happened in our case. I presented my university adviser with autoethnography as the appropriate research form. I believed that it could express the full meaning of indigenous research as related by an indigenous person who wanted to share her findings not only with the academe, but with the indigenous community where the data came from and for which the results were intended.

Bochner and Ellis (2006) described autoethnography as "… the look through an ethnographic wide angle lens, focusing outward on social and cultural aspects of… personal experience. Then the look inward, exposing a vulnerable self… As they zoom backward and forward, inward and outward, distinctions between the personal and cultural become blurred, sometimes beyond distinct recognition" (p. 119). Autoethnography "plunges the reader into the interior, feeling, hearing, tasting, smelling, and touching worlds of subjective human perception" (Denzin, 1997, p. 46).

Despite the significant number of autoethnographic authors that has enriched academic research beginning in the 80's, my adviser denied me its use, insisting that it was not the prescribed format sanctioned by the university. She said that I should keep to the rules of the five chapters composed of: 1) introduction, 2) review of related literature, 3) method, 4) results, and 5) discussion of results. I complained that this was an imposed Western construct which impinged on my right to freely express myself as an indigenous researcher with a distinct non-Western framework and methodology.

"Do you want to finish your degree?" she asked. Her question was a prison sentence delivered. The dissertation that I regarded as my bliss expressed suddenly became the chains that bound. How could I touch the truth of the expressive arts therapies when I was myself denied the healing of my own artistic expression? I was the supposed healer who could not heal herself because of academic rules that dictated a theory disconnected from practice. From that time on, I dragged myself from day to day, month into the next month and the next, groaning with the weight of this imposition that immobilized all creativity and paralyzed my writing. It seemed like torture, and I was assailed with piercing migraines that I could not shake off, a coma of spirit that rendered me lifeless and numb to the world.

I realized that the battle for decolonization, as inspired by Leny Strobel's (1996) seminal work, appeared like a losing one. Here I was, terrorized once more by the White oppressor, just like my ancestors and the healers or babaylans they tried to annihilate centuries ago. And then at that moment, it suddenly dawned on me: what was happening was a waking dream, in slow motion. I was part of the historical strand, I was the native denied fulfillment, her story of oppression stretching throughout our people's colonized past spiraling into the present. My physical body was reacting with the violence it remembered, the head splitting, the heart dismembering, the soul identity fragmenting. I needed to go through the experience so I may know the truth of colonial oppression that was still ongoing. I could choose to either wither and die from the challenge or use it as a path for defining the life ahead.

CONNECTING WITH THE ENEMY

I gathered my strength and pulled the support of family, of colleagues, of friends, and of allies. They were the light rays who reminded me through their proverbs, advice, tales, inspiring acts, wisdom, and compassion, of the luminescence inherited from my ancestors, of the healing of the *makkatta* and the elders. Here was the collective weaving that melded my life journey with theirs, spanning the past and present and projecting to the future. We were the voice, the threads of consciousness plaited to unfold the indigenous people's continuing quest for freedom.

I did more research and came up with indigenous authors who could support my stand, speak in my tongue, chant with my songs. In other words, I gave my adviser references to their works and the need for the indigenous viewpoint. Patti Lather in commending Linda Tuhiwai-Smith's (2008) book, *Decolonizing Methodologies: Research and Indigenous People*, reaffirms the need "...for a counter story to Western ideas about the benefits of the pursuit of knowledge," noting that by "[l]ooking through the eyes of the colonized, cautionary tales are told from an indigenous perspective, tales designed not just to voice the voiceless but to prevent the dying—of people, of culture, of ecosystems" (in Tuhiwai-Smith, p. ix).

> *I shall raise the voice of the indigene as researcher and healer, the link that connects communities and people together.*

Fortified with renewed resolve, I engaged my adviser in a discursive exchange about indigenous people's rights until finally, a compromise was reached. She agreed that I could write my autoethnography as part of the chapter on methodology. It was a victory, albeit, a minor one, but it was a foot that opened the door to the academe a bit. It will not be long before that foot will be followed by the other, and together dance a story that will tell once more of a people's resilience and triumph in the face of seemingly insurmountable odds.

EPILOGUE

I am set to face my dissertation committee in a few weeks for the dissertation defense. It is indeed a battle, and I see it as a continuing one, especially in the academic arena. I believe that the indigenization movement now sweeping critical parts of the globe indicates a raising of consciousness to respect our relationships with fellow beings, including non-humans. The university cannot afford to alienate itself by clinging to its secluded stance as an ivory tower, devoid of relevance in people's lives. I shall raise the voice of the indigene as researcher and healer, the link that connects communities and people together. The journey from balance and fullness to fragmentation, and again to fullness, recreated as a collective myth with other Filipino Americans and indigenous groups, will weave its magic of transformation and inspiration. I intend to use intergenerational mythweaving with more groups, both young and old, in various communities here and beyond, to foster stronger cultural identity and emerge as living Bernardo Carpio heroes fulfilling their authentic strength. With our myths rediscovered and constantly recreated, we shall arrive with our fellow beings, not in a nowhere land, but in a land lit by clarity and purpose.

References

Boal, A. (1985). *Theater of the oppressed.* New York: Theatre Communications Group.

Bochner, A., & Ellis, C. S. (2006). Communication as autoethnography. In G. J. Shepherd, J. S. John & T. Striphas (Eds.), *Communication as…: Perspectives on theory* (pp. 110–122). CA: Sage Publications.

Campbell, J. (2008). *The hero with a thousand faces.* California: New World Library.

De Guia, K. (2005). *Kapwa: The self in the other.* Pasig City: Anvil Publishing.

Denzin, N. K. (1997). *Interpretive ethnography. Ethnographic practices for the 21ˢᵗ century.* Thousand Oaks: Sage Publishing.

Freire, P. (1970). *Pedagogy of the oppressed.* New York: The Continuum International Publishing Group Inc.

Heathcote, D. (1967). *Drama in the education of teachers.* England: University of Newcastle upon Tyne.

Houston, J. (1996). *A mythic life: Learning to live our greater story.* New York: Harper-Collins Publisher.

Jung, C. G. (1976). *The portable Jung.* New York: Penguin Books.

Smith, L. (2008). Decolonizing methodologies: Research and indigenous peoples. New York: Palgrave.

Strobel, L. (1996). Coming full circle: The process of decolonization among post-1965 Filipino-Americans. In M. P. P. Root (Ed.), *Filipino Americans: Transformation and identity* (pp. 62-79). California: Sage Publications.

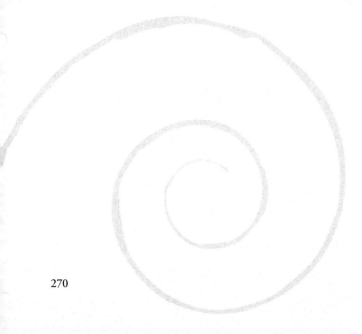

Pagbabalikloob[1], Cyberactivism, and Art

Babaylan Provocations and Creative Responses

Perla Paredes Daly

Create what you want to exist in the world.

—WorkIsNotaJob.com

BEGINNINGS

There came a time in my life when I could no longer ignore the call of the *babaylan.* Thus began what was to be a deep and wide exploration that would open up not only my creativity, but also my life.

My creative efforts in various media, such as prose poetry, art and web pages, are attempts to search for, find, and live out the "essence" of my Filipino self and a link to my ancestry. My soul exploration work became intrinsically woven with the *Babaylan* spirit and things ancient and forgotten. These were thrilling things, fulfilling things, and at times, scary or painful things while the impetus was, and is always, love and longing.

Let me tell you about my life passage with words and imagery in the following pages.

---

[1] *Pagbabalikloob* comes from two root words *balik* meaning "return" and *loob* meaning "depths of self" and the whole word is translated to mean a "returning to home" or to to one's True Self.

My journey involved listening to something deep inside me. It involved reaching into the depths of my psyche through dreams and heeding the visions and guidance in those dreams. It also involved taking inspiration from my friendships with those I admired in real life. These energies and elements along with my creative abilities enabled me to bring into being things that I did not yet see in the world, but that I so wanted to see and experience for myself.

I am a mother, graphic designer, multimedia artist, and I am a Filipina living in the United States diaspora. But in the mid 1980s, I was a college student at the University of the Philippines, Diliman, the hotbed of student activism. There my eyes were opened to corruption and oppression and an ability was awakened within me to speak up against injustice. The university honed my sense of what was wrong in society and so at the time, I learned how to identify, take a stand, and voice an opinion against these things. This included the subtle but strong undercurrent of the legacy of colonial mentality in our society.

I became a young enrollee of colonial mentality at the age of ten when my widowed mother moved our young family from California to Bacolod City on the island of Negros Occidental, Philippines. Growing up there I observed how much my grandmother, whom we called Lola Clotilde (with her refined ways), and my mother believed that all products stateside or from abroad were superior to anything made in the Philippines—things like Tide and Palmolive shampoo, Australian butter in a tin can, Chinese apples, Spanish cheese and turron, and American spam and corned beef. I began to realize that this fawning over foreign things was rampant in Philippine society and that the middle to upper class Filipinos admired European racial features, bloodlines, and cultures over their own. This, at times, annoyed me. Nonetheless, I began to subscribe unconsciously to these beliefs and it was thus that I began taking on a sense of false pride.

Foreign bloodlines were deemed to be nobler. In the early 1900s my grandfather Lolo Pisyong went to school at Ateneo de Manila while my Lola went to Assumption College, both exclusive Catholic schools. My Lola grew up in the Assumption boarding school for girls in Iloilo City and was thus educated among the daughters of the wealthy clans in the Visayas. Lola was not a snobby woman, but she would comment on women or men who were "aristokrata" or "aristokrato" (Spanish for those possessing aristocratic qualities) and I observed that these people she spoke of were wealthy, European mestizo, or those who either received boarding-school or higher education training in Europe, or those whose houses were furnished with European chandeliers, furniture, and other imported household items.

I myself am a *mestiza* with lighter skin, so my Lola would scold me if I came home with a tan because I had gone swimming with my friends. She would exclaim in dismay "*ay kalaway na sa imo, ah!*" (Oh, you are so ugly now!). I would just happily laugh because I was doing the same as all my high school girl friends who loved to tan their light skins.

I sensed that my *Lola* was being old fashioned and didn't want me to look dark like a *hacienda* (plantation) worker.

I loved and grew close to my Lola Tilde so despite having grown up first in the United States, and despite only having come to the Philippines at the age of ten, I started believing this type of conservative, upper class social upbringing and conforming to these old fashioned standards of beauty and cultural constructs.

By the time I reached my senior year in high school, this snobby attitude did not altogether sit with me anymore because I had begun to feel fragmented and disconnected somehow. I felt discomfort at the way attractive Filipino women and men with dark skin were deemed ugly, and dark skinned actors in Philippine movies and TV were relegated to comedic, and other demeaning, roles. I felt distinctly annoyed by Philippine music and dance that were influenced by Spanish culture such as the *rondalla* and the *fandango*. On the other hand, I found that my favorite Philippine music and dance were those that were least touched by Spanish culture, such as the *kulintang* and gong music, the *kappa malong* dance and the Kalinga *Banga* pot dance. I knew that these were from Mindanao and the mountains of the Cordilleras, respectively, and that those remote areas of the Philippines were those that had remained largely untouched by foreign colonial power and thus still retained their indigenous character and cultural integrity.

By the time I had reached college, the Filipino penchant for all things foreign was finally given a name by a professor in my history class with the phrase "colonial mentality." As a student of Visual Communications at the College of Fine Arts at the University of the Philippines, I decided to verbalize my young adult observations in an essay on "Colonial Mentality in Philippine Advertising." In that student writing, I merely provided evidence for how paler skin, mestiza features, and foreign products dominated Philippine TV and movie screens. My English professor asked me, "But do you have a solution?" Thus was I struck by the daunting challenge. What? Me? Provide a solution? I couldn't. I had none. From then on, I yearned for possible answers on how I and my fellow Filipinos could find an antidote to, and overcome, colonial mentality.

> *It was years later that my own personal work began unlocking a creative realm... [that] made me feel more whole and deeply connected to something sweet and fulfilling.*

It was years later that my own personal work began unlocking a door that opened up to a creative realm of answers to overcoming my personal colonial mentality. As I began to create websites online that represented myself as a Filipino, and as I created online discussion groups for Filipino netizens[2], I had a sense of at last beginning to gather lost pieces of myself together. I went on to write and create art to formulate more answers for myself. These acts of creating websites and art made me feel more whole and deeply connected to something sweet and fulfilling.

Strangely enough, I ran into the *Babaylan* figure found in many Philippine indigenous tribes after discovering the shameful stereotyping of Filipina women on the internet and creating a website to counter those narrow representations. Type in "Filipina" in any search engine and you're invariably led to dating sites, "mail-order bride," or Asian pornography and sex tour, sites. In the 1990s, Filipina presence online was shaped mainly by Western male desire and by these online services that enabled men to fulfill their sexual orientalist fantasies. I was sure that Filipino men and women were probably finding the same pornographic sites when searching the term "Filipina." By then, I was already working as a graphic designer in print, multimedia and web design, so I decided to use my spare time to create a strong, multidimensional cyberpinay presence to counter such powerful, global, commercially viable industries that profited from the trafficking of women and the peddling of sexist images. I wrote about this in an essay "Creating NewFilipina.com and the Rise of CyberPinays," published in Melinda de Jesus' *Pinay Power* anthology:

> I began using the Internet in 1991. In 1995, having lived away from the Philippines for a while, I began to check out the Web and to use it to reconnect with my roots. This is how I found www.filipina.com, a website whose homepage title was "mail order brides from the Philippines." I was stunned and upset.

> This site spoke only for a small percentage of Filipinas. Hoping to find better websites than this one, I did a Yahoo! search for the word *Filipina* but became disheartened when I found numerous site results that were just the same thing—Filipinas looking for foreign pen pals, friends, and husbands. My dismay grew into horror when I also found many explicit websites about Philippine bar girls, sex-tours, and pornography. I was miserable how these sites used *Filipina* within their domain names.

> I researched online and found that many of these sites are owned and operated by males; some matchmaking sites are owned and operated by married couples. These sites' customers were men from the United States, Germany, Australia, the United Kingdom, and some from Japan...

---

[2] The term coined from "internet" and "citizens" and used during the 1980s and '90s to refer to those who used and communed on the Internet.

Within these sites I see marketed two icons of men's notion of idealized femininity, the *domestic goddess* and the *sex goddess*: Beyond promulgating sexist stereotypes, these sites are disturbing for the following reasons: they exploit Filipina beauty and femininity for online profit; they idealize Filipinas through commodification, commercialism, and chauvinism. They further exploit women who are already economically and socially disadvantaged, and many traffic in underaged women.

In 1995, I knew the Internet was a powerful medium by which people connected with people, goods and services, as well as with knowledge and ideas. And so, when I found these sites, I understood that their presence on the Web was establishing an unfair generalization of Filipina behavior and was thus creating an Internet stereotype of Filipina women—a Filipina *cybermyth*. (Daly, 2005, p. 221)

In 1998 I founded *BagongPinay* at http://www.NewFilipina.com, a new Filipina website that would not only represent Filipinas and their interests but also define the evolving identity of Filipinas. *BagongPinay* became the first online community for Filipinas and by Filipinas. During those years the homepage featured an editorial, along with links to various sections that stood for diverse Filipina perspectives around the world, e.g., features on lifestyles and personal stories, tips on successful personal relationships, recommended books, and other web links having to do with religion and spirituality, sociopolitical topics, current events, sexuality and gender issues, notable quotes, discussion boards, and finally, poetry and an art gallery. *BagongPinay* grew and became an established online presence, representing and connecting Filipinas throughout the world.

By 2004, after six years online, *BagongPinay* finally found its way to top results in Yahoo and Google searches for "Filipina." Traffic to the site had steadily increased to over 60,000 hits a year. The *BagongPinay* site attracted a Filipina audience from around the world. There was even a small male audience, a global mix of Filipinos and foreign men who were related, married, dating, or interested in meeting, Filipinas. The site of NewFilipina.com was fighting not only the imbalanced images of Filipinas online but also subtly bringing awareness to myself and others that there were larger, patriarchal, and imperial worldviews that were at work in shaping and skewing Filipina image online towards objectified mail-order brides, and sex tour and porn targets. *BagongPinay,* with its carefully written articles and discussions proved to be thought-provoking and empowering to site readers. I believe that *BagongPinay* was also working to provide more balance to the Filipina image online by creating a Filipina collective presence on the Web and by deliberately reclaiming Filipina identity online and defying cybermyths about Filipinas.

While publishing and writing for *BagongPinay*, I became more involved with Filipino-American community events by promoting them at the site, and at times, attending those events in New York City when I was able. It is also at this time that I began to delve

275

deeper into my Filipino roots. In many ways, working on *BagongPinay* initiated my own process of healing and decolonization. After a few years of being published, I realized that *BagongPinay* was also doing the same for others who participated in the site. Writing to *BagongPinay*, Erlou Penado observes:

> Opening the website always makes me feel good and proud of being a Filipina. Not only that it presents a positive image of us Filipinas but it tells more of who we are, what we think, and what we have in our hearts. Thank you for keeping the site alive and for constantly reaching out to other Filipinas. (Daly, 2005, p. 230)

And so I wrote about what this could mean in a bigger context:

> Nationalism—in the sense of being Filipino, of other Filipinos, of our ancestors' heritage, of *Inang Bayan*— needs to be drawn upon to fight the cybermyth, to resist misrepresentations of who we are. Filipinas reclaiming and embracing their identity are experiencing a form of healing and decolonization. Moreover, when Filipinas consciously produce web content to reclaim their identiy, they are expressing a form of Filipina feminism in cyberspace–a cyberPinay feminism. (Daly, 2005, p. 230)

My interactions with other Filipino organizations and leaders flourished after publishing *BagongPinay*. In 1999, I took the online efforts of *BagongPinay* to the next level and began organizing actual events and constituent gatherings in New York City and thus the entity of NewFilipina, Inc. (NFI) was created. It was named so in honor of establishing a new Filipina cyber-identity through the domain of NewFilipina.com. The organization relied on the efforts of volunteers who could give some dedicated, steady time when they were available and who also believed in NFI's goals: to broaden Filipino women's horizons and to allow them discover and harness the power and strengths that they have within themselves; and to connect Filipinas to other Filipinas around the world, to ideas old and new, and to encourage users to take action for themselves and for others. The organization aimed not only to empower Filipinas but to uphold a more balanced personification of Filipina identity(ies) and, ultimately, to promote a sense of Filipina pride and community healing.

"FEMINIST" IS NOT A DIRTY WORD

As part of my work to for *BagongPinay* I would attend various Filipino American organization events in New York City. Going to such an event meant I would take a 4-hour round train trip down to New York City and then spend a full day away from a hilly, rural area of Connecticut where our home was. These trips took me away from my husband and our young children. One day, I was preparing to attended yet another of these events. My husband, Kenneth, was raised by an at-home-mom and, at that the time, was quite conservative in his opinion of women's roles. It wasn't surprising then that when I announced my plans to leave home for a day, he criticized me by blurting out these words—"You've become a feminist!" He used the word "feminist" as if it was an insult. I was hurt and dismayed by the tone and belittlement in his voice and eyes. I felt in my heart that "feminists" are committed to doing good things and that there was a higher, purpose to feminism—that of healing and bringing wholeness to gender relationships, to society and ultimately to humanity. My husband's negative response spurred me to search, contemplate, and articulate the nobility of being a feminist. (It was years later that Ken finally accepted my role as a feminist.)

As it turned out, my work with *BagongPinay* enabled many synchronous meetings and interactions with Filipina feminists. At events and online, I engaged with dynamic, brilliant, profound, spiritual, to-be-reckoned-with Filipinas. I was eager to share their work and their personalities online by promoting their events or by posting articles and links about their work at *BagongPinay*. Through the pro-women work of *BagongPinay*, I deepened my understanding of feminism and, in the process, broke down my own previous anxieties of "*what* a feminist is" by coming to know "*who* a feminist is" and why I myself was claiming the label. I was also connecting with the terms of Filipina feminism such as "pinay power," "pinayism," and "peminism,"[3] that, for me, meant all the different ways of reclaiming pride in being Filipina, addressing the challenges facing Filipino women anywhere in the world, and bringing about acts of resistance against all forms of domination and exploitation. I began to understand the following about Filipina feminism and feminism in general and wrote in the essay "Creating NewFilipina.com and the Rise of CyberPinays":

> …when we consciously produce Internet content [to reclaim our identity] then we certainly bring about a form of Filipina feminism in cyberspace — a cyberPinayism.

> Filipinas defying all gender and race stereotypes and myths, and taking an active part in creating and presenting their identity and transforming it for themselves, regardless of cyberpsace–are part of the larger struggle of Filipino people reclaiming their identity. The deeper significance of Filipina feminism is that it is intrinsic to the process of Filipinos everywhere realizing themselves as a healthy, whole and progressive people. (Daly, 2005, p. 231)

---

[3] "Choosing Pinay+ism rather than Filipina Feminism or Pilipino Peminism challenges the old debate around the P versus the F. It allows for a space to be created influenced by feminism but not limited to feminism. It also allows for Pinays [Filipino women] to claim an identity in the United States while also providing a forum to make transnational connections to the issues of F/Pilipinas/os in Diaspora" (Allyson Goce Tintiangco-Cubales, Pinayist Self Expression Through Art. Blog at http://pinayism.wordpress.com/faq/).

KNOCK THREE TIMES...

While publishing *BagongPinay*, between 1999 and 2000, the Babaylan *diwa* (Tagalog word for "idea," "concept," "consciousness," "essence," "cause of inspiration," and "energy,") began to catch my attention. In promoting Filipinas' work online, I came across Eileen Tabios who was about to publish a book with Nick Carbo called *Babaylan: An Anthology of Filipina and Filipina American Writers*. As Carbo's (2000) introduction states: "The tradition of women's writing in the Philippines can be traced back to the Pre-Hispanic Era of the archipelago wherein certain communities' priestesses-poets called *babaylan* (Bisayan) and *catalonan* (Tagalog) held sway in the spiritual and ritualistic lives of the people. These women provided healing, wisdom and direction with morality stories, myths, poems, prayers, and chants" (p.vii). This is how I first met the *babaylan* archetype of the storyteller and culture bearer.

My second encounter was when I promoted another book written by a Filipina in Germany, *Trans Euro Express: Filipinas in Europe,* edited by Mary Lou Hardillo-Werning and published in 2000 by Babaylan-Philippine Women's Network in Europe and Philippine Women's Forum Germany-Book. The book was about the issues faced by Philippine women who were overseas Filipino workers (OFW) in Europe and how the Babaylan Network organization worked to help these women overcome their challenges of being far away from their families and traditional support systems while working in foreign countries. This is how I encountered the symbol of the *babaylan* as protector, warrior, and bringer of justice.

...the Babaylan from the ancient past had grabbed me by my shoulders, looked me deep in the eyes until I could not turn my head away to ignore Her. She said very clearly in my dream, "I am important, too. Find me. Tell the world about me, too.

In the early spring of 2000, the third encounter with "*babaylan*" took place when the site of *BagongPinay* was honored with the Babaylan community award at the 2000 Filipino American Women's Network (FAWN) Conference in San Mateo, California. The conference was put together by two key women and their organizations: Mona Lisa Yuchengco, publisher of Filipinas Magazine, and the publication staff; and by Virna Tintiangco, the president of the Filipino Women's Network (FWN) in San Francisco. This contact taught me about the *Babaylan* as caretaker and community leader. Receiving the award was a confirmation for me that the online community work was significant and important and that I should continue and develop it even more.

Along with that award, Mona Lisa Yuchengco passed the baton of the FAWN conference leadership to me and requested that I be the volunteer chair of the next FAWN conference the following year. I realized that this would be possible only with the concerted efforts of the volunteers of NewFilipina, Inc. and that together we had to increase our efforts in networking and organizing.

By this time, I was, also practicing yoga, meditation, and contemplation and these disciplines highlighted even more the significance of this third encounter for my vocational calling. The brushes with the figure of the *babaylan* became a metaphor, a gradually unfolding waking dream. In this dream, it was as if the *Babaylan* from the ancient past had grabbed me by my shoulders, looked me deep in the eyes until I could not turn my head away to ignore Her. She said very clearly in my dream, "I am important, too. Find me. Tell the world about me, too."

I knew that the spirit of the Babaylan was calling to me beyond the ocean, beyond time, to discover her meaning, her work, and her modern-day children, who continue to do babaylan-inspired work in the world today.

So early on, during the work of *BagongPinay*, I had already decided that I would find out more about the *babaylan* and what she was supposed to mean for me and what she could mean for the Filipino community. This began the deep and wide exploration that opened up my creativity, my heart and my life. It led me to a new community of Filipino folk who served their *Kapwa* (kindred beings) and their communities, with the rippling resonances from the Philippine homeland and no matter where these people were in the world. From within the core of my being, I knew that the spirit of the *Babaylan* was calling to me beyond the ocean, beyond time, to discover her meaning, her work, and her modern-day children, who continue to do *babaylan*-inspired work in the world today.

Thus it was that the networking work of *BagongPinay* supported the effort towards organizing the next FAWN conference. Through *BagongPinay* I would continue to meet strong, intelligent, and community-active Filipinas from around the world. I encountered Filipina artists, writers, teachers, students, business women, leaders, activists and more, whose lifeworks and commitments supported my exploration the meaning of the babaylan.

Throughout the online community work of *BagongPinay*, I began to reflect carefully on my alliances with Filipina leaders, their different styles of leadership, and the issues and challenges they faced. In this way, I began to see patterns and the common one I saw in these Filipinas' practice of leadership was that they functioned, regardless of context and field of work, as women who restored balance to individuals and communities. For example, there is a sense in which sex trafficking, injustice, and exploitation could be considered forms of social imbalance. These Filipina leaders were working to counter those imbalances, through works of healing, correcting imbalances in power and resource allocation, and freeing people from all manner of oppression.

FILIPINO IDENTITY AND DECOLONIZATION

Around 1998, through the work of *BagongPinay*, a young woman whose character and work I personally admired, told me that she saw me as a role model and community leader. I was surprised. Feeling unworthy, I scoffed at the notion, yet her insistence impressed upon me that I should be worthy of being looked upon this way. Thus, I began the process of becoming worthy by taking on the mantra—"Never out of Ego. Always out of Love." This meant that I would always endeavor to let Love of *Kapwa* be the reason I took on any project. I decided that my ego was always to take a back seat in all my work. At the time, I was in my late 30s, and had I begun looking for answers and calling myself a Seeker. I was led to pray more, meditate, study yoga, and seek an animist spiritual path. And that is how I took on the practice that the higher Self must always guide the little self, otherwise known as the ego.

Soon after practicing how to quiet my ego, I grew in my ability to read dreams (my own and those of others) and I also began to have visions or waking dreams. At first this was a strange experience to me but over time I got used to the gift, learned to embrace it and began paying attention to how this intuitive sense had relevance in my work. This is not something that I could ever tell my readers at *BagongPinay* at the time, though. I was only ready to talk about this ability with closest family and friends, and then only later amongst people that formed a *babaylan*-inspired community made up of kindred spirits whom I instinctively trusted. My dream journeys and my waking dreams were very personal and intimate, and they were significant keys, unlocking expansive meaning and creativity, and beckoning me deeper into endeavors of service to my *kapwa* Filipinos and people of the world.

Early on, when I was publishing *BagongPinay*, I connected with Leny Strobel and her work on decolonization through Eileen Tabios who had recommended that Leny's work be included at the site. I contacted Leny by way of email and she consented by contributing an intelligent, mind-blowing essay that was published within the first year of the site's launch. I actually can't remember the title that was used for this essay but it later became the introduction to her book, *Coming Full Circle* (2001). It wasn't until about a year later that I finally got a copy of her book and began reading it, and I was enthralled. By the time I had reached the middle of her book, I knew I had found the answer that I had been searching for since my college days when I first longed for what could possibly release colonial mentality's stranglehold upon the Filipino people's ability to be true to themselves. Strobel's answer was decolonization!

The thoughts of *babaylan* kept on echoing in my head as I read this book because it reminded me of the courage and strength of the women revolutionaries as they resisted the colonizers. These women were *babaylan* leaders aiding their people to freedom. This writer, this thoughtful, intelligent Filipina was proposing a form of psychological freedom and of healing—a communalized healing of the Filipino wounded identity from the blows of colonial rule! Even before I finished reading the book, I emailed her immediately and begged her for her phone number and the chance to talk to her that very night. We connected and I spilled out my enthusiasm to her. This was to begin a long friendship and collaboration. This is the point in time when I urged Leny to create an online interactive listserve. She seemed surprised by my enthusiasm, but she allowed me to set up the online discussion group called *Pagbabalikloob*. The purpose of the group was to discuss colonial mentality and decolonization. These concepts were very important to deepening my own path of spirituality, learning more clearly what it meant to be a Filipino. Through discussions in this group, I learned more about the following indigenous concepts: *diwa*, (consciousness), *loob* (deepest inner being), *kapwa* (self in the other) and *pakikipagkapwa* (sacred interconnection). It was also here that I realized that my own decolonization was a shedding of my colonized heritage—a programmed mentality of racial and cultural inferiority. My decolonization was a purging of false beliefs fed to me by limited human beings with a domination agenda or those victimized by such ideology of domination. My decolonization was a spiritual awakening. It was a process that allowed me to become a better Filipino.

Learning about Filipino *pakikipagkapwa* enabled me to see that the highest goals of feminism and of movements for social justice, liberation, and equality, regardless of gender emphasis, have the same goals—to compel balance in society and to heal and make whole

Pakikipagkapwa has become for me a worldview that within one's loob *or deepest inner being, there is not just a shared humanity but also a shared inner life that connects us with each other and with all cosmic existence. I took this worldview to heart and began to understand better the opposing worldview of patriarchy and imperialism.*

individuals as well as collective humanity. *Pakikipagkapwa* has become for me a worldview that within one's *loob* or deepest inner being, there is not just a shared humanity but also a shared inner life that connects us with each other and with all cosmic existence. I took this worldview to heart and began to understand better the opposing worldview of patriarchy and imperialism. This is what I wrote in "Creating NewFilipina.com and the Rise of CyberPinays":

> [Our colonizers and the developed countries today still] operate from a worldview based on a hierarchical order that establishes status and competition and justifies oppression and exploitation. This philosophy creates notions of superiority and privilege that underlie antagonism, colonization, racial discrimination, and male dominance. The philosophy is that of the Oppressors and Conquerors of world history. It is a philosophy based on external power and is, in fact, the exact opposite of what the deepest values of Filipino ancestry really are—that of *loob* and *kapwa* (connection and oneness with others). Filipinos today must therefore realize that the antithesis of patriarchy's worldview is the Filipino consciousness of *pakikipagkapwa*. The philosophy is based on awareness of *lakas ng loob* (internal power) and spirit how they give way to healing, compassion, and wholeness. To recall this ancestral way of being enables Philippine people to embrace their identities and not look down upon themselves as inferior to their colonizers or to any other nationality, culture or religion. Subscribing to the worldview of *pakikipagkapwa* and unsubscribing from the patriarchal worldview are inherent in decolonizing not only of the colonized, but also of the colonizer. (Daly, 2005, p. 233)

Thus, in my experience, the journey of *BagongPinay* has surfaced from deep within me a bond of connection with my ancestral home of the Philippines. It had come to signify: connection with homeland and ancestry, energy for creative endeavors, and inspiration to re-create Filipino culture, both on cyberspace and in the real. In many ways, this spiritual rejoining with homeland and ancestry assuaged the pain of my geographical dislocation as a Filipino American.

Over the years, the *diwa (essence)*[4] of *BagongPinay* deepened my journey into the significance of Filipina feminism and the challenge of realizing its promise. In this journey I came to a conscious *pagbabalikloob*, return to self or self-discovery, and found the power of being Filipina and the gifts of my feminine strengths. I also found the spirituality of being a mother, wife, daughter, soul sister, woman, Filipina, and feminist. Through my engagement

---

[4] Diwa is a Philippine term I've come to understand as meaning "essence," "consciousness," "spirit," "thread of thought," or "soul." In some places, it also refers to "cause of inspiration and energy."

with other Filipina sisters, I came to know personalized elements of Filipina empowerment as communicating *loob* in one's choices and actions, e.g.: Reclaiming dignity and freedom for oneself; Expressing creativity and using one's talents and resources to support others' in finding their own dignity and freedom; Enhancing awareness and clarity through meditation, prayer and spiritual practice; Believing in one's own feminine traits (intuition, compassion, wisdom) and balancing it out with one's masculine traits (analysis, single-mindedness, assertion); Being the best woman that one is capable of being; Believing that one is here on Earth as a Filipina for a reason; Owning one's identity as a Filipina; and finding a way to contribute to Philippine community healing and empowerment.

The spiritual aspects of my journey taught me that at every moment, one must discern whether one is making a decision out of ego or out of love. I am mindful now that one can make decisions based on either the notion of separation from others (Western patriarchal worldview) or that one is connected to others (*pakikipagkawa* indigenous worldview). Along the way, I developed an awareness of the mysterious, spiritual aspects of

Along the way, I developed an awareness of the mysterious, spiritual aspects of Feminism— the awakening of the Sacred Feminine in humanity's minds and hearts and the rise of women's roles in societies being part of the process of healing for our planet.

Feminism—the awakening of the Sacred Feminine in humanity's minds and hearts and the rise of women's roles in societies being part of the process of healing for our planet. I sensed the parallelism between Filipina Feminism and the Babaylan tradition and how both are committed to *kapwa* (mutuality) and to the overall healing and wholeness of the larger community.

THE FIVE POWER ROLES OF THE BABAYLAN

It took take a few years of community work for me and the volunteers of NewFilipina, Inc. to be ready to host the next FAWN conference. The preparations included my personal internal work so that I could lead this conference with integrity and assuredness. Then come June 2005 we successfully staged the FAWN 2005 Conference at the Kimmel Conference Center of New York University. The theme for the conference was "Coming into Our Own: Spirit, Leadership & Success."

A key consideration defining the theme was empowerment—understood not in terms of gaining privilege, recognition, and status but rather as a process of finding *lakas ng loob* (strength of the heart) or inner power. This was empowerment that strengthened one's capacity to make choices not only for oneself but in the interest of the greater good. Along with developing this capacity, it was important to also tap into the cultural resources of our rich Filipino heritage.

For the *Spirit of Babaylan* art exhibit featured at the FAWN Conference, I submitted a one-off fine art print titled, "How Shall I Serve?" based on my conception of Tagipusuon sg Babaylan (Heart of the Babaylan) —a collection of art and prose poetry I published around 2003 at Babaylan.com.

Figure 1. How Shall I Serve[5]

Made from a collage of my digital artworks, this fine art print was my gift offering at the FAWN2005 conference to my fellow Filipina and Filipinos for our collective healing, growth and transformation. It was derived from Babaylan.com.

The Babaylan.com website was a result of the publishing efforts from working on *BagongPinay* at NewFilipina.com coming out of my interaction with dozens of Filipinas around the world who contributed content and participated in the discussions. Influenced by the gentle and compassionate writing in *A Woman of Wisdom: Honoring &*

---

[5] The Spirit of Babaylan Open Art Exhibit was coordinated by Marv Velando and shown between June 2-24, 2005. The exhibit began before the 2005 Filipino American Women's Network conference (FAWN) 2005 conference and continued to be shown thereafter.

Celebrating Who You Are by Caroline Joy Adams (1999). I made it one of the objectives of NewFilipina.com to convey the strengths and qualities of Filipino women including their feminine wisdom. I became inspired. For over a year, I had also been intensely reading and rereading *The Four-Fold Way: Walking the Paths of the Warrior, Teacher, Healer, and Visionary* (1993), by Angeles Arrien. For months, after reading these books, my hands became very warm as I lay awake at night thinking about the qualities I found in the various remarkable Filipino women I met.

I began to recognize in these Filipina leaders five archetypal figures: the Warrior, the Teacher, the Healer, the Sage and the Priestess. I began sensing and feeling out each one of these archetypal figures, envisioning them in my *kapwa* Filipinas and Filipinos. Thereafter, it was an emotional and physical urge to transmit these intuitions, thoughts and visions in physical form. Thus the following images and words came about:

THE POWER ROLE OF WARRIOR

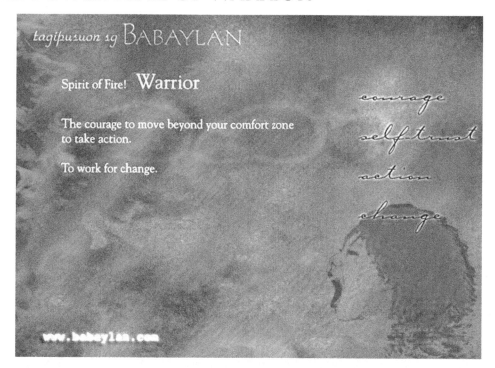

Figure 2: Warrior: *Diwatang Apoy*/Spirit of Fire[6]

Spirit of Fire!
Warrior

---

[6] Originally published at http://babaylan.com/fire.html, 2003.

The courage to move beyond your comfort zone
To take action.
To work for change.

The responsibility of the Warrior archetype is to take action not only for survival, but also for stability and change for the better. The warrior fights for and protects her family, her loved ones, her communities, and the poor and vulnerable. I see the fiery elemental qualities in the Warrior— heat, combustion, burning, forging. I also see the fiery elemental effects in the Warrior's works — transformation, transmutation, ignition, power, empowerment and more. In *The Four-Fold Way*, Arrien (1993) writes that the Warrior is the archetype of leadership. The Warrior archetype within us brings us into leadership skills by helping us stay in our power, by showing up and choosing to be present, by extending honor and respect, and by being responsible and accountable. A warrior's leadership skills include the ability to honor and respect, to align words with actions, to respect limits and boundaries, to be responsible and disciplined, and to demonstrate right use of power.

THE POWER ROLE OF TEACHER

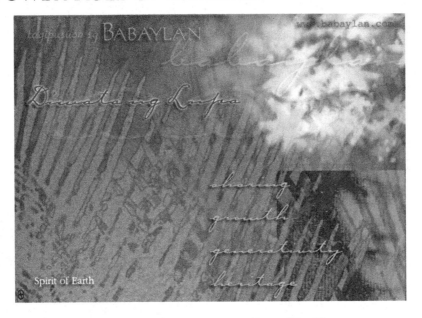

Figure 3: Teacher: *Diwatang Lupa*/Spirit of Earth[7]

Spirit of Earth!
Teacher
The generosity to share knowledge

---

[7] Originally published at http://babaylan.com/earth.html, 2003.

The foresight to pass on heritage
The desire to cultivate learning and growth.
To work for our children and their children and theirs...

The responsibility of the Teacher archetype is to take action for regeneration and growth, to create a lineage of generativity. They create systems of storing/holding/ keeping, cultivating and conveying knowledge, experience, culture, and heritage. They are vehicles of teaching and learning. I see the Earthy elemental qualities in the Teacher— soil, fertility, fecundity, planting, growth, flowering, fruits, seeds, nurturing, cycles, and the earthy elemental effects in the Teacher's works — regeneration, nurturing, growth, harvest, bounty and more. The teachers are our culture bearers, our dancers, musicians, artists, writers and our storytellers. They make sure that our heritage is passed down from generation to generation and that our culture lives on, thrives, and evolves. Arrien (1993) writes that the Teacher is the archetype of that is open to outcome, but not attached to outcome, that when we act as a Teacher, we develop our capacities for detachment, we honor our heritage, we become flexible and fluid, like the ancient and wise ocean, and that we demonstrate wisdom and its components of clarity, objectivity and discernment.

THE POWER ROLE OF HEALER

Figure 4: Healer: *Diwatang Ulan at Tubig*/Spirit of Rain and Water[8]

---

[8] Originally published at http://babaylan.com/water.html, 2003.

Spirit of Water!
Healer
The gift to bring wholeness,
and to wash away dis-ease,
The realization of integration...
The compassion to forgive...
To work for healing.

The responsibility of the Healer archetype is the promotion of healing and wholeness and the preservation of health and well-being of the community. I see the Watery elemental qualities in the Healer archetype— cleansing, washing, quenching, soothing, and the Watery elemental effects in the Healer's works —fullness, cleanliness, fulfillment, well-being, and health (Arrien, 1993, p. 47).

THE POWER ROLE OF SAGE

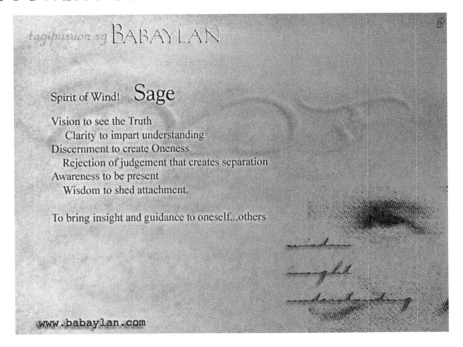

Figure 5: Sage: *Diwatang Hangin*/Spirit of Air/Wind [9]

Spirit of Wind!
Sage
Vision to see the Truth

---

[9] Originally published at http://babaylan.com/air.html, 2003.

Clarity to impart understanding
Discernment to create Oneness
Rejection of judgement that creates separation
Awareness to be present
Wisdom to shed attachment.
To bring insight and guidance to oneself and to others

The Visionary is also a Sage. The responsibility of the Visionary archetype is to provide access to visions, ideas, wisdom, and understanding, and to relate that which is appropriate and timely so that others may benefit and act upon the received knowledge or vision. I see the Airy elemental qualities in the Visionary/Sage archetype. Air is light in physical mass/density. Clouds are physically located higher than ground, and, being positioned high up in the air, one is given sight of the bigger picture and things that can't be seen from lower on the ground. I also see the airy elemental effects in the Sage's works —Wind, or moving air, possesses strength & energy that can move and affect objects and climate and enable travel across the earth (Arrien, 1993, p. 77).

THE POWER ROLE OF PRIESTESS

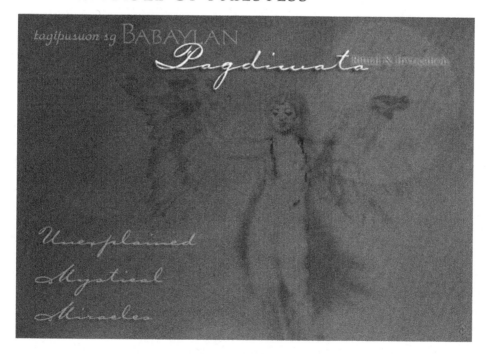

Figure 6: Priestess: *Pagdiwata[10]*

---

[10] Originally published at http://babaylan.com/pagdiwata.html, 2003.

Pagdiwata-Invocation of Diwa
Bridge between the
Seen and Unseen

Remind us! Of the Union
Of spirit and matter
Around us and within us

To give practice to that which
Increases our Awareness
Harmonizes Logic with Intuition
Marries our hearts with our minds
Uplifts us and inspires us

Connects us to that which
Fires us... heals us
Guides us... nourishes us
Strengthens us

The responsibility of the Priestess archetype is to take action by creating ritual that bridges the Seen and Unseen, the Spirit World and the Physical World. The Priestess archetype gives spiritual meaning to all aspects of Life and Earthly Existence and creates practices and events for raising awareness and consciousness.

By the opposing terms Seen and Unseen, the Physical World and the Spirit world, I am also referring to the metaphor of Light and Dark—that which is illuminated and in the Light can be seen, and that which is not illuminated or is in the Dark and cannot be seen and is thus unseen. The Seen, or illuminated dimension also corresponds to the Physical World. The Unseen, or un-illuminated dimension corresponds to the Spirit World or the mysterious and mystical. When the two dimensions of Seen/Unseen, Light/Dark, Physical/Spirit touch, it does not have to be a collision of catastrophe or even conflict, but rather it can be a dance that is magical and miraculous. By defining Light and Dark in this manner, I see the dance of Light and Dark as the elemental quality in the Priestess' archetype and her way of bridging the Physical World with the Spirit World through ritual as her solemn and sacred work.

POWER ROLES IN SERVICE OF KAPWA

From observing the patterns of qualities in the Filipina leaders I had the opportunity to meet in my work, I have come to associate the foregoing archetypal roles (or what I call Power Roles) with the indigenous Philippine babaylan fulfilling her duties to her community.

I realized that an individual leader may be acting out a power role or several power roles at a time. I also found that advocacy groups too may embody one or more of the power roles at any given moment. For example, an environmental activist group could embody the Warrior power role (for change and stability) and the Teacher role (for generativity and growth). A person such as a spiritual activist or writer may embody the power roles of the Healer (wholeness and healing) and the Visionary (wisdom, ideas received from spirit world). A person called to public service may embody the power role of the Visionary and the Warrior. Non-indigenous Filipino men and women can act out these 5 power roles no matter where they are in the world. I took these power roles and archetypes and wove them into the structure of the FAWN2005 conference. The pre-conference retreat embodied the priestess. The five speaker panels were based on Warrior, Teacher, Healer and Visionary. I also mentioned these five power roles in the conference program (Daly, 2005, p. 6). Sister Mary John Mananzan, a well known third-world feminist theologian and president of St. Scholastica College in Manila, spoke of these archetypes in her work in her keynote address at the 2005 FAWN Conference. In our few personal conversations, she expounded more on how she felt that the archetypes of Warrior, Teacher, Visionary, and Priestess are embodied in her life work in places as diverse as the streets of the Philippines, the theological universities of Germany, and the libraries of the Vatican. I was so touched by the stories that she imparted to me that when I visited Sr. Mananzan in Manila, I gifted her with the Spirit of Babaylan Fine Art Print that had been on exhibit at the FAWN2005 conference art exhibit.

I believe that today, the figure of the babaylan exists not just as a reclaimed icon. Filipino men and women, real persons in our living, breathing communities, have always enacted the power roles that could have been those of the babaylan in her time—warrior, teacher, healer, visionary, and in some cases, even priestess. Modern Filipino society and communities around the world can benefit from the spirit of the babaylan as it manifests in acts of community empowerment towards restoring harmony and balance, justice and transformation.

THE SEARCH FOR THE INDIGENOUS

> Indigenous peoples are one of the world's most persistent voices of conscience, alerting humankind to the dangers of environmental destruction. As the world searches for alternative strategies to deal with global problems, it is turning more and more to indigenous peoples. Much of their respect for nature, their methods of resource management, social organization, values and culture are finding echoes in the writings of scientists, philosophers, politicians and thinkers. (Burger, 1990, p. 166)

In our modern world, the powers that be see the world in arranged in a hierarchy of four worlds: the First World which refers to developed, industrialized countries such as the United States and the western European nations; the Second World, which refers to the socialist block countries; the Third World to the so-called "developing" countries, and finally, the Fourth World countries or the indigenous peoples who are descended from the aboriginal populations who do not own land titles or material riches. The people of the First, Second and Third world mostly believe that land belongs to people. The people of the Fourth World believe that people belong to the land. The ideals of ownership and material wealth and power that underlie the developed world order have already created a massive imbalance on a planetary scale and ecological catastrophe worldwide through unsustainable lifestyles that promote economies that can collapse in on themselves through financial world crisis and the reaching of all kinds of ecological limits. Arrien (1993) conveys on a gem in The Four-Fold Way: "A new world order can be created once all four worlds create a bridge that is truly healing. Perhaps the bridge can be the interface where these four worlds meet in joining together to heal and restore Mother Earth" (p. 4).

In her writing, Leny Strobel (2001; 2005; 2010) talks of decolonization and indigenization as indispensable to any work of repairing the damage caused by the ideology of conquest and domination. I believe in these things because strangely enough, as an artist, I feel the pain and loss that our ancestors underwent. Yet some would critique a desire to recover indigenous roots as nothing more than a romantic ideal dreamed up by alienated Filipinos in their faraway diasporic places of exile. Many Filipinos today (both abroad and in the homeland) scoff at any notions of reclaiming one's indigenous roots as a bogus return to anachronistic traditions that, as far as they are concerned, exist more as quaint tourist attractions than having cache as vibrant and living lifeways.

Philippine independent film maker Kidlat Tahimik, knows the grief of some Filipinos over the loss of their indigenous heritage as a result of western colonization and so-called "progress" and "development." So Kidlat picked up the word "indio genius" from an Ifugao elder who was his mentor in *katutubong kaalaman* (native knowledge), and who always mispronounced the word "indigenous." Kidlat adapted the term for Filipinos who, despite their colonized history and their westernized reality, still retain a sense of their indigenous wisdom. Kidlat urges Filipinos, "We must find and cultivate our indiogenius strengths. We must tell our indio- genius stories" (Alwin, 2010).

So the question remains, how do we cultivate indigenous/indio-genius strengths? What indio-genius stories do we relate to each other in the community?

As I finish writing this essay I know that my own close friend Rhodora "Bing" Veloso is one of the critics of those of us who talk about reclaiming spirituality or practices that are termed "indigenous." She is pained at the perceived appropriation of indigenous practices only because of the loss and difficulties that Philippine indigenous people are going through. As someone who lives in the homeland and is closely related to the struggles of indigenous communities, Bing wondered aloud to me whether Filipinos who are in the diaspora can relate to those struggles as well so that they do not merely "consume" indigenous culture. I shared with her my journey of how I came to my knowledge and awareness of indigenous struggles in the homeland. I responded with shared emotions and asked her,

I responded with shared emotions and asked her, "What is indigenous, Bing?" And she replied to me, "It's who YOU are, Pearl." ...She helps me clearly see that I am walking this path and creating works that are coming out of my deepest Loob *and Being...*

"What is indigenous, Bing?" And she replied to me, "It's who YOU are, Pearl." I know Bing accepts my personal work and spiritual practices as genuinely indigenous to me. She helps me clearly see that I am walking this path and creating works that are coming out of my deepest *Loob* and Being and that I am striving to be true to who I am.

I believe that Filipinos today who awaken and stand strong in their identity, history, heritage, and the center of their being (*Loob*), will find their inner light and compass that is indigenous to themselves. So when the Babaylan Spirit rises within us, we know we are guided to assist and support our *Kapwa* in finding their own Light and compass within themselves.

THE BABAYLAN MANDALA

Figure 9: Babaylan Mandala I.I[11]

The creation of the Babaylan Mandala series is a recent artistic expression in honor of the The Babaylan and babaylan service. It was originally created to be on the cover of *Babaylan: Filipinos and the Call of the Indigenous* (Strobel, 2010). Three versions came from that exercise. The one shown above is the gold version. I know that the Babaylan Mandalas are not only an outcome of my personal longing but also an unspoken message from our ancestors on how to connect with something deep within ourselves.

Here is how I first described the Babaylan Mandala for the Center of Babaylan Studies:[12]

> With the coming of Western colonizers over 400 years ago, the conquerors shaped the identity of Filipinos. As the gold of our ancestors and the motherland were wrested away and loaded upon Spanish galleons to be delivered to the conquerors' home across the seas, so too was the richness of Filipino identity and spirituality replaced with dysfunctional perceptions of the superiority of the Westerner's race, religion and ways and the innate inferiority of the indios.

---

[11] Babaylan Mandala website is found at http://www.babaylanmandala.com.

[12] Daly co-founded the Center for Babaylan Studies along with Leny Mendoza Strobel and Baylan Megino in 2009 in order to bring about the First International Babaylan Conference held in April 17-18, 2010 at Sonoma State University (California). http://www.babaylan.net.

I believe that Filipinos today who awaken and stand strong in their identity, history, heritage and the center of their being (*Loob*), find their inner light, their inner gold. The Babaylan Mandalas and all their symbols of the 4 elements and *baybayin* scripts represent the reclaiming of the Filipinos' Inner Gold. (http://babaylanfiles.blogspot.com/2009/12/babaylan-mandala-fine-art-series.html)

I was born a Filipina and I believe in the beauty of the Filipino people. I want Filipinos to know that when the Babaylan Spirit rises within any one of us, then we are guided to help our selves and our *Kapwa* find an inner Light and precious gold within. I am grateful for this divine gift.

References

Alwin, I. (2010, June 5). Conversation with Kidlat Tahimik, Indio Genius. *The Daily Tribune*. Manila, Philippines.

Adams, C. (1999). *A woman of wisdom: Honoring & celebrating who you are*. Berkeley, California: Celestial Arts.

Arrien, A. (1993). *The four-fold way: Walking the paths of warrior, teacher, healer and visionary*. San Francisco: Harper.

Babaylan Files Blog, http://babaylanfiles.blogspot.com

Burger, B. (1990). *The Gaia atlas of First Peoples: A future for the indigenous world* (p. 166). Garden City, New York: Doubleday.

Carbo, N. (2000). Introduction. In E. Tabios (Ed.), *Babaylan: An anthology of Filipina and Filipina American writers* (pp. vii). San Francisco, CA: Aunt Lute.

Daly, P. (2005). Creating NewFilipina.com and the rise of CyberPinays. In M. L. de Jesús (Ed.), *Pinay Power: Peminist Critical Theory* (pp. 221-238). New York, NY: Routledge.

Daly, P. (2005). *Paths of service of babaylan work, babaylan spirit and power roles*. Souvenir Program for Filipino American Women's Network 2005 Conference (FAWN2005), New York City. Retrieved from http://fawn2005.com/pdfs/archetypes_leadership.pdf

Hardillo-Werning, M. (Ed.). (2000). *Trans Euro Express: Filipinas in Europe*. Babaylan-Philippine Women's Network in Europe and Philippine Women's Forum Germany.

Mangahas, F. & Laguno, J. (Eds.). (2006). *Centennial crossings: Readings on Babaylan feminism in the Philippines*. Quezon City, Philippines: C & E Publishing.

Strobel, L. (2001). *Coming full circle: The process of decolonization among post-1965 Filipino Americans*. Quezon City, Philippines: Giraffe Books.

Strobel, L. (2005). *A book of her own: Words and images to honor the Babaylan*. San Francisco, CA: Tiboli Press.

Strobel, L. (2010). *Babaylan: Filipinos and the call of the indigenous*. Davao City, Philippines: Ateneo de Davao University Research and Publications Office.

Perla Daly's other sites and blogs:

http://www.bagongpinay.org

http://www.bahalanameditations.com

http://www.FAWN2005.com

http://www.baybayinalive.com

http://www.pinay.com

http://www.fabulousfilipinas.net

http://www.pakikipagkapwa.net

Notes on the Contributors

Jane Alfonso holds a Master of Arts degree in Somatic Counseling Psychology from the John F. Kennedy University. A Bay Area native raised by a tribe of strong-willed women, she draws upon her experiences in Orgonomic psychotherapy, bodywork, meditation, and other mindfulness practices to help others develop and deepen their awareness of "body-as-self." Jane has been leading groups and workshops for the past several years in hospital and community mental health settings and specializes in treating trauma, anxiety, and cultural identity issues. She tends to her dreams, garden, and family when not studying for her Marriage and Family Therapist license.

Ethelyn (Mila) Anguluan-Coger is an Itawit native of Tuao, Cagayan, in Northern Philippines. She graduated with degrees in Journalism and Family Life and Child Development from the University of the Philippines, Diliman, Quezon City. She is currently a PhD candidate in Expressive Arts Therapies at Lesley University in Cambridge, Massachusetts. Her continuing bliss, aside from loving her six children and four grandchildren (with more forthcoming), is the intergenerational mythweaving method and process that she developed and has been sharing with Los Angeles communities in California. She is a Co-Director at the Center for Babaylan Studies (www.babaylan.net) where she finds her deepest fulfillment in serving her *Kapwa*.

Perla Ramos Paredes Daly is a multimedia artist and activist who collaborates with artists, healers, and activists around the world in digital art, poetry, photography, painting, jewelry, online communities & new media publications. She chaired the Filipino American Women's Network FAWN2005 conference, *Coming Into Our Own Spirit and Success*, built around her original conceptualization of the five *babaylan* power roles or archetypes (www. fawn2005.com and www.babaylan.com). She is also the founder of *BagongPinay* the first online community for, and by, Filipinas aimed at creating a positive and empowering Filipina identity online (www.newfilipina.com). She publishes Pinay.com, BahalaNaMeditations. com, BaybayinAlive.com, BagongPinay.com, and pakikipagkapwa.com and is the creator of the *Babaylan* Mandala fine art series. In 2009 she co-founded the Center for Babaylan Studies based in California. For her online publishing and her mentoring of young Filipinas, she received the Fillipino American Women's Network FAWN2000 *Babaylan Award* and the *100 Most Influential Filipinas in America* award in 2011.

Nenita Pambid Domingo is a Lecturer of Filipino language and culture at the University of California, Los Angeles since 2000. She has taught Filipino language, literature, and culture at Peking University (as a Government Exchange Professor), the University of the Philippines (Quezon City and Manila), Loyola Marymount University, California State University at Long Beach, and the University of Southern California. She holds a PhD in Philippine Studies from the University of the Philippines, Diliman, Quezon City. Among her publications are *Anting-Anting o Kung Bakit Nagtatago sa loob ng Bato si Bathala (Amulet or Why the Tagalog God Bathala is Hiding Inside a Stone* (UP Press, 2000). She co-authored *Elementary Tagalog Tara, Mag-Tagalog Tayo! (Come On, Let's Speak Tagalog) Book and Workbook* (Tuttle, 2012). She also manages the yearly e-magazine *Liwanag at Dilim (Light and Darkness)* that showcases the works of students in Filipino language classes from the different UC campuses, Osaka University, University of the Philippines, University of Hawaii at Manoa, and San Diego State University.

Maria Joy Ferrera is a Licensed Clinical Social Worker and an Assistant Professor in the Masters in Social Work program at DePaul University in Chicago. Her areas of practice and research include decolonization methods; the influence of colonization on ethnic identity development; community-based, socially just practices and mixed methods research with ethnic minority youth; and health disparities and the impact of the Affordable Care Act on new and undocumented immigrants in Chicago. She received her Master's degree and PhD in Social Work at the University of Chicago School of Social Service Administration.

Margarita Garcia is a Filipino American artist born in Chicago. She served as the former Executive Director of the Pacita Abad Foundation based in Basco Batanes, Philippines and Washington DC, and was a recipient of a United States Fulbright grant in fine Arts. She is also a Cannes Bronze Lion awardee, a senior project manager in New York City for IBM, Reebok and Pfizer, a muralist, the photographer of *Bomb the Suburbs* (a hip-hop classic), and the art editor of *Another World is Possible*—an anthology that included work by Noam Chomsky, Arundahti Roy and Sebastiao Salgado. At the Pacita Abad Center for the Arts, she founded an indigenous youth arts organization and has published, exhibited, and worked, on three continents. She graduated cum laude from Brown University and was awarded a Rektorate grant to complete her MFA in Public Arts and New Artistic Strategies at the Bauhaus University in Weimar, Germany. Her work focuses on global migration and the Philippine diaspora.

Michael Gonzalez teaches history, anthropology, and music in City College San Francisco, a vocation he has found more satisfying than his former work in the information industry. He has also taught Ethnic Studies at the University of California Santa Cruz, Cal State

East Bay and Tagalog courses at Stanford University, aside from being a former faculty at the University of the Philippines Diliman where he taught history and classical guitar. As a guitarist, he played for numerous school, radio, and television programs in the Philippines. He has published essays on Philippine culture and history in several journals and magazines both in English and Filipino. He is currently a doctoral candidate in Education at Fielding Graduate University and his dissertation research focuses on digital literacy in Silicon Valley schools.

Tera Maxwell holds a PhD in English from the University of Texas at Austin (2011). Her areas of specialization are Filipino Studies, trauma studies, and archival studies. Her dissertation titled, *Imperial Remains: Memories of the United States' Occupation of the Philippines,* is a critical examination of the intimate details of the United States' occupation in the Philippines through the recuperation of an alternative archive that includes family stories, museum sites, and other repositories of personal memories in order to track what she calls the "inexplicable legacy of imperial trauma." She currently runs her own professional practice as an energy coach and intuitive.

Maria Christine Muyco is an Assistant Professor and Chair of the Composition and Theory Department of the University of the Philippines College of Music. Besides being a music composer (B.M. Music Composition, University of the Philippines; M.Mus. Music Composition, University of British Columbia), she is also an ethnomusicologist and music anthropologist. She finished her PhD in Philippine Studies at the University of the Philippines, Diliman, Quezon City and received a grant to take Ethnomusicology and Dance Theory courses at the University of California, Los Angeles, U.S.A. from 2006-2007. Her research on the Philippine *binanog* music-dance tradition received the Best Dissertation Award from University of the Philippines and a book-length publication on the subject is forthcoming with the Ateneo University Press. Aside from her academic work, she is an active supporter of the Schools of Living Traditions in Panay, Western Visayas dedicated to the strengthening and continued thriving of indigenous traditions among the tribal peoples in the area.

Grace Nono is a multi-awarded Philippine music performing artist, author, and grassroots cultural worker. She received her Bachelor's degree in Humanities and Masters in Philippine Studies from the University of the Philippines. Currently, she is a doctoral candidate in the Ethnomusicology Program of the New York University Department of Music, As a performing artist, Grace has toured the world in the past two decades. She is the recipient of arts fellowships and trainings from the Asian Cultural Council, the Asia-Pacific Performance Exchange, the Asia-Pacific Cultural Center for UNESCO, and the

Asian Institute of Management. As a cultural worker, Grace heads the Tao Foundation for Culture and Arts, a non-government organization engaged in cultural regeneration and holistic development initiatives, for which she has received support from the Toyota Foundation, UNESCO, AusAid, and local communities, among others. To date, Grace has won over 40 awards, including The Outstanding Women Award in the Nation's Service Award, the Ten Outstanding Young Men Award, National Book Award, Outstanding University of the Philippines Alumni Award, Catholic Mass Media, Katha, Awit, National Press Club, and other awards for her artistic and cultural contributions.

James W. Perkinson is a long-time activist and educator from inner city Detroit, currently teaching as Professor of Social Ethics at the Ecumenical Theological Seminary and lecturing in Culture and Communication Studies at the Oakland University, Rochester, Michigan. He holds a Ph.D. in theology from the University of Chicago and is the author of *White Theology: Outing Supremacy in Modernity* (Palgrave, 2004) and *Shamanism, Racism, and Hip-Hop Culture: Essays on White Supremacy and Black Subversion* (Palgrave, 2005) and *Messianism Against Christology: Social Movements, Folk Arts and Empire* (forthcoming, Palgrave). Jim has also written extensively in both academic and popular journals on questions of race, class, and colonialism in connection with religion and urban culture, and regularly performs on the spoken-word poetry scene.

Lane Wilcken is the author of *Filipino Tattoos Ancient to Modern* (Schiffer Publishing, 2010) and the forthcoming volume, *The Forgotten Children of Maui* (2013). He is also a traditional Filipino hand-tap tattoo practitioner, an artisan of ancient technology and art, Co-Director of the Center for Babaylan Studies, and the Editor-in-Chief of 808ink, Hawaii's premier tattoo magazine. For the past two decades, Lane has researched the indigenous past of the Philippines and the Pacific Islands. His interest in cultural tattooing is borne out of a desire to strengthen cultural pride among Filipinos and to reunite Filipinos symbolically and spiritually with their estranged ancestors. He has given presentations and lectures on the tattooing and other cultural traditions of the Philippines at several universities and private forums. His audience has included social clubs, university professors, students, and scholars. Lane comes from a Filipino, English, and Scandinavian ancestry.

About the Editors

S. Lily Mendoza is Associate Professor of Culture and Communication at the Department of Communication and Journalism, Oakland University, Rochester, Michigan. She is the author of *Between the Homeland and the Diaspora: The Politics of Theorizing Filipino and Filipino American Identities* (Routledge, 2002; Revised Philippine Edition by University of Santo Tomas, 2006) and has published in various communication and cultural studies journals and anthologies. Her academic interests include critical intercultural communication, questions of identity and subjectivity, cultural politics in national, post- and trans- national contexts, discourses of indigenization, race, and ethnicity, and more recently, culture and ecology. She is a native of San Fernando, Pampanga, Philippines and is a passionate lover of all things indigenous.

Leny Mendoza Strobel is Professor and Chair of the American Multicultural Studies Department and Coordinator of the Native American Studies Program at Sonoma State University. She is the Project Director of the Center for Babaylan Studies. Her books – *Coming Full Circle: The Process of Decolonization Among Post-1965 Filipino Americans, A Book of her Own: Words and Images to Honor the Babaylan,* and *Babaylan: Filipinos and the Call of the Indigenous* – are widely referenced. Her essays and other writings have been published in scholarly journals, book chapters, anthologies, online ezines, and other media. Academic credentials aside, her greatest joy derives from her grandson's delight in her Kapampangan cooking.

Made in the USA
Coppell, TX
02 May 2020